The Conscious Mind
and the Material World

The Conscious Mind and the Material World

On Psi, the Soul and the Self

Douglas M. Stokes

McFarland & Company, Inc., Publishers
Jefferson, North Carolina, and London

LIBRARY OF CONGRESS CATALOGUING-IN-PUBLICATION DATA

Stokes, Douglas M., 1947–
The conscious mind and the material world : on psi,
the soul and the self / Douglas M. Stokes.
p.   cm.
Includes bibliographical references and index.

ISBN 13: 978-0-7864-3004-8
(softcover : 50# alkaline paper) ∞

1. Mind and body.   2. Consciousness.   I. Title.
BF161.S76   2007   128'.2—dc22   2007014629

British Library cataloguing data are available

Cover illustration ©2007 Imageshop

Manufactured in the United States of America

*McFarland & Company, Inc., Publishers
Box 611, Jefferson, North Carolina 28640
www.mcfarlandpub.com*

To Iris, Rachel and Bessie,
my closest companions
in this strangest of journeys.

Acknowledgments

I would like to thank all those who have pushed, prodded and led me to construct the Person I am (even though I will be shortly arguing that this very construction is ultimately an illusion).

These people include the faculty members of Tabor Academy (including my parents), Harvard University and the University of Michigan. They provided me with the tools I needed to embark on this journey. Ultimately, however, I refused to enter the dark and narrow tunnel into which these last two institutions guided me.

I am especially indebted to the editors of parapsychological journals who have guided my writing and given me a voice in parapsychology over the years, including K. Ramakrishna Rao, Dorothy Pope, Laura Dale, Betty Shapin, Rhea White, Stanley Krippner, John Palmer, Suzanne Brown and Nicola Holt.

I would also like to thank those who have helped me formulate my views, including J. B. and Louisa Rhine, Karlis Osis, John Beloff, Susan Blackmore and too many more to mention here. At least one will be surprised to find herself on this list. Sometimes you learn the most from those whose ideas you initially find foreign and wrong-headed. These ideas have a way of chipping an entrance into one's thick skull, slowly but surely. It may take decades, but one's inner sanctum is eventually penetrated.

Contents

Preface

This is a book about the self, the soul as it were (to use two terms with all the wrong connotations). It argues for the view of the self as a field of pure consciousness or "Cartesian theater" (to use the dismissive terminology of Daniel Dennett). It draws conclusions about the self and its relations to the physical body and the physical world that the reader may find unorthodox and surprising.

This book will explore many familiar areas, perhaps in an unfamiliar way. These areas include the perennial mind-body problem, the role of consciousness in quantum mechanics, the anthropic principle, the evidence for Intelligent Design, and parapsychology (the investigation of ostensible paranormal abilities such as ESP and psychokinesis).

The reader may find the ultimate conclusions drawn to be unsettling and disconcerting, as did I in arriving at them. Once they begin to worm their way into your brain, however, they may provide you with a sense of peace greater than that offered by the dogmas hawked by religions that are still mired in the concept of the Person.

Introduction: Dreams and Awakenings

The Dream of Matter

You are born into the world as a blob of protoplasm, the astronomically improbable result of a random recombination of genes and the confluence of a (literal) uncountable infinity of random events. Had just one or two of these billions of random events had a different outcome, you would in all likelihood never have been born. Your very existence could not be more improbable.

You are nothing but your body and brain. Your inner self, your aspirations and strivings, your deepest emotions, and innermost thoughts are nothing more electrical discharges and chemical secretions in the wetware of your brain. When that brain and body are gone, decomposed once more into their constituent elements, dispersed back into the Mother Earth, and finding new homes in her countless new creatures, plants and minerals, you will be no more. Aside from your works, influences on others, and the continuation of the myriad other causal chains in which you once participated, it will be as though you never existed.

Such is the dream of modern science and indeed of many modern enlightened religions that, perhaps prematurely, have rushed to embrace the materialist worldview of modern science, not wanting to be left behind in the dark ages from which they sprang.

Awakening from the Dream of Matter

According to the physicalistic philosophies underlying modern science, one's self is nothing more than one's physical body and the physical world is all that exists. We are identical to our physical bodies, our selves nothing more than the electrochemical activity of billions of neurons housed in calcium skulls. In the *Weltanschauung* of modern science, the world/universe is comprised of a collection of blindly careening elementary and not-so-elementary particles, a spacetime stage for them to perform their antics in, and little else. The behavior of these material particles is governed by the mathematical laws of physics and nothing else.

But, if each of us does have a self that endures from moment to moment, from day to day, and year to year (however much it may be extinguished at death), then that self cannot be identical with any specified collection of material particles. The material particles that make up our bodies are constantly changing. Atoms and molecules are continually entering into and exiting from your body, so that the collection of material particles that comprises your body of today is a completely different assemblage of material particles from that which comprised your body of several years ago. For instance, Burruss (2006) computes that some of the atoms in your body were part of the sun only months ago, having been driven to Earth by the solar wind, and that hydrogen atoms that were a part of your body only months ago have exited from the Earth's atmosphere and are on a course toward interstellar space. Yet you perceive that you are the same self you were several months ago. If this perception is correct, then you cannot be identical to any particular collection of material particles, including your present physical body.

If each of us is identical with his or her physical body, it is most surprising that we would find ourselves conscious at the present moment of time. A human lifespan is only several decades long. On the other hand, the universe has existed for approximately 13.7 billion years and will likely exist for billions more to come (to say nothing of the age of any "multiverse," of which the universe may be only a part). Thus, the probability that the moment in time that has somehow been mysteriously selected to be the "present" (something for which physics, by the way, has no explanation whatsoever) would correspond to a moment in one's lifetime would seem to be vanishingly small. Also, if one is to be identified with a particular physical body, the probability that the set of genes that formed the blueprint for that body would ever have come into combination is virtually zero (and still smaller is the probability that the particular configuration of material particles that comprises one's present physical body would ever have formed, much less exist at the present moment). Yet here you find yourself (a field of consciousness that is unique and special to you at any rate) existing at the present time. This is most surprising—indeed, virtually impossible—based on the view that you are identical with, or dependent on, the presence of a particular collection of material particles at a particular moment in time. Hence, by a quick pseudoapplication of Bayes' theorem in statistics, the probability that the standard view (that you are your physical body) obtains is also virtually zero.

There is much merit in the worldview of modern physical science, and its current avatar is supported by a wide array of scientific evidence. However, scientists seem always to hope that their work is complete and that leisurely island life is only just around the corner. Sometimes they are quite adamant in their defense of this position.

This attitude is exemplified in a statement by the Nobel prize–winning physicist Albert Abraham Michelson, made twenty years after his paradigm-shaking experiment on the velocity of the Earth relative to the aluminiferous ether. Michelson's experiment (conducted in collaboration with Edward W. Morley) established the speed of light as a fundamental constant of nature and eventually led to the downfall of Newtonian mechanics and its replacement with Einstein's special theory of relativity. Michelson's remarks are as follows:

> The more important fundamental laws and facts of the physical universe have all been discovered and these are now so firmly established that the possibility of their ever being supplanted in consequence of new discoveries is exceedingly remote [quotation taken from Feuer, 1974, p.253].

Michelson added that, although there were apparent exceptions to most of these laws, these were due to the increasing accuracy of measurement made possible by modern apparatus and that the system of known physical laws would be adequate to deal with the "apparent exceptions." He went on to assert that "future discoveries must be looked for in the sixth place of decimals" (Feuer, 1974, p. 254.)

What is most noteworthy about these statements is that they preceded rather than followed the publication of Einstein's paper on special relativity, a paper that caused a revolution in science and that received its main immediate empirical support from the results of Michelson's own experiment. The development of quantum mechanics was another major revolution Michelson did not anticipate.

In fact, the discoveries and revolutions just keep on a-coming. For instance, *Science's* "Breakthrough of the Year" for 2003 was the discovery that 96 percent of the energy in the universe is comprised of dark matter and dark energy, the existence of which was not even suspected a few decades ago, rather than the matter-energy that is visible to us, which comprises a mere 4 percent of the energy in the universe. A full 73 percent of the universe is comprised of dark energy, the existence of which was not even suspected until 1998 (Seife, 2003). Many more surprises may be in store for us.

There is no real place for mind or consciousness in the great World Machine of modern physicalistic science (leaving aside for the moment certain interpretations of quantum mechanics, which will be discussed in more detail in Chapter 2 and elsewhere in the book). Indeed, physicalistic science is at a loss to explain how the human brain, composed like everything else of supposedly insensate matter, can give rise to conscious experience (as contrasted with mere information-processing). To be sure, modern cognitive neuroscience has achieved remarkable insights into the nature of the brain activities that are associated with various forms of cognitive experience. What it has not thus far achieved is any explanation of how a three-pound hunk of meat can give rise to conscious experience in the first place.

Finally, there is a smattering of (hotly contested) evidence that conscious minds have powers such as precognition, telepathy and psychokinesis (collectively referred to as psi) that cannot be accounted for in terms of the known principles of physics. This evidence will be discussed in detail in Chapters 3 and 4. As modern science clings to the delusion that its grasp of the nature of reality is complete, it has steadfastly resisted the work of parapsychologists.

If psi phenomena are real, they have major implications for our understanding of the place of mind in the cosmos. Psi phenomena appear to transcend spacetime separations and to violate the normal temporal ordering of causation (such as in the case of precognition, or the ability to foresee the future, and retroactive psychokinesis, or the ability to influence events that have already occurred). Because of their importance, a large portion of this book will be devoted to a discussion of psi phenomena and their implications for our understanding of the mind and the cosmos. As they appear to represent phenomena that cannot be accounted for in terms of current theories of physics, psi phenomena have often been taken as pointing to the existence of an "immaterial" mind. Many parapsychologists believe that psi phenomena may eventually be given an account in terms of an extension of current physical theories. If so, psi phenomena may point to the existence of new physical entities and principles rather to an immaterial realm.

As we shall see, the existence of psi phenomena has not been conclusively established. If the critics are correct and psi phenomena do not exist, the principal conclusions in this book regarding the nature of the conscious self will not be invalidated. For instance, our recent awakening from the Dream of Matter was achieved without the "alarm clock" of psi. Whether psi phenomena exist or not, our conscious selves cannot be identified with our physical bodies or brains.

The Dream of the Person

You are your mind, not your body, not even your brain. You are your thoughts, your personality, your memories, your emotions. In short, you are a person, not a blob of pulsating neurons. While your body and brain might decay into dust, you may survive by being

- brought to Heaven (or Hell, Valhalla, Hades, or the Dreamtime) in an angelic (or demonic) ethereal body;
- reincarnated with some of your memories, emotions, thoughts and much of your personality intact, at least at a subconscious level;
- transformed into an astral ghost capable of monitoring the events in this work and, occasionally, manifesting yourself to the living;
- resurrected in your present body or a replica thereof at the time of the Day of Judgment; or
- transferred to a cybernetic "brain" by having your memories, thoughts and personality traits downloaded into a supercomputer or robot, or perhaps etched into the neuronal connections of willing or non-so-willing volunteers (or possibly even a mass of stem cells growing in a beaker in some remote laboratory).

The first and fourth alternatives above are subscribed to by certain adherents to the Judeo-Christian-Islamic religious tradition, as well as the great mythological traditions of the pre–Christianized world, who look forward to reunion with the deity (or deities) and loved ones in some type of post-mortem realm such as the Christian heaven. In the fourth alternative above, the resurrection is thought to take place right here on Earth or in some Resurrection World in a parallel universe. Besides having one's personality recreated, we will all be generously provided with idealized resurrection bodies as well (see Edwards, 1997, pp. 53–62, for an entertaining discussion of beliefs regarding the resurrection of the body within the Christian tradition). Many resurrectionists believe that these will be the same physical bodies we occupied in life (although as noted above, each of us has already occupied several different physical bodies). If this is the case, I hope I will not have to fight with the likes of Socrates and Jack the Ripper over who owns a particular set of atoms that we shared during our respective physical lives. (It is estimated that every minute, each of us inhales an atom once expelled in Julius Caesar's dying breath.) This process of sharing recycled atoms might well result in a heated game of "musical atoms," much like musical chairs, at the time of the resurrection. Thus, the resurrectionists are not only lost in the Dream of the Person, they are still lost in the Dream of Matter.

The third alternative, reincarnation, is subscribed to by many shamanistic traditions, by Eastern religious traditions such as Hinduism and Buddhism (although as we shall see later, many of the more sophisticated adherents to the Eastern religious tradition have awakened from the Dream of the Person), and by as much as one-quarter of the people in the highly Christianized United States. There is even empirical evidence for reincarnation in the form of children who report seemingly accurate memories of past lives (Stevenson, 1987).

Additional empirical evidence for the survival of the person has been provided by psychical researchers studying apparitions and hauntings, purported massages from the dead communicated by mediums or in dreams, as well as near-death experiences and the related phenomenon of out-of-the-body experiences. We will duly consider this empirical evidence for the survival of the personality in Chapter 6, presenting both the proponents' and skeptics' evidence and arguments.

As for the fifth alternative, some writers, including Hans Moravec (1988), Grant Fjermedal (1987), and Frank Tipler (1994) among others, have suggested that one's thoughts, memories and personality could be "downloaded" into a computer or robot, allowing one's essential self to survive after death in a cybernetic world or as a cybernetic simulacrum operating in the physical world. This survival could be for eternity, or at least until the heat death of the universe (after which the universe may not be that much fun to play in anyway).

Awakening from the Dream of the Person

Just as the collection of atoms and elementary particles making up your physical body undergoes continual change and replacement, so do your thoughts, emotions, memories and personality traits. Your essential self persists, despite these continual changes in the contents of your consciousness (and, we might add, subconscious and unconscious minds as well). Hence you cannot be your personality or its "contents," such as your thoughts, emotions, and memories.

During the past three decades neuroscientists have amply demonstrated that one's sensations, feelings, thoughts, emotions, memories, ideas, and even personality can be radically altered through electromagnetic, surgical, chemical, and accidental interventions in the brain. Because of these demonstrations we live in a different world of knowledge than did the psychical researchers of a century ago, who searched for some trace of the continuing existence of the dearly departed in the garbled words of mediums uttered during séances.

If relatively minor modifications of brain states can substantially alter the nature of one's experience and personality, how could your personality and experiences manage to continue on in a more or less an uninterrupted fashion after the far more drastic event of the destruction of your entire brain? Also, many of the concerns that drive the structure of your personality have to do with the preservation of your own physical body and the bodies of people who are closely related to you (or perhaps to the propagation of your "selfish genes"). What would be the point of the continuance of these concerns once your physical body has been returned to dust and your ability to intervene in the physical world perhaps radically curtailed?

Of course, there is the possibility, as suggested by Tipler (1994), that your personality may be resurrected by a benevolent and almost omnipotent Programmer that is so enamored of you that She creates a simulacrum of your personality in a semi-eternal cyberspace. However, there is nothing in principle stopping a sufficiently ardent fan of your personality from constructing a computer or robot to simulate your personality while you are still alive. Surely it would be absurd to think that your self would then reside both in the computer and in your physical body. The computer or robot is just a replica of you. It is not you. You are not your personality traits and behavior patterns.

Along similar lines, it could be argued that, if you are not the particular collection of physical particles that make up your present physical body, perhaps you are the particular *pattern* of molecules that make up your present body (including your brain configuration and thus personality). You would then remain the same person even if the physical particles that make up your body changed, so long as the general pattern remained the same. This is the basis of the famous beaming technique in the *Star Trek* television and movie series. In *Star Trek*, one can "beam" to a new location by undergoing a process in which one's physical body is atomized, information about the pattern of the physical particles that make up one's body is sent to a distant location, and a new body is reassembled (presumably out of new atoms) at the second location. Peter Oppenheimer (1986) and Derek Parfit (1987) have independently concluded that this beaming process would result in the death of everyone who used it as a form of transportation, followed by the construction of a replica of the person at the destination site. This replica may not be the original person any more than identical twins are the same person as one another. To make this example more compelling, assume that more than one copy of the person is assembled at the destination site. Surely it would be difficult to believe that one's self could simultaneously inhabit all the replicas of one's physical body that are constructed at the destination site, insofar as a conscious self cannot have several separate and independent streams of consciousness occurring at the same time.

Thus, you cannot be the pattern of your neural activity, your emotions, your memories, your personality traits, or your present hopes and dreams. We have now awakened from both the Dream of Matter and the Dream of the Person. If we are not our physical bodies and not our personalities, then what can we be? What further dreams await us?

The Dream of Atman and Brahman

The self that (seems to) persist over long time periods (from birth to death in the popular, common view) would appear to correspond to what Hornell Hart (1958) called the "I-thinker," that entity that thinks one's thoughts (although it may not have a primary role in generating them), feels one's feelings, remembers one's memories and senses one's sensations, rather than being the conglomeration of the thoughts, feelings, memories, and sensations themselves. After all, these contents of consciousness are fleeting and do not persist from one moment to the next. One outlives one's current emotional state, and one's self may survive the demise of myriad personalities. After all, how could we be the contents of our streams of consciousness when these contents change from moment to moment while we ourselves seem to persist unchanged from moment to moment, day to day and even from year to year?

What seems to persist, at least from an introspectionist point of view, is the (contentless) field of consciousness itself. Perhaps, as suggested above, our real selves are fields of pure consciousness, the "contentless consciousness" of Indian philosophy, as described by Rao (2002), among others. In other words, we are the vessel of consciousness rather than the contents of that vessel.

Of course there are those, such as Daniel Dennett (1991), Susan Blackmore (1991a, 1993, 2002) and Thomas Metzinger (2003), who deny the very existence of a continuing self, or "Cartesian theater," as Dennett calls it. The self, they maintain, is a convenient "story" we tell ourselves in an attempt to render our experiences coherent and consistent. As such, the self is an entirely fictional concept, and "we" are nothing more than the scattered contents (fleeting sensations, thoughts, and emotions) of "our" minds. To most people the existence of a continuing self is immediately given and obviously true. It is an integral part of our essential existence. However, if thinkers such as Blackmore and Dennett are correct, there is no need to worry about whether the self will survive death; the "self" does not even survive moment to moment and in fact does not even exist at all.

The Zen doctrine of "No Mind" also denies the existence of a continuing self. However, the Buddhist doctrine seems more directed at the concept of the self as one's personality, comprising one's aspirations, motivations, cravings for material possessions, lusts, pride, and so forth, rather than at the existence of a field of pure consciousness. A goal of Buddhist practice is to distance oneself from these transitory elements. In order to achieve a state of peace and tranquility, the Buddhists teach that one must suppress and eliminate one's cravings and greed, which, unfulfilled, are the root of all human misery and suffering.

As we have seen above, most branches of Buddhism and Hinduism teach that the true self is pure consciousness, not the contents or objects of consciousness. Thus, rather than clinging to the hope that one's personality will survive relatively intact in some sort of afterlife, the Eastern philosophies teach that our personalities are transitory and not our true selves. One's true self in this view is the pure consciousness that in Hindu philosophy is taken to be identical with all consciousness, including that of the World Soul or Brahman. Under the Vedantic worldview, there is only one pure consciousness, and we are all the Universe looking at itself from different perspectives. Thus, according to this view, when persons temporarily abandon their individual identities and perceive themselves as merging with the Cosmos or as being in perfect union with God, as in the mystical experiences described by William James (1902) and others, they are seeing directly into their true selves. All consciousness is the one Consciousness that underlies this and all other worlds. We are fragmented splinters of the World Soul, our selves at once separate from, and yet identical to, one another.

It should be conceded that survival in the form of pure consciousness with little continuity of memories, emotions, and predispositions from one's previous biological life may not be what most persons would consider survival in the true sense (i.e., survival with one's memories and personality completely intact). It would, however, be survival of one's essential self, the central core of one's existence.

If our true self is Atman, pure consciousness, is there any Brahman, any larger Consciousness for it to merge in, or be identical with? In recent times, most scientists have turned their backs to the concept of deity and a creator, with the possible exception of such doddering old fogies as Erwin Schrödinger and Isaac Newton. Arguments for a designer have largely been abandoned as regressive. After all, if there was a designer, who designed Him? If there was a "preuniverse," then what preceded that?

The noted mathematician and physicist Sir James Jeans, pondering the subtleties of the mathematics of laws of physics and the seeming dependence of material events upon observation by conscious minds, observed that the "universe begins to look more like a great thought than a great machine" (Jeans, 1937, p. 122). Another great physicist, Sir Arthur Eddington, remarked, "The stuff of the world is mind-stuff" (Eddington, 1920/1959, p. 200).

Indeed, the base reality of the world appears to be one of quantum probability waves inhabiting an abstract, multidimensional mathematical space rather than the solid, marble-like electrons and protons zipping around in a four-dimensional spacetime continuum that we imagine to be the firm underpinnings of our material existence. The mathematical complexity and beauty of the laws of the quantum mechanics are remarkable. It does indeed seem as though the creator is, as both Jeans and Einstein thought, a great mathematician. As Henry Stapp says, under quantum mechanics, the world has "an essentially 'idea-like' structure" (Stapp, 2005a, p. 73). Stapp's remarks are echoed in a recent editorial in *Nature*, the flagship journal of orthodox science, in which Richard Conn Henry points out that modern physics has demonstrated that the universe is "entirely mental" in nature and that "nothing exists but observations" (Henry, 2005, p. 29).

But if the universe is a thought, whose thought is it? In recent years, a seemingly endless succession of physicists have observed that the laws of the universe and the initial conditions set at the time of its creation seem extraordinarily finely tuned to support the evolution of complex life forms and hence conscious observers (see Barrow & Tipler, 1986, or Livio and Rees, 2005). This seeming evidence of intelligent design is often referred to as the anthropic principle. Was the universe created as a vast cosmic amusement park? And why go to trouble of designing such an elaborate "roadside attraction" unless one intended to enjoy it oneself, if only vicariously? Are our individual consciousnesses just aspects of the creator's (or creators') consciousness, lost in an unimaginable form of contemplation of the myriad creatures it has managed to generate from its mathematical inventions, much as we may become lost in the adventures of a goldfish in the bowl in our living room or in the adventures of the cybernetic "life" forms we may create when we implement the mathematician John Conway's "Game of Life" on our computer?

The anthropic principle is based on the support of life as we know it (i.e. carbon-based life forms). But there may be other forms of life (e.g., nucleon-based) that may arise under different conditions. Also, there may be multiple universes created, so that we necessarily find ourselves in a universe capable of supporting conscious observers, with initial conditions and laws that would seem improbable had only one universe been created with a random assortment of physical laws and initial conditions. Guth and Kaiser (2005), for instance, note that cosmic inflation (the currently favored model of cosmogenesis) may produce "pocket universes" in each of which the fundamental laws of physics might be different. Again, we of necessity inhabit a pocket universe that is capable of supporting the existence of conscious observers. Still, one must explain the laws and initial conditions that gave rise to cosmic inflation in the first place.

One might imagine that a consciousness so complex and vast as to be able to create (perhaps literally dream up) such a startlingly wonderful (and frightening) world as this one might well become bored with its omniscience and may wish to lose itself in its creation, if only temporarily. It may need to fragment itself and temporarily shed much of its omniscience to accomplish this. We too might well begin to stagnate and become bored if we were to somehow become immortal and become trapped in our present bodies and mired in our present personalities and situation for all eternity. Death may be the rope thrown to free us from the quicksand of our current identities.

Beyond the Veil of Maya

We awake from the Dream of Atman and Brahman to find ourselves in still yet another, but this time possibly the final, dream. We are, exactly as in the dream from we have just awakened, each of us specks of consciousness adrift in a universe whose vastness defies our understanding (if we can even be said to have an "understanding" in any real sense of the word). There are as yet no planets, no stars, only a rapidly expanding rush of matter and light. The universe is but seconds old. We may have come from a place before the universe, but being disembodied with no notepad or brain on which to record and preserve the events of this prelife, our memories of such a place are lost. For all we know—and we don't know much at his point—we may have just been fused together in some great computer of our own construction, of unimaginable computational and physical power, in a "Manhattan project" designed to produce a very Big Bang indeed (at least from our present perspectives). We are adrift in a rapidly expanding spacetime designed to captivate us in a way that is even more amusing and terrifying than any Hollywood concoction our current primitive technologies can produce. However, that all lies in the distant future. Now, with our memories lost along with our cosmogenic computer, we drift among the beautiful clouds of quantum waves, admiring their beauty, touching them, drawing them this way and that as the potential universe is actualized. Our consciousness is like that of a quark lost in a swarming buzz of photons and gluons.

As Tim Hill points out in a letter to the editor of the *Skeptical Inquirer* (Hill, 2005), the vast emptiness of space is totally hostile to human observers with its lack of air, pockets of intense radiation and unimaginably high temperatures, not to mention the total absence of fast-food establishments. If the anthropic principle is valid, Hill suggests, the overwhelming evidence surely suggests that the universe was created for beings that exist in the vacuum of space, not for the amusement for a handful of abnormally smart "geek" apes confined to one tiny speck in a cold dark corner of a comparatively uninterested and desolate cosmos.

Perhaps, then, we are more akin to antiprotons than to angels, small islands of consciousness born to force the amorphous clouds of quantum possibilities into the crystallized raindrops of actualized events. In the view of many interpreters of quantum mechanics, observation by consciousness is what causes such quantum collapse (i.e., collapse of the state vector containing an array of possibilities into one definite outcome). Walker (2000) has even proposed the existence of "mini-consciousnesses" or "proto-consciousnesses" that govern the collapse of quantum vectors that are remote from human observers.

Indeed, some physicists (e.g., Wheeler, 1983) have suggested that the universe itself, conceived as a quantum process, could not have come into existence without some conscious observer to force the collapse of state vectors and thus to give rise to a definite history of the universe. Wheeler terms this view the "participatory universe." Wheeler notes that this view may explain the fact that the initial state and physical laws of the universe seem finely tuned to support the existence of conscious observers. Potential universes that do not support the presence of conscious observers could not become actualized in Wheeler's view, as there would be no conscious observers to collapse their state vectors in the proper "direction" to create such a history.

But perhaps those observers are more akin to Walker's "proto-consciousnesses" than to human beings. If physics suggests anything, it is that the fundamental constituents of the universe are more likely to be very small in comparison to the human observers that formed the center of the medieval view of the cosmos. Our essential selves are more likely to resemble an electron than a human body.

After our dispersal at the time of the Big Bang, we have surfed the quantum waves, finding our selves in neutron stars, methane oceans on moons of gas giants, exploding in supernovae (the matter comprising our physical bodies was formed in such explosions), shooting out of volcanoes, condensing into rocks, shepherding the bodies of amobea, gazing out of worried eye of a stegosaur, stretching with the leaves of a sequoia. Through much of this, our consciousness would be dim, as we float in a universe largely separated from our fellow monads, deprived of any physical template to hold our memories or any hormones to drive our wishes and aspirations. But time is on our side.

As the debris of supernovae cooled and their ashes condensed once again into stars and planetary systems, on one remote outpost (and probably on a virtual infinity of outposts), the physical templates (and the complex assemblages of our essential selves) grew more complex. With the first protozoa, we began to gather, and after eons we were collected in assemblages in whales and crows and octopodes and in at least one malcontented bipedal ape.

Our common conception, and one that forms part of the Dream of Atman and Brahman, is that we are each a single conscious self (field of consciousness) which in some mysterious manner became attached to our brains shortly after our conceptions and will persist in those brains until we die. But our brains are powerful and unimaginably large in comparison to our single-celled ancestors, who, we might suppose, had the glimmerings of consciousness. Our brains and bodies are in essence a colony of billions of amoebas. Many of us may ride in a single brain. Indeed (as discussed in more detail in Chapter 7), when a human brain is split into its two hemispheres by severing the corpus callosum (the primary bundle of neural fibers connecting the two hemispheres), two fields of consciousness seem to exist, sometimes with such differences in motivation that the right hand (controlled by the left hemisphere) may forced to grab the left hand (controlled by the right) in order to prevent the latter from carrying out an assault on one's spouse.

In fact, the findings of split-brain research are precisely the evidence Patricia Churchland uses to refute the existence of a nonphysical self or soul in human beings (Churchland, 2002, pp. 46–47).

Churchland is likely correct so far as the "single soul" theory goes; but the evidence suggests that multiple centers of consciousness or "souls" may exist within a single brain, with each of them falling under the delusion that they are the single center that is "in charge of" the body. Jonathan C. W. Edwards (2005) and Willard Miranker (2005) have even proposed that that each single neuron in the brain is associated with its own center of consciousness. Due to the complexity of the input to each neuron, each such center of consciousness would likely identify with the body as a whole and fall under the delusion that it is the single, central conscious self "in charge" of the whole body.

We directly experience ourselves as single unified fields of consciousness that persist through changes in our brain states and bodily composition over periods of at least hours. We think we persist as the same selves over the lifetimes of our bodies. In this we may be wrong. If memories are, as an overwhelming body of scientific evidence indicates, stored as patterns of synaptic connections among neurons in our brain, how do you know that you are the same field of consciousness that inhabited your body when you fell asleep? If you can become attached to your brain shortly after conception (or in the view of some people at birth) and become detached from it at the moment of death, it stands to reason that you can also become attached to it long after birth and leave it well before death. Our association with our bodies may be only temporary. We may be breathed out and breathed in like so many oxygen atoms. Indeed, while many philosophers (such as Descartes) have thought that minds or souls are not extended in space and time and hence immaterial, the fact that we find ourselves stuck in physical bodies occupying in particular locations in space and (even more mysteriously) located at a particular moments in time, suggests that we too must (at least partially) be residents of spacetime ourselves, if only temporarily.

Elementary particles such as electrons and quarks may become embedded in physical brains; these particles persist and remain stuck over "long" time intervals such as minutes and hours. These particles appear, like our individual consciousnesses, to be indivisible (leaving aside the possibility of subquarks for the moment). If an electron can "incarnate" in a body for a period of time, then be expelled, and then be "reincarnated" in another body or physical system, then so might we. We may ourselves be material or quasi-material entities that can become stuck in individual brains on a temporary basis. We may be a particle or field already known to physical science, although it is more likely we are an entity yet to be discovered and explained. In the latter case we could be called "nonphysical" or "immaterial" in the sense that we are not identical to any particle or field already known to modern physics; however, if the theory of physical science were to expand to accommodate us, perhaps the label of "physical" could then be applied. As Noam Chomsky once remarked, as soon as we understand anything, we call it physical; thus, "anything in the world is either physical or unintelligible" (Lipkin, 2005, p. 55).

The evidence for psi phenomena, to be discussed in Chapters 3 and 4, suggests that the mind may have abilities that transcend those of entities located at a single spacetime location. Such spacetime transcendence, if proven, may make the label "physical" more difficult to apply to minds (but not impossible, in view of the nonlocal behavior of material particles under the theory of quantum mechanics, to be discussed more fully in Chapter 2).

If we are continually being recycled, then when we wake in the morning, we may not be in the same bodies (or objects or plasma fields) that we were in the day before. If, as the overwhelming body of modern research in neuroscience indicates, our memories, thoughts and emotions are largely a function of our brain states, we would not remember our existence as, say, a crow the day before. Our previous "memory pad," namely the crow's brain, is lost to us. We cannot find those memories, just as we cannot find a telephone number written on a misplaced piece of paper. The telephone number and the pad it was written on are not parts of our essential selves. Neither are we the memories stored in the brain of the crow that now perches outside our window, nor the memories and personality traits stored in the new human brain in which we have just awakened. What we will remember are the memories stored in that new human brain (sometimes after a momentary period of confusion upon awakening). We will feel the emotions caused by the intense firing of our midbrain neurons and the hormones and neurotransmitters rampaging through our cerebral cortex. Accessing the brain's memories of our sixth birthday party, we will immediately come to the conclusion that we have inhabited this brain and body for decades. The brain has evolved to serve the body and we are now made to serve that purpose as well, overwhelmed by the delusion that we are the Person, that is to say, the body and the memories, thoughts and emotions that result from the neural activity of that body's brain. We think we are in sole command of the body, whereas in fact our nerves, the neurochemical soup in which they bathe, as well as numerous other centers of pure consciousness also mired in the same brain, may have as much or more to say about the fate of the body than we do. In short, we fall under the illusion that we are the Person, the physical body that continues from birth to death, and the stream of memories, thoughts and emotions that courses through it, rather than the centers of pure consciousness that we are. Blackmore and Dennett are correct in their analysis that the "person" is just a story that we tell ourselves (although it would be more accurate to portray it as a story that is screamed at us by a billion pulsating neurons). Where Blackmore and Dennett err is in denying that there is any self or center of conscious that persists from moment to moment (i.e., a "Cartesian theater"). The existence of a conscious self is given to each of us in our direct experience (or at least to me—I can't speak for Blackmore and Dennett). If I am to doubt that I am a center of consciousness persisting through macroscopic time intervals, then I must doubt everything and enter a state of total solipsism and nihilism. However, I do agree that it is likely that spheres of consciousness are, just like electrons and quarks, continually being recycled, joining first one aggregate body and then another. We are somehow stuck to our brains like an oxygen atom stuck to two hydrogen atoms, a view I once called the "chewing gum" theory of personal identity (Stokes, 1988). But it is likely that such centers enter and leave the brain at times other than birth and death. The idea that the conscious self enters into the body at some time shortly after conception and then persists in that body until death is just an aspect of the illusion produced by identifying ourselves as the Person. We are not the Person, we are not even Atman (in the sense of a sphere of pure consciousness inhabiting the body from birth until death), and are likely no longer Brahman (although it is possible that we were once conjoined in an aggregate of consciousnesses that may have somehow "designed" the world, implemented that design, and are now walking through our "art gallery").

As we have seen, through replacement of atoms, the body we inhabit today is a totally different body from that of a decade ago, and the spheres of consciousness that inhabit it (including ourselves) are likely themselves different as well. There is no Person in the sense of a continuing aggregation of matter or a continuing self. The Person is likely to be, as Blackmore and Dennett insist, a story we tell ourselves. However, it is a useful story, just like the story of my car or my kitchen table. It helps credit card companies to obtain payments for purchases we made the preceding month and guides our interactions with former classmates at a high school reunion. But in an absolute sense, the Person is only a cognitive construct, a very vivid hallucination. We may be eternal, but "we" (the People) have only a momentary time in the sun and may only be cognitive constructs, much like the ever-changing body of water that is now called the Mississippi River.

We cling to our present form of existence thinking that there is no other; but when you think about it, human bodies, with their ills, needs and subjugation into mindless repetitive jobs, may not be the best places in the universe to inhabit. In fact, they may be "mini-hells," aberrations in a great cosmic scheme. But we may not inhabit such hells (or such heavens as there might be) for as long as we think. The best thing for us to do is likely to take the poet Robert Frost's advice and momentarily stop the horses we are currently riding to enjoy the beauty of the falling snow. As Frost suggests, there may be miles to go (although perhaps not so many as one might think) before we sleep (and enter yet another dream).

The Game Plan

The remainder of this book further develops the themes outlined above (and defends the foregoing thesis regarding the relationship between conscious selves and the physical world). In Chapter 1, we well will explore the nature of the relationship between mind (consciousness) and matter. Chapter 2 continues this exploration with a consideration of the implications of quantum mechanics regarding the role of mind in the cosmos. In Chapters 3 and 4, we will consider the evidence for psi phenomena, such as ESP and psychokinesis, in some detail. The defense of the primary thesis regarding the role of conscious observers presented above will in no way rest on the existence of psi phenomena. However, such phenomena, if they exist, have profound implications regarding the role of mind in the physical world (and they are entertaining and instructive to explore in their own right). Chapter 5 is devoted to an exploration of the implications of psi phenomena, if they exist, for our views of reality in general and the nature of mind-matter interaction in particular. Chapter 6 presents the existing evidence for the survival of the Person (including memories, emotions, and even physical appearance) of the death of the human body. In Chapter 7, we will explore in further detail the nature of the self and the nature of mind-brain interaction. In Chapter 8, we will turn again to a consideration of the role of mind in the physical universe, this time on the grandest of scales, by considering the anthropic principle and arguments that the universe may to designed to support the existence of (and possibly to entertain) conscious observers. Chapter 9 contains a final summing-up of the evidence and conclusions presented in the main body of the book.

1

Mind and Matter

We begin with our journey with an examination of the relationship between conscious minds and physical matter (traditionally called the "mind-body problem").

Historical Roots

Before launching into a discussion of modern views on the mind-body problem, it is helpful to consider the historical processes that gave rise to those views. In particular, an historical perspective will enable us to understand the almost religious vehemence with which some positions are held.

In the history of human thought up until surprisingly recent times, it was much more common to attribute mental or psychological properties to seemingly inanimate matter than it is today. Jonathan Shear, the founder and editor of the *Journal of Consciousness Studies*, notes that the problem of accounting for the existence of conscious experience that confronts modern science was not a problem for the ancient Greeks, as they viewed the material world as being imbued with mind, which served as a force governing the behavior of matter (Shear, 1995). Aristotle taught that the natural state of any body was one of rest. He asserted that the crystalline spheres which carried the planets and stars on their celestial voyages in his cosmology were associated with incorporeal "movers" that provided the force needed to maintain their motion. He viewed these movers as being spiritual in nature and conceived of the relation of a mover to its sphere as "akin to that of a soul to its body" (Mason, 1962, p. 42).

Aristotle's view was given a Christian interpretation by Christian philosophers such as Dionysius in the fifth century and Thomas Aquinas in the thirteenth century, with Aristotle's "movers" being equated with the angels described in the Scriptures. Aristotle also attributed psychological properties to baser matter, ascribing the tendency for a terrestrial object to fall to the Earth to its "aspiration" to reach its natural place.

Even as late as 1777, the English chemist Joseph Priestley asserted that physical matter was akin to "spiritual and immaterial beings" because of its properties of attraction and repulsion.

These animistic views of matter gradually crumbled under the onslaught of scientific advances. The law of the conservation of angular momentum (earlier called the doctrine of "impetus") led John Philoponos in the sixth century and William of Ockham in the fourteenth to deny the need to assume the existence of angels to keep the planetary spheres in motion. After all, if you spin a top, it keeps spinning by itself. (Philoponos was rewarded for this observation by being denounced as a heretic by the Church.)

In rejecting Aquinas' angels, William of Ockham was led to formulate his famous injunction "not to multiply entities beyond necessity," which has since become known as "Ockham's Razor." In fact, Ockham's Razor, which was originally formulated to justify the exclusion of a class of spiritual beings (Aristotle's angelic movers), is still one of the primary justifications used by modern scientists and philosophers to deny the existence of a realm of mental experience that is independent of physical events in the brain. With regard to Ockham's original application of his principle, the historian of science Herbert Butterfield (1957) viewed the impetus doctrine (in the form of the modern laws of conservation of momentum) as the primary factor underlying the banishment of a spiritual realm from scientific accounts of the world and the establishment in seventeenth century of the view of the universe as a huge impersonal machine governed by strictly mechanical principles.

One of the contributors to this mechanistic cosmology was, paradoxically enough, the seventeenth century philosopher and mathematician Rene Descartes, who is widely regarded as being the prototype of the modern dualist (a dualist being one who regards the realms of mind and matter as having independent reality). Among the phenomena that had most strongly indicated a mental aspect to matter were those suggestive of the operation of action-at-a-distance, such as gravitation and magnetism. Descartes was able to eliminate this stumbling block on the road to a totally mechanistic outlook by proposing theories of magnetism (the vortex theory) and gravitation (the plenum theory) that avoided the problem of action-at-a-distance by assuming that these two types of force were transmitted through a physical medium.

Descartes extended his mechanistic philosophy to encompass living creatures as well as inanimate matter. He viewed animals as mere machines. He did not, however, question the existence of minds in humans; indeed, he thought one's primary and most direct knowledge was of one's own mind. He viewed mind as a totally different kind of entity from matter. In Descartes' view, one's mind (or ego) was indivisible and hence lacked a basic character of matter—that of extension in space. Thus, the mind inhabited a different plane of existence from the physical world and could not be said to have a spatial location.

Despite their different natures, Descartes proposed that the mind interacted with the physical body by deflecting the motion of the "animal spirits" flowing through the brain. He thought the pineal gland was the area of the brain in which this mind-matter interaction took place (as the pineal gland was the one structure that was not duplicated in the cerebral hemispheres and thus seemed appropriate to house a unitary and indivisible mind). Because Descartes' law of inertia held merely that the total quantity of motion in a system remains constant (but not necessarily its direction), he proposed that the soul acted upon the body by altering the direction of motion of the animal spirits, while not changing the intensity of that motion.

The mathematician G. W. Leibniz, however, demonstrated that Descartes was in error and that directionality was conserved in the law of momentum. Thus, Leibniz demonstrated that the physical body (as modeled by Descartes) was a deterministic system. There was therefore no room left for an influence of the mind on the body, and the mind was totally excluded from influence on the physical world. (It should be noted that mind retained a place in Leibniz' own "monad" cosmology, although that cosmology never gained ascendancy in Western thought.)

As a deterministic clockwork physical universe allows no room for mind-action, it is not surprising that Cartesian dualism soon yielded to the materialism of Hobbes and La Mettrie (and more recently of Watson, Skinner, Dennett and the Churchlands).

Once again, an application of the law of inertia led to the exclusion of the spiritual realm from scientific models of the world, only this time it was not angels being banished from the heavens, but the human soul itself being banished from its body. Indeed the historian of science Richard Westfall (1977) viewed the rigid exclusion of the psychic from physical nature as the "permanent legacy" of the seventeenth century.

However, since the emergence of the theory of quantum mechanics early in the last century, the brain is no longer viewed as a deterministic system. Thus, the argument from determinism no longer works, and there is now the possibility that an immaterial mind could interact with a physical brain by selecting which quantum state the brain enters out of the many states that are possible at any given time.

The philosopher Michael Lockwood (1989) has noted that the prejudice in favor of matter was grounded in the apparent solidity of the former in the Newtonian worldview. Lockwood points out that the solidity of matter has disappeared in the theory of quantum mechanics (material particles exist as probability waves in an abstract mathematical space until they are observed) and that mind and matter are now both equally mysterious.

The tenacity with which some scientists resist the idea of an autonomous realm of mind is perhaps understandable in light of history. The emerging mechanistic picture of the world was fiercely resisted by the religious establishment, notable examples being the condemnation of Galileo for the crime of propounding the heliocentric (sun-centered) model of the solar system and the resistance to the theory of biological evolution that is still being mounted by Christian fundamentalists. Thus, any mention of an immaterial soul may raise fears of a descent back into religious irrationalism (and a consequent lack of funding) on the part of many scientists.

Edge (2002a) in fact attributes Descartes' proposal of his theory of mind-matter interaction in part to his desire to remove the authority of the Church over the scientific investigation of matter. Edge notes that science could only investigate matter with the tools available in the seventeenth century and that it was (and still is) "not equipped" to deal with mentalistic phenomena. Edge (2002b) also attributes science's embrace of the ancient Greek philosophy of atomism (in which the universe is conceived as being composed of microscopic, discrete elementary particles) as another move to reject, or circumvent, the authority of the Church.

Modern Views

Let us now turn to an examination of modern views on, and "solutions" of, the mind-brain problem.

MONISTIC PHILOSOPHIES

Monistic solutions to the mind-brain problem are those that postulate that the universe is composed of only one type of "stuff." That "stuff" is usually taken to be mind, matter, or some sort of "tertium quid" having both mental and physical properties. Monism stands in contrast to dualism and pluralism, which comprise those philosophical positions that postulate the existence of two or more distinctly different types of "stuff," with one of them typically being mind and another being matter.

Idealism. The monistic position that contends that the world is composed solely of minds and mental events goes by the name of idealism. According to idealists, all that exists is mental experience. People consciously or unconsciously construct the hypothesis of a physical world in order to account for certain regularities in their sensory experience, but this is only a convenient fiction. The contention that the physical world may be an illusion is logically irrefutable. For instance, you may think you are a human being holding a book on the mind-brain problem in your hand; however, you could be merely dreaming or hallucinating. Following the Taoist philosopher Chuang Tzu, the reader might legitimately wonder whether she or he might be a butterfly temporarily dreaming about being a human being reading a sentence about butterfly dreams.

All you can be certain of is your own existence. Seeking certain knowledge, Descartes found that he could not doubt his own existence as a thinking being. In perhaps his most famous quote, he was led to exclaim, "I think, therefore I am." All you can be absolutely certain of is your own existence and that you are now thinking certain thoughts, remembering certain memories, feeling certain feelings and sensing certain sensations. The inferences you make about your external environment based on these mental events may not be valid, as you may be hallucinating, remembering falsely, having groundless feelings and thinking delusional thoughts. The doctrine that only one's self exists or can be proven to exist is a special case of idealism that goes by the name of solipsism.

The various agencies presumed by idealists to be responsible for producing the illusion of the physical world have included God (in the view of the prototypical idealist, the eighteenth century philosopher Bishop George Berkeley, for whom Berkeley University was named), a collective mind or collective unconscious, and the illusion-producing state of craving and ignorance (according to certain schools of Buddhism).

The reply of most modern scientists and philosophers of science to idealism is that scientific theories that postulate the existence of an objective physical world have produced more exact predictions about possible human observations than have idealistic theories and therefore should be preferred over the latter for that reason. (Such theories are even covertly preferred by most solipsists, who seem strangely reluctant to step in front of illusory oncoming trains. Dr. Samuel Johnson said of idealism, "I refute it thus," and then he proceeded to kick a rock with his foot. Johnson's "refutation," while actually proving nothing, did show his dedication to the anti-idealist cause.)

Idealism is not merely an historical curiosity, but even has its advocates today. The physicist Amit Goswami (1993) has contended that an idealist conception of the world is required in order to render modern theories of physics, in particular quantum mechanics, coherent.

Radical materialism. Radical materialism is the polar opposite of idealism. Radical materialists deny the existence of mental events, insisting that the world of physical matter is the only reality. Incredibly enough, this philosophy held sway in the discipline of psychology itself in the early part of this century (at least in the United States). Behaviorism emerged as the dominant force in psychology in this country as a reaction against the fallibility of the method of introspection that predominated in the earliest days of psychological investigation. Behavior was publicly observable and scientifically measurable, whereas the vague mental images that form, say, a particular individual's idea of the number seven are not. Some of the leaders of the behaviorist movement, such as John Watson (1924/1970) and the earlier versions of B. F. Skinner (e.g., Skinner, 1953), went so far as to deny the existence of mental events altogether. This denial of course flies in the face of the fact that the reader and I (if I am not a figment of the reader's imagination) have directly experienced such mental events as sensations, thoughts, feelings and memories. Skinner's position essentially contains its own refutation. Skinner could not consistently claim that he believed that mental events do not exist, as that belief would itself constitute a mental event. Therefore by his own theory (and reportedly by his own contention), Skinner's expressions of belief in the doctrine of radical materialism were merely forms of physical behavior than he had been rewarded for displaying in the past (through royalties, academic honoraria, etc.). If the books produced by Skinner are in fact merely the product of conditioned typewriter-pecking responses and the sentences within them do not express ideas, there is no need to take these books seriously. It should be noted that Skinner did eventually retreat from this early radical version of his theory.

Materialism is not dead as a philosophy in modern cognitive neuroscience, however. The philosopher Paul Churchland has recently proposed doing away with "folk psychology" (talk of mental events such as beliefs and desires) in all human discourse (Churchland, 1989, 1995). He would replace "folk psychology" with a strictly neural account of behavior. Thus, instead of a wife telling her husband that she is really angry at him, she would say instead, "The neurons in my amygdala seem to be firing at an unacceptably high rate."

Churchland has in fact gone so far as to assert that truth might cease to be an aim of science! This assertion is implicitly based on the assumption that the concept of truth presupposes the existence of propositions capable of being true or false, which in turn presupposes the existence of mental events such as thoughts, ideas and beliefs that are expressed in such propositions. Churchland proposes that scientific theories should no longer be expressed in terms of sentences but rather in terms of patterns of connections among neurons (or among the pseudoneurons in a computerized "neural net," as discussed below). But now we are right back where we started. Unless human knowledge is to be given up entirely, Churchland must at least be able to entertain propositions such as "neural net A diagnoses diseases more accurately than does neural net B." Such propositions, however express beliefs. If Churchland seriously wishes to give up the "folk psychological" concept of belief, then his philosophy self-destructs in the same way that Skinner's did.

Skinner, incidentally, was by no means the last modern thinker to deny the very existence of private conscious experience, or "qualia" in the terminology of philosophers. The prominent materialist philosopher Daniel Dennett has asserted that "contrary to what seems obvious at first blush, there simply are no qualia at all" (Dennett, 1988, p. 74). This statement may go a long way toward explaining Dennett's reasoning. However, I imagine that reader (like me) has personally experienced a great number of qualia, such as brilliant patches of red and pangs of hunger. Qualia may be both beautiful and horrifying. Dennett doesn't know what he is missing.

Quasi-dualistic materialism. More sensible versions of materialism concede the existence of mental events, but contend that mental events arise solely from physical events and that a complete scientific description of the world can be given in terms of physical processes alone. In one version of this theory, mental events are thought to be brain events experienced from the "inside." This view goes by the names "central state materialism" and "neural identity" theory, among others. A related doctrine is double-aspect theory. Double-aspect theorists contend that mental and physical events are merely two aspects of a single underlying reality. As the vast majority of double-aspect theorists implicitly or explicitly assume that this single underlying reality is essentially physical matter, this theory is basically equivalent to the previous two.

Panpsychism. A similar doctrine is panpsychism, which asserts that all matter, not just living organisms, has a mental aspect. This view has been advocated by the prominent Western philosopher Alfred North Whitehead (1929/1978), among others.

Panpsychism, with its contention that rocks and toothbrushes enjoy some form of consciousness, strikes one as absurd at first brush (or even more clearly upon a secondary cursory inspection of one's toothbrush). However, when you carefully consider it, the doctrine begins to grow on you.

A prominent recent proponent of this position is the philosopher David Ray Griffin (1988a, 1988b, 1994, 1997), although he prefers to call his doctrine "panexperientialism" rather than "panpsychism," as he does not contend that rocks and other inanimate collections of material particles possess a highly unified and structured consciousness, but rather ascribes only vague "feeling-responses" to them. More highly complex and structured forms of consciousness, in Griffin's view, are restricted to "compound individuals." Such compound individuals are composed of, or arise from, a hierarchical collection of more primitive selves or "individuals." For instance, a neuron would be a compound individual in relation to its individual constituents such as molecules, and a "suborgan" such as the hippocampus of the brain that is composed of neurons would be a compound individual somewhat further up the hierarchy. All such "individuals" would have both mental and physical aspects under the panexperientialist view, although only hierarchically-ordered structures would be assumed to have a highly organized and structured consciousness. Less well-organized structures, such as rocks, would be ascribed only vague "feeling responses" according to Griffin's panexperientialist theory. Griffin's theory raises the possibility that human societies may achieve a global consciousness that is beyond our ken, with each of us playing the role of a neuron in some sort of global "hypermind," much as each of our neurons is essentially a specialized cousin of unicellular organisms such as amoeba.

David Skrbina (2003, 2005) has recently provided a comprehensive and brilliant defense of the doctrine of "panpsychism." Skrbina argues for instance that an electron must somehow sense the presence of a proton in order to respond to its attractive force. (An electron may even enjoy a certain degree of freedom of action due to quantum indeterminacy and may be able to sense a quantum field that is highly complex and global in nature.)

As does Griffin, Skrbina associates more complex forms of consciousness with aggregates of matter, such as single neurons, or large assemblies of neurons such as hippocampi and cerebral hemispheres. (However, it should be noted that, as discussed in the Introduction, such aggregates of matter, much like one's personality and physical body, do not persist over time and thus cannot form the basis of a continuing self. Also, fields of consciousness appear to be unitary and indivisible, much more like a quark than like a molecule or a neuron.)

As Skrbina points out, the panpsychist position solves the problem of "emergence" or the need to account for how organisms acquired consciousness in the course of evolution (i.e., how insensate matter gave rise to consciousness). As he notes, there is no definitive line of demarcation that can be drawn between conscious and nonconscious organisms, in either the present world or in the course of evolution. If all matter is imbued with consciousness or if fields of consciousness are fundamental constituents of the universe that have existed throughout its history, then the problem of evolution of consciousness (and of how a three-pound "hunk of meat" like the human brain could generate conscious experiences in the first place) does not arise.

It should, however, be noted that panpsychism still faces the difficulty of accounting for the emergence of a unified mind and global consciousness out of a myriad of psychic elements, as was pointed out long ago by William James and, more recently, by William Seager (1995).

Epiphenomenalism. Epiphenomenalism is technically a form of dualism, insofar as it grants separate reality to the realms of mind and matter; however, I will classify epiphenomenalism as a form of quasi-dualistic materialism, as it denies that mental events have any influence whatsoever on the physical world. Mental events are considered to be mere "epiphenomena" of physical events in the sense that, while mental events are caused by physical events, they are themselves incapable of causing or influencing physical events. A prominent advocate of epiphenomenalism was the biologist Thomas Henry Huxley (1874, 1877), the grandfather of the noted writer Aldous Huxley, who was perhaps most noted for his tireless defenses of Darwin's theory of evolution (so much so that he earned the nickname "Darwin's Bulldog").

Several writers, including the noted mathematician Roger Penrose (1987) and Karl Popper and John Eccles (1977), have noted that epiphenomenalism in fact goes counter to Darwinism. Why should a conscious mind have evolved, they ask, if it did not play an active role in benefiting the organism?

Also, and perhaps most amusingly, the mere existence of epiphenomenalist theories is in itself sufficient to refute the doctrine of epiphenomenalism. After all, epiphenomenalism was developed as an attempt to explicate the role of mental events; therefore, the theory has been created in response to (i.e., has been caused by) mental events; otherwise, epiphenomenalism could not claim to be a theory of mental experience. Thus, the theory of epiphenomenalism is refuted by the fact of its own existence.

The physicist Heinz Pagels (1988) raised the question of whether the universe could be a giant computer, much as a personal computer screen can become transformed into a mini-universe with quasi-organisms evolving on it when a program realizing mathematician John Conway's "game of life" is run on it. This idea had previously been suggested by Ed Fredkin of M.I.T. and explicitly endorsed by Tomasso Toffoli (1982). This view has been most recently revived by the noted mathematician Stephen Wolfram (2002), who suggests that universe is best understood as a giant cellular automaton (computerized grid of cells following prescribed rules of behavior). If this suggestion that the universe is in fact the product of a giant computer has any validity, we cannot equate ourselves with the godlike programmers who created the universe and assume that we have simply each become entranced in the life of one of our three-dimensional creations (which we have come to regard as our physical body). Because of the arguments against epiphenomenalism, we cannot be mere spectators in the world. Our consciousnesses have a more active role in the universe than that.

Physicalism. The philosophical positions that I have grouped together under the heading of quasi-dualistic materialism would seem to be equivalent to one another as scientific theories, insofar as they all apparently make the same scientific predictions (mainly that no violations of the known laws of physics will occur in the brain and that no successful predictions regarding the behavior of the brain can be generated from theories involving nonphysical entities such as souls or minds that could not in principle at least be derived from theories referring solely to physical entities and processes).

The empirical findings that most directly challenge the doctrine of physicalism derive from the parapsychologists' investigations of ostensible psi phenomena such as the clairvoyant reading of ESP cards and psychokinetic influence of the fall of rolling dice. Because of their importance in this debate and because of the controversies surrounding parapsychological research, these findings and their implications will be discussed in some detail in Chapters 3 through 5. However, as we have seen in the Introduction, this evidence is not needed in order to build a strong case that one's individual self or consciousness is something other than one's physical body and may be capable of surviving the death of that body, or (perhaps more likely) of departing the body and becoming associated with a new physical system well prior to the death of the body.

It is commonly held, both by parapsychologists and skeptics, that psi phenomena are inexplicable on the basis of current physical theories and are thus evidence against the doctrine of physicalism, if the latter is construed as the contention that all phenomena can be ultimately accounted for in terms of present theories of physics or relatively minor extensions thereof.

Joseph Banks Rhine (the researcher who is largely regarded as the progenitor of modern parapsychology and who established the first major research program in experimental parapsychology at Duke University in the 1930s) in particular was highly skeptical that psi phenomena could be explained on the basis of any physicalistic theory. In fact, Rhine suggested that psi was nonphysical in nature, due to the lack of dependence of experimental psi-scoring rates on spatial or temporal separations and the lack of attenuation of the psi signal by physical barriers between the percipient and the target object (e.g., ESP card or die) that would block most known forms of physical signals (such as electromagnetic radiation). Rhine also cited the fact psi success appears to be independent of the physical nature of the target object, as well as the apparent backward causation in time involved in precognition (and, we might now add, retroactive psychokinesis), as further evidence against any physicalistic explanation of psi phenomena.

Michael Levin (2000) has made the argument that if psi abilities are based on physical processes grounded in the biomechanical properties of the body, then surely these abilities would be selected for in the process of evolution and would by now be readily apparent in animals' behavior. The fact psi is an elusive and rarely observed ability, Levin asserts, constitutes further evidence that it is not derived from the biomechanical workings of animals' bodies.

Because it appears to be difficult to account for psi phenomena on the basis of known physical theories or principles, it is often believed that the existence of psi phenomena would falsify physicalism (where "physicalism" denotes the class of theories encompassing radical materialism and quasi-dualistic materialism). As the vast majority of working scientists subscribe to some form of physicalistic solution to the mind-body problem, it should not be surprising that they would choose to reject the claims of parapsychology, insofar as those claims tend to threaten their worldview.

Some of the resistance of establishment science toward accepting the existence of psi may stem back to the fact that Western science has relatively recently (in the vast scheme of things) emerged from a battle with the Church over who would hold the authority regarding determining the nature of reality, the trial of Galileo being only one prominent example. There are those who believe that some sort of truce should be declared between science and religion, such as Stephen J. Gould, who asserted that science and religion should be considered as "separate magisteria," with science holding reign over matters of empirical fact and religion holding reign over ethics and matters of the spirit (Gould, 1999). However, despite Gould's contentions, science and religion are in many cases still in conflict over empirical questions, as is evident in the ongoing battle of religious creationists in the United States to have Darwin's theory of evolution either removed or downplayed in high school biology curricula.

Even if it is assumed that the explanation of psi phenomena will require the postulation of entities and principles beyond those currently known to physicalistic science, it may be a mere issue of terminology whether such entities are to be considered material or nonmaterial. If the former, the physicalist can claim victory; if the latter, the dualist can claim the same. Obviously, if mind and matter interact, they form one united system. Whether one chooses to call that system the physical universe may be a matter of semantics rather than substance. (Some of the theoretical concepts already employed by physicists, such as the quantum-mechanical wave function discussed in the next chapter, already seem more mind-like than material in any event.)

DUALISTIC INTERACTIONISM

We are thus led to consider dualist interactionism, which grants independent reality to both mental and physical events, Unlike epiphenomenalism, in interactionism the causal highway is a two-way street. Not only do events in the physical realm cause mental events, but mental events are capable of influencing physical events as well. As we have mentioned, since the advent of the theory of quantum mechanics, the brain is no longer considered to be a completely deterministic system and therefore could be open to influence from a mental realm. (In this context, however, it should be noted that some die-hard materialists such as philosopher Daniel Dennett [1991] continue to reject dualism on the basis of arguments involving the outmoded concept of a deterministic brain system.) In fact, the brain seems almost designed in such a way as to maximize its receptivity to such influence from a nonmaterial mind. Neurophysiologist John Eccles has called the brain just "the sort of a machine a 'ghost' could operate," as its functioning is dependent on minute electrical potentials and the motions of neurotransmitter molecules and calcium ions (Eccles 1953, p. 285). Several prominent physicists, including Niels Bohr (1958), Arthur Eddington (1935), Henry Margenau (1984), Euan Squires (1990) and Henry Stapp (1992), have explicitly proposed that the mind interacts with the brain by influencing the outcome of quantum processes within the brain.

There have been many who have had difficulty conceptualizing how such different entities as mind (which Descartes and many subsequent philosophers regarded as immaterial and lacking any spatial extension) could interact with matter. For instance, in regard to Descartes' notion that the mind interacted with the human brain through the deflection of the animal spirits as they passed through the pineal gland, the philosopher Thomas Metzinger says:

> Something without any spatial properties cannot causally interact with something possessing spatial properties *at a specific location*. If Descartes had taken his own premises seriously, he could never have come up with this solution, which is so obviously false. If the mind truly is an entity not present in physical space, it would be absurd to look for a *locus* of interaction in the human brain [Metzinger, 2003, p. 381. Emphasis in original].

As each of us seems to be somehow "stuck" in a human brain, however temporarily, it would in fact seem that the self, construed as a field of consciousness, does have some spatial properties, if only the property that it is, at least temporarily, somehow stuck to (or under the panpsychistic hypothesis, part of) a human brain occupying a particular region in space.

From this it does not follow that the self in its entirety is confined to a spatial location in the human brain or circumscribed region of space. As we shall see in the next chapter, even the elementary particles of matter such as electrons and protons typically do not have any particular spacetime location until they are forced to adopt one through an act of observation. Even physical matter lacks the material properties ascribed to it by Metzinger.

Another conceptual objection to interactionism is that mind-brain interaction would involve violations of the laws of physics. Many writers, including Mohrhoff (1999), Wilson (1999), Levin (2000), Jaswal (2005) and Clark (2005a), have argued that any action of a nonphysical mind on the brain would entail the violation of physical laws, such as the conservation of energy and momentum and the requirement that the outcomes of quantum processes be randomly determined.

Levin (2000) argues that dualist interaction would involve a violation of the law of the conservation of energy. However, the noted philosopher Karl Popper has suggested that the mind may have its own source of (presumably physical) energy. Under this view, the mind would be a sort of quasiphysical object that might be capable of greater influence on the brain than that allowed by the Heisenberg uncertainty principle of quantum mechanics. Popper even went so far as to assert that the law of energy is only "statistically valid" (Popper & Eccles, 1977, p.541). Without going to this extreme, it could be argued that mind is capable of exerting some force on some of the material particles in the brain. Also, we are a long way from having measured with precision every minute energy transaction in human brains. In the process of doing so, it is conceivable that some unexpected energy transactions may be observed. If science should progress to the point where the action of spheres of consciousness on energy transactions within the brain can somehow be mathematically (or otherwise) described, this might be a victory for the contention that immaterial minds can exert physical force. If such spheres of consciousness are identified with known material particles and system, the physicalists could claim victory. If not, the dualists could so declare.

If spheres of consciousness could exert some sort of physical force, it is likely that they would be declared as a new form of physical matter or energy, resulting in a victory for the physicalists. If the present day physicalists opine that all physical particles have already been discovered, this may only be evidence for the psychological tendency toward premature closure, in that they fervently wish to believe that they already possess virtually complete understanding of the universe. But such a declaration could only be the worst form of arrogance in view of the fact, already noted, that physicists have only recently discovered the existence of dark energy, which is now believed to comprise three-quarters of the matter-energy in the universe.

Physicist Henry Stapp (2005b) asserts that quantum mechanical laws must be used to describe the process of exocytosis (the emission of neurotransmitters into the synaptic cleft), citing empirical research in support of this assertion (Schwartz, Stapp & Beauregard, 2005). In particular, Stapp notes that the "quantum Zeno effect" (maintaining a quantum state through repeated observation) provides a means whereby conscious minds could act on the physical brain, namely by holding the brain in a particular state. He cites William James' observation that the role of conscious attention is to preserve brain states in support of this view. He also notes that Pashler (1998) has observed that consciousness may act as an information-processing bottleneck in this regard.

Contrary views have been expressed by Jaswal (2005) and Clark (2005a), among others, who argue that any such influence on quantum mechanical processes would lead to a violation of the statistical predictions of quantum mechanics and the principle that the outcome of quantum mechanical processes are randomly determined. Such influence would therefore constitute a violation of the laws of physics.

First of all, it should be noted, as many observers have argued, that description of the universe afforded by the laws of quantum mechanics is incomplete. Also, no one has provided, or likely ever will provide, a complete description of the quantum state of any brain at any time. We may discover new entities or processes that may be identified with the so-called "hidden variables" that determine the outcomes of quantum processes. Also, quantum mechanical outcomes may indeed be random in simple physical systems, but may be less random in certain complex systems, such as human brains, in which the observing consciousnesses may have a more vested interest. It may also be that such consciousnesses enjoy a closer physical proximity to physical brains, on the view that quasi-physical spheres of consciousness may be, at least, temporarily, somehow "stuck" in physical brains.

Thus, it might turn out that the outcomes of quantum processes inside complex systems such as brains are not randomly determined but are governed by fields of consciousness, whereas those in simpler systems are not so governed. Also, many parapsychological researchers, going back to Schmidt (1969, 1970), have produced evidence that conscious minds may be capable of determining, or at least biasing, the outcomes of quantum processes, as will be discussed in more detail in subsequent chapters.

Having discussed the general framework, we will now consider specific versions of dualistic interaction that have been proposed in recent times. This discussion will be an introductory one, and a more detailed discussion of some of the philosophical and scientific issues raised by modern models of dualistic interaction will be postponed until Chapters 2, 5 and 7.

Eccles' theory of mind-brain interaction. There are few adherents to the doctrine of dualistic interaction among working scientists today. John Eccles was perhaps the most prominent example of such a scientist in the second half of the twentieth century. Eccles was a renowned neurophysiologist, who in 1963 shared the Nobel prize in medicine and physiology with his coworkers A. L. Hodgkin and A. F. Huxley.

Eccles progressively elaborated his dualistic model in a series of publications spanning several decades (e.g., Eccles, 1953, 1970, 1977, 1979, 1980, 1983, 1987, 1989; Eccles & Robinson, 1984; Popper & Eccles, 1977). Eccles felt that it is necessary to postulate the existence of a mind separate from the brain in order to explain the integration of mental activity. In particular, Eccles felt that the integrated perception of objects and visually presented scenes cannot be explained in terms of known neurological processes, in view of the fact that the nervous impulses related to visual experiences appear to be fragmented and sent to divergent areas of the brain. For instance, Christof Koch and Francis Crick count from 30 to 40 different cortical areas specializing in different aspects of visual processing (Koch & Crick, 1991). Similarly, Wilson, Scalaidhe and Goldman-Rakic (1993) have described the separation of the neurons dealing with the spatial location and identity (color and shape) of an object in the prefrontal cortex of the brain of a monkey. Hodgson (2005) notes that red circles are experienced as a whole (or "gestalt") despite the fact that the neurons "reporting" "red" and "circle" are located in different areas of the brain.

In view of the fact that the perception of any single object involves the firing of neurons in widely dispersed areas of the brain, it is difficult to understand how this neural activity can possibly result in a unified perception of an object. This conundrum is generally termed the "binding problem" (Koch & Crick, 1991). In Hodgson's view, the experience of gestalts such as his example of the red circle indicates that consciousness may be nonlocal in the quantum mechanical sense (Hodgson, 2005). The relationship between quantum nonlocality and consciousness will be revisited several times in the chapters to follow.

Stacia Friedman-Hill, Lynn Robertson and Anne Triesman (1995) report an instance in which a breakdown of this perceptual unity was apparent in a patient who miscombined colors and shapes from different objects and who was unable to judge the locations of objects. This patient had bilateral lesions in the parietal-occipital areas of the brain, suggesting that these brain regions may be centrally involved in generating unified perceptions of experience.

Francis Crick (1994) ascribed the unity of perception to rhythmic oscillations in the brain resulting in the synchronous firing of large populations of neurons.

Two other neurophysiologists, Gerald Edelman and Giulio Jononi (1995), have contended that the binding of perceptions and the unity of experience is achieved thorough reentrant signaling pathways in the brain.

Eccles, on the other hand, saw the integration of neural activity as the raison d'être of an immaterial mind, and he suggested that the evolution of consciousness may have paralleled the emergence of the visual processing mechanism. He endorsed William James' conjecture that brains may have had to acquire conscious minds because they had grown too complex to control themselves.

Eccles contended that the mind interacts with only certain groups (or "modules") of neurons, which he called "open neurons." He used the term "liaison brain" to refer to the regions of the brain containing these open modules, and he asserted that this liaison brain lies in the cerebral cortex rather than in the deeper areas of the middle brain.

Libet's CMFs. Benjamin Libet (1989, 1991a) views the supplementary motor area (SMA) of the cerebral cortex as being one of the primary areas that is involved in voluntary acts. In this he agrees with Eccles, who at one point went so far as to say that "there is strong support for hypothesis that the SMA is the sole recipient area of the brain for mental intentions that lead to voluntary movements" (Eccles, 1983, p. 45). Libet notes that patients with damaged supplementary motor areas are often incapable of spontaneous voluntary movement; while they may listlessly respond to suggestions from others, they seldom initiate movements on their own. In this sense their will is curtailed. Libet's view is underscored by Goldberg's observation that lesions of the supplementary motor area lead to repetitive hand movements, such as buttoning and unbuttoning a shirt, that are experienced as ego-alien and occurring independently of the subject's will (Goldberg, 1985). Libet further observes that blood flows into the supplementary motor area when movements are merely being contemplated.

Libet's own experiments indicate that subjects' decisions to initiate motor movements (flexing the hand) typically do not occur until 350 milliseconds after a readiness potential has begun to build in the brain, indicating that the brain itself has already been preparing for movement at the time of the subject's experienced decision. Libet notes, however, that mind-brain interaction must be a two-way street, and he found that subjects could change their mind about flexing their hands during the final 150 milliseconds preceding the actual physical act. He also found that this veto decision seemed to coincide in time with a drop in the voltage of the readiness potential. Libet infers from this that the conscious mind has the ability to block an already initiated movement or to let it occur. In this view, the brain is seen as generating courses of action, while the mind or a "free will" decides on the options. He sees the inhibition of action as one of the central roles of a conscious mind.

Levy (2005) has interpreted Libet's results in a somewhat different manner. Levy notes that Libet's subjects may have delegated the task of deciding when to flex their hand to processes occurring in the "unconscious" regions of their minds. Levy also notes that it is reasonable to doubt whether Libet is correct in identifying the unconscious brain activity with the intention to or decision to act rather than with the generation of an urge or desire to act.

To explicate the process of mind-brain interaction, Libet (1994) postulates the existence of a "conscious mind field" (CMF), which he sees as being produced by brain activity. The CMF is not capable of being detected by physical measuring devices, nor is it reducible to neural processes; nevertheless, Libet proposes that the CMF is capable of exerting a causal influence on brain processes and that it provides the means whereby diverse neural activity can give rise to unified perceptions and experiences. Libet contends that his view of the CMF is compatible with a variety of different philosophical positions on the mind-body problem. Libet's views are discussed in more detail in Chapter 7.

Other views on mind-brain interaction. It would almost seem that no region of the brain has been omitted from the list of brain regions that form the primary center of consciousness according to one researcher or another. In addition to the candidates listed above we have the thalamus (Cotterill, 1995), nonrandom, coherent deviations of the brain's electromagnetic field from its resting state (John, 2003), and, last but not least, quantum-mechanically entangled water in the microtubules composing the cytoskeletons of neurons (Penrose, 1994; Hameroff, 1994). Each of these authors presents a cogent argument in favor of their candidate for the area of the brain (or brain process) that is the center of consciousness (or of the interaction between consciousness and mind).

With this many candidates for the *primary* center of consciousness (or of interaction between the conscious mind and brain), it may begin to seem that no center is primary, that many different brain centers and processes may be associated with their own conscious activity, and that these centers of consciousness may not be mutually accessible to one another, at least in a direct sense. This possibility will be discussed in much further detail in Chapters 5 and 7.

MYSTERIANISM

Last, but by far not least, there is strangely appealing doctrine of "mysterianism," whose most notable proponent is Colin McGinn (1999). McGinn contends that the biological wetware of our brains has evolved to enable us to reason about and understand the physical world rather than to solve such esoteric problems as the nature of consciousness and the fate of the soul. Our globs of 10^{11} pulsating amoeba-like neurons are more likely designed to discover how to better secure a stone axe head to a stick to beat upon our neighbor's brain than to enable us to understand the realms to which our neighbor's consciousness has fled after we have completed our handiwork.

In McGinn's view, the role of consciousness and the nature of the soul will forever remain beyond our cognitive grasp as our primate brains have evolved to seek fruit and elude tigers and deal with other concrete concerns in the physical world. McGinn opines that the nature of consciousness and its relation to the physical world must remain outside of the grasp of consciousness, at least of those consciousnesses inhabiting our primitive primate brains, which are unequal to the task of understanding their true nature. Perhaps McGinn is right. Perhaps that is why consciousness is often referred to as the "hard problem" of philosophy. But, unlike our ape brethren, we have been to the moon and plumbed the creation of the universe down to the first femtosecond. It is premature to give up trying to understand the nature of our conscious mind. As we shall see, such understanding may require us to relinquish core beliefs about the nature of our selves and the quasi-permanence of our association with any particular body.

Once we have shed our present body and the "self-cocoons" we have wrapped around us to keep us firmly fixed to our present personalities, who knows what wonders may await us?

2

Mind and the Quantum

As discussed in the previous chapter, under the theories of physics developed by Isaac Newton that dominated Western thought about the physical world from the late seventeenth to very early twentieth century, the physical world was seen as a great impersonal clockwork mechanism. Under this classical, Newtonian view, the physical world was deterministic in the sense that, given the present state of the world, including the position and velocity of every single particle of physical matter, the future states of the universe were completely determined by the laws of physics. Thus, given the (completely described) state of the universe on July 15, 2012, the events of, say, November 23, 2013, are completely determined. As the mathematician and cosmologist Pierre Simon Laplace put it, a Divine Calculator who knew the position and velocity of every material and particle in the universe could deduce the entire history and future of the universe down to the smallest detail.

Obviously in such a clockwork universe, there is no room for intervention by a nonphysical mind. The soul, or atman, had no place in the theory of physics developed by Newton, despite the fact that Newton himself was a devout believer in the Christian God (unless of course the soul were conceived to be a material particle under some type of double-aspect theory).

All this changed with the development of quantum mechanics around the beginning of the twentieth century. Under the quantum mechanical view, the world is no longer completely deterministic, even (especially) at the subatomic level. Given the present state of the universe, under the laws of quantum mechanics, many different futures are possible. This view of reality opens a crack in the cosmic egg (to borrow a phrase from Joseph Chilton Pearce, 1973) for the influence of a nonmaterial mind or soul to creep into the picture.

Quantum Nonlocality

Also, the classical determinism of Newtonian physics saw the world as composed of whirling buzz of mindless submicroscopic particles, careening blindly about in space, sometimes joining and sometime repelling one another, their behavior governed by the impersonal laws of physics. In this universe there seems only room for the parts and little room for the whole as exemplified in conscious minds that are somehow aware of activity of vast (on the elementary particle scale of things) regions of the brain. In the classical view of the universe, each particle of matter responds only to its local surroundings. It does not respond to its compatriot particles until it quite literally "bumps into them." This notion that the behavior of physical particles is governed completely by events in their local spacetime regions is called "local realism." Despite the deluge of popular books that have been written about quantum mechanics in the second half of the twentieth century (not to mention those published in the infancy of the new millennium), "local realism" is still the view that undergirds our intuitive understanding of the universe, both laymen and scientists alike (although perhaps both groups should know better by now).

As noted above, under the theory of quantum mechanics, indeterminism reigns. Given the present state of the universe, many different futures are possible. Take, for instance, the case of Schrodinger's hapless cat, imprisoned in a box together with a radioactive source that will kill it (through some sort of Rube Goldberg device) if a Geiger counter detects a radioactive decay. After a fixed period of time there is a 50–50 chance that when we open the box we will find a cat that has been sent to that Great Alley in the sky. According to the standard interpretation of quantum mechanics, the variables that determine the instant of the first decay, if indeed there are any, are "hidden" to us. The best we can do is compute the probability that the cat is still alive. If there are "hidden variables" that determine the cat's fate, we cannot know them.

The most startling and remarkable thing about such hidden variables is that, if they exist, they must be nonlocal in nature. To understand what "nonlocality" means in this context, consider the case of two protons that are initially united in a state of zero spin (what physicists call the "singlet state"). Suppose that the protons have become separated from one another and are moving in opposite directions through space. If the spin of one of these protons is measured along a spatial axis and the proton is found to be spinning "upward" along that axis, the other proton must be spinning "downward" along that axis (as their total spin along any axis must sum to zero). Thus, it seems that when you measure the spin of one proton and find it to be "up," the second proton is somehow instantly informed that it should adopt the "down" state on that axis.

It might be assumed that the Newtonian framework in which the protons are viewed as separate, isolated particles could accommodate this phenomenon through postulating that, when the protons separated, one of them possessed some property that made it spin "down" on the axis and the other one possessed some property that made it spin "up." In other words, there is no need to assume any mysterious interconnection between the protons. This is view under the doctrine known as "local realism."

It can be shown that if protons really do posses such local properties, the numbers of proton pairs exhibiting various combinations of spins on certain predefined axes must satisfy a class of inequalities called Bell inequalities after the physicist John Bell, who derived them. The theory of quantum mechanics, on the other hand, predicts that Bell inequalities will be violated if certain combinations of spatial axes are chosen.

Against my better judgment, I am not going to force the reader to take my word for it this time, but I am going to walk those readers that are able to recall their high school trigonometry through the actual mathematics used to establish that the "hidden variables" of quantum mechanics must be nonlocal in nature. (They say that each equation a book contains halves its sales. If so, here go 99.95 percent of my royalties.) The math phobic reader may however ignore the equations and inequalities that follow and quite literally "read between the lines" to follow the gist of my argument. However, for those readers who can follow the actual mathematics, the demonstration of quantum nonlocality is all the more compelling, startling and, to use a hackneyed phrase, awe-inspiring when you appreciate and understand the beauty and simplicity of the mathematics behind it. The mathematical exposition to follow is roughly along the lines set forth by Bernard d'Espagnat (1979) in his highly lucid explanation of quantum nonlocality.

We begin our story with two protons blissfully united in the "singlet" state, a state in which their collective spin is zero. (A proton's spin may be oversimplistically imagined as the spin of a top; its units are expressed in term of angular momentum. Unlike a top, however, the proton is only able to manifest distinct units of spin, unlike a skater who can go smoothly from a slowly spinning state with her arms extended to a fast-spinning state with her arms pulled in or slowly turn a clockwise rotation into a counterclockwise rotation. In quantum mechanics, these states are discrete; there is no intermediate spin in which the spinner's arms are half pulled in so that she is spilling at an intermediate rate. A proton goes directly from one spin state to another in what is often termed a quantum leap. The proton, like all free quantum spirits but unlike skaters, also may be found in a mixture of states in which it is spinning "clockwise" (also known as "downward") with probability, say, 0.6 and spinning counterclockwise with a probability of 0.4.

Thus, in quantum theory, the properties of material particles are not specified deterministically, but only probabilistically. For instance, one may measure the spin of a proton along any spatial axis A of one's choosing, and its spin will be found either to be in the upward direction with regard to that axis (A^+) or in the downward direction along that axis (A^-). The quantum mechanical description of the particle's state does not determine the spin direction along any axis, but only gives the probabilities that the spin will be found to be either "up" or "down" with regard to the given axis.

If the quantum mechanical description is complete, then the proton does not have any definite, well-defined spin with regard to any axis until a measurement is made, after which the proton's spin will either be up upward along the axis or downward along the axis. If the spin of a proton along any particular axis A has been measured, its spin along any other axis B is indeterminate according to quantum theory. The proton is said to be in a "superposition" of the "spinning upward on B" and "spinning downward on B" states. The proton is not definitely in one state or the other, and quantum theory can only yield the probability that it will be found to be spinning upward on B rather than being able to predict in advance which way the proton will be found to be spinning when measured along axis B.

At the point of measurement or observation, the proton acquires a definite spin on axis B, through a process known as "the collapse of the state vector." The nature of this process is not adequately specified by quantum theory, and state vector collapse seems to be due to factors not adequately defined in present day quantum theory.

The lack of any provision for the state vector collapse in the formalism of quantum mechanics formed the inspiration for Hugh Everett's Many-World, interpretation of quantum mechanics in which all possible outcomes of quantum mechanical processes are postulated to occur in some alternate future (Everett, 1957). Thus, there may alternate universes alongside of ours in which you are no longer a quadriplegic because President Al Gore's Secretary of Transportation enacted policies leading to schedule changes in your local bus service so that the bus did not locate itself in the same spacetime region as your body when you stopped to tie your shoe on April 1, 2003. Under Everett's Many World hypothesis, all events that are possible under the laws of quantum mechanics actually occur in some alternative future.

Many theorists (e.g., Wheeler, 1983; Walker, 2000) have proposed that observation by a conscious mind, an entity outside of physical science altogether (barring the truth of reductive physicalism), may be necessary to force state vector collapse and to ensure that only one of the many futures allowable under quantum mechanics actually occurs.

If a proton's spin is determined (through measurement) along one axis, its spin along any other axis is undetermined according to quantum theory and does not take on any definite value until an act of observation occurs. Einstein, Podolsky and Rosen (1935) argued that quantum theory is simply incomplete in this regard. For instance, it may be possible in some sense to measure the spin of a proton along two directions at once. If two protons are initially united in a state of zero spin (e.g., the "singlet" state) and then allowed to separate, their spins as subsequently measured on any chosen axis must have opposite values. Thus, if the spin of the first proton is measured to be upward along an axis A (A^+) and its partner's spin measured to be upward along a second axis B (B^+), it can be argued that the first proton must have been an A^+B^- proton (i.e., having properties causing it to spin upward on the A axis and downward on the B axis) prior to the act of observation.

Thus, Einstein, Podolsky and Rosen argued, particles do have definite properties prior to any act of measurement and the probabilistic description provided by quantum theory is simply an incomplete description of reality.

John Bell (1964), on the other hand, was able to use a simple mathematical argument to show that the empirical predictions of quantum theory are in conflict with any theory assuming that the outcome of quantum measurements are determined by the local properties of particles and do not depend on what occurs in distant regions of space.

A simplified version of Bell's argument is as follows. Assume that protons have localized properties that determine the outcomes of spin measurements (i.e., the proton has "really" been spinning upward on the A axis all along, although we didn't know it until we observed it). An A^+B^- proton would then be a proton that has a property that ensures that it will be found to be spinning upward when measured along axis A and downward if measured along axis B. Such A^+B^- protons must come in two varieties: those that will be found to be spinning upward when measured along any third axis C (the $A^+B^-C^+$ protons), and those that will be found to be spinning downward when measured along axis C (the $A^+B^-C^-$ protons). Thus, the probability $p(A^+B^-)$ that a proton will have spins A^+ and B^- must satisfy the following equation:

$$p(A^+B^-) = p(A^+B^-C^+) + p(A^+B^-C^-) \qquad (2.1)$$

By a similar reasoning process, we have:

$$p(A^+C^-) = p(A^+B^+C^-) + p(A^+B^-C^-) \qquad (2.2)$$

But as $p(A^+B^-C^-)$ is greater than or equal to 0, Equation (2.2) implies:

$$p(A^+C^-) \geq p(A^+B^-C^-) \qquad (2.3)$$

Similarly,

$$p(B^-C^+) \geq p(A^+B^-C^+) \qquad (2.4)$$

Adding inequalities (2.3) and (2.4), we obtain:

$$p(A^+C^-) + p(B^-C^+) \geq p(A^+B^-C^-) + p(A^+B^-C^+) \qquad (2.5)$$

Substituting from equation (2.1), we have:

$$p(A^+C^-) + p(B^-C^+) \geq p(A^+B^-) \qquad (2.6)$$

Inequality (2.6) is known as a Bell inequality, and it must be obeyed if the proton's spins are determined by local properties of the protons themselves and do not depend on events happening in remote regions of space and time. Inequality (2.6) is, however, in conflict with the predictions of quantum theory. According to quantum theory, if the positive directions of two axes A and B are separated by an angle φ_{AB}, the probability that a proton will display opposite spin orientations on the two axes is given by $\sin^2(\varphi_{AB}/2)$. As either the A^+B^- or the A^-B^+ orientations are equally likely given the singlet state, we have:

$$p(A^+B^-) = \tfrac{1}{2} \times \sin^2(\varphi_{AB}/2) \qquad (2.7)$$

Suppose we orient detector A so that the positive pole points in the "north" direction (in a plane). Suppose also that we point detector B in the "southeast" direction and detector C in the "northeast" direction (in the same plane). Then we have φ_{AB} = 1350, φ_{AC} = 450, φ_{BC} = 900. (Now is the time to reach back into your memory for whatever tidbits of high school trigonometry may be remaining there or, better yet, to dust off that scientific calculator you have been keeping in the attic.)

Using the probabilistic laws of quantum mechanics as described above, we have:

$$p(A^+C^-) = \tfrac{1}{2} \times \sin^2(45°/2) = \tfrac{1}{2} \times \sin^2(22.5°) = .073 \qquad (2.8)$$
$$p(B^-C^+) = \tfrac{1}{2} \times \sin^2(90°/2) = \tfrac{1}{2} \times \sin^2(45°) = .250 \qquad (2.9)$$
$$p(A^+B^-) = \tfrac{1}{2} \times \sin^2(135°/2) = \tfrac{1}{2} \times \sin^2(67.5°) = .427 \qquad (2.10)$$

These probabilities are in violation of the Bell inequality (2.6), as can be seen by substituting the values given in equations (2.8) through (2.10) into inequality (2.6) to obtain:

$$.073 + .250 \geq .427 \qquad (2.11)$$

Inequality (2.11) is obviously false, thus revealing that the laws of quantum mechanics are in conflict with the philosophy of "local realism" from which inequality (2.6) was derived (i.e., the view that the outcomes of quantum measurements are determined by properties of the particles and the local spacetime regions in which they reside).

Experimental evidence by Alain Aspect and his coworkers (e.g., Aspect, Dalibard, & Roger, 1982) has shown that in a test of quantum mechanics against local realism, the Bell inequalities are violated, and the evidence is strongly against the doctrine of local realism. It should be noted that Aspect's experiments were conducted using photons rather than protons, and the mathematics underlying the Bell inequalities is somewhat different and a little more complex than that for protons. A very readable exposition of the mathematics underlying Bell inequalities for photons is given in McAdam (2003).

Aspect et al.'s results imply that two quantum particles such as protons may not be the isolated objects separated from each other in space that they appear to be. Instead, they may form one united system even though they may be separated by light years of space. The protons do not have defined spins on a spatial axis until a measurement of one of their spins along that axis is made, at which point the measured proton's partner suddenly adopts the opposite spin. After the first proton "chooses" a spin (up or down) along the measured axis, the second proton is somehow mysteriously informed that it should adopt the opposite spin if measured along that same axis. It cannot be the case that the first proton manages to send a message to the second proton telling it which spin to adopt, as the protons may be sufficiently far apart that no such signal could be sent between them unless it exceeded the speed of light, which is regarded as impossible in standard theories of physics. Thus, the protons, two seemingly separated and isolated little billiard balls, turn out not to be separated from one another after all.

Even single physical particles are not the localized, isolated entities that they appear to be. Consider the case of the classic "double-slit" experiment, in which electrons must pass though one of two slits in order to reach a detecting mechanism. Electrons are always detected as point-like entities; thus, it is reasonable to assume that the distribution of the locations of electrons detected when both slits are open will simply be the sum of the distributions obtained when the slits are opened one at a time. However, as streams of electrons possess wavelike properties, an interference pattern (bands of darkness and light) will be manifested at the detecting device when both slits are open, and this interference pattern will differ markedly from the distribution expected by summing the distributions obtained when the slits are opened one at a time. The most amazing thing is that the interference effect manifests itself even under conditions in which only one electron can pass through the diffraction grating at a time. Thus, it appears that a single electron somehow manages to go through both slits at once! Any attempt to determine which slit is actually traversed by the electron reveals, on the other hand, that the electron passes through only one slit. Furthermore, this determination destroys the interference pattern and results in a distribution equal to the sum of the distributions from each slit.

Thus, although an electron is always detected as a point-like entity, it appears to manifest itself as a nonlocalized wave function under circumstances in which we do not attempt to determine its location. The modern interpretation of this wave is that it is a "probability wave" existing in an abstract mathematical space called Hilbert space rather than in physical space. The electron, an apparently solid point-like entity when we observe it, is apparently a ghostly vibration in an abstract, almost mind-like, space when we are not looking! Perhaps the universe is telling us something here. Maybe the message is that there is no consistent physical description of the elementary particles that make up the universe. The message may be that the physical universe is in some sense "unreal" at the most basic level, in Jeans' terminology more like a thought than like a machine. Or perhaps the message is to lie back, don't ask so many questions, and enjoy.

Chris Clarke (2004) notes that the phenomenon of quantum nonlocality as demonstrated in Aspect's experiments strikes the death knell for the philosophy of atomism (the notion that one must look to the scale of the universe's smallest particles in order to find ultimate reality). He notes that atomistic and mechanistic metaphors lead to dualistic approaches to the "mind-body" problem such as those derivative from Descartes' model, rather than to an approach that would truly integrate the mental and physical worlds. Clark concludes that contemporary physics cannot provide any sort of ultimate reality at all, although it points the way to a more complete understanding of reality.

Quantum Holism

Science has generally proceeded by the analysis and dissection of complex systems into their parts, the ultimate parts being of course elementary particles such as electrons and quarks. Higher-order phenomena, such as the activities of the mind, are to be explained in terms of lower-order entities such as molecules and electrons, at least according to the "orthodox" (that is, outmoded Newtonian) view of the world. This type of explanation is known as "upward causation." The philosophy upon which it is based is called "reductionism," as it assumes that the properties of complex systems, such as people, can be reduced to the properties of their components (such as atoms).

However, as we have seen, even the behavior of our two entwined protons, seemingly the simplest of physical systems, is not governed by their local properties but rather by the more encompassing system that includes them both.

The physicist David Bohm (Bohm, 1980; Bohm & Peat, 1987) has referred to the universe as a "holomovement," invoking an analogy to a hologram (a three-dimensional photograph in which the entire picture may be reconstituted from each part). Bohm has termed the world of manifest phenomena or appearances the "explicate order" and the hidden (nonlocal) reality underlying it the "implicate order." Bohm laments the tendency of modern science to fragment and dissect the universe and to focus on parts rather than wholes. He proposes a new mode of speaking in which "thing" expressions would be replaced by "event" expressions.

K. Ramakrishna Rao (1978) has noted the similarity of both Bohm's concept of an implicate order (in which all events are interconnected) underlying the manifest world to the Vedantic doctrine of the identity between atman (or a person's individual consciousness) and Brahman (the Supreme Self or World Mind). Transcendental and mystical states of consciousness may involve the direct experience of Brahman in Rao's view.

Based in part on quantum mechanical considerations, astrophysicist David Darling (1995) proposes that our individual, encapsulated egos are illusions and that, when a person dies, this illusory self is dissolved and the person's consciousness merges with the world consciousness (or Brahman, in Rao's terminology).

In a similar vein, the physicist Evan Harris Walker (2000) has proposed that all observers are in fact one and that this single observer is responsible for the collapse of all quantum mechanical state vectors. Walker, like Eccles, Stapp and many other mind-brain theorists, proposes that the mind acts on the body through determining the outcome of quantum processes in the brain.

Consciousness and Quantum Collapse

There is no provision within the theory of quantum mechanics itself for the collapse of the quantum probability vector into a definite outcome. According to the theory of quantum mechanics, the quantum probability wave will be happy to go on deterministically evolving, never settling in to a definite outcome. But we do not experience the world as a fuzzy blob of half-dead/half-alive Schrödinger's cats. When we open the box, we observe either a live cat or a dead cat.

Many observers ascribe the collapse of the state vector to the act of observation itself. To some, this means that it is observation by a conscious mind that forces the quantum vector to collapse and take on a definite outcome. In a "speciesist" version of this theory, the cat will be suspended in a mix of the alive and dead states until a human observer opens the box, at which point the quantum vector will collapse and the cat will assume either the alive state or the dead state and will remain in the state, to misquote Poe's raven, "evermore" (so long as we either keep bringing food and water and providing it the most advanced feline geriatric care or, in the nonfavorable scenario, make no attempts at a Frankensteinesque revival). To a nonspeciesist observer, however, observation by the cat's conscious mind would be sufficient to collapse the state vector. To exalt the human mind as the only conscious agent capable of collapsing state vectors in to commit the same act of hubris as our ancestors who place the earth at the center of the universe and proclaimed man to be the divine ruler over all beasts. Human beings, despite their industrious natures, cannot be all places at all times. In fact, we have only been around for a lousy few million years, which is but a blink of an eye in comparison to the 13.7 billion years our universe (or local portion of a much vaster "multiverse") has been around. In that time, we have been confined to a nondescript (but thankfully wet) piece of rock in the boondocks of a galaxy that is not particularly distinguished from the myriad other galaxies that float through our cosmos.

Try though we might, human beings (and animals for that matter) cannot be everywhere at all times. A quantum-collapsing consciousness's work is never done. This is why some theorists, such as Walker (2000), have postulated that the universe comes complete with "proto-consciousnesses" that collapse quantum vectors in regions of space and time that are remote from human presence. (And, if such conscious observers are out there in the "void," they are likely to be here among us as well.) These are the considerations that led Hill (2005) to propose that, from the looks of things, the universe is devised for creatures or consciousnesses that inhabit the vast, inhabitable regions of outer space. Could Hill's beings and Walker's proto-consciousnesses be one and the same?

The view that quantum collapse is brought about through observation by consciousness has led Henry Stapp (2005a) to proclaim that quantum mechanics replaces the material world with a world of experience. Indeed, if conscious minds are what force quantum processes to assume a definite outcome, it may be that mind plays a fundamental role in the process of "becoming," the process whereby an undetermined future becomes the experienced present and then the determined past. Perhaps consciousness is responsible for the flow of time, the process by which the future becomes the "now" and then recedes ever more distantly into the past. Theories of physics are at a loss to explain the phenomenon of the "moving present" that treks its way into the future at a paradoxical speed of "one second per second." Physicists dismiss the concept (and experience) of "time flow" as subjective, and hence (perhaps like consciousness itself) not worthy of serious consideration. And yet still, Time's finger, having writ, moves on. If conscious minds are the major players in generating the flow of time and determining the location of the "present" (a concept denied in relativistic physics) along the axis of time, then role of consciousness in the cosmos may be truly fundamental.

While the view that acts of observation by conscious observers are what cause quantum probability vectors to collapse to a definite outcome is a common one, not all quantum physicists subscribe to that view. Some scientists assert that a recording of the outcome on a macroscopic recording device (e.g., computer printout) is sufficient to cause collapse. However, technically speaking, the deterministically evolving quantum probability function applies to such macroscopic systems and there is no provision for collapse within quantum theory itself. Such macroscopic recording devices could exist in a state of undecided superposition until Hell freezes over (i.e., about 10^{100} years from now, but not to worry) as far as the laws of quantum mechanics are concerned.

Other quantum theorists assert that at reasonably warm temperatures (say, -200 C°), the quantum waves of macroscopic outcomes (such as the breaking or non-breaking of the glass vial of cyanide and the last few pages of the autobiography of Schrödinger's unfortunate cat) cannot remain in a state of superposition due to interactions with external systems. Penrose (1994), for instance, hypothesizes that when a physical system reaches a certain mass, it can no longer remain in a state of quantum indecision (superposition), as the effects of gravity come into play.

Other physicists (e.g., Hugh Everett, 1957) take the "easy" way out and deny that quantum collapse occurs. Under Everett's "many worlds" interpretation of quantum mechanics, all possible outcomes of a quantum process occur, which fractures the universe into multiple worlds at each moment of a quantum decision. If Lee Harvey Oswald had flipped a quantum mechanical coin to decide whether to enter the Marines to receive rifle training or become a scuba diver instead, there might now be a parallel universe existing alongside of ours (in an abstract mathematical space called Hilbert space) in which Oswald receives his demise, not at the hands of a crazed Jack Ruby seeking to avenge the death of President Kennedy, but rather in the mouth of a famished great white shark. Of course there are countless quantum decisions taking place at each instant of time, so every second the universe we reside in splits into a (literally and mathematically) uncountable infinity of universes existing alongside each other in Hilbert space. Unfortunately, however, there is no way for us (at least at present) to leave our mundane universe and travel through Hilbert space to catch up with the fascinating adventures of our other selves in these parallel worlds.

Most physicists think that the countless multiplying of universes in Everett's "many worlds" interpretation of quantum mechanics is simply too uneconomical (in terms of the number of unobservable universes that must exist) and too fantastic to be taken seriously. However, Everett's model does have the beauty of not having to account for what causes the collapse of quantum mechanical state vectors. They simply don't collapse.

The Mind's Influence on Quantum Outcomes

As well as causing the collapse of quantum mechanical state vectors, there is a smattering of evidence that the mind can influence the outcomes of such collapse. This evidence is controversial and has not as yet been accepted by the majority of the scientific community, but rather falls under the rubric of parapsychology.

A series of experiments directed at detecting the psychokinetic ("mind over matter") influence of such quantum events as radioactive decay, begun by Helmut Schmidt in the 1960s and since continued by many other investigators, has been quite successful by parapsychological standards (e.g., Schmidt, 1970, 1976, 1981, 1984, 1985, 1986, 1993). In a typical such experiment, a subject might be given the task of increasing the number of radioactive decays in a sample of strontium-90 that occur during odd microseconds rather than even microseconds. Schmidt's typical finding is that subjects are able to slightly to increase the number of events that are in line with their goal (e.g., decays detected during odd microseconds rather than even microseconds). The typical effect is a slight bias in the target direction (e.g., 50.3 percent of decays detected during an odd microsecond vs. the 50 percent that would be expected by chance according to the laws of quantum mechanics). However, owing to the large number of trials, the odds against even such a small deviation happening by chance are generally quite large (on the order of a million to one). This line of evidence directly suggests that the mind may indeed be the source of some of the hidden variables that govern the outcomes of quantum processes. A more detailed discussion of the nature and strength of the experimental evidence for such parapsychological phenomena as psychokinesis, precognition and telepathy will be postponed until Chapter 4.

One of Schmidt's more intriguing findings is his evidence for retroactive psychokinesis (e.g., Schmidt, 1976, 1981, 1985, 1993). In such an experiment, a series of quantum events is recorded in a computer's memory bank, but not observed by anyone. At some time in the future, a human (or animal) subject is asked to influence these events, which would normally be regarded as falling into the fixed past. Schmidt and his coworkers have found such observers to be successful in their attempts to manipulate the past. Thus, if acts of conscious observation are indeed the cause of "time flow," it seems that events of last week, already stored on a computer, may still be part of the "future" until they are consciously observed and the quantum mechanical state vector collapsed to a specific outcome. Incidentally, the same effect is obtained in more orthodox areas in physics. For instance, light emitted from a quasar billions of years ago may be "gravitationally lensed" by a galaxy sitting between the Earth and quasar, producing a double-image of the quasar. Much like the quantum mechanical "two slit" experiment with electrons described above, a decision to observe whether the light took the "left" or "right" path around the galaxy, will show no interference pattern, only the bimodal "two humped" distribution one would expect from photons following one path or another. A decision not to monitor the path, will result in the typical interference pattern suggesting that the photon (or its quantum state vector) somehow took both paths. Thus, a decision as to the type of measurement to be made in the present may seemingly influence events happening billions of years ago, suggesting that these events in the infancy of the universe may be part of the as yet to be determined "future" until they are observed by a conscious entity.

Quanta and the Mind

Many scientists have proposed that the mind acts on the brain through the influence of quantum processes. The views of Hameroff, Penrose, and Eccles have been discussed in the previous chapter. Another prominent theorist to propose such a view is the physicist Evan Harris Walker (Walker, 1975, 1984, 2000, 2003), who, like Schmidt, has also developed mathematical theories regarding psychokinetic effects on quantum processes.

Walker asserts that the quantum probability wave (i.e., state vector) constitutes a complete description of the physical system of the brain, but does not specify the outcomes of quantum processes. He asserts that the conscious mind, or "will" in Walker's terminology, corresponds to the "hidden variables" that determine the outcomes of quantum events. As the will falls outside of the physical description of the brain, it is nonphysical in Walker's view. He further asserts that the will is nonlocal and atemporal (not located at a particular instant of time). He hypothesizes that the will has a channel capacity (ability to influence events) of 6×10^4 bits per second. However, in Walker's view, the will is far from being all-powerful as it is embedded in a physical system processing 5×10^7 bits per second.

Bierman and Walker (2003) report some empirical evidence in support of Walker's theory. Specifically, they report a difference in brain waves between human subjects who were the first to observe a quantum event and those who observed outcomes of quantum mechanical events that had already been observed by another human observer. They note that their results go counter to an earlier finding by Hall, Kim, McElroy and Shimoni (1977) that subjects could not guess which quantum events had been observed previously. Bierman and Walker argue that the inter-observational interval was too short in Hall et. al.'s experiment for the first observer to consciously perceive the outcome, citing Libet's finding that 300–500 milliseconds of brain activity is required before a stimulus is consciously perceived (Libet, 1991b). Bierman and Walker found a difference in brain waves between subjects who observed "new" and "preobserved" quantum outcomes in the first 100 milliseconds of brain activity, but no differences in the late brain potentials (after 1000 milliseconds). Bierman and Walker note that their failure to find an effect of preobservation in the late evoked brain potentials of their subjects is consistent with Hall et al.'s finding of no *conscious* differences in the perceptions of "new" and preobserved quantum processes.

A somewhat more passive view of the mind's role in influencing the outcomes of quantum mechanical processes in the brain, at least in terms of its timing, is proposed by the theoretical physicist Henry Stapp (2004, 2005b). As discussed in the previous chapter, Stapp postulates that the conscious mind waits for the quantum probability wave to favor a desired outcome and then stabilizes it. This would involve an ability on the part of fields of consciousness to sense the mathematically abstract quantum wave function and then to stabilize that function through continued observation. This is a somewhat more esoteric level of influence than the more or less direct influence on the physical processes themselves proposed by Walker and others.

It should be noted that many of the theories and empirical findings regarding the mind's influence on quantum mechanics discussed in the preceding passages fall outside of mainstream science. In particular, the findings of Schmidt and others that conscious minds may influence the outcomes of quantum processes occurring outside of the subject's physical body are controversial, have not been universally (or easily) replicated, and have been relegated to the outcast field of parapsychology, a field whose status in regard to the mainstream scientific community is marginal at best. The mainstream scientific/philosophical community has been somewhat more receptive to notion that the conscious minds may influence quantum processes within the brains in which they are (however temporarily) imprisoned. Thus, despite Bell's and Aspect's demonstrations of quantum nonlocality, most scientists/philosophers operating at the fringes (but within the borders) of mainstream science are more comfortable with the idea that the mind's action is confined to the physical brain than with the notion that its influence may extend beyond the borders of the physical body. Of course, those physicalists who are deeply embedded within the orthodox core of mainstream science would deny the mind any influence on quantum mechanical processes at all, even those within the physical brain it inhabits.

It should be noted that the hypotheses as to the nature and eventual fate of one's essential self set forth in the Introduction to this book are in no way dependent on the existence of the paranormal phenomena studied by parapsychologists. Neither are they dependent on the hypothesis that the conscious mind directly influences the outcomes of quantum processes in a way that would be incompatible with the laws of physical science. (There also may be physical or quasiphysical processes yet to be discovered that may have a considerable bearing on this debate. The vast majority of scientists and philosophers have, in all historical eras, basked in their supreme confidence that their knowledge of the world was essentially complete. It has never been so in the past, and there is no good reason to believe it is now.)

It is, however, to the study of alleged paranormal such as precognition and psychokinesis that we turn in the next two chapters, because of their importance in the contemporary debate of the nature of the mind and the self. In Chapter 5, we will consider the implications of psi phenomena, if they exist, for our understanding of the fundamental nature of reality. In Chapter 6, we will consider the evidence that, not just the self, but some aspects of the personality, survive the death of the physical brain.

3

Spontaneous Phenomena
as Evidence for Psi

This chapter and the next will examine the evidence for psi phenomena such as telepathy (direct mind-to-mind, or at least brain-to-brain, communication), precognition (the ability to "see" the future), clairvoyance (the ability to gain direct knowledge of a physical object by means other than the recognized physical senses) and psychokinesis (the ability of mind to directly influence matter remote from the physical body). Collectively, these ostensible phenomena are called "psi phenomena," a term introduced by the parapsychologists Robert Thouless and B. P. Wiesner (Thouless & Wiesner, 1948; Wiesner & Thouless, 1942).

As the reader is no doubt aware, there is a vast (or, by orthodox science standards, moderately large) literature regarding attempts to demonstrate the existence of paranormal phenomena such as extrasensory perception (ESP) and psychokinesis (PK) in experimental studies. As will be discussed in detail in the next chapter, there is a great deal of controversy surrounding this literature. Many observers within the field of parapsychology contend that the existence of psi phenomena has been conclusively established and that the task of experimental parapsychology should now be to explore the nature of psi and the conditions that facilitate or inhibit the expression of psi rather than to amass further evidence that such phenomena exist. Skeptics, who comprise the vast majority of the orthodox scientific community, assert that the existence of psi phenomena has not been conclusively established and that the existing body of experimental evidence for psi can be explained away by a combination of procedural and statistical flaws or outright fraud.

We will discuss this controversy in considerable depth in the next chapter. To do so now would be getting ahead of our story and putting the cart in front of the horse. The true story begins with a discussion of apparent instances of psi that occur in everyday life outside of the laboratory. Such cases of "spontaneous psi" have occurred throughout recorded history. Studies of such cases preceded experimental investigations of psi and formed the rationale and motivation for experimental investigations.

Subtypes of Spontaneous Psi Phenomena

One of the foremost investigators of spontaneous psi phenomena was Dr. Louisa Rhine, the wife and colleague of Dr. J. B. Rhine, the man who is widely regarded as the founder of the field of experimental parapsychology. Over a period of several decades, she amassed a vast collection of over 10,000 cases of apparently paranormal events, which were mailed to her, often in response to articles in the popular press, over a period of several decades. Her anecdotal, theoretical and statistical studies of such cases led to a long list of publications, spanning several decades (e.g., Rhine, 1951, 1955, 1961, 1962a, 1962b, 1963, 1970, 1977, 1978, 1981). She partitioned the experiences suggesting the operation of an ESP capacity into four main groups: hallucinatory experiences, intuitive experiences, realistic dreams and unrealistic dreams. She established a fifth, "wastebasket" category of "indeterminate type" for experiences that were difficult to assign unambiguously to one of the four previously mentioned categories. Cases involving hallucinations while falling asleep (hypnagogic imagery) or while waking up (hypnopompic imagery) might fall into this indeterminate category, along with cases involving mixed features.

Hallucinatory cases sometimes involve auditory, tactile, or olfactory hallucinations. However, visual hallucinations are by far the most predominant mode in such cases (unlike in schizophrenia, where auditory hallucinations predominate). One famous subcategory of visual hallucinations comprises "crisis apparitions," in which someone has a vision of another person at the time that the appearing person is undergoing a crisis (often death).

Intuitive cases involve a sense of foreboding or "hunch" that something has occurred. For instance, a woman may be driving to work and be overcome with a sense of foreboding that something is wrong at home. She turns her car around and drives back to her house, only to find it on fire, her toddler and babysitter huddled on the front lawn.

Louisa Rhine's third category of spontaneous ESP experience was that of realistic dreams. Such dreams involve a more or less literal and accurate portrayal of the confirming event. Unlike intuitive experiences, which primarily involve contemporaneous events, dreams are more often precognitive, that is to say involve events that have yet to happen at the time of the dream. For instance, a mother may dream that her son is a fiery car crash on the night before the actual crash occurs.

Rhine's fourth category is that of "unrealistic" dreams, which appear to represent events symbolically rather than literally. For instance, rather than dreaming of the car crash in more or less realistic detail, the woman in the last example might dream that her son hands her a single rose and then begins walking into a dark cave.

Some spontaneous cases involve puzzling physical effects such as clocks that stop or portraits that fall off the wall at the time of a persons' death. There are also cases that involve anomalous physical phenomena that occur repeatedly over a longer time period. These are known as poltergeist cases or, in the parapsychologists' parlance, recurrent spontaneous psychokinesis (or RSPK for short). Poltergeist cases may involve anomalously moving objects such as cups that fly off the kitchen counter or rocks that pummel the house from outside as well as strange behavior of electrical apparatus, such as radios that seem to turn themselves on or phones that malfunction in odd ways. Even stranger phenomena have been reported, including bite marks appearing on a victim's skin. While the term "poltergeist" literally translates as "noisy ghost," most modern observers attribute poltergeist phenomena to living agents. In a typical poltergeist case, there is a "focal person" or "poltergeist agent" involved. Anomalous physical phenomena generally occur in close proximity to the focal person and few, if any, phenomena are observed in the focal person's absence. For this reason, the RSPK effects are generally thought to be caused either through the focal person's psychokinetic powers or through fraudulent behavior on the part of the focal person.

Examples of Spontaneous Psi

Having outlined the major categories of spontaneous psi, I will now present examples of each of the major subtypes listed above.

HALLUCINATORY EXPERIENCES

Hallucinatory experiences are perhaps the most dramatic category of spontaneous experiences that are suggestive of the operation of ESP. They may involve visions of persons at the time of death (crisis apparitions), auditory hallucinations (often of a voice calling one's name), and even olfactory and tactile hallucinations.

MacKenzie (1995) reports a case involving a seemingly precognitive vision of a fatal fire. On October 27, 1971, a six-year-old boy reported seeing a fire out of the front window of his aunt's house. According to his aunt, the boy shouted, "Look at that fire over there—get some water quick!" The aunt went to the window and saw nothing and took the boy home because she thought that he must be tired.

The boy's sister, then nine, corroborated this story, saying that she had gone to her uncle's house after school on that day and her brother was looking out of this window at the house across the street at about 3:30 PM on October 27. She stated that her brother had a vision of the house being on fire, including fire engines and stretchers being brought out of the house with the bodies covered by blankets. She noted that it seemed to be nighttime in the boy's vision, as he stated that it was dark outside. She stated that her brother ran out into the street and urged his uncle to get some water. She stated that her brother then ran home and later got smacked for making up stories. (Note that this account is at variance with the aunt's on this point. This indicates that not all the witnesses' memories have remained perfectly intact and undistorted between 1971 and McKenzie's interviews in 1995.)

The boy himself (by then of course a man) reported to MacKenzie that he was looking through the window of his uncle's house and saw the house across the street on fire. He said that he could see a pram under the window, with glass and wood falling into it. He could hear people screaming and could see smoke. He states that, though it was daylight in reality, the events seemed to be taking place at night. He said that he called his uncle, but by the time he had looked out, the scene had reverted back to normal. He said that he was smacked for telling lies and that the actual fire happened the next evening. (A report in the October 28, 1971 number of the Bolton *Evening News*, the local evening newspaper, confirms that a fire in the house in question did take place. The blaze was described as an inferno, and two brothers, aged two and three, perished in the conflagration. MacKenzie notes that it is odd that the fire is described as having occurred "today" in the account in the evening newspaper. He speculates that the paper was a very late edition or that the fire had in fact occurred the previous evening.)

That the fire occurred at night was corroborated by the boy's father, who stated that his son had in fact run into his shop on the afternoon of the day in question, talking about the fire and telling him to come quickly. He also confirmed that the boy said that the fire was occurring at night despite the fact that it was late afternoon. He also stated that the actual fire occurred the next day while his son was fast asleep in bed.

This case is of interest in view of the large number of corroborating witnesses. As noted above, however, the memories of at least some of these witnesses appear to have become somewhat distorted over time.

The boy's father stated that he had heard that the fire had been investigated as a possible arson. Thus, there is the possibility that the boy had subconsciously picked up cues from the arsonists' activities, which were then manifested as a vision. Such possibilities aside, this case is suggestive of a precognitive hallucination. This is somewhat unusual in that most ostensible psi experiences taking place in the waking state involve contemporaneous events, whereas dreams are much more likely to be precognitive.

As noted above, hallucinatory experiences frequently involve senses other than vision. However, vision is the most frequent modality among seemingly psi-induced hallucinations, whereas the hallucinations of psychotics most frequently involve the auditory modality. A typical auditory hallucination suggestive of the operation of psi might consist of hearing your mother's voice calling you at the exact time that she is experiencing some sort of physical crisis at a distant location. Smell, kinesthesia (muscle sense), pain and other sensory modalities may also be involved. The Finnish folklorist Leea Virtanen (1990) notes that cases involving the parallel experiencing of physical symptoms of disease and injury are quite common and most often occur between parent and child. The following is such a case taken from the early investigations of the SPR:

> I woke up with a start, feeling I had had a hard blow on my mouth, and with a distinct sense that I had been cut and was bleeding under my upper lip, and seized my pocket-hand-kerchief and held it (in a little pushed lump) to the part, as I sat up in bed, and after a few seconds, when I removed it, I was astonished to not to see any blood, and only realized it was impossible anything could have struck me there, as I lay fast asleep in my bed, and so I thought it was only a dream!—but I looked at my watch, and saw it was seven, and finding Arthur (my husband) was not in the room, I concluded (rightly) that he must have gone out on the lake for any early sail, as it was so fine.
>
> I then fell asleep. At breakfast (half-past nine) Arthur came in rather late, and I noticed he rather purposely sat further away from me than usual, and every now and then put his pocket handkerchief furtively up to his lip, in the very way I had done. I said "Arthur, why are you doing that?" and added a little anxiously "I know you have hurt yourself! But I will tell you why afterwards." He said, "Well, when I was sailing, a sudden squall came, throwing the tiller suddenly around, and it struck me a bad blow in the mouth, under the upper lip, and it has been bleeding a good deal and won't stop." I then said, "Have you any idea what o'clock it was when it happened?" and he answered, "It must have been about seven."
>
> I then told what happened to me, much to *his* surprise, and all who were here at breakfast.
>
> I happened here about three years ago at Brantwood to me [Gurney, Myers, & Podmore, 1886a, pp. 187–189].

This woman's story was corroborated in a statement made by her husband.

A very similar case was provided to me by one of my students. According to the student, his father was suddenly knocked off the bench he was sitting on by an invisible blow to the jaw. A few minutes later, he received a call from the health club where his wife was working out informing him that his wife had just broken her jaw on a piece of gymnastic equipment.

One skeptical explanation of psi experiences is that they are the product of coincidence. For instance, women may frequently dream of their husbands' deaths, so one would expect that some of these dreams may occur at or shortly before the husband's death. In the case of my student's father, such an explanation is much less plausible, as the baseline probability of the event is virtually zero. It would be absurd to argue that men are frequently knocked off benches by invisible blows and that some of these blows are likely to coincidence with an injury to a family member by chance.

INTUITIVE EXPERIENCES

The second major category of experiences that are suggestive of the operation of ESP is that of intuitive experiences. Intuitive experiences typically occur in the waking state and most often involve a feeling that something is wrong at a distant location that is later corroborated. The following intuitive experience is taken from Stevenson (1970b).

> Around the middle of June, 1964, Linda and I decided to visit the Travis' [*sic*] to congratulate them on their new child. After supper we put the children to bed and we asked Linda's grandmother to babysit for a while.
>
> We arrived there and Paul Travis fixed our drinks. As he was showing me the blueprints of his new house I stopped and had a feeling as if something bad had happened at home, the nature of which I was not aware.
>
> I asked Linda to call home. She said: "I will in a few minutes." I said: "You'd better call now. Something is wrong."
>
> Linda went into the bedroom where the phone was and I followed and my feelings were then of distress. Our ... neighbor answered the phone. Both children were screaming in the background. She informed us that Linda's grandmother had hurt her back just a few minutes earlier and [that] the children were so frightened ...
>
> We arrived home and the neighbor met us at the door, saying that Linda's grandmother had called upon her after she hurt her back.
>
> Scott, my son, was frantic and refused to go to Linda and clutched me for comfort.
>
> What is surprising about this incident is the sudden feeling of distress and my insistence on Linda to call home and my premonition that something bad [had] happened [Stevenson, 1970b, pp. 49–50].

This statement was corroborated by the informant's wife, who added that the informant had never previously displayed strong anxiety about something being wrong at home and had never previously asked her to telephone a babysitter while they were away.

DREAMS—REALISTIC AND UNREALISTIC

The third major mode of psi experience is that of dreams. In her classification system, Louisa Rhine divided such cases into those involving realistic dreams, which correspond closely in detail to the confirming event, and unrealistic dreams, which she defined as containing "a bit of imagination, fantasy and even symbolism" (Rhine, 1977, p.71). As an example of symbolism, she offered the case of a woman who dreamed of heavy black smoke prior to tragic events. Virtanen (1990) in her study of spontaneous psi experiences used a category that she called "symbolic dreams," which is analogous to Louisa Rhine's unrealistic dream category. As examples of symbolic dreams depicting death, Virtanen cites dreams of a person going on a journey, ascending to heaven, departing toward black trees, swimming in black ice, and well as the snuffing out of a candle and a black butterfly flying by. About one-third of Virtanen's dream experiences fell into this category.

The following account, taken from Louisa Rhine's collection, is an example of a realistic dream. It was provided to Rhine by the district manager of a sheet and tin plate company. The experience occurred shortly before he and several business associates were to return home from a two-week vacation in the wilderness, where they had been cut off from all news sources.

> The night before they were to return home, the district manager had a dream, so clear, so

vivid, he could not sleep afterward. In it, he writes, "one of our locomotive cranes that was unloading a car of scrap iron, together with the car, was on the track near the bank of a river alongside the water tower which served the locomotives. For some unaccountable reason, as the huge magnet swung around with a heavy load of scrap, it suddenly toppled over the river bank. The operator, whom I called by name, jumped clear of the crane and landed below it as it came bounding, tumbling and bouncing down the river bank, and he finally disappeared from view as the crane came to rest twenty feet below at the water's edge. I particularly noted the number of the crane and the number and positions of the railroad cars, and was able to tell how the crane operator was dressed. Furthermore, I noticed the approximate damage done to the crane. I did not know, however, what had finally happened to the operator. He had disappeared under or behind the crane after it had come to rest. In other words, I was observing the accident from somewhere in or across the river.

"Upon my return to the mill the following day, the first man I met was the master mechanic. He told me to come with him to inspect the crane of my dream, to talk with the operator who had emerged from the accident without a scratch. The operator explained his lack of injury by the fact that the crane had fallen over in front of him as he made his last jump and as it made its last bounce. The record showed the smallest detail to be as I had dreamed it, with one exception. The exception was that the accident had happened two hours after the dream" [Rhine, 1961, pp. 43–44].

ANOTHER POSSIBILITY: PSI-MEDIATED INSTRUMENTAL RESPONSE

Stanford (1974, 1990a) has pointed to one possible type of psi experience that may be missed in Louisa Rhine's classification scheme. This category encompasses cases in which a person takes an action that is appropriate to a situation when the person has no normally acquired knowledge (or any conscious paranormally-acquired knowledge) that the situation even exists. Presumably, in such cases the person is acting on the basis of information provided by ESP at an unconscious level. Stanford uses the term "psi-mediated instrumental response," or PMIR, to describe such events. As an example, he cites the case of a retired New York attorney who was traveling to Greenwich Village to drop in on two artist friends. He had to change subway trains, and upon leaving the first train, he claimed that he "absent-mindedly" walked out through the gate and was halfway up the stairs to the street before he realized that he had intended to switch trains. Not wishing to pay another fare, he decided to walk the additional six blocks south. He then ran into his friends, who had left their home and were walking north along the same route on their way to an appointment.

One reason why examples of PMIR may be relatively rare in collections of spontaneous cases may be that the people involved in such cases do not typically have any awareness of possessing paranormally-acquired knowledge and are consequently likely to attribute their experiences to luck or coincidence rather than to the operation of ESP or PK (psychokinesis). Stanford suggests that cases of PMIR may be occurring frequently without the people involved being aware that anything unusual is going on.

Physical Effects

Louisa Rhine's second major category of paranormal experiences involves puzzling physical effects, such as the stopping of a clock at the time of the owner's death or a person's portrait falling off a wall at or near the time of the person's death. One of her cases involved a man in Wisconsin who died in an easy chair in his living room. The watch in his vest pocket and the large clock in the living were both found to have stopped, each at the approximate time of the man's death (Rhine, 1961, p. 243).

Not all of Rhine's clock cases involved the stopping of timepieces. Occasionally, time-pieces were reported to have behaved aberrantly at the time of a death. One woman gave an account of a case in which a clock that normally chimed only on the hour chimed once at 7:20 P.M., surprising the woman and her parents. Five minutes later, they received a phone call informing them that their mother's sister had died of a heart attack at 7:20. This was the only occasion on which the clock chimed at a time other than on the hour (Rhine, 1961, p. 244).

Ian Wilson describes a similar case involving the late Pope Paul VI. At the time of the Pope's death (9:40 P.M. on August 6, 1978), his bedroom alarm clock, which had always been set to 6:30 A.M., inexplicably rang (Wilson, 1987, p. 183). However, Mary Roach (2005), in a detailed investigation of several famous cases suggestive of survival after death, interviewed several witnesses in connection with this case. In the course of those interviews, Archbishop Pasquale Macchi, one the pope's associates, stated that on the morning of the Pope's death, he had rewound the pope's clock, as it was stopped, and likely inadvertently set the alarm time to correspond with the pope's death. Of course, even if this explains the anomalous ringing of the alarm, the fact that it was accidentally set to the moment of the pope's death could be another instance of Stanford's PMIR.

Objects are occasionally reported to fall or break at the time of a significant crisis to a person associated with the object, as in the following case from Louisa Rhine's collection:

> A woman in Nevada tells of an experience which centered on her elder brother Frank. He was an especially thoughtful boy who did many things to please his mother, to whom he was very close. She says: "One day he came home with a beautiful cut-glass dish. Mom thought it was just about the most wonderful thing that ever happened to her and put it on our sideboard.
>
> "When the rest of us had chicken pox, my brother Frank was sent down to my grand-mother's in Grand Haven, Michigan, which was about forty miles from where we lived, although Mother was reluctant to have him go. Two days after Frank left, Mom and our neighbor were having their morning coffee and talking, and we children were told to be quiet. All of a sudden, this cut-glass dish that Frank had given Mother popped and broke right in two. It was just sitting on the sideboard. Mother screamed and said, 'My God! Frank has just been killed.' Everyone tried to quiet Mother, but she said she just knew.
>
> "About an hour after, or a little more, we received a telegram from Grandpa which said to come right away, something had happened to Frank. Mom said, 'I know.' She cried all the way going to Grand Haven, and Grandpa met us at the train. Before Grandpa could tell us what happened, Mom cried, 'At what funeral parlor is he?' Grandpa just stood there with his mouth open and Mom ran right up the street and went to the place Frank was without being told. They wouldn't let her see him because a terrible thing had happened.
>
> "The boy next door to Grandfather was home from school and his parents were not at home, so he started playing with his father's shotgun, and came outside, showing it to Frank. The boy, not knowing it was loaded, pulled the trigger and killed my brother. The strange thing—Frank was shot at the same time the dish broke" [Rhine, 1961, pp. 245–246].

Cases involving physical effects are relatively rare. Rhine (1963) noted that her case collection at that point contained only 178 physical effect cases, in comparison to over 10,000 ESP cases.

Skeptical Explanations of Spontaneous Cases

Critics of spontaneous case investigations are quick to point out that there are many explanations besides ESP and psychokinesis that might account for apparent cases of paranormal phenomena. First, the cases may be due to coincidence. For instance, consider a case in which a man is overcome by a sense of impending doom, breaks out in a cold sweat and refuses to board an airplane, and then later learns that the plane crashed upon landing at its destination. It might be quite plausible to assume that many people back out of imminent airplane flights because of sudden feelings of nervousness and anxiety. Occasionally, the planes involved in some of these flights may crash, thus producing what looks like a spontaneous case of intuitive ESP when really all that is involved is simple coincidence. Similarly, people may frequently dream of the death of one of their parents. When such a dream happens by chance to fall on the night preceding the parent's actual death, another spurious precognition case is generated.

Richard Broughton (1991), a former Director of the Rhine Research Center in Durham, has noted that explanations in terms of coincidence are not particularly plausible when applied to experiences involving hallucinations or psychosomatic pain. For instance, recall the case of my student's father who was knocked off a bench by an "invisible blow to the jaw" at the time that his wife broke her jaw on a piece of gymnastic equipment. Surely, it would be absurd to argue with regard to such a case that men are constantly being knocked off benches by invisible blows to the jaw and that sooner or later one of these events is bound to occur simultaneously with the breaking of the jaw of a member of the man's immediate family.

Despite the implausibility of coincidence explanations in hallucination cases, the early investigators of the Society for Psychical Research attempted to perform a statistical analysis to rule out the coincidence hypothesis in the case of crisis apparitions. They conducted what they called a "Census of Hallucinations" in order to find out how often people experienced apparitions of human figures. (Sidgwick et al., 1894). They found that, of the apparitions reported to them, one in 63 occurred within 12 hours of the death of the person whose apparition was experienced. Based on existing death rates, the investigating committee concluded that only 1 in 19,000 such hallucinations would occur so close to the death of the appearing figure by chance. One could certainly quibble with this analysis. For instance, it could readily be imagined that cases in which a person's apparition was experienced in close proximity to the time of his death would make a deep impression on a person and might therefore be more easily remembered than other hallucinations of human figures, thus artificially inflating the proportion in the sample.

A second, more informal statistical argument is provided by the Italian investigators Rinaldi and Piccinini (1982), who conducted a door-to-door survey related to psychic experiences in the South Tyrol region of Italy. By interviewing informants about deaths in the family, they found that one in twelve deaths were accompanied by a paranormal experience related to the death. When only sudden deaths were considered, one in six deaths were the target event in a reported psi experience. It strains one's credulity, they argue, to assume that such a high proportion can be accounted for by chance coincidence.

In general, any attempt to assess the actual probability that the evidence from spontaneous cases is due to chance coincidence, whether performed by the proponent of psi phenomena or the skeptic, is fraught with pitfalls. Such calculations rely on too many debatable and hidden assumptions, and the data are subject to too many distorting factors to allow any definitive assessment to be made. This is one of the reasons why parapsychologists have largely turned from the study of spontaneous cases to the study of psi processes in experimental situations, in which the probability that the results are due to chance can be more or less precisely calculated.

A second problem pointed out by critics of spontaneous case investigations is that what appears to be anomalously acquired knowledge may in fact represent information that has been consciously or unconsciously acquired through the normal sensory channels or may be based on unconscious inference from such information. For instance, a woman's husband may be exhibiting a depressed mood, increasingly reckless driving, and a decidedly morbid interest in automobile accidents on the evening news while polishing off his final two six packs of beer. She may then unconsciously infer that he is becoming suicidal or at least dangerously alcoholic, and her unconscious mind may present this conclusion to her in the form of a dream in which her husband is involved in a fatal car accident. If her inference is accurate and her husband is subsequently killed when his car collides with a pickup truck, an apparent case of spontaneous psi, which is really due to unconscious inference, is generated. Similarly, a trapeze artist may subliminally perceive a frayed wire and consequently have an apparently premonitory dream of her partner's fall to his death.

Sometimes no direct signal may be involved in an apparent case of ESP, but rather a third factor may cause both the percipient's mood and the target event. For instance, the parapsychologist Ed Cox, famous for his invention of innumerable Rube Goldberg–like devices for testing for psychokinesis, found that trains involved in accidents tend to carry significantly fewer passengers than comparable trains not involved in accidents (Cox, 1956). Cox interpreted this finding as evidence that people use their precognitive powers (consciously or unconsciously) to avoid being involved in accidents. Physicist John Taylor (1980) on the other hand points out that a third factor, such as bad weather, may contribute to both the passengers' decisions not to travel and to the increased probability of an accident.

A third line of criticism of spontaneous case evidence centers around the possibility that the testimony provided by the informant may not be an accurate portrayal of the events as they occurred, due to distortions of memory, delusions, conscious or unconscious embellishment of a case to make it seem more impressive, and possibly even outright fabrication of a case in a conscious effort to perpetrate a hoax. For instance, in the fictional case considered above, the woman may merely have dreamed of a car accident, but reported that she dreamed of her husband being killed in a collision with a pickup truck because she viewed her dream as a premonition of that event and wished to communicate that fact. Alternatively, she may have consciously added the details regarding the truck to make the dream more impressive to the researcher, a form of falsification which she may take to be benign. A third possibility is that her memory of the dream and the actual event may have been confused, so that she came to believe that she saw a pickup truck in the dream when in fact she had not. This process is known as confabulation as (or, more often these days, as "false memory").

In some instances, the testimony of independent witnesses can help bolster one's confidence that the experience occurred as the informant described it. For instance, a percipient may have related a precognitive dream to her family before news of the confirming event was received. In such a case, the family members may be interviewed to obtain independent confirmation that the dream in fact occurred. Such independent testimony would then constitute evidence against the hypothesis that the percipient simply made up the precognitive dream after hearing of the confirming event or that she came to believe falsely that she had had such a dream through a memory distortion process. It was the practice of the early psychical researchers, who sought to prove the existence of ESP through the analysis of spontaneous cases, to obtain such independent testimony when available, and that is still the practice of a large proportion of case investigators today. As a result, there are many cases on record in which such independent testimony corroborates the existence of the ostensible psi experience.

Memory distortion can also be minimized if written descriptions of the experience are made as soon as possible. This criterion is met by dream diary studies in which the dreams were immediately recorded, such as those reported by Schriever (1987), Sondow (1988) and de Pablos (1998). The subject in Schriever's study sent all her dream reports to a research institute, and Schriever eliminated all reports that did not reach the institute before the confirming event occurred. This method carries the advantages both of allowing corroboration by witnesses and of immediate recording of the experience.

Schouten (1981) found that the number of details in case reports and the length of such reports fell off as the time interval before reporting the case increased. He attributes this effect to the percipients' forgetting of details over the course of time. This finding could be cited as evidence against the hypothesis that spontaneous case informants tend to "improve" their testimony or embellish their reports over time.

Recent research by Elizabeth Loftus and her colleagues has amply demonstrated that false memories may easily be implanted in people's minds through the use of leading questions and the provision of misleading information (e.g., Loftus, 1995; Lynn, Loftus, Llienfeld & Locke, 2003). Loftus and her associates have obtained evidence in support of this view from several studies they have conducted (e.g., Hall, McFeaters & Loftus, 1987; Loftus, 1981; Loftus & Greene, 1980; and Loftus, Miller & Burns, 1978). In one such experiment, subjects were lead to believe that they had once been lost in a shopping mall as a child. In a second study, they found that subjects' memories could be biased by questions about a stop sign when in fact a yield sign had been presented to them. In another study, subjects were misled by questions about a nonexistent mustache. Clearly, psychical researchers must be wary about altering their informants' testimony and possibly even their memories through the use of leading questions.

A less innocent possibility is that the informant may fabricate the case. Harris (1986) notes for instance that one story, in which British troops were said to have been helped in battle by an apparition of St. George and some accompanying angels, was shown to be a falsification concocted by persons not present at the battle. In a study of reported premonitions, Hearne (1984) found that his respondents had elevated scores on the Lie-scale of the Eysenck Personality Inventory, which is designed to detect dissembling subjects. Furthermore, the Lie scores correlated with the alleged accuracy of the reported premonition. Such findings provide fuel to skeptics wishing to ascribe much of the spontaneous case evidence to fabrication.

Of course some cases of reported psi phenomena are the product of delusion or even outright insanity, as in the case of a schizophrenic man who believes that his garbageman is the reincarnation of Noah and is telepathically commanding him to build a second Ark. Such cases rarely, if ever, find their way into the serious parapsychological literature.

Conclusions Regarding Spontaneous Cases

Most parapsychologists today do not feel that the existence of ESP and psychokinesis can be proven on the basis of spontaneous cases, as skeptics can always explain away such cases by ascribing them to coincidence, sensory cues, delusion, memory distortion, and outright falsification. While the construction of such skeptical explanations for any given case is frequently possible, often such constructions involve so many mental gymnastics that the brusque dismissal of spontaneous case material seems far too cavalier an approach to take. It is sometimes argued that, while each individual spontaneous case is like a twig that may be broken by counterexplanations in terms of normal processes, when taken as a whole the spontaneous case evidence constitutes an unbreakable bundle of sticks. Tyrrell (1953) termed this the "faggot" theory, using the word "faggot" in the British sense as denoting a bundle of sticks. It is true that spontaneous cases follow certain patterns (the events foreseen in precognition cases are predominantly serious health crises to close relatives, for instance) and that they do not resemble the consciously invented ghost stories that appear in the fictional literature. It could still be maintained, however, that the similarities are simply due to common patterns of human thought and behavior rather than reflecting the characteristics of an anomalous channel of information transmission.

Poltergeists

Poltergeist phenomena will be considered separately from the spontaneous cases described above in that poltergeist outbreaks are more rarely reported than the types of spontaneous cases considered above and in that poltergeist outbreaks last over a longer period of time, typically weeks or months, but sometimes several years. A poltergeist disturbance typically involves strange physical events that occur repeatedly in a specific location or in the vicinity of a specific person or group of people.

These physical phenomena generally include inexplicable movements of objects, such as a glass spontaneously flying off a kitchen table and hitting the kitchen floor at a considerable lateral distance from the table. Sometimes quite large objects such as heavy cabinets are involved in such movements. Frequently the motion of the object is described as being unusual in terms of curved trajectories or abnormal slowness of flight. Levitation effects have also been reported. In such cases, the beginning of the object's motion is hardly ever observed. This is sometimes called the "shyness effect," and some observers have interpreted it as evidence for an inhibiting effect of observation, while for others it suggests the possibility that the motions may have been fraudulently produced. William Roll (1977), perhaps the world's foremost investigator of poltergeists, attributes the failure to observe the beginnings of movements to the fact that people do not typically attend to an object until after it is already moving.

Apparent materialization and teleportation effects are also reported. Occasionally, rocks are reported to materialize inside a room and drop to the floor. An apparent teleportation event might involve the sudden disappearance of an object at one physical location and its reappearance at another. Objects in poltergeist cases are usually inferred to have been teleported when they are found at an unexpected location. Again, the actual moments of disappearance and rematerialization are almost never witnessed.

Another frequently occurring poltergeist effect is the aberrant behavior of electrical apparatus. In some instances, machines such as radios, lights, and dishwashers are inexplicably turned on or off. Strange sounds, most prominently including rapping, are sometimes heard in poltergeist cases. Less frequently, apparitions or disembodied voices are perceived, although these are more commonly a feature of hauntings, as will be discussed below. Truly strange phenomena such as showers of rocks or even frogs on or toward a house, as well as the spontaneous ignition of fires, have been reported.

The term "poltergeist" literally means "noisy ghost," and poltergeist phenomena were sometimes suspected to be caused by such entities. (Some writers still assert that spirits of the dead may be involved in some poltergeist cases, as will be discussed below.) It has been discovered that poltergeist phenomena generally tend to center around a single person or group of persons in that the phenomena only occur in their presence and in their immediate spatial vicinity. Such a person is called a focal person or, less commonly nowadays, a "poltergeist agent." The prevailing view among those parapsychologists who believe that some poltergeist effects are truly paranormal is that the focal person or persons cause the poltergeist phenomena through the (largely unconscious) use of their psychokinetic powers. For this reason, many parapsychologists use the term "recurrent spontaneous psychokinesis" or "RSPK" to describe such outbreaks. Skeptics, on the other hand, maintain that the focal person produces such effects through fraud and trickery. They also believe that some residual effects may be due to the witnesses' misinterpretation of normal physical events.

Case Study: The Rio Tercero Poltergeist

An example of a rock-throwing poltergeist is reported by Parra (2004). The phenomena occurred in the city of Rio Tercero in the province of Cordoba, Argentina and began on February 15, 2004 and continued through May 18, 2004 (the date when Parra's article was written). The phenomena consisted entirely of the anomalous appearance and movement of stones. The size of the stones involved were typical of those found in the Cordobese hills as well as on the road to the family's house. The stones increased in weight as the phenomena progressed, eventually reaching a weight of 1.3 kilograms. The stones broke several windows and blinds, including the windscreen of the family's car.

The family initially thought that someone was throwing the stones and had the house surrounded by 16 policemen. No stone thrower was detected and several policemen observed that the stones sometimes followed "impossible trajectories." All the family members, the sheriff and many of the neighbors attributed the events to the psychic powers of Andres, an 18-year-old boy living in the house. The stones only entered the house when Andres was present and awake. Also, no phenomena were reported during a 17-day period during which Andres was hospitalized.

At one time, Andres' 44-year-old mother Monica was reading to her son Ezequial when a stone passed between them without hitting either of them and then came to a sudden stop on the table. In Monica's view, the momentum of the stone should have caused it to continue to slide on the table rather than coming to a sudden stop.

At one point, the family heard a loud noise and then found a stone embedded in the television set. All windows and doors were shut at the time of this incident, and Andres was standing in the living room. Shortly later, another stone broke a large window and curtain. Another impact on the television screen occurred when Andres and the family dog were playing in the kitchen. Andres' sister Denise felt a strange sensation, which she described as somewhat like a breeze, just prior to hearing the impact of the stone on the television set. An older sister, Veronica, reported that a stone came from behind her (Andres was visible at the time) and left a small scratch on the television set and cabinet before hitting the window violently. She described the trajectory of the stone as highly anomalous.

Andres was taken to a psychiatrist, who found that Andres frequently manifested aggression toward family members, but seldom were these aggressive impulses directed toward strangers. Parra's own psychological testing indicated that Andres manifested emotional instability, irritability, impulsivity and feelings of inadequacy. Andres has also been diagnosed as hyperactive as well as suffering from neurological disorders involving the frontal lobes. Parra also notes that Andres suffers from photosensitive epilepsy and has been subject to convulsions since age 12 and "blank spells" since age 9. At the time of the disturbances, he was taking anticonvulsive and antiepileptic drugs and receiving neuropsychological treatments.

Actuarial Investigations

Some of the poltergeist cases displayed features that are more commonly associated with hauntings. Twenty-three percent of the Roll's 116 cases involved apparitions or "hallucinations." These visual hallucinations included human figures, animals, demons and amorphous shapes. In eleven percent of the cases, intelligible voices were heard; often these were associated with apparitions. In five cases, one or more persons were wounded or slapped by an unknown agency or displayed stigmata (spontaneously appearing wounds). In five cases people were pulled or lifted by an unseen force. In most instances the victim was the poltergeist agent (or focal person).

One recent such case with mixed features has been reported by Kokubo and Yamanoto (2003). This case occurred in an apartment complex in Tomika-cho, Gifu Prefecture, Japan in 2000. Among the phenomena reported were noisy footsteps (heard in more than half the apartments), sounds similar to the sonar signals of a submarine, the rapid death of flowers, two sightings of "ghosts," anomalous movements of curtains and cans, a fan and a hair dryer that worked despite the absence of a power supply, the turning of a doorknob, the spontaneous opening of doors to two cupboards, the movement of a rice bowl from a cupboard, resulting in its being chipped, a television set that switched channels, a gas cooking stove that spontaneously turned on, the breakdown on several machines, the rotations of magnetic compass needles, and the malfunctioning of cameras. The phenomena were reported by a variety of tenants occupying at least twelve apartments. Notably, this case investigation did not identify a focal person.

THE PROBLEM OF FRAUD

Skeptics contend that most, if not all, poltergeist effects are produced by trickery on the part of the apparent poltergeist agent, often in an attempt to gain attention. In some cases direct evidence of such fraud on the part of the focal person has been obtained. Roll (1969, 1972) used a one-way mirror to observe a 12-year-old focal person in another room together with his grandmother. His coinvestigator (J. G. Pratt) saw the agent hide two measuring tapes behind his shirt and then later throw them after his grandmother. The grandmother then reported this as another poltergeist incident, evidencing no suspicion of any fraudulent activity. The boy was later administered a polygraph test. That test indicated that he was telling the truth when he was in fact lying in denying that he had thrown the tapes (which shows you why the results of polygraph tests are not admissible as evidence in most courts). Roll (1977) reports another case in which the poltergeist agent was found to be producing "knocks" by stamping his foot.

James "the Amazing" Randi (1985), a skeptical magician who has written several books debunking parapsychology, has presented photographic evidence suggesting that one of Roll's subjects, Tina Resch, the focal person in a poltergeist case in Columbus, Ohio, threw a phone when no one was looking and produced an apparently anomalous movement of a couch by hooking it with her right foot. A videotape also suggested that she pulled a lamp toward her in order to make it fall. Roll (1993) has, however, continued to argue for the genuineness of the RSPK phenomena in this case, noting that Tina was not in the area when many of the events occurred. He also documents an apparent attempt by the prominent skeptic Paul Kurtz to doctor the evidence in this case by implying that two photographs that were actually taken an hour apart were taken within seconds of each other. On the other hand, the fact that Resch was recently sentenced to life in prison for the murder of her daughter does nothing to enhance her credibility as a poltergeist agent (see Frazier, 1995, and Roll & Storey, 2004, for the details of the circumstances surrounding this murder). Roll and Storey (2004) also note that Resch's phenomena displayed the "shyness effect" that is characteristic of many poltergeist cases in that no ostensible psychokinetic phenomena were observed if Tina knew she was being filmed. More generally, the term "shyness effect" is used to denote the fact that the beginnings of object movements are rarely observed in poltergeist cases. The "shyness effect" is consistent with what would be expected if the poltergeist phenomena were being produced through fraudulent means. The shyness effect is thus evidence in favor of the fraud hypothesis.

SUMMARY OF POLTERGEIST PHENOMENA

Poltergeist cases constitute a dramatic and striking category of possible spontaneous psi phenomena. The number of agents who have been detected in fraud together with the "shyness effect," wherein the beginnings of motions are rarely observed, suggest that RSPK phenomena will have to be approached cautiously and investigated thoroughly from a skeptical viewpoint before they can be accepted as genuinely anomalous phenomena. Investigations of the personalities and other characteristics of poltergeist agents will have to be conducted more rigorously and with more appropriate experimental blinds before they can be considered definitive.

Psychic Healing

"Psychic healing" is a generic term employed to describe a variety of techniques whereby diseases and other ailments are healed or alleviated by an apparently paranormal process.

FAITH HEALING

The term "faith healing" will be used primarily to refer to healing carried out in the context of a (usually Christian) religious meeting in which ailments are ostensibly cured by the power of God or the patient's own religious faith rather than the cure being ascribed to any "energy" emanating from, or physical manipulation performed by, the healer. Faith healing may be accomplished with or without any physical contact between the patient and the healer. Extensive physical contact between the healer and the patient would probably result in the classification of the technique as either psychic surgery or the laying-on-of-hands (to be discussed below). Examples of modern day faith healers would be Kathryn Kuhlman, Oral Roberts, Peter Popoff, Ernest Angley, the noted Christian broadcaster and former presidential candidate Pat Robertson, and the more infamous Jim Jones.

Some cures that occur in the context of faith healing may be due to the fact that the original ailment was psychogenic in origin. Some apparently serious conditions, such as paralysis and blindness, may have no organic basis but may merely be hysterical symptoms that reflect the patient's psychological distress. Even apparently genuine physical conditions such as visible rashes, ulcers and asthma attacks may be aggravated or even caused by psychological factors. Such illnesses are typically referred to as psychosomatic illnesses to distinguish them from hysterical ailments. Obviously, as both types of conditions are at least partially caused by psychological factors, it would not be surprising if a religious ritual, which may have a considerable emotional impact on the patient, had the effect of alleviating these symptoms.

Sometimes people with a genuine physical illness may experience a surge of excitement, possibly involving the release of endorphins (the brain's "natural opiates"), during a religious ritual and may overcome their symptoms for a brief time. (The alleviation of pain through the administration of placebos or hypnosis is a well-known effect and is thought to be governed by the release of endorphins in many cases.) The symptoms may, however, return once the fervor of the ritual has waned. For instance, Hines (2003) cites a case in which the faith healer Kathryn Kuhlman "healed" a woman who had cancer and who could only walk with a back brace. The woman threw off the back brace and ran across the stage. However, two months later the woman died from the cancer that Kuhlman had supposedly cured.

Cases in which documented serious physical illnesses, such as cancer and lupus, were cured through faith healing do exist, although they are extremely rare; however, cancer and other serious illnesses do sometimes improve without medical intervention, in a process known as spontaneous regression. What is needed in order to document the efficacy of faith healing are controlled studies showing that such spontaneous regression occurs more frequently among patients undergoing religious rituals than for control patients not undergoing such rituals. Such studies have not been done.

The activity of the immune system and the course of diseases are known to be affected by psychological conditions such as stress. It is well established that physical diseases occur more frequently following traumatic life events such as the loss of a job or the death of a spouse. There are cases on record of voodoo death, in which a victim who learns that he has been cursed by a witchdoctor suddenly dies. It is commonly thought that this is an example of what is known as parasympathetic death or "death by helplessness," as described by Martin Seligman (1975). In such a death, a person facing what he perceives to be a hopeless situation essentially relaxes himself to death, stopping the heart. The central nervous system is also known to interact directly with the immune system through the hypothalamus, and immune responses in animals have been conditioned to occur in response to certain tastes or even in response to the presence of particular persons (Ader, 1981). Thus, it might not be too surprising if participating in a faith healing ritual served to bolster a patient's immune system. This would not be a paranormal phenomenon, however, as the bolstering of the immune system could be due to the brain's normal channels of influence over the immune system operating in response to suggestion. Some evidence against the hypothesis that all forms of psychic healing are placebo effects or due to suggestion is provided by a survey conducted by Haraldsson and Olafsson (1980), in which they found that prior belief in the efficacy of psychic healing did not correlate with the perceived benefit the patient received from the healing session. Their study was not specific to faith healing, but encompassed healing in general.

Several faith healers have been exposed in using fraud to aid their practices. James Randi's book *The Faith Healers* (Randi, 1987) contains an extensive documentation of such fraudulent activity. Perhaps the most common ploy used by faith healers is to "heal" a stooge sitting in the audience who is only faking an illness. Morris (in Edge, Morris, Palmer & Rush, 1986) describes how the Reverend Jim Jones used such stooges and other forms of deception to dupe his followers into believing he had magical powers. Some of these people later followed Jones into death in the infamous Jonestown massacre in Guyana, in which hundreds of Jones' followers drank cyanide-laced Kool Aid at his command.

In general, there is no compelling evidence that any paranormal process is involved in faith healing. The more spectacular miracles are chiefly the result of fraud, and other cures may be due to the effects of suggestion and normal psychosomatic and psychoimmunological processes.

PSYCHIC DIAGNOSIS

Some healers claim the ability to diagnose illness by psychic means. One such person was Edgar Cayce. Given the name and address of a patient, Cayce would enter a trance, diagnose the patient's ailment and prescribe a (typically unorthodox) method of treatment. Cayce's recommended cures have been the subject of study by physicians at the Association for Research and Enlightenment, an organization dedicated to the study of Cayce's readings based in Virginia Beach, Virginia. James Randi (1979) has provided a skeptical analysis of Cayce's diagnoses, pointing out that Cayce was often inaccurate and even provided diagnoses of people who were in fact already dead. However, this negative evidence may not prove much, as Cayce's proponents concede that he was accurate in only about one-third of the cases he attempted to diagnose. A well-controlled statistical study might have settled the issue of whether Cayce displayed any paranormal ability in his diagnoses, but unfortunately Cayce died before any such study was conducted.

Randi (1987) has cast more definitive doubt on the paranormal diagnostic capability of the faith healer Peter Popoff. In his services, Popoff claimed the ability to obtain the names and medical conditions of people in his audience through paranormal means (described as a revelation from God). Randi and his associates were able to intercept a radio signal transmitted from Popoff's wife to an earpiece worn by Popoff giving him names and medical data for various audience members. In this instance at least, the psychic diagnosis was achieved through fraud.

Ray Hyman, a well-known skeptic regarding psi phenomena, and his associates Richard Wiseman and Andrew Skolnick conducted a controlled experiment in which the claimed psychic diagnostic capabilities of a seventeen-year-old Russian girl, Natasha Demkina, were put to the test (Hyman, 2005). However, despite the fact that at least two of the investigators (Hyman and Wiseman) are known for their criticisms of flawed procedures in parapsychological experiments, their own experimental procedure allowed Natasha to see the subjects she was attempting to diagnose at short range. Thus, she could have picked up sensory cues (e.g. breathing and movement patterns) that could have her helped to match medical diagnoses to subjects. Interestingly, Hyman declared the experiment a "failure" despite the fact that Natasha successfully matched four of the seven diagnoses to the correct subject. Such success would happen less than two times out of one hundred experiments by chance. As one could not reasonably expect lower probabilities in any experiment with only seven trials, the results would actually seem to support the claim that Ms. Demkina can provide more accurate diagnoses than would be expected by chance. While this experiment is inconclusive regarding Ms. Demkina's psychic diagnostic abilities due to the investigators' failure to screen our sensory cues, it serves as a cautionary example regarding the interactions between parapsychologists and their critics.

PSYCHIC SURGERY

In the technique of psychic surgery, the healer purportedly enters the patient's physical body, sometimes using only his bare hands, as in the case of the Philippine healer Tony Agpaoa, and in other cases using an unorthodox implement, such as the rusty knife wielded by the Brazilian healer Arigo (see Fuller, 1974, for a comprehensive discussion of the phenomena produced by Arigo). In a typical psychic surgery session, the healer might massage the patient's stomach muscles, seemingly penetrate the abdominal cavity with his bare hands, and apparently remove a "tumor" (which is frequently immediately destroyed because of its "evil" nature). Although bleeding may be profuse during the surgery, the alleged incision usually heals immediately, without a trace of a scar.

Psychic surgery is now widely regarded by scientists both within and outside the parapsychological research community as a fraudulent activity. The illusion of an incision is thought to be produced by kneading the patient's skin. The illusion of bleeding is achieved by the psychic surgeon's releasing blood or some other red liquid from a source he has palmed as if performing a cheap magic trick. The tumors removed by the surgeons are thought to be samples of animal tissue that have also been palmed by the surgeon. An early investigation of psychic surgery by the American physician William Nolen (1975) failed to uncover even one case in which a physical illness that had been documented to exist before a psychic surgery session was found to be absent following the session. Nolen also detected many instances of fraudulent activity on the part of the psychic surgeons he observed. In one case, a "kidney stone" was found to be composed of sugar. In an earlier investigation, Granone (1972) had found such "kidney stones" to consist of table salt and pumice stone. David Hoy (1981) also describes sleight-of-hand techniques he witnessed during psychic surgery sessions, including the palming of objects. Lincoln and Wood (1979) identified "blood" produced from a patient during psychic surgery as pig blood rather than human blood. Finally, Azuma and Stevenson (1987) analyzed two more kidney stones removed from patients during psychic surgery and found them to be pebbles. By now it should be apparent that the rampant fraudulent activity on the part of psychic surgeons casts extreme doubt on the hypothesis that any paranormal effect has been demonstrated in this procedure.

LAYING-ON-OF-HANDS AND REMOTE HEALING

In both the technique known as the "laying-on-of-hands" and in the technique I will call "remote healing," the healer is conceptualized as being the source or channel of a healing effect or healing "energy." The chief difference between the two techniques is that the laying-on-of-hands involves more or less direct physical contact between the patient and the healer, whereas the healer is isolated from the patient in remote healing. In practice, the distinction between the two techniques becomes blurred by the fact that many experimental studies of healers who would normally use the laying-on-of-hands in their daily practice have of necessity used experimental protocols that remove the healer from direct physical contact with the patient to be healed or from the biological system to be influenced. Unlike other forms of healing, a great many experimental tests of the efficacy of these two techniques have been performed. A surprisingly high proportion of these experiments have yielded evidence of some sort of healing effect. Healers have been found to be able to retard the growth of goiters in mice and to accelerate the recovery of such goiters (Grad, 1977), to speed the healing of experimentally induced wounds in mice (Grad, Cadoret & Paul, 1961), to accelerate the recovery of mice from anesthesia without physical contact (Watkins & Watkins, 1971; Watkins, Watkins, & Wells, 1973; Wells & Klein, 1972; Wells & Watkins, 1975), to speed the regeneration of salamander forelimbs (Wirth, Johnson, Harvath & MacGregor, 1992), to heal malaria in rats, remotely and retroactively (Snel & Van der Sijde, 1990–1991), and to facilitate the healing of surgically induced wounds in humans. (Wirth 1989, 1990, but see also the nonsignificant study of the effect of healing and prayer on diabetes mellitus by Wirth & Mitchell, 1994).

Radin, Taft and Yount (2003) report a study on the influence of practitioners of Johrei, a Japanese spiritual healing practice, on the proliferation of cultured human brain cells (astrocytes). Radin et al. report a significant increase in treated cells relative to control cells, although this difference was only significant on the third day of treatment. They also found that the Johrei healers could influence the output of a quantum-based random event generator (REG). The psychokinetic effect on the REG declined with distance, which the authors interpret as supporting the hypothesis that the healing effect involves some sort of radiation.

Bengston and Krinsley (2000) report a significant difference between healers and skeptics as they attempted to inhibit the growth of transplanted breast cancer cells in mice. However, this study was flawed in that the healers were allowed to place their hands just outside of the mice's cages, which would allow the transmission of sensory cues (e.g., the movements of the hands of the healers might be gentler and less threatening that those of the skeptics). Another flaw in this experiment is that the control group of mice were housed in a different city than the treated group; thus, the differences between the treated and control mice might have been due to differences in weather, pollution levels, or other factors.

A large number of studies have shown that the growth of plants may be accelerated when they are irrigated with water previously held by healers or when they are grown from seeds held by healers (Grad, 1963, 1964; MacDonald, Hickman & Dakin, 1977; Solfvin, 1982; Saklani, 1988a, 1988b, 1989, 1990, 1991, 1992; Scofield & Hodges, 1991; and Roney-Dougal & Solfvin, 2004). There have also been claims of changes in the light absorption properties of samples of water held by healers, (Grad 1964, 1965; Dean 1983a, 1983b; Dean & Brame 1975; Grad & Dean, 1984; Schwartz, De Mattei, Brame & Spottiswoode, 1987; Saklani, 1988a, 1988b; Rein & McCraty, 1994: but see also Fenwick & Hopkins, 1986). Healers have also been found to produce effects on the activity levels of enzymes (Smith, 1968, 1972; Edge, 1980b; Bunnel, 1999).

Experiments have shown that even ordinary citizens may be able to influence biological systems at a distance. Ordinary subjects in such bio-PK experiments have been found to be capable of affecting the growth rates of fungal and bacterial cultures (Barry, 1968a, 1968b; Tedder & Monty, 1981), the mutation rates of bacterial genes (Nash, 1984b), the electrical activity of plants (Dolin, Davydov, Morozova & Shumov, 1993), the electrodermal and brainwave patterns of human subjects (Braud & Schlitz, 1983, 1989; Braud, Schlitz, Collins & Klitch, 1985; Dolin, Dymov & Khatchenkov, 1993; Radin, Taylor & Braud, 1993), the firing rate of individual neurons of the sea snail Aplysia (Baumann, Stewart & Roll, 1986), and the rate of hemolysis of red blood cells (Braud, 1988, 1990; Braud, Davis & Wood, 1979), to name only a few of the effects that have been reported.

To be sure, not all investigators who have looked for such effects have found them, but the success rate is rather substantial. In a "meta-analysis" of 149 psychokinesis experiments using living organisms as targets, Braud, Schlitz and Schmidt (1990) found that 53 percent of them produced significant evidence of a psi effect. As in any other area of research, the methodological quality of the studies is uneven. While the procedures in many of the studies are quite sound, others suffer from various defects. One common defect is that the person caring for or measuring the target organisms may not be blind as to which experimental group the organisms are in. If the person watering a plant or placing a fungal colony in an incubator knows whether the plant or fungus is in the "healed group" or the control group, this may affect his treatment of the organism. This was in fact a problem in some of the plant and fungus experiments (e.g., Nash, 1984b; Saklani, 1988a, 1988b). Another defect occurs when the target and control organisms are not housed in the same areas or under comparable conditions, as was the case in some of the wound-healing experiments with mice (e.g., Grad, Cadoret & Paul, 1961), or when the healing and control procedures are carried out at different times or locations, as was the case in some of the mouse anesthesia experiments, some of the enzyme studies, and some of the human wound experiments (e.g., Watkins & Watkins, 1971; Rein, 1986; Wirth, 1989, 1990). In such cases the target organisms or systems may simply be responding differently to different locations or times of day rather than to the treatments. A third defect occurs when the healer is allowed to be in close physical proximity to the patient or target organism, as the possibility then arises that any effects may be due to suggestion or to the comforting of an animal.

One criticism that has been leveled against parapsychological experiments in general is that the results may be due to experimenter dishonesty. Flamm (2004, 2005) raises such questions regarding the investigator Daniel Wirth. Flamm notes that Wirth and his coworkers conducted a study in which infertile women who were prayed for in Christian prayer groups became pregnant at twice the rate of women in a control group (Cha, Wirth,

& Lobo, 2001). It should also be noted that Wirth's work has been widely cited above in connection with other areas of psychic healing. Flamm notes that Wirth has received a five-year prison sentence on thirty counts of fraud and that he often assumed false identities in connection with his embezzlement schemes. Joseph Horvath, who collaborated with Wirth on some of his psychic healing studies (e.g., Wirth, Johnson, Horvath & Mac-Gregor, 1992), has also gone to prison for embezzlement and the use of false identities. Among their crimes, Wirth and Horvath were convicted of bilking the Aldelphia Communications Corporation out of $2.1 million by infiltrating the company and then having it pay for unauthorized consulting work. Flamm also notes that Horvath posed as a medical doctor when performing biopsies on human subjects and that Dr. Rogerio Lobo, who was listed as a coauthor on the study regarding the effect of prayers on infertility in fact had no involvement in the study.

Nonetheless, when the work of Wirth and his collaborators is removed from consideration, there remains a large number of seemingly methodologically sound studies that appear to show that humans are capable of affecting biological systems at a distance, and that therefore there may well be reason to believe that there could be some validity to the claims of laying-on-of-hands or remote healing. The reason this evidence is largely ignored by the medical and scientific community is probably related to scientific community's general rejection of psi research; the data just do not fit into established theories. On the other hand, while there may be prejudice against this research, any person seeking treatment should understand that the magnitude of the healing effects found in these studies tends to be far less than the effects produced by orthodox medical treatment, and they are also much less reliable.

Summary of healing studies. In conclusion, there is not much solid evidence for the existence of paranormal effects in the areas of faith healing, psychic diagnosis, or psychic surgery. With regard to the techniques of laying-on-of-hands and remote healing, there are hints from the existing experimental evidence that some sort of paranormal effect could be involved in these techniques.

Forteana

There are a wide variety of truly strange phenomena that are sometimes linked, albeit tangentially, with phenomena that form the subject matter of more "orthodox" parapsychology. These bizarre occurrences are sometimes designated "Forteana," in honor of the early twentieth century paradoxer Charles Hoy Fort, who amassed a large catalogue of anomalies that seem to fly in the face of modern science. Forteana include such diverse subjects as UFOs, sightings of Bigfoot and the Loch Ness monster, weeping statues, the Bermuda triangle, and spontaneous human combustion.

One of the more lucrative phenomena in this category is an image of the Virgin Mary that recently manifested in a grilled cheese sandwich that fetched a price of $28,000 in an eBay auction. However, the human brain is hard-wired to detect human faces, and it seems that, whenever anything remotely resembling a human face appears, Marian enthusiasts interpret it as an image of the Blessed Virgin. In recounting the tale of the grilled cheese sandwich icon, Nickell (2005b) notes that the Virgin's likeness has also appeared on a cinnamon bun in a coffee shop and that Jesus has appeared in a tortilla as well as in a giant forkful of spaghetti. Lest it be thought that divine appearances are restricted to food items, it should be noted that the Blessed Virgin has also recently manifested Herself in a salt stain on a highway overpass in Chicago (Associated Press, April 20, 2005).

The list goes on and on, and encompasses bleeding statues, sightings of the Virgin Mary, UFOs, Sasquatch, crop circles and cattle mutilations. It would take us too far afield to give a comprehensive review of such fields as ufology and cryptozoology here. Readers interested in such phenomena are invited to consult such specialty journals as the *Journal of Scientific Exploration* and *The Skeptical Inquirer*.

General Summary of Field Investigations

The evidence discussed in this chapter has been largely of an anecdotal nature. A determined skeptic might be inclined to dismiss all of it on the basis of coincidence, unconscious inference, memory distortion, delusions, hallucinations and outright fraud. It is largely because of these counterexplanations that parapsychologists have turned to experimental investigations as the primary means of establishing the existence of psi phenomena and investigating their modus operandi. These investigations form the subject of the next chapter. It should be noted, however, that these experimental studies have themselves been subject to repeated attacks by skeptics on the basis of methodological errors, lack of repeatability, and possible experimenter fraud. Sometimes spontaneous case material may be more convincing than an array of experiments. I have talked to several skeptics who, while dismissing experimental investigations, were left with a nagging feeling that psi might be real after all due to their own personal psi experiences or those of their acquaintances.

A summary dismissal of the evidence from spontaneous cases as nonrigorous and hence unworthy of serious consideration is not appropriate. Not only may spontaneous cases provide unique insights into the operation of psi in naturalistic settings, which may not be obtainable from contrived and artificial experimental situations, but they may provide important clues as to possible productive lines of experimental investigation. Also, many skeptical counterexplanations of spontaneous cases are quite implausible. Thus, spontaneous cases form an important body of evidence for psi in their own right, and supplement the evidence obtained by experimental parapsychologists. A past president of the Parapsychological Association, Rhea White, has even gone so far as to urge the abandonment of the experimental approach in psi research in favor of the study of spontaneous cases (White, 1985, 1990). She has contended that reliance on statistical and laboratory methods may lead to a suppression of awareness of clues to the nature of psi arising from spontaneous experiences and informal practices, and she suggests adopting a "depth psychology" approach to the investigation of parapsychological phenomena. She has further contended that sounder data have arisen from surveys of spontaneous experiences than from unreliable laboratory effects. In all probability, however, it will take evidence of both types to convince a skeptical scientific community of the existence of psi. A total abandonment of the experimental approach would probably disqualify parapsychology from any claim to be a real science in the eyes of the scientific establishment. Experimental approaches must be an integral part of any science of parapsychology. It is to an examination of such laboratory studies that we now turn.

4

Experimental Investigations of Psi Phenomena

As noted in the last chapter, most parapsychologists have adopted the view that spontaneous cases cannot provide a "clean proof" of the existence of psi due to the various possible skeptical explanations of these cases, such as those invoking coincidence, delusion, unconscious inference and fraud. Therefore, they have turned to experimental approaches to establish the reality of psi effects. In the early days of parapsychology, such experiments typically involved attempts by human subjects to use their powers of extrasensory perception to discern the identity of a playing card hidden from their view or to use their psychokinetic abilities to influence the fall of mechanically thrown dice. When a subject is guessing a randomly selected card held in a separate room, the problems of sensory cues and unconscious inference are presumably removed. If contemporaneous records of the experiments are made, one need not rely on the fallible memory (or deceiving testimony) of the people involved, save of course for the experimenters themselves. Thus, the problems of memory distortion or fraudulent testimony on the part of informants in spontaneous cases are likewise eliminated when the experimental approach is adopted.

Perhaps the chief benefit of the experimental approach is its ability to deal with the objection that apparent cases of psi are simply due to coincidence. For instance, if a person attempts to guess the order of the cards in a well-shuffled and hidden deck of ESP cards and guesses 13 of the cards correctly (as opposed to the five she would be expected to get right on the average by chance), the mathematical theory of probability can be invoked to show that this would happen in fewer than 1 in 10,000 such experiments by chance. We would conclude that it is very unlikely that we would have obtained such a result by chance unless we were to run thousands of such experiments.

The philosopher Francis Bacon was perhaps the first on record to suggest that psi phenomena could be investigated through the statistical analysis of card-guessing and dice-throwing experiments (Bell, 1956). Charles Richet of France (1884, 1888) was the first to initiate anything approaching an actual research program in this area, using card-guessing as a technique for investigating ESP. In the early part of the twentieth century, experimental studies of ESP involving the guessing of cards were performed by Leonard Troland and George Estabrooks at Harvard University and J. E. Coover at Stanford University (Troland, 1917; Coover, 1917; Estabrooks, 1927). Estabrooks' very successful experiment was conducted while completing his doctorate under William McDougall, a prominent psychologist who had an interest in psychical research.

In 1927, McDougall moved to Duke University to assume the chairmanship of the psychology department. He was followed soon thereafter by an enthusiastic young psychical researcher, J. B. Rhine, and his wife, Louisa. During the academic year 1929–1930, Rhine began his program of experimental research on psi phenomena. This program eventually evolved into the sustained and continuous research tradition that has become known as experimental parapsychology. For this reason, Rhine is usually regarded as the founder of the field of parapsychology (in the sense of the experimental study of psi phenomena).

Rhine's initial methods for investigating ESP relied heavily on the standard "ESP cards," which were designed for Rhine by the Duke perceptual psychologist Karl Zener. (This deck was known for a long time as the "Zener deck," somewhat to the consternation of Zener, who later abandoned parapsychological research for work in more mainstream and less controversial areas of psychology.) The ESP deck consists of 25 cards, with five cards representing each of the following five symbols: circle, star, cross, square and wavy lines. When a subject guesses the order of the cards in a well-shuffled ESP deck, he has a one-fifth chance of guessing any particular card correctly, and it can be shown mathematically that the average score he would expect to achieve by chance is five correct guesses.

In 1934, at the suggestion of a young gambler, Rhine began to investigate psychokinesis (PK), using dice as target objects. Initially, Rhine investigated the ability of human subjects to influence dice to roll in such a way that a given "target" face would come up. Because of the controversy surrounding his ESP results, Rhine withheld publication of his PK research until 1943.

In the modern era, the targets of psychokinetic influence have expanded to include living organisms, red blood cells, thermistors, and quantum-mechanically based random event generators (REGs). REGs have also been used to generate ESP targets. In ESP research, there has been a move in the direction away from forced-choice experiments (in which the subject's response on each trial is restricted to a finite set of specified alternatives, as in guessing a deck of ESP cards) and toward free-response experiments, in which a subject is free to describe his impression of the target in any manner he chooses.

A free-response methodology is employed in modern ganzfeld experiments, in which a subject is typically seated in a comfortable chair with ping-pong balls placed over his eyes to produce a uniform visual field. Frequently, white or "pink" noise played in the subject's ears to produce a homogeneous form of auditory stimulation as well.

The subject may then try to describe a target picture that is being viewed by a human sender or agent, this target having been randomly selected from a target pool consisting of, say, four potential target pictures. The subject or an outside judge then ranks the pictures in the target pool against the subject's descriptions. Obviously, given the random nature of the target selection, the probability that the subject's description will be matched against the correct target by chance is one-fourth.

Other examples of free-response experiments include remote viewing studies, in which a subject attempts to describe the location to which a human sender has been sent, and dream studies, in which a subject's dream reports are matched against, say, art prints viewed by a human sender attempting to influence the subject's dream.

Forced-choice Experiments

Perhaps the foremost forced-choice ESP experiment performed in the heyday of the card-guessing era of Rhine's early research group at Duke University was the Pearce-Pratt series conducted on the Duke campus during the 1933–1934 academic year (Rhine & Pratt, 1954). In this experiment, the subject, a divinity student named Hubert Pearce, attempted to guess the identity of cards held in a separate building by J. G. Pratt, a graduate student in psychology. In each session, the men would synchronize their watches, and then Pearce would leave for a cubicle in the stacks of the library. Pratt then shuffled a deck of ESP cards and placed one card face down each minute on a book on a table in his building, which was either the Physics Building (100 yards distant from the library) or the Medical Building (250 yards distant). Pearce attempted to guess the identity of the card located on the book at the specified time. Two decks were guessed per session. In all, 1850 cards were guessed, and Pearce averaged 7.54 cards guessed correctly per deck, where 5 would be expected by chance. These results were significant at the $p < 10^{-22}$ level, meaning that this level of success would occur by chance fewer than once in 10 sextillion such experiments. Clearly chance coincidence cannot account for these results, and they have been taken as strong evidence of ESP.

A more modern form of forced-choice experiment was pioneered by physicist Helmut Schmidt (1969) in his study of the precognition of radioactive decay, a quantum process that is in principle unpredictable under modern theories of physics. Schmidt's study relied on a type of quantum-mechanically based REG that has since become known as a "Schmidt machine" and is now a widely-used and basic tool in parapsychological research. With Schmidt's original machine, the subject was confronted with an array of four differently colored light bulbs. The subject's task was to guess which bulb on the display was going to be the next to light up. The subject signaled his or her guess by pushing a button in front of the chosen bulb. During this process, an electronic counter was constantly cycling through the values 1, 2, 3, 4, 1, 2, 3, 4, 1, 2, 3, 4 ... at the rate of a million steps a second. After the subject pressed a button indicating his or her guess, the counter stopped when a Geiger counter detected a decay electron emitted from a sample of strontium 90 and the corresponding lamp was lit. The subject's task could thus be construed as one of predicting the time of future radioactive decay of a strontium 90 atom to within an accuracy of a millionth of a second. (However, more plausibly from a psychological and sensory-motor point of view, the subjects were simply foreseeing which lamp would be lit.) The subjects' guesses and the lamps actually lit were automatically recorded on counters and punch tape, eliminating the possibility of directional errors by human recorders. Extensive randomness tests were run on the REG to ensure that its output was indeed random. In Schmidt's first experiment, three subjects made a total of 63,066 guesses and scored 691.5 more hits than they would have been expected to by chance. This level of success could be achieved through sheer luck in only two out of every billion such experiments. In a confirmation study, Schmidt had the subjects attempt to achieve high scores in some prespecified trials and low scores in others. 20,000 trials were run, and the subjects obtained 401 more hits (in the prespecified direction) than they would have been expected to by chance. Results this good would occur by chance only once in 10 billion such experiments.

Free-response Experiments

In free-response experiments, the target is generally not chosen from a small pool of targets known to the subject, but instead may be drawn from a small pool of targets that is unknown to the subject at the time of the trial. Much more rarely, the target may be created uniquely for each trial. The subject in turn does not simply select a guess corresponding to one of a fixed number of alternatives, but rather describes her impressions of the target, which may be in the form of dreams, visual imagery, or a free-association monologue. The subject typically uses verbal descriptions or drawings to communicate these impressions.

The most commonly used techniques in modern free-response experiments are the ganzfeld and remote-viewing procedures. A highly successful series of remote-viewing trials was conducted in the late 1970s by the team of Targ and Puthoff at Stanford Research Institute (Puthoff & Targ, 1979; Targ & Puthoff, 1977; Targ, Puthoff & May, 1979). To give the reader the flavor of the remote-viewing procedure, a single trial from a five-trial long-distance series will be described. Unlike most of Targ and Puthoff's trials, the target was not chosen randomly but rather was selected by a skeptical scientist. The scientist then took the remote-viewing team to the target site, which was a series of underground chambers in Ohio Caverns in Springfield, Ohio, which were filled with stalagmites and stalactites. The subject remained behind in New York City and was told only that the remote-viewing team was located somewhere between New York City and California. After the remote-viewing team had spent 45 minutes touring the caverns, the skeptical scientist then called the subject in New York, whereupon a transcript of the subject's impression of the target area was read to him. The opening passage of the transcript was as follows:

> 1:50 PM before starting—Flat semiindustrial countryside with mountain range in background and something to do with underground caves or mines or deep shafts—half manmade, half natural—some electric humming going on—throbbing, inner throbbing. Nuclear or some very far out and possibly secret installation—corridor—mazes of them—whole underground city almost—Don't like it at all—long for outdoors and nature. 2:00 PM— [Experimenters] R and H walking along sunny road—entering into arborlike shaft—again looks like man helped nature—vines (wisteria) growing in arch at entrance like to a wine cellar—leading into underground world. Darker earth-smelling cool moist passage with something grey and of interest on the left of them—musty—sudden change to bank of elevators—a very manmade [sic] steel wall—and shaft-like inserted silo going below earth— brightly lit [Targ, Puthoff & May, 1979, p. 88].

The above correspondence is of course quite impressive. But it is important that targets in free-response experiments be chosen randomly (as they were in most of Targ and Puthoff's research). For instance, a depressing global event (or increasing sunspot activity, etc.) may have caused both the skeptical scientist and the percipient in this experiment to be in a gloomy mood, and that may account for both the scientist's selection of a dark underground cave as a target area and for the percipient's descriptions.

In the early 1970s, Montague Ullman and Stanley Krippner conducted an experimental study of "dream telepathy" at the New York Maimonides Medical Center (Ullman, Krippner & Vaughn, 1973). This research employed a fully-equipped sleep laboratory and was designed to investigate the possibility that a subject's dreams could incorporate elements of an art print chosen as an ESP target. The subject went to sleep in the laboratory, with the usual EEG electrodes affixed to his head. He was then awakened toward the end of each rapid eye movement (REM) period, which is known to be associated with dreaming, and asked to give a dream report. Several such reports would be elicited from a given subject in a typical night. The art print to serve as the ESP target was randomly chosen from a set of possible targets. A person who served as sender or "agent" then attempted to "send" the picture to the sleeping subject, so that the latter might incorporate the target material into his or her dream. Usually, one art print served as the target for an entire night. After the subject's sleep period was concluded, the subject's dream reports were compared to the target as well as to a set of control art prints, which served as foils. The pictures were then ranked as to degree of correspondence with the dream reports, both by the subject and by outside judges. In several series, the foil pictures consisted of the remaining targets in a small target pool from which the actual target was chosen. Some subjects obtained highly successful results. For instance, a woman named Felicia Parise obtained 34 "direct hits" (meaning that the target picture was rated first among the pictures in an eight-target pool in terms of correspondence with the subject's dream) out of 66 trials, as determined by her own ratings of the targets. Only 8.25 direct hits would be expected by chance, so this is a clearly significant result. Strangely enough, the independent judges gave Ms. Parise only nine direct hits (about what would be expected by chance). Another subject, Dr. Robert van de Castle, himself a dream researcher, spent eight nights in the laboratory as a subject and scored a "hit" (target print ranked in the top half of the eight-target pool) on each night by his own evaluations. The independent judges gave him only six hits, but five of these were direct hits, where only one direct hit would be expected by chance. Many other subjects were less successful.

Sometimes rather striking correspondences between the target print and the subject's dream were obtained. For instance, on one night the art print chosen as target was Goya's "The Duelers," which portrays two Spaniards engaged in a duel with swords. One of the participants has succeeded in making a thrust into the other's abdomen. The first dream report of the subject, Dr. Robyn Posin, a psychologist, was as follows:

> [I was] in the office of a man who is sort of waiting for this woman to arrive. He's actually ... talking about her in the sense that the venom and anger that I experience in him is reserved for her.... And he has this thing that's like a bullwhip ... and he hits the wall with the whip and makes a crack ... and then thinks of a woman. There was something very impotent about this man's rage.... It wasn't a bullwhip that he had, it was really a cat-o'-nine tails.... It had its origins ... in Spain.... It was a very frightening experience [Ullman, Krippner & Vaughn, 1973, p. 131].

The researchers go on to report that

> In her seventh dream, she was at a Black Muslim rally. "They were really raging, and all of a sudden some doors from an auditorium opened and out came Elijah Mohammed and a bunch of his followers.... He had on this huge flaming torch with which to set some more stuff on fire, and I got very scared." Her associations to this were "It was like a real chaos scene ... the terrorism, that same kind of lack of control, I guess, that seemed to me to be anger and hostility and acting out in it.... It's some sort of conflagration, either symbolically or realistically ... something rather violent" [Ullman, Krippner & Vaughn, 1973, p. 131].

Subconscious Psi

The above experimental procedures are aimed at detecting the conscious use of psi. In the past few years, there have been an increasing number of experimental investigations of the unconscious or subconscious detection of psi signals. For instance, McDonough, Don and Warren (2002) ran an experiment in which the subject attempted to guess which of four playing cards sequentially presented on a video monitor had been selected as the ESP target. They found a greater amplitude of slow wave brain potential 150–500 milliseconds after the target card was presented compared to that following the control cards.

Similarly, Satori, Massaccesi, Martinelli, and Tressoldi (2004) found subjects' heart rates were accelerated when the ESP target picture was presented compared to the heart rates when the nontarget pictures were presented. This effect occurred even though the subjects' scores on the conscious ESP guessing task did not differ significantly from chance.

Radin (1997b, 2003, 2004) has carried out a series of studies in which he found that subject's heart rates and electrodermal activity (a measure of stress, anxiety or excitement) increased prior to the presentation of emotional pictures when compared to the same time periods prior to the presentation of control pictures. Across all four of Radin's studies, this effect was statistically significant at the .001 level. Radin terms this effect "presentiment." It would appear to be a case of subconscious precognition, manifested in physiological activity rather than in the subjects' consciousnesses. Radin (1997a) attributes Libet's finding that a widespread buildup in brain potential precedes the conscious experience of a voluntary decision to initiate a finger movement (Libet, 1991a) as a presentiment "presponse" (as opposed to "response") of the brain's own decision-making.

In a similar vein, May and Spottiswoode have found an increased startle response (as measured by skin conductance) in three-second epochs (time periods) prior to a startling stimulus (a blast of white noise) relative to control trials in which no startling stimulus was presented (May & Spottiswoode, 2003; Spottiswoode & May, 2003).

Darryl Bem, a prominent social psychologist, has devoted much of the past ten years of his career to parapsychological research. Bem (2003) has recently conducted an experiment in which he presented pairs of positively-valenced (i.e., pleasant) pictures and pairs of negatively-valenced (unpleasant) pictures to human subjects. He asked the subjects which picture of the pair they preferred. Then one picture from each pair was chosen as the target and these targets were then subliminally presented to the subject. Bem found that subjects presented with a pair of positively-valenced pictures preferred the picture that would not be chosen as the target and that subjects presented with pairs of negatively-valenced pictures preferred the picture that would be chosen as the target. Bem attributes his results to "precognitive habituation," postulating that the repeated subliminal exposure in the future diminished the subject's affective responses to the targets in the present (i.e., both the positive and negative targets became more neutral in comparison to the nontarget pictures). In short, repeated subliminal exposures of the picture in the future diminished the subject's emotional/aesthetic responses in the present. Bem also found a precognitive habituation effect for targets that were supraliminally presented to the subject (i.e., the subjects could perceive the pictures consciously), but only for negatively-valenced pictures.

As with most lines of parapsychological research, these results have not been universally replicable. For instance, Broughton (2004) failed to replicate Radin's "presentiment studies." Broughton also reported a very poor test-retest reliability score, indicating that his subjects failed to manifest a consistent psi effect. Similarly, Sarra, Child and Smith (2004) failed to replicate Bem's "precognitive habituation" effect using pictures of spiders as the negatively valenced targets.

PK Tests

PK tests may be divided into roughly two types: "micro-PK" tests, in which the evidence for PK is primarily based on deviations from statistical distributions expected by chance (such as those governing the fall of dice) and "macro-PK" tests, in which the subject attempts to create a macrophysical change in the target object (such as by bending a spoon).

MICRO-PK

In the early days of parapsychology, dice typically served as the target objects in micro-PK experiments. In the modern era, quantum-mechanically based random event generators (REGs) and living systems have been the most frequently used target objects.

In one typical experiment involving animals as subjects, Schmidt (1970) enclosed his pet cat in a cold shack. In the shack was a 200-watt lamp, which served as a source of heat for the cat. Once each second, a quantum-mechanically based REG of the type described previously sent either an "on" or "off" signal to the lamp. The REG was designed in such a way that the probability of an "on" signal was 50 percent. Thus, the cat could obtain more heat by using its psychokinetic abilities to influence the REG to output more "on" signals than would be expected by chance. In fact, in 9000 trials, 4,615 "on" signals were generated, indicating that the cat may have used its PK to increase the probability of an "on" signal from 50 percent to 51.2 percent, admittedly a very slight increase, but one which would occur by chance in only eight of a thousand such experiments. To check the randomness of the generator, Schmidt ran the REG over a period of 24 nights without the cat in the shack and found no departures from chance levels in a total of 691,200 signals generated.

In recent years, there has been a flurry of research reports relating to the effects of global consciousness on the output of REGs. Specifically, it is asserted that events that produce a state of widespread excitement through the world (or smaller region), resulting in a coherent state of consciousness involving many individuals, are associated with the anomalous behavior of REGs. One research initiative to study this phenomenon is called the Global Consciousness Project (GCP) and involves the continuous monitoring several REGs paced at different locations around the world.

Radin (2002) reported that the GCP REGs showed a high degree of correlation in their behavior on September 11, 2001 (the day of the terrorist attack on the World Trade Center) as well as on other days involving major news events over a 250 day-period. Similarly, Nelson (2002) reports that the behavior REGs at 40 host sites became more correlated with one another at the time of the September 11 attack, with this effect being statistically significant at the 10^{-7} level. He notes that some global events are accompanied by the anomalous behavior of REGs, while others are not (e.g., widespread flooding in Nicaragua resulting from the collapse of the Casaitas volcano). It should, however, be noted that Scargle (2002) has criticized both Radin and Nelson for reporting exploratory analyses as if they were preplanned and for "lying with statistics" by presenting misleading graphs.

Hirukawa and Ishikawa (2002) report evidence of anomalous deviations in the output of an REG toward the end of the Aomori-Nebuta summer festival in Japan.

Experiments on the effects of global consciousness on the behavior of REGs in fact predate the September 11, 2001 tragedy. Radin, Rebman and Mackwe (1996) report evidence for increased variance in the output of an REG during times of high group coherence in a Breathwork workshop, but no increased variance during times of low group coherence. Radin et al. also report a correlation in the outputs of two REGs separated by 12 miles during the first half of the broadcast of the 67th annual Academy Awards. This correlation declined in the second half of the broadcast, as did the television audience, and the strength of the correlation was significantly related to the decline in the size of the television audience.

Bierman (1996) found an increased variance in the output of an REG during time periods in which disturbances occurred in a poltergeist case in the Netherlands. He also reports deviations in the output of an REG during the time of a soccer match between the Dutch and Italian teams. The REG's behavior returned to normal after the winning score by the Dutch team with two minutes left in the game.

Nelson, Bradish, Dobyns, Dunne and Jahn (1996) report significant deviations in the output of an REG during periods of high attention, intellectual cohesiveness, and shared emotions of a discussion group. In a review of 61 field REG experiments, Nelson, Jahn, Dunne, Dobyns and Bradish (1998) report highly significant deviations from chance expectation in REG output during intense emotional events during small group interactions, but no such deviations during times of less emotional events. In a recent summary of this line of research, Jahn and Dunne (2005) state that in general, they have found high deviations from the distribution of REG outputs expected by chance at times of highly cohesive events producing "resonance," but low deviations from chance during time of more "mundane" events.

Of course, it is difficult to see why a coherent state of group consciousness should have an effect on the behavior of an REG that is otherwise not connected to the group. As Palmer (1997) points out, the success of these "field REG" experiments is more likely due to psi influence by the experimenter, who has a vested interest in the experiment's outcome than to psi influence by the group members, who are generally not focusing on, and in many instances are unaware of, the REG.

Macro-PK

The subject of macro-PK is much more problematic. Macro-PK, which may involve the bending of metal specimens, the ostensibly paranormal production of images on photographic film, or the movement of small objects across the surface of a table, usually involves special subjects having the status of semiprofessional psychics. Because the psychic himself to a large extent determines the nature of the phenomena he may produce and the conditions under which he feels comfortable in producing them, the investigator does not have the same control over the experimental procedure that she would have in a micro-PK experiment instigated and designed by herself. In fact, in macro-PK research, experimental procedures and conditions often must be negotiated with the psychic if he is to perform at all. Consequently, proper procedures are much less well-defined in macro-PK research than they are in micro-PK research. As most special macro-PK subjects are suspected of, and accused of, fraud by skeptical scientists and writers, the suspicion arises that these psychics will not perform unless they have succeeded in negotiating conditions and procedures that will allow them to produce the alleged macro-PK phenomena fraudulently. Thus, there is considerable debate, both within and outside the parapsychological community, over the adequacy of the methods and safeguards taken in macro-PK research. In fact, several macro-PK subjects have indeed been detected in fraud, as will be discussed in greater detail in the section on subject fraud below.

Separation of Psi Modalities

In the beginnings of experimental parapsychology, it was thought possible to separate psi abilities into several component subtypes: telepathy (the ability to read the mind of another person or being, usually assumed to involve direct contact between minds at the mental, rather than physical, level), clairvoyance (the paranormal ability to acquire information directly from objects, such as when a subject is able to identify a card which has been hidden in a container and whose identity is known to no one at the time), precognition (the ability to foretell events that are yet to happen), retrocognition (the direct paranormal knowledge of past events), and psychokinesis (the ability of mind to influence matter directly). To this list could be added retroactive psychokinesis, the rather outlandish ability to influence events that have already occurred in the past. This seemingly implausible psi power was first proposed to exist by Helmut Schmidt (1975a, 1975b, 1984), who has since gone on to amass a considerable amount of experimental data in its support (see Schmidt , 1976, 1981, 1985, 1986, 1993; Terry & Schmidt, 1978; Gruber, 1980; Schmidt, Morris & Rudolph, 1986; and Schmidt & Schlitz, 1988). In a typical retroactive-PK experiment, a subject may be asked to use his mental abilities to increase the rate at which one of two lights comes on. Unknown to the subject, the behavior of the lights is governed by the output of a random event generator (REG) of the "Schmidt machine" type that was generated two weeks previously. Thus, the subject's covert task is to extend his PK influence backward in time to influence the behavior of the REG two weeks in the past. Schmidt has actually provided a fairly plausible account of why such retroactive PK effects might be expected to occur, based on his reading of quantum mechanics. Schmidt, along with many other theorists, believes that the outcome of a quantum process does not take on a definite value until it is observed by a conscious being (even if a considerable period of time elapses before the observation takes place).

Early on in parapsychology, it became apparent that it was difficult to establish the existence of any of these pure forms of psi in a definitive manner. For instance, in Schmidt's four-button precognition experiment, instead of using precognition to guess the identity of the correct lamp, the subject may rather be pushing a button and then using her psychokinesis to cause the correct lamp to light up.

There is a similar difficulty in separating telepathy (direct mind to mind interaction) from clairvoyance (direct knowledge of a target object). For instance, in a telepathy experiment in which a percipient attempts to guess what card a sender is looking at, it is quite possible that the percipient may use her clairvoyant powers to read the card directly rather than reading the mind of the sender. Alternatively, if the sender is merely thinking of a card, the identity of which he will announce later, the percipient might use precognitive clairvoyance to access whatever physical record of the target is later made. Also, even if a seemingly pure test of telepathy could be devised, any alleged telepathy on the part of the percipient could be interpreted as clairvoyant perception of the brain state of the agent. Such considerations led J. B. Rhine (1974) to call the existence of telepathy an "untestable hypothesis" and to recommend that the problem of proving the existence of pure telepathy be "shelved."

Because of the difficulty of obtaining an experimental separation of the various types of psi phenomena, the parapsychologists Robert Thouless and B. P. Wiesner suggested adopting the neutral term "psi" to designate parapsychological phenomena of unspecified type (Wiesner & Thouless, 1942; Thouless & Wiesner, 1948).

Parapsychologists continue to use terms such as precognition, clairvoyance, telepathy and psychokinesis in describing their own experimental procedures, but these typically refer to the experimental task as described to the subject rather than implying that a particular set of experimental results is definitely due to, say, precognition rather than PK.

Criticisms of Parapsychological Research

We will now turn to an examination of the controversies surrounding experimental work in parapsychology, the lessons that may be learned from them regarding proper methodology and the reasons for the continuing resistance of the scientific establishment to experimental psi research.

SENSORY CUES

When one is attempting to establish the existence of an ability to identify target material that lies outside of the normally recognized channels of the physical senses, it is obviously important to exclude the possibility that the subject's knowledge of a target is based on "sensory cues" (that is, information acquired through the usual physical senses). The early days of experimental parapsychology were not characterized by the stringent safeguards against sensory cues that are (usually) employed today. For instance, an "agent" might sit at one end of a table, pick up an ESP card and attempt to project its identity into the mind of a percipient seated at the other end of the table. Under these circumstances, the percipient might learn the card's identity by seeing the card reflected in the agent's eyes or by picking up on cues unconsciously provided by the agent (such as tilting the head when viewing a "star," etc.). The behaviorist B. F. Skinner pointed out that the cards in the Zener ESP deck used by Rhine in his early experiments could be read from the back under certain lighting conditions, invalidating any experiment in which the percipient could see the backs of the cards. Parapsychologists were quick to respond to such critiques by totally isolating the subject from the targets (such as by having them in a separate building, as was done in the Pearce-Pratt series discussed previously, for instance). Most forced-choice experiments in parapsychology today are characterized by adequate shielding of the target from the percipient. Exceptions do of course still occur, as no field is immune from methodological errors committed by its practitioners. For instance, Don, Warren, McDonough and Collura (1988) report an experiment in which the ESP cards used as targets were placed directly on the hand of the special subject (Olof Jonsson), allowing him access to possible sensory cues arising from the back of the cards, as well as possible glimpses of the fronts of the cards. The random number table used to generate the targets was also in the room with the subject and could have been a source of additional cues.

Rupert Sheldrake (1998b) reports an experimental investigation of the hypothesis that people know when someone is looking at them and that this knowledge is mediated by ESP. However, in Sheldrake's experiment, the "starer" was sitting directly behind the "staree." This allows for the possibility of sensory cues, in that the starer's breathing and body movements may be different during staring trials from those during non-staring trials. The subject might be able to use to such cues to differentiate between staring and non-staring trials.

In an attempt to placate his critics, Sheldrake (2001) repeated his experiment with the subjects blindfolded and trial-by-trial feedback eliminated (i.e., the subject was not told immediately after the trial whether the trial had been a staring or non-staring trial). However, this halfhearted attempt at sensory shielding still leaves open the possibility that the subject could be responding to differences in the starer's breathing patterns and bodily movements between staring and non-staring trials.

Lobach and Bierman (2004a) repeated Sheldrake's experiment with improved sensory shielding. Also, to eliminate artifacts due to response bias (e.g., a subject who calls "staring" on 80 percent of the trials would be expected to have a hit rate of 80 percent on staring trials, not the 50 percent rate that would be expected to obtain across all trials by chance), Lobach and Bierman did not analyze staring and non-staring trials separately, as did Sheldrake. In three attempts to replicate Sheldrake's findings, Lobach and Bierman found no evidence that subjects could distinguish between staring and non-staring trials at a rate significantly greater that what would be expected by chance. They conclude that Sheldrake's staring detection effect is not as easily replicated as claimed by Sheldrake.

Sheldrake (2005), however, points to the success of experiments in which the "starer" watches the "staree" over a closed television circuit in a separate room as evidence against the hypothesis that the remote detection of staring is due to sensory cues. In this regard, he cites meta-analysis of 15 such experiments by Schmidt, Schneider, Utts and Walach (2004) indicating that there was overall statistically significant evidence of psi under such conditions.

Sheldrake and Smart (2003) investigated the hypothesis that people sometimes know who is calling on the telephone before even picking up the phone. Of course, as a spontaneous phenomenon, this sort of guessing may be mediated by knowledge who is likely to call at which time of day, ongoing crises and other daily events that may involve some friends (possible callers) more than others, and the amount of time that has elapsed since the person last called. In Sheldrake and Smart's experiment, subjects had to guess which one of four target persons was calling on the phone during a preassigned time interval. Sheldrake's subjects were able to identify the caller before picking up the phone with a frequency that would occur by chance less than four times in a million.

A similar experiment was run by Lobach and Bierman (2004b). In their experiment, one of four target persons was randomly assigned to call the subject during a preassigned five-minute time interval. The subjects were able to identify the caller on 29.4 percent of the trials compared to the 25 percent rate that would be expected by chance (and this difference was statistically significant at the .05 level).

Both the study conducted by Sheldrake and Smart and that conducted by Lobach and Bierman are susceptible to explanation in terms of a time-delay code. For instance some callers may call early in the five-minute trial interval and others may call late. The subject may learn to use such differences in calling times to identify the caller. The possibility may also exist that different phones produce different rings on the receiving phone.

It should also be noted that Schmidt, Muller and Walach (2004) attempted to replicate Sheldrake and Smart's phone-calling experiment, but they obtained nonsignificant results.

In the same vein, Sheldrake and Smart (2000) report an experiment in which Pam Smart's dog Jaytee seemed to know when its owner was coming home and would go to the window or the porch to await her arrival. However, Wiseman, Smith and Milton (2000) failed to confirm Sheldrake and Smart's results when strict quantitative criteria were used to define the event "Jaytee goes to the porch." They attribute Sheldrake and Smart's results to Jaytee's becoming more anxious regarding Pam Smart's absence as time went on, resulting in more frequent trips to the porch and window.

Trial-by-trial feedback. The mathematician Persi Diaconis (1978) pointed out the danger of giving trial-by-trial feedback to a subject guessing a target pool that is being sampled without replacement, such as might occur if the subject is guessing a deck of ESP cards and being shown each card after every guess. Such feedback would enable the subject to improve his chances by avoiding guesses corresponding to already sampled targets (e.g., if the subject guessing an ESP deck has already seen all five circle cards, he can improve his chances by not guessing "circle" again). This is of course correct, but Diaconis' implication that this was a typical testing procedure in parapsychology at that time is misleading. In fact a search conducted by Charles Tart two years prior to the publication of Diaconis' article revealed only four studies using such a procedure, three of them appearing in an unpublished master's thesis. Tart had labeled all four studies as methodologically defective in his review of the literature pertaining to studies employing trial-by-trial feedback (Tart, 1976).

While it is rare for forced-choice experiments to employ trial-by-trial feedback with such a "closed deck" procedure, this does occur more often in free-response experiments, in which subjects give their subjective impression of a target rather than guessing it directly. In one type of procedure, these subjective impressions are ranked or matched against all the targets used in the experiment. For instance, Puthoff, Targ and Tart (1980) conducted an experiment in which a subject attempted to use her ESP to describe ten different target objects. Because the subject was shown the target object after each trial, she could, on subsequent trials, avoid giving descriptions corresponding to previously seen targets, thus artifactually inflating the probability that her descriptions would be correctly matched to the targets by the judges. Diaconis' criticism is clearly applicable to this sort of free-response experiment. In a similar vein, Marks and Kammann (1978, 1980) have argued that in Targ and Puthoff's main remote viewing research (e.g., as reported in Targ & Puthoff, 1977) the subjects' remarks contained clues as to trial order (by referring to "two previous targets," for example) and target identity (by explicitly referring to previously seen targets, which the judges would then know not to match with the present transcript). Tart, Puthoff and Targ (1980) attempted to respond to Marks and Kammann's critique by conducting an analysis showing that the results were still statistically significant even after these cues had been edited out of the transcripts. One can of course quibble about the efficacy of the editing process, and Marks and Scott (1986) have argued that statements left in the transcripts after the editing that referred to the subject's location could constitute residual order cues that might be used by judges. For instance, in one trial Targ asked the subject if he noticed "any difference being in a shielded room rather than in the park." This was the first trial done in a shielded room. In any event, the basic problem (namely, the avoidance by the subject of responses descriptive of previously seen targets) that arises from use of trial-by-trial feedback under conditions of sampling without replacement remains, no matter how effective one assumes the editing process was.

Cuing of judges. A related problem in free-response experiments involves the nonverbal sensory cuing of judges. For instance, in remote viewing experiments conducted by Bisaha and Dunne (1979), judges were provided with pictures of the target location taken on the day of the remote-viewing trial. Thus, cues as to weather conditions, seasonal variations (e.g., foliage conditions), time of day, and so forth, could have been present in both the subject's transcripts and the pictures, and the judges could then use these cues, consciously or unconsciously, to match the transcripts to the targets. Bisaha and Dunne deny that such cues exist, but in the only two picture sets they reproduce from their first experiment, the leaves are still on the trees in one, whereas the trees are bare in the other. Also, Marks (1986) has pointed out that, in Bisaha and Dunne's experiments, the decision as to whether the subject's drawings of his or her impressions of the target site would be presented to the judges was made on an ex post facto basis (that is, after examination of the drawings), which may have biased the information presented to the judges in favor of correct transcript-target matchings. Marks goes on to note that the choice of which photographs of the target site to present to the judges may have been a further biasing factor.

Most of the feedback-related problems discussed above arise from the fact that the experiments in question used a procedure involving sampling without replacement from a finite target pool, often combined with a procedure involving judging the entire set of transcripts for a series against the actual targets used in that series. In most free-response experiments, such as the well-known research line of ganzfeld experiments, the responses are judged against a different target pool for each trial and do not suffer from the problem of sensory cuing of judges to the extent that the above-discussed studies do.

Violations of blindness. It is important in parapsychology, as in other disciplines, that measurement of certain variables be done by a person who is blind as to the values of other variables.

It is also important that anyone interacting with a subject prior to his description of an ESP target be blind as to the identity of that target. For instance, Palmer and Lieberman (1976) report an "out-of-body experience" study in which an experimenter who knew the identity of the target was in the room with the subject. This experimenter might have been able to exert some sort of subtle influence to predispose the subject to give a description corresponding to the target, without even being aware of doing so.

As a general principle, recording or measurement of experimental conditions and targets and of the related psi effects should be carried out under conditions of mutual blindness in both PK and ESP experiments.

Due to the defensive stance parapsychologists must take in light of criticism by a community of hostile skeptics, parapsychologists tend if anything to be more careful about blindness violations than most scientists. In a review of the recent scientific literature, Sheldrake (1998) found that blinding procedures were used more often by parapsychologists than by researchers in other fields.

Nonrandom target selection. In order to eliminate the hypothesis of chance coincidence, it is important that the targets in parapsychological experiments be selected randomly. It will not do, for instance to have a person select a target by thinking of a number between 1 and 10, as certain numbers are more likely to pop into his mind (and the guesser's) than are others, raising the probability to a correct guess above the chance level of 0.1

As an example of nonrandom target selection, in the "volitional mode" technique employed in the "remote perception" studies by Jahn and Dunne (1987) and conducted at the Princeton Engineering Anomalies Research (PEAR) center, the target to be visited was merely selected by the agent rather than chosen randomly from a prepared target pool (no such pool even existed on these trials). Also, in Jahn and Dunne's experiments, the agent was frequently allowed to wander from the assigned target area, to take photographs and to write descriptions of the target area. As these materials were provided to the judges, they essentially constitute the target. The agent was therefore free to construct a target that might match the verbal transcript likely to be provided by the percipient on that particular day. In 211 of Jahn and Dunne's 336 formal "remote perception" trials the agent was free to choose or construct the target in a nonrandom manner.

In the most recent work on "remote perception" conducted by the PEAR team, as described in Dunne and Jahn (2003), the procedure is to have the agent and percipient check off a list of "descriptors" regarding the target location (e.g., whether the scene is "confined or expansive," whether it is "noisy or quiet," whether it involves the presence of water, is indoors or outdoors, etc.). The degree of match between the descriptors checked (or rated) by the percipient and agent are then compared to the statistical distribution of matches between the percipient's descriptor list and those provided for other locations on other trials. However, the same problems exist as for the pictures taken by the agent in Dunne's early research. The location is not the target, rather the target is the agent's description of the location. Common thought processes and common experiences could thus lead the agent and the percipient to provide similar descriptions. For instance, if they are in glum mood, they may both rate the location as "confined and quiet" rather than as "expansive and noisy."

The procedure of comparing descriptor lists for the target to the descriptor lists of the targets used on other trials also runs into the problem that the percipient may consciously or subconsciously avoid given descriptions that correspond to previously seen target locations.

THE PROBLEM OF FRAUD

One reason for critics' reluctance to accept the experimental findings of parapsychologists is the possibility that they may be the result of fraud, either by subjects or by the investigators themselves. We will discuss each in turn, beginning with the former.

Fraud by subjects. In certain types of parapsychological experiments, fraud by subjects is a possibility that must be carefully guarded against. This is especially true of experiments employing "special subjects," a term used to designate persons with a reputation for having extraordinary paranormal abilities and whose livelihood often depends on the exhibition of such abilities. Subject fraud is much less of a concern in situations in which a group of supposedly average citizens participates in an experiment initiated and designed by the parapsychological investigator, although even in this type of experiment it is prudent to take precautions against the possibility of deceit by subjects.

Several instances of subject fraud occurred in the very early investigations of "mind-reading" teams. Hansel (1966, 1980) describes how such fraud occurred in the Society for Psychical Research's (S.P.R.s) investigations of the mind-reading team of Douglas Blackburn and G. A. Smith, which were conducted over the time period from 1882 to 1894. Blackburn served as the telepathic agent in a series of apparently successful picture-drawing experiments in which Smith was the receiver. Blackburn confessed in 1908 that these results had been due to fraud. He as agent had transferred the target drawings onto cigarette paper and then was able to get this paper to Smith when Smith reached for his pencil. Smith himself never admitted to his involvement in the fraud.

The subjects in another one of the S.P.R.'s investigations, the Creery sisters, likewise admitted six years after the investigation that they had used auditory and visual codes to transmit the identity of playing cards to one another. (Gurney, 1888–1889). Similarly, Hansel (1966, 1980) describes how two Welsh schoolboys, Glyn and Ieuan Jones, used signals involving coughs and leg movements to transmit the identity of cards from one to another during experiments run by the British parapsychologist S. G. Soal and his coworkers. The alleged telepathic effects ceased when the door joining the boys' rooms was closed, illustrating the importance of eliminating the possible use of sensory codes by members of alleged mind-reading teams. This is of course merely a special case of the elimination of sensory cues, which is a necessary feature of any properly designed parapsychological experiment.

Subject fraud becomes a central concern in experiments on "macro-PK." Macro-PK experiments involve the production of macrophysical effects, as opposed to subtle influences on random event generators that may only be detectable through statistical analysis. Such macrophysical effects include the bending of metal specimens, the levitation or anomalous movement of macrophysical (that is, nonmicroscopic) objects, the starting or stopping of watches, and the apparently paranormal production of photographs. Macro-PK experiments typically but not always involve "special subjects" (persons with prior reputations regarding their ability to manifest extraordinary physical effects of an apparently paranormal nature). It is of course quite possible that such subjects may use fraudulent means to simulate paranormal effects, and it is thus very important that every precaution be taken to eliminate the possibility of such fraud. Unfortunately, macro-PK experiments have frequently lacked the kind of rigorous conditions that would enable the fraud hypothesis to be definitively ruled out. For instance, in the research on metal-bending conducted by physicist John Hasted (1981), the subjects were allowed physical contact with the target object. One subject, Masuaki Kiyota, was even allowed to carry a spoon he was attempting to bend psychokinetically around with him in his pocket. Such lax conditions allow the subjects the opportunity to bend the metal specimens through covert muscular action. Hasted eschewed the use of a video camera, as he felt that such a device with its implied mistrust would decrease his rapport with the subject.

Martin Gardner, the noted writer of popular books on mathematics and a staunch critic of parapsychology, has criticized macro-PK researchers for their failure to employ traps such as a one-way mirror to detect cheating (Gardner, 1986). That such devices may be effective in detecting fraud is borne out by the research of Pamplin and Collins (1975), who used a one-way mirror to observe several young subjects using fraudulent means to bend metal specimens.

James Randi, who is a professional magician as well as being a prominent critic of psi research, sent two young magicians to a parapsychological laboratory in St. Louis to pose as special macro-PK subjects in an operation Randi (1983a, 1983b, 1986) dubbed "Project Alpha." Randi found that the researchers had ignored his own advice as to what precautions should be taken against subject fraud. Objects were marked with tags that could be switched. The subjects were allowed to handle sealed envelopes containing ESP targets when they were alone and unobserved. They were able to remove the targets and return them, replacing the staples on the envelope. They were able to remove metal specimens and other target objects from containers supposedly designed to prevent their removal. They were also able to introduce a gap in the sealing of a bell jar, allowing movement of a rotor inside to be produced through air puffs.

Thus, it is clear that investigations of special macro-PK subjects have all too often fallen short of ideal standards of rigor and sometimes lack necessary precautions against subject fraud. It is important that the control of experiments reside with the experimenter; the subject simply must not be allowed to dictate conditions to the extent that all precautions and safeguards are abrogated.

Experimenter fraud. There remains the possibility that the experimenters themselves might engage in fraud. Certainly, some parapsychological researchers have been caught red-handed in such activity. Experimental studies of telepathy by S. G. Soal (Soal & Bateman, 1954), long regarded as among the studies providing the most impressive evidence for ESP, have been demonstrated through statistical analyses by Scott and Haskell (1974) and a computer analysis of Soal's target series by Markwick (1978) to be due to a crude form of fraudulent alteration of the experimental data by Soal.

The second major scandal involving investigator fraud in parapsychology involved Walter J. Levy, a young medical school graduate, who had recently been appointed as director of J. B. Rhine's research institute and whom many people regarded as Rhine's heir-apparent. When I joined Rhine's research staff in 1974 shortly after completing my own doctorate, one of the primary things that lured me to the lab was Levy's active and hugely successful program in investigating the psi powers of animals. In one experiment, rats had to use their PK to convince an REG to send them a jolt in the pleasure center of their brains. This was this experiment that proved to be Levy's undoing. His fellow researchers noticed him frequently puttering around the equipment when experiments were in progress and there would normally be no reason to be interacting with the experimental apparatus. To see if he were up to some monkey business, they secretly wired up the computer to make a duplicate record of the output of the REG. This second record showed the output of the REG to be perfectly random, while Levy's official record showed that the rat was getting jolt after jolt to his pleasure center and obtaining truly prodigious PK scores in the process. It transpired that Levy was disconnecting the wire that recorded the trials on which the rat was unsuccessful and shorting it out on the side of the computer for brief periods of time, thus making it seem as though the rat was achieving remarkable PK success. Confronted with the evidence of his crimes, Levy was forced to resign as the director of Rhine's lab and returned to the practice of medicine.

It should be borne in mind that parapsychology is by no means unique in having had investigators exposed in fraudulent activity. Few areas of science have escaped the problem of experimenter fraud, as is evident to anyone reading the pages of *Nature* and *Science* over the past few decades. Even archskeptic Martin Gardner has stated that he believes that such cheating by experimenters is not much more of a problem in parapsychology than it is in more orthodox areas of science (Gardner, 1986). However, in view of the fact that most investigators are not able to obtain reliable and replicable experimental evidence for psi, the possibility that the most striking evidence for psi is due to experimenter fraud should not be completely discounted. If such is the case, parapsychology would stand head and shoulders above the typical run-of-the-mill case of experimenter fraud in terms of the large number of investigators and studies involved. It would be fraud on a scale that is unprecedented in the history of science.

STATISTICAL CONTROVERSIES

The use of improper statistical tests. In parapsychology as in any other science, researchers do occasionally apply inappropriate statistical tests to their data or commit other statistical errors. As universal perfection is not likely to be achieved in any field of study, the rate at which such errors occur is not likely to be reduced to zero. In recent years, however, parapsychologists have been fairly meticulous about ensuring that the statistical tests they perform are appropriate to their data. They have been held to higher standards than the practitioners of other disciplines due to unrelenting and vigorous attacks by critics. Thus, the statistical practices of parapsychologists tend, if anything, to be a little more rigorous than those of many other scientific disciplines. Some researchers will always be more competent than others, and some errors are bound to occur from time to time.

The repeatability problem. One of the reasons why parapsychology has not been embraced by the scientific establishment is that many or most researchers have been unable to obtain reliable evidence of psi. In the critic's mind, this raises the suspicion that the evidence for psi may be due to undetected methodological errors or possibly even fraud on the part of the experimenters. Parapsychologists have been quick to point out that many naturally occurring phenomena, such as ball lightning and meteorite landings, are not reproducible on demand but are nonetheless real. Interestingly, both ball lightning and meteorites were initially disputed by many scientists in much the same way as current scientists reject psi phenomena.

Meta-analysis. Recently a statistical technique known as "meta-analysis" has played an extraordinarily active role both in parapsychological research and debates about the reality of parapsychological effects. A meta-analysis consists of a statistical examination of a group of experimental studies, sometimes consisting of an entire line of research, in order to determine the strength, direction and statistical significance of any overall effects as well as the possible influence of moderator variables (e.g., barometric pressure or the sex of the experimenter) on the size and direction of the effect in question.

One of the earliest uses of meta-analytic techniques was in the now classic debate over the significance and replicability of the ganzfeld line of research between the parapsychologist Charles Honorton and the critic Ray Hyman (Honorton, 1985; Hyman, 1985). Since that time, meta-analyses of a great many lines of parapsychological research have been reported, including forced-choice precognition experiments (Honorton & Ferrari, 1989), free-response ESP experiments (Milton, 1993), bio-PK studies (Braud, 1985; Braud, Schlitz & Schmidt, 1990; Walach & Schmidt, 2005), PK experiments with REGs (Radin, May & Thomson, 1986; Steinkamp, Boller and Bösch, 2002; Pallikari, 2004; Jahn & Dunne, 2005; Ehm, 2005), PK experiments with dice (Radin & Ferrari, 1991), and experiments investigating the effects of hypnosis on ESP (Schechter, 1984; Stanford & Stein, 1994), studies with subjects recruited via the mass media (Milton, 1994), the relationship between ESP scores and the psychological trait of defensiveness (Watt, 1991; Haraldsson & Houtkooper, 1994), the relationship between ESP and extraversion (Honorton, Ferrari & Bem, 1990), and detection of being watched over a closed television circuit monitor (Schmidt, Schneider, Utts & Walach, 2004), to name just a few.

Among other things, meta-analysis offers a means of deciding whether a given line of research has produced overall results that differ significantly from what would be expected by chance. For instance, in a vote-counting type of meta-analysis (that has now gone out of fashion), Radin, May and Thomson (1986) analyzed 332 PK experiments with random event generators that had been published between 1969 and 1984, finding 71 of them to have produced statistically significant evidence of psi. They compute the probability of this happening by chance to be less than 5.4×10^{-43}.

Meta-analysis also provides a means for answering the charge of data selection. For instance Radin, May and Thomson compute that, in order to reduce the overall REG-PK effect to nonsignificance, it would have to be assumed that 7,778 nonsignificant studies had been conducted but not reported.

Similarly, Honorton (1985) performed a meta-analysis of 28 ganzfeld studies and concluded that, in order to reduce the cumulated ESP effect to nonsignificance, it would have to be assumed that a "filedrawer" containing 423 nonsignificant and unpublished studies would have to exist into order to reduce to overall ESP effect to nonsignificance.

The traditional "filedrawer" computation in meta-analysis assumes that the overall chance distribution is replicated in the unpublished studies in the filedrawer. Scargle (2000) has noted that this assumption may be invalid, in that if all the positive, statistically-significant studies are published, the file drawer will consist of studies that do not fall in the upper "tail" of the distribution. Hence, the average psi effect in the studies in the filedrawer will tend to be slightly negative rather than zero as assumed in the traditional filedrawer calculation. Stokes (2001) performed a Monte Carlo analysis and determined that if one takes 90 ganzfeld "pseudoexperiments" simulated using random numbers to simulate chance performance and then selects the 28 highest experiments, the odds against chance for the 28 highest experiments will typically be more than one billion to one (as found in Honorton's meta-analysis). Thus, one would only have to assume the existence of 62 unpublished studies, rather than 423 studies as computed by Honorton (1985). While it stretches the mind to think that there are 423 unpublished ganzfeld studies given the small size of the parapsychological research community, it may not be so unthinkable that there are 62 unpublished studies.

As a way around the filedrawer problem, Bösch (2004) suggested that psi experiments be preregistered before the data collection process. Kennedy (2004) proposes that parapsychology adopt the standard used in the pharmaceutical industry (in which Kennedy works) and that research protocols be developed and registered and calculations of statistical power (the ability to detect an effect of the predicted size) be performed prior to the data collection process. Kennedy questions the value of post hoc meta-analyses in that meta-analyses may be manipulated to produce a desired outcome (such as when a judgment of study quality is made after the results of the study are known.)

Statistical calculations can go a long way toward settling the question of whether the significant results reported in a line of research could have arisen by chance or as a result of data selection. There are, however, other ways significant effects could arise and still not be due to psi. Procedural errors and fraud are two possibilities. What might satisfy the critics would be something approaching repeatability upon demand. If virtually anyone could produce psi effects under conditions he or she found acceptable, there would certainly no longer be much debate about their reality. Perhaps, if a certain minimal proportion of all investigators could obtain evidence of psi, then the critics would be satisfied. Or possibly, if certain individual critics obtained evidence for ESP, the battle for the acceptance of psi would be won. Replication may well be at heart a political process rather than an issue that can be decided by statistical analysis.

Conclusions

After the review of the evidence for psi in these past two chapters, the reader undoubtedly finds himself or herself in the position of a spectator in a 125 year long prize fight. The skeptics have delivered a few good blows, perhaps even a few knockdowns. They are likely ahead on points. Both sides are glassy-eyed. But the parapsychologists sit in their corner, apparently more than ready for yet another round.

The existing evidence does not compel the conclusion that psi phenomena exist. The determined skeptic who wishes to ascribe all the experimental evidence to a combination of experimenter incompetence, methodological errors and outright fraud can rest easy knowing that, given the poor replicability of psi results, his or her position will not easily refuted. However, to attribute the existing evidence for psi is to such factors is to postulate a level of experimenter malfeasance/incompetence that is unparalleled in the history of science.

Spontaneous phenomena may also be explained away in terms of memory distortions, embellishments, runaway fantasies, coincidence, psychosis, and outright falsification and collusion on the part of the witnesses involved. Again the skeptic can rest easy, knowing that such attributions cannot easily be disproved. The case for psi has not been conclusively established. Conclusive proof will likely await the development of repeatable means of eliciting psi.

If psi phenomena exist, their implications for our fundamental understanding of the nature of reality are profound. These implications form the subject of the next chapter.

It should be stressed, however, that the nonexistence of psi would not alter in any important way the core conclusions put forth in these pages regarding the fundamental nature of the conscious self, its interactions with the physical body, its likely central role in the causation of physical phenomena, and its likely survival of the death of the physical body as outlined in the Introduction and in later portions of this book.

5

The Implications of Psi

If psi phenomena exist, they likely have major implications for our understanding of the role of mind in the physical universe, of the nature of the interaction between the mental and physical realms (if these in fact are separate realms), and of the very nature of time and space.

This chapter is devoted to an examination of some of the various theories that have been proposed to explain psi phenomena. Some attempts have been made to explain psi phenomena in terms of the classical Newtonian physics that implicitly underlie the metaphysical mindset of the majority of the "orthodox" scientific community (with the exception of the physicists themselves, of course). In general, these attempts have not met with success. Other attempted theories involve extensions of our current views of space and time and quantum mechanics. A third genre of theories proposes the existence of a collective unconscious or collective mind. We will consider each of these theoretical genres in turn.

Our focus will be on theories that have been proposed to account for ESP and PK. Theories that are primarily directed to the problem of the relationship of the mind to the physical brain—and to the possible survival of the mind (or some portions thereof) of the death of the physical body—will be addressed in the ensuing chapter.

Models of Time

There are quite a few spontaneous cases on record that seem to indicate that one can foresee an unpleasant event in the future and then perform some action to avoid that event. Thus, it seems that one might be able to change the future. This raises interesting philosophical and scientific questions about the nature of time. Louisa Rhine (1955) published a collection of such cases, and we will consider two of her cases here to give the reader a better sense of nature of such experiences. The first case is taken from her book *Hidden Channels of the Mind*:

> In Washington State a young woman was so upset by a terrifying dream one night that she had to wake her husband and tell him about it. She had dreamed that a large ornamental chandelier which hung over their baby's bed in the next room had fallen into the crib and crushed their baby to death. In the dream she could see herself and her husband standing amid the wreckage. The clock on the baby's dresser said 4:35. In the distance she could hear the rain on the windowpane and the wind blowing outside.
>
> But her husband just laughed at her. He said it was a silly dream, to forget it and go back to sleep; and in a matter of moments he did just that himself. But she could not sleep.
>
> Finally, still frightened, she got out of bed and went to the baby's room, got her and brought her back. On the way she stopped to look out the window, and saw a full moon, the

weather calm and unlike the dream. Then, though feeling a little foolish, she got back into bed with the baby.

About two hours later they were wakened by a resounding crash. She jumped up, followed by her husband, and ran to the nursery. There, where the baby would have been lying, was the chandelier in the crib. They looked at each other and then at the clock. It stood at 4:35. Still a little skeptical they listened—to the sound of the rain on the windowpane and wind howling outside [Rhine, 1961, pp. 198–199].

In another case in Rhine's collection, a streetcar operator braked as he approached a one-way exit in order to avoid an accident that he had dreamed about that morning. At that moment, a truck containing the very same people who had been injured in the dream shot out into the street, having gone the wrong way through the one-way exit.

In both of these cases, it would seem that two different futures were involved. In the first (precognized) future, a negative event took place. In the second future, the one that actually occurred, the negative event was avoided.

BRANCHING TIME MODELS

In branching time models, it is assumed that at the "present" moment many possible futures exist. For instance, in the case of the baby and the chandelier, in one possible future (the one that was precognized) the baby was killed by the falling chandelier, whereas in a second possible future (the one that actually occurred) the baby escaped injury.

In the classical, Newtonian view of the universe that prevailed until early in this century, it would be unthinkable that two different alternative futures could both be possible. Under the Newtonian worldview, the universe was seen as governed by laws that preordained the state of the future. This deterministic outlook of classical physics led the famous mathematician and cosmologist Pierre Simon Laplace to propose that a Divine Calculator who knew the position and velocity of every particle in the universe could deduce the entire history and future of the universe down to the last detail.

The development of the modern theory of quantum mechanics has overthrown this deterministic outlook. Under modern theories of physics, given the present state of the universe, many different futures are possible. An atom of radioactive material may or may not decay during a given time period. It is impossible in principle to predict whether it will or not. Under quantum theory, different futures may have different probabilities assigned to them. For instance, it may be more likely that the above-mentioned radioactive decay will occur during the next half-hour than that it will not.

Thus, in the case of the falling chandelier, both the "baby dead" and "baby alive" futures may be compatible with the laws of physics. Which future occurs may depend on indeterminate quantum events in the mother's brain; if her brain enters a favorable quantum state (through precognition?), she will act to avert the disaster.

While most scientists hold that only one of the possible alternative quantum futures is actually realized, the physicist Hugh Everett (1957) has proposed that all the possible futures are actualized, albeit in alternate universes. Everett's theory has become known as the "many worlds" interpretation of quantum mechanics.

The branching time model is easily capable of accommodating cases of precognition followed by intervention. One could assume, say, that in our "chandelier" case the mother foresaw the most probable future, that her baby would be killed, but was able to act in such a way as to ensure the occurrence of a less probable future.

THE LINEAR TIME MODEL

It is also possible to account for such cases with a model postulating only one time dimension and one future, should one prefer such a pedestrian and colorless approach. One could for instance simply state that the mother accurately foresaw that the chandelier was going to fall. Her premonition of her baby's death was simply an error, as that death never occurred. The mother's unconscious mind was merely dramatizing to her the consequences of not moving the baby out from under the chandelier.

One parapsychological theorist to recently propose a linear time model is Jon Taylor (1995, 1998, 2000). Taylor subscribes to a "block universe" model in which there is only one future, corresponding to the events that actually happen. (Such a block universe model is also inherent in the spacetime manifold of Einstein's special and general theories of relativity, as will be discussed in more detail below). Thus, in Taylor's view, it is impossible to "change the future" through an act of intervention, insofar as the future contains events that will happen, not those that might happen. He proposes that extrasensory contacts only take place between living brains in similar emotional states, which create a "resonance" between the two brains. He asserts that people can only precognize events that they do not intend to influence, as any attempt to change or alter the future would destroy the resonance that formed the basis of the interaction between the brains of the person's present and future selves.

Taylor (1995) asserts that this view of precognition is compatible with "free will," as the person only precognizes those events that he or she does not chose to prevent through an act of intervention. Taylor hypothesizes that the absence of precognitive feedback, or resonance, between the present self and future events that the subject does intend to influence or prevent provides the basis for nonspecific intuitive experiences that "something is wrong." This lack of resonance is subconsciously noticed as a sense of foreboding and thus enables the subject to make decisions based on intuitive feelings. Taylor postulates that psi phenomena are due to the creation of quantum fields in human brains that are emanated both in space and time. Psi-mediated information transfer occurs when similar thoughts in one's present and future selves give rise to a resonance between the quantum field of the present and future brains. Intuitive psi experiences occur when there is a lack of resonance between the present and future selves (thus implying that some sort of expectancy, such as that one will live through tomorrow's subway ride, will not be fulfilled). Taylor predicts that there is no such thing as clairvoyance, in view of the dissimilarity of the quantum fields associated with brains and those associated with objects, and that telepathy and precognition should only be able to occur over limited space-time separations. Here Taylor may be underestimating the nonlocal nature of quantum fields, as discussed in Chapter 2 and elsewhere in this book. Also, the existing evidence for information transfer followed by intervention to prevent the precognized event, such as the dream of the falling chandelier discussed above, would seem to constitute strong evidence against Taylor's theory that intervention can only occur with intuitive experiences.

THE SKEPTICAL MODEL

Under this view, there is no such thing as ESP. The mother probably subliminally perceived some dust falling from the unstable chandelier support as she was about to go to bed and then dreamed about the probable consequences.

"TIME FLOW" AND THE PSYCHOLOGICAL EXPERIENCE OF "BECOMING"

The preceding discussion leads us directly into another unsolved fundamental mystery of the universe that ranks right up there with the problem of the relation between conscious experience and material events in terms of its apparent intractability to human analysis. We seem to find ourselves located at a particular instance in time called the present (or for those philosophers who prefer a thin "slab" of time, the specious present). The "present" and our consciousnesses seem to be traveling along the time dimension in the direction of the future. Another, perhaps relativistic, way to put it is that time seems to be "flowing" from the future through the present moment and into the past. Once an event has receded into the past, it is lost to us forever.

Yet modern theories of physics, at least those that incorporate variants of Einstein's special and general theories of relativity, have no place for a set of events that are uniquely distinguished as the present moment or for the phenomenon of time flow. In fact, relativity theory does away even with the concept of the "present" as we intuitively understand it; there is no unique set of events (or cross-section of spacetime) that be unambiguously identified as belong to the present or the "now."

One of the lesser known paradoxical results of Einstein's special theory of relativity is that observers in motion relative to one another will disagree on which sets of events (locations in spacetime) should be taken as being simultaneous with one another (i.e. assigned the same time coordinate). A result of this "relativity of simultaneity" is that two observers in motion relative to each other will disagree on what sets of events (i.e., cross-section of spacetime) should be taken to be the "present." It is even possible that two observers will differ as to what they perceive the temporal order of events to be. In one reference frame, an event X may precede an event Y, whereas in a second reference frame Y is seen to precede X. In the absence of signals traveling faster than light, such a reversal of time coordinates will be achieved only between events that are "spacelike" connected (i.e., no signal moving at light speed or slower can travel between the two events). Thus, if events A and B are "timelike separated" and one observer sees A as being the cause of B, a second observer will also perceive that B is later than A and that the causal chain extends from A forward in time to B. This prohibition against "backward causation" (i.e., an effect preceding its cause in some reference frame) only holds so long as no causal signal may travel faster than light and thus (as we shall see shortly) backward in time in some reference frame.

To illustrate, the relativity of simultaneity, consider Einstein's famous train example. Suppose an observer O is at rest with respect to the Earth (let's give the pre-Copernican motionless flat Earth theory its due, just for the sake of this example). Further suppose that O is standing at a railroad track and is being passed by the train. At the moment she is adjacent to the exact center of the train, lightning strikes both ends of the train. As the speed of light is a constant (and is the same in all reference frames) the light flashes from the two lightning bolts will reach her eyes (or recording equipment) at the same instant. She will therefore judge them to be simultaneous, as they have both traveled the same distance (half the length of the train) at the same speed (the speed of light is a consequence of the laws of physics and is the same in all reference frames).

Consider however the situation of a second observer O,' who is sitting on top of the train and at the middle of the train. As the speed of light is finite and as he is moving in the direction of the lightning bolt at the front of the train, the light from that bolt will have to travel a shorter distance to reach him (from the perspective of the observer on the ground), and therefore the light from that bolt will have to travel a shorter distance to reach him than the light from the bolt at the rear of the train. But, *in his reference frame*, both bolts have traveled the same distance, namely half the length of the train. As the speed of light is a constant in his reference frame, he deduces that the bolt at the front of the train must have happened earlier than the bolt at the rear of the train. Thus, observers O and O' differ in their judgments regarding the temporal order of the two lightning bolts.

An even more cognitively disturbing example of the relativity of simultaneity involves the case of a woman, possible on a very high dose of steroids and quite likely to win the decathlon in the next Olympics, who is running at nearly the speed of light while carrying a very long javelin toward a barn with a front and a back door. From the point of view of the farmer standing beside the barn, the pole has shrunk in length due to the Lorentz-Fitzgerald length contraction. (Another strange consequence of Einstein's theory of relativity is that stationary observers perceive that the length of objects in motion shrink along the direction of the motion.) Thus, even though the javelin was longer than the barn just before the woman began her run, because the javelin has shrunk in length (from the farmer's perspective) due to the woman's high speed, the farmer is able to open the front door and allow the woman to enter the barn and to close the door behind her. Thus for a brief time the woman and javelin are contained in the closed off barn. A *very* short time after the front door closes, the farmer's daughter opens the rear door of the barn and is startled to see a very quick woman carrying a javelin come flying out of the barn.

Consider, however, the situation from the standpoint of the Olympian hopeful. As she is running, in her reference frame the barn is in motion relative to her; thus, its length has shrunk so that it is now much shorter than her javelin. Not being one to shy away from a collision and possibly owning a spare javelin or two, she continues her rush at the barn and to her amazement is able to pass through it without mishap. Due to the relativity of simultaneity, she sees her javelin sticking out of both doors of the incredibly shrunken barn at the same time. In her reference frame, due to the relativity of simultaneity, she sees the farmer's daughter open the rear door *before* the farmer closes the front door, so that both doors are open at the same time.

Because observers in motion with respect to one another will in general disagree about which set of events (spacetime locations) constitute the "present moment," it is impossible to speak about the absolute existence of a three-dimensional space at a single moment in time (a notion that formed one of the fundamental underpinnings of classical, Newtonian physics). Different observers will select different "slices" of events as being simultaneous with one another, depending on their state of motion. Thus, rather than proposing a model involving the existence of a three-dimensional space at a particular time, relativity theorists work with a four-dimensional continuum involving three spatial dimensions and one time dimension. However, observers in motion relative to one another will not in general agree on the assignments of the spatial and temporal coordinates of events. If an observer is in motion relative to me, she may see events in my future as having occurred in her past or events in my past as occurring in her future. Thus in some sense, in relative theory, the future "already exists" and the past "still exists" (in the sense that both the future and the past may be in the present for some observer in motion relative to me but whom I regard as being part of my "now").

Lawrence LeShan (1969) noted the compatibility of this view of physical reality with such psi phenomena as precognition and "retroactive" psychokinesis (the mental influence of events that have already occurred). This view is, however, somewhat at odds with the worldview of quantum mechanics, in which the future is not determined and many alternative futures are possible. Some writers, such as Randall (1998) have argued against theories of the "block universe" type, in which the future is viewed as in some way already existing and thus predetermined, in favor of a model based on quantum indeterminism. In Randall's view, models of the latter type are more compatible with philosophies based on "freedom of will." (However, one can argue that the "will" may be free to act, but that its actions will be guided by desires and values that are themselves determined. Thus, the concept of "free will" and a block universe model of reality need not be fundamentally incompatible.)

What modern physics cannot explain, any more than it can at present explain the existence of conscious experience, is the psychological experience of "time flow" and "becoming." In fact, the experience of "time flow" may be as fundamental a mystery as the existence of conscious experience itself. Indeed, as "time flow" is a subjective experience, it quite likely dependent in some unfathomable manner on consciousness. The two mysteries may thus be somehow intertwined.

Our experience of time is dynamic and anisotropic. We are apparently somehow being propelled forward in time. Alternatively, we experience time flowing past us. Yet the concept of "time flow" has no place in theories of physics. As we have just seen, in Einstein's theory of relativity, all past, present and future events are viewed as a timeless array of points in four-dimensional Minkowski spacetime. And, as pointed out above, no single cross-section of spacetime can be uniquely defined as the present for all observers.

Neither can theories of physics, for the most part, distinguish the directions of the future from that of the past. Most physical processes are (theoretically at least) reversible. An electron and a positron (the antimatter counterpart of the electron) may collide and annihilate one another, producing two photons. However, it is also possible for two photons to collide, producing an electron-positron pair, and this process appears to be the same as the first process, but reversed in time.

A ball being thrown upward in the air loses velocity due to gravity. A film of this process, if reversed, would show a falling ball picking up velocity due to gravitational attraction, a process that may occur in the forward direction of time. The film of a more complicated process, such as a swimmer diving into a pool of water, would appear to represent an impossible sequence of events when run backward (i.e., the swimmer being mysteriously propelled out of the water, instantly drying and landing on the diving board). Actually, even the reversed film of the dive does not represent an impossible sequence of events, only a very improbable one (it requires a collections of water molecules all to suddenly converge on the swimmer's body in just the right manner that, through the collective force, the swimmer is propelled vertically out of the water, among other improbable coincidences).

Similarly, if the door between a hot and a cold room is opened, heat will tend to flow from the warmer room into the cooler room, so that the rooms will become more equal in temperature as time goes on. The reverse process, wherein one of two equally warm rooms suddenly grows hotter and the other suddenly grows colder (in the absence of any external energy sources) is not impossible, but only very improbable (as it would require most of the faster-moving gas molecules to go randomly into one of the rooms and most of the slower moving gas particles to go into the other, a very unlikely event). Isolated physical systems will thus tend to evolve from more highly ordered states to more disordered states. In physics, this is known as the "law" of entropy increase.

While some physical processes, such as the growth of a flower from a seed appear to involve the creation rather than the destruction of order, it should be remembered that terrestrial life forms are not isolated physical systems, but obtain their energy from external sources (e.g., the sun and decomposing organic matter) and thus the law of entropy increase does not apply to them.

Some philosophers, such as Adolf Grünbaum (1964) have argued that time is inherently anisotropic (behaves differently in the past and future directions) and that the future direction of time may be identified as the direction in which the entropy (disorder) of most "branch systems" (isolated physical systems) increases. Many other philosophers have been skeptical of this proposal, seeing entropy increase as an artifact of the highly improbable initial state of the universe.

Closely related to the entropy increase criterion for the direction of "time's arrow" is the observation that, in general, wavefronts diverge from their source rather than converge upon them. For instance, a sphere of light may expand from a point light source or a series of concentric ripples may spread out from the point of impact of our irreversible diver into the swimming pool. Although the differential equations governing the production of such wave allow solutions corresponding to waves converging to a point (i.e., a sink rather than a source), such contracting waves are never seen to occur, perhaps again because of their improbability. Later in this chapter, we shall see that several parapsychologists have postulated that such converging waves moving backward in time (usually referred to as "advanced waves") may provide a means of explaining such phenomena as precognition.

Another criterion to differentiate the future from the past is the quantum mechanical criterion proposed by Denbigh (1981). As discussed earlier, in the theory of quantum mechanics, microscopic events (and, through the amplification of their effects, macroscopic events) are not determined prior to an act of measurement or observation. Thus, the position of a photon is not defined until an attempt to measure it (such as capturing it on a piece of film).

Similarly, in a quantum mechanical random event generator of the type used in modern parapsychological experiments, the random number or other display feature to be generated (which is often based on the time of a radioactive decay) is not determined by the laws of physics and is free to take on any (permissible) value prior to the act of observation. Thus, the random number to be generated or the position at which the photon will impact the film are indeterminate prior to the act of measurement, and determined thereafter. The process by which these events are determined is often referred to as "the collapse of the state vector." Thus, quantum events, and by implication all events, might be partitioned into two categories—those that have been determined (the observed past) and those that have yet to be observed (which, depending on which interpretation of quantum mechanics one prefers, may include events in the yet-to-be-observed "past," the present and the future). This would allow specification of the future and the past relative to any point in time. However, it does not provide a noncircular definition of the (absolute) present, insofar as what is "now" and "what is yet to be determined" may depend on the observer's location along the time line. However, quantum mechanics may provide a physical basis for the sense of "time flow" and "becoming." Perhaps the process of becoming is inherently related to or perhaps identical with the collapse of the state vector. If so, conscious minds may a fundamental role in the generation of "time flow." The existence of conscious experience and the subjective experience of time flow, two fundamental mysteries that modern theories of physics have yet to explain, may be intimately related if not identical. (In this context, it should be noted that the experience of "time flow" and its incompatibility with the essentially deterministic Minkowski spacetime of Einstein's theory of relativity, may be related to physicists' current difficulties in relating quantum theory to Einstein's theory in general and constructing a quantum theory of gravity in particular.)

According to the "observational theories" in parapsychology, such as those proposed by Schmidt (1975a, 1975b, 1984) and Walker (1975, 1984), as well as some mainstream interpretations of quantum mechanics, quantum events are not determined prior to their observation by a conscious observer. Thus, a series of random numbers generated by a quantum process is in an indeterminate state prior to inspection. (This interpretation differs from that of many physicists, who would consider the numbers to be determined at the point where they are irreversibly registered on a macrophysical apparatus such as a punch tape or a computer memory store.) According to the observational theorists in parapsychology, a sequence of random numbers may be generated, stored in computer memory, and then later displayed to a subject, who may at this later time influence which numbers have been produced through retroactive psychokinesis. Thus, the generation of these numbers, which would have occurred in the past according to most orthodox accounts of time, would fall into the present (at the time of the PK experiment), if one uses the quantum collapse criterion to distinguish the past from the future.

Under the observational theories' interpretation, the quantum mechanical criterion for distinguishing the events that fall into the "future" from those that fall into the "past" might lead to a model of time similar to that implicit in some Native American languages (such as Wintu and Hopi) studied by Lee (1938) and Whorf (1956). These Indian languages assign tenses to verbs according to whether the events to be described are "manifested" (the outcome is known to the speaker) or "unmanifested" (the outcome is unknown or, in observational theory terms, the event is unobserved, at least from the speaker's standpoint), rather than according to whether the events are in the past, present or future in the Western (or from Wintu's and Hopi's point of view, Eastern) sense of those terms. Thus, the unmanifested tense might be used to describe the outcome of a battle fought three days ago, if the outcome is unknown because the raiding party has not yet returned to the village. The observational theory, in its Wintu and Hopi versions, might provide a somewhat solipsistic criterion for demarcating the future from the past, but this division in not likely to result in a clean "slice" of events, as the future would have to include many events that are regarded as belonging to the past based on other criteria. Nonetheless, the criterion does have the attractive feature of potentially uniting the subjective experience of time flow or "becoming" with the more "objective" (or should one say "subjective?") notion of the collapse of the quantum mechanical state vector through observation.

LeShan (1969, 1976) suggests that, in mystical states involving the experience of unity with all things, one may see the past, present and future as one ("all things are now"), much the same as in the Minkowski spacetime of special relativity. LeShan asserts that this perception of timelessness, in which all things are perceived as one, would be an especially psi-conducive state, and the self-other boundary as well as spacetime separations would no longer exist, at least psychologically.

Thus, the psychological experience of time may be one of the fundamental bedrocks of existence, yet is inexplicable on the basis of current theories of physics. Some writers have suggested that a profound alteration in the experience of time flow or of spacetime itself may temporarily allow such events as precognition and psychokinesis to occur. The subjective experiences of the "now" and of "time flow" may point to the mind as a fundamental component of the universe. The observational theories, with their suggestion that the mind governs the collapse of the quantum mechanical state vector, even hint that the mind may be a primary agent in causing the future (the indeterminate) to become the past (the determinate). Thus, implicit in the observational theories is the image of the mind as a cosmic "time tractor" plowing indeterminate probability waves into actualized events.

Signal Theories

Several attempts have been made to explain psi phenomena in terms of the exchange of some type of physical signal. Some theories assume that ordinary physical particles carry the psi message. Such particles are typically conceived of as "traveling forward in time." To explain cases of precognition, some theorists have resorted to more exotic particles that travel backward in time. We will consider each in turn.

THEORIES EMPLOYING SIGNALS "TRAVELING FORWARD IN TIME"

Particle theories. Several theorists have proposed that the transfer of information in cases of ESP is accomplished through the exchange of some signal already known to contemporary physicists, such as electromagnetic radiation and neutrinos.

Electromagnetic radiation. One of the earliest proponents of an "electromagnetic" theory of psi was Joseph Glanvill, a contemporary of Newton, who proposed that telepathic exchanges were caused by the vibrations of the "ether" (see Jaki, 1969). More modern proponents of electromagnetic theories of psi include Kazhinsky (1962), Becker (1990, 1992), MacLellan (1997), and Vasilescu and Vasilescu (1996, 2001). Taylor (1975) proposed an electromagnetic explanation of paranormal metal-bending, although he later retracted it (Taylor, 1980).

Severe difficulties confront any attempt to explain psi phenomena on the basis of electromagnetic waves. These difficulties include the apparent ability of psi signals to penetrate barriers normally impervious to electromagnetic radiation, the apparent failure of psi phenomena to obey the usual the usual inverse-square law governing the falloff in electromagnetic effects with distance, the feeble strength of the electromagnetic signals emanating from the brain compared to the power that would be required to send a telepathic signal or perform a psychokinetic feat over any reasonable distance, and the lack of any plausible neurological mechanism whereby such a signal could be encoded, generated, received, and decoded. Each of these difficulties will be discussed in turn.

Regarding barriers, successful telepathy experiments have been reported in which the subjects were electromagnetically shielded from one another by Faraday cages and other types of barriers, ruling out the exchange of most electromagnetic signals (e.g., Vasiliev, 1976; Targ & Puthoff, 1977; Ullman & Krippner, 1969). Some theorists, including Michael Persinger (1979) and I. M. Kogan (1968), have proposed that psi signals are carried by extremely low frequency electromagnetic radiation, also known as ELF waves. ELF waves would be able to penetrate some of the electromagnetic barriers used in these experiments. ELF wave theories are discussed in a separate section below.

Distance independence. If ESP and PK effects are due to electromagnetic waves transmitted between the subject and the target person or object, it would be expected that psi success would decrease with increasing distance between the subject and target (as the intensity of electromagnetic information emitted from a point source is inversely proportional to the square of the distance from the point). The small electrical power of the brain (discussed in the next section) combined with the inverse square law for electromagnetic radiation, would seem to imply that psi effects could not occur over large distances if they are due to electromagnetic radiation. However, successful remote viewing experiments have been conducted with the percipient (viewer) in Detroit and the agent (sender) in Italy (Schlitz and Gruber, 1980, 1981), and a successful dream telepathy experiment with the agent in Edinburgh and the percipient (dreamer) in London (Markwick & Beloff, 1983). A series of successful PK experiments, with distances ranging from 10 miles to 1,100 miles separating the PK agent from the target apparatus has been reported by Tedder and his associates (Tedder & Monty, 1981; Tedder & Braud, 1981; Tedder and Bloor, 1982). Nelson, Dunne, Dobyns and Jahn (1996) and Jahn And Dunne (2005) report that the size of the PK and remote viewing effects obtained by the Princeton Engineering Anomalies Research (PEAR) team were independent of the spacetime separations between the subjects and the target. Many more examples could be cited.

The apparent lack of dependence of psi effects on spatial and temporal separations is evidence not only against electromagnetic theories of psi, but against all theories of psi based on known or currently postulated physical signals. Indeed, the lack of dependence of psi on spacetime separation was one of the factors that led J. B. Rhine, the founder of experimental parapsychology, to proclaim that psi phenomena indicate that the mind has a nonphysical component. Thus, psi phenomena have long been regarded as evidence against physicalist theories of mind. As a physicalistic metaphysics underlies current "orthodox" scientific theories, this may explain why the debate over the existence of psi has been so heated and why the evidence for psi phenomena is so strongly rejected by the scientific establishment. In this regard, one might recall the comments of Anthony Freeman, the Editor of the *Journal of Consciousness Studies*, who recently noted that "orthodox science is orthodox religion's true heir" (Freeman, 2005, p. 6).

The existence of long-range psi effects and the failure of psi effects to obey an inverse-square law pose grave difficulties for any electromagnetic theory of psi (assuming all psi effects will be subsumed under one theory or mechanism). So too does the phenomenon of precognition. If the ultimate explanation of precognition involves signals traveling backward in time (as discussed below), then the normal forward-traveling ("retarded") electromagnetic waves will not suffice (although theories involving "advanced" electromagnetic waves, which travel backward in time, have been constructed).

The weakness of the brain's electromagnetic signals is another problem. The electromagnetic theory of psi was originally inspired by Hans Berger's detection of electrical currents emanating from the brain through the use of the electroencephalograph (which was invented by Berger), as well as by the invention of the radio. However, Berger (1940) thought that changes in the electrical potential of the brain were too small to account for telepathy over reasonable distances and so was led to postulate some sort of hitherto undetected "psychical energies" as the carrier of telepathic message.

In fact, several parapsychologists (e.g., Dobbs, 1967; Millar, 1975; Vasiliev, 1976: Bigu, 1979) have performed calculations of the power of the electromagnetic radiated by the human brain. These estimates have varied widely, from a millionth (Millar) to a quintillionth (Dobbs) of a watt. However, even electromagnetic radiation at the high end of this range would appear to be far too weak to account for reported ESP or PK effects.

Finally, proponents of electromagnetic theories of psi have proposed no plausible mechanisms whereby such signals could be encoded, generated, transmitted, received, and/or decoded. Large areas of physical musculature and cerebral cortex are devoted to the production of sound waves to carry messages in speech. So too, the detection of sound and light waves requires the existence of elaborate external receptors (the eyes and ears) and the involvement of large areas of the cerebral cortex. As Vasiliev (1976) points out, the fibers and fluids surrounding the brain possess greater electromagnetic conductivity than do the nerve tissues themselves. It is implausible that the brain would have evolved in such a manner if it is to serve as a direct and sensitive detector of electromagnetic radiation. In any event, the analysis of information and pattern detection that would be required in order to receive and decode an electromagnetically-encoded telepathic message would presumably require an organ at least approximating in complexity that of the human eye or ear. The generation of electromagnetic telepathic signals, besides surpassing the brain's electrical power capacity, as noted above, would also undoubtedly require the existence of a specialized organ (whose location inside the brain would be most unstrategic).

ELF wave theories. Thus, insurmountable difficulties seem to confront any attempt to explain psi phenomena on the basis of electromagnetic radiation at typical wavelengths. Some (but not all) or these objections can be overcome if it assumed that the radiation involved is of extremely long wavelength (or equivalently, extremely low frequency). Some theorists, most notably Kogan (1968) and Persinger (1979), have hypothesized that psi signals are carried by such extremely low frequency radiation (ELF waves). Such radiation has a frequency of less than 3 kHz (3000 cycles per second). Persinger notes that many periodic biological processes occur with frequencies in the ELF range, such as the heart rhythm (less than 4 Hz, or four cycles per second), brain waves (less than 30 Hz), and muscular rhythms (1 Hz to 1 kHz). He also observes that geological and meteorological processes produce standing waves in the earth-ionosphere cavity with a frequency of 7–8 Hz, which Persinger notes corresponds to the alpha rhythm of the brain, which has been found to be a psi-conducive state (see Honorton, 1977, for instance). Persinger proposes that "biogenic-environmental interactions" could occur through a "resonance-like" mechanism, in cases in which the frequencies of the geological/meteorological waves and biological cycles are similar.

Persinger essentially proposes two theories of telepathy. In the first, the agent (i.e., sender of the psi message) would impose an ELF wave on a geophysical system, which would carry the psi message to the recipient. In the second theory, the brains of the agent and percipient would resonate with an existing physical wave, producing a similar state in both (such as a depressed mood in the percipient and an act of suicide by the agent). Persinger's second theory is thus a theory to explain "pseudopsi" events rather than the "real" psi that might occur in an experiment with randomly determined targets. Stevens (2005) discusses evidence that geomagnetic fields may directly influence the REGs used in psi experiments, which may be responsible for observed correlations between psi success and geomagnetic activity.

Puthoff and Targ (1979) point out that the information channel capacity of ELF waves is very low (they estimate it to be between .005 and .1 bits per second). As a way out of this difficulty, Persinger (1979) suggests that a subject may be exposed to the signal for a long time before the total message is received, as which point it emerges into the percipient's consciousness fully formed. He also suggests that a percipient may learn subtle codings through experience, facilitating ESP communication between family members and friends. As he acknowledges, the amount of time required for an agent to encode a message (around 100 minutes for 60 bits of information) may be a telling blow against the ELF wave theory. Persinger concludes that the information transmission rate is too slow for the "real psi" version of the ELF wave theory to be viable (due to short-term memory demands on the percipient), although the "pseudopsi" version may still be tenable. (Interestingly enough, however, he notes that the ELF wave information rate compares favorably with the information transmission rate in many psi experiments.)

In addition to the above objections, the problems of accounting for the encoding and decoding of any intricate psi message and accounting for precognition confront the ELF wave theory as surely as they do the general electromagnetic theory.

Resonance theories. Some theorists have proposed that psi effects constitute some sort of "resonance" phenomena similar to that which occurs when one tuning fork is struck and transmits sound waves to a second tuning fork of similar construction, which then starts to vibrate also. (Note that the resonance in this case is mediated by a signal, in this case the sound wave. Many resonance theories can be construed simply as theories involve signals and/or interacting fields. What sets resonance theories apart as a special case of signal/field theories is that resonance theorists propose that the psi exchange is facilitated by similarities between the "sending" and "receiving" systems.) Some theorists have proposed that similar minds (i.e., minds containing shared experiences, thoughts, etc.) may resonate with one another, resulting in the transmission of thoughts, perceptions and emotions from one mind to the other.

As previously noted, Jon Taylor (1995, 1998, 2000) has also proposed a theory in which psi effects are caused by a resonance between two brains in similar states and denies the existence of pure clairvoyance, attributing the evidence for clairvoyance to trans-temporal telepathy.

The basic problem with these resonance theories is that they explain one mysterious similarity between two complex systems (psi) in terms of another (resonance). Unless the signal underlying the resonance (analogous to the sound wave in the case of the tuning fork) and/or the specific types of mental similarities that give rise to resonance can be given a sufficiently exact characterization to yield testable predictions about psi, these theories are unfalsifiable and merely substitute a prejudicial term ("resonance") for a more non-committal term ("psi"). At best, they yield the prediction that psi effects will occur more frequently if there is greater similarity between the minds of the percipient and the agent, a prediction that is yielded by several other theories (such as Whately Carington's association theory, which is discussed later in this chapter).

Theories Employing Signals "Traveling Backward in Time"

Retrocausal signals. Some theorists have proposed that phenomena such as precognition and retroactive psychokinesis, in which the future appears to influence events in the present (or, as in the case of retroactive PK, events in the present appear to influence events in the past), may be explained on the basis of physical signals that travel backward in time.

Helmut Schmidt, the designer of the quantum-mechanically based random event generators that are widely used in parapsychological work today, postulated that a psi source (typically a conscious observer) may influence the outcome of a quantum-mechanically based process (such as the output of a Schmidt-type REG) and that this influence is independent of the spatiotemporal separation between the subject and the target events (Schmidt 1975a, 1975b, 1984). Even if the target events are generated and recorded on a punch tape prior to the subject's attempt to influence them, the subject is postulated to be able to influence the earlier behavior of the REG at the time the target events are presented to the subject (e.g., as flashing lights on a Schmidt four-button machine

Statistically significant evidence for retroactive PK has been reported by many investigators, including Schmidt (1976, 1981), Terry and Schmidt (1978), Gruber (1980), and Schmidt, Morris and Rudolph (1986). However, most or all of the actual experimental evidence for retroactive PK can be explained away in terms of "forward causation." In this regard, retroactive PK may enjoy an even murkier status than precognition. For instance, an experimenter who wants to run a retroactive PK experiment, in which the subject will attempt to influence a previously recorded target sequence to obtain more "0s" than "1s" may simply exert a direct psychokinetic influence on the REG at the time the targets are generated. In some cases, as in precognition experiments, such counter-explanations in term of forward casual chains can become quite convoluted and thus implausible.

The Observational Theories

However, as discussed in Chapter 2, experiments in the quantum mechanical realm indicate that the universe does not consist exclusively of discrete, mutually isolated and localized particles and objects. In fact, the theory of quantum mechanics paints a picture of the universe that is not at all hostile to psi phenomena. Indeed the principle of nonlocality in quantum mechanics would almost lead one to anticipate the existence of psi. If not even two protons separated by light years can be conceptualized as separate objects, perhaps it is also incorrect to consider persons as encapsulated, spatially isolated entities. Seeming separate persons may in fact merely be different facets of a higher nonlocal entity. The mysterious connections between apparently isolated elementary particles in field of quantum mechanics make the prospect of psi interactions between people much more palatable.

As noted in Chapter 2, science has generally proceeded by the analysis and dissection of complex systems into their component parts, the ultimate parts being of course elementary particles such as electrons and quarks. In the orthodox scientific view, higher-order and holistic mental phenomena, such thoughts and beliefs, will ultimately be explained in terms of the activity of "lower order" entities such as neurons and synapses, whose activity is in turn explained by still lower entities such as molecules and quarks. At least this is the view according to the "orthodox," Newtonian view of the world that is still (consciously or unconsciously) clung to by most mainstream scientists, despite the fact that quantum mechanical evidence indicates that such a view is outmoded and incorrect in fundamental ways.

Several parapsychological theorists (e.g., Roll, 1982b; Villars, 1983; Nash 1983, 1984a; Giroldini, 1986; and Shan, 2002) have explicitly proposed that psi phenomena may due to nonlocal quantum connections between the elementary particles in someone's brain and particles in another person or object. Shan, for instance, hypothesizes that telepathy may be mediated by quantum entanglement between brains and suggest that psi might be facilitating by inputting entangled photons into the subjects' eyes.

This hypothesis that psi effects are due to quantum entanglement at the particle level runs into difficulties on several fronts. First, it is difficult to believe that pairs of particles could be maintained in a coherent quantum state while residing in separate physical objects, including brains, for any reasonable amount of time. Second, this hypothesis assumes an ability of a person or brain to track the past history of particles that is far more miraculous than the psi powers it is invoked to explain. Third, no psi message can be sent through such nonlocal connections under standard interpretations of quantum mechanics, as the behavior of both particles in a pair is apparently random at each site (although they are correlated with each other). The only way a psi message could be sent or a PK influence exerted would be for the mind to force the quantum process to occur in a preferred manner (such as by sending a message in Morse code by making protons spin up or down with respect to a selected spatial axis). This would implicitly equate the mind with the so-called "hidden variables" that determine the outcome of quantum processes. As these variables must necessarily be nonlocal, why not simply assume that the mind exerts its influence on the object directly rather than through particles in the brain that happen to be correlated with particles in the target? The latter view seems to be mired in a view of the mind as a localized entity, despite its explicit appeal to quantum nonlocality.

Several theorists, including Helmut Schmidt (1975a, 1975b, 1984), Harris Walker (1975, 1984, 2000, 2003) and Richard Mattuck (1977, 1982, 1984), have in fact taken the position that the mind should be equated with the hidden variables of quantum mechanics and that the mind should be seen as capable of directly influencing the outcome of quantum events. Their theories are collectively known as the "observational theories." This term derives from the fact that, as discussed in Chapter 2, attributes of quantum particles, such as the position of an electron, only take on definite values when an act of observation is made to determine what those values are.

If being observed by a conscious mind somehow causes the electron's position to assume a definite value, the observational theorists reason, perhaps the conscious mind can also somehow determine what particular position the electron will adopt. As discussed in the previous chapter, parapsychologists have amassed a large body of evidence suggesting that the mind may be able to influence the outcomes of quantum processes in the form of significant PK influences on quantum mechanically based random event generators. So the observational theories are not without experimental support.

The Collective Mind

If individual persons cannot be thought of as separate and autonomous from one another, perhaps it would make sense to abandon the assumption that their minds are entirely separate from one another and to raise the possibility that individual psyches may be aspects of a group mind or collective unconscious. In fact, several parapsychological thinkers have postulated the existence of a collective mind in order to explain telepathy and other forms of psi phenomena. Some of these theorists, such as G. N. M. Tyrrell (1953) and C. G. Jung (1973), have postulated that individual minds may share common regions at a deep level of the unconscious. Steinkamp (2002) has noted that the existence of psi phenomena imply that our "selves" are not entirely separate from one another and that precognition suggests that one's own present and future selves may not be separate. William Roll (1988, 1989) has suggested that the Iroquois' concept of the "long body" (a kind of collective mind encompassing one's family and other intimate acquaintances) might usefully be employed in attempting to understand psi phenomena. More recently, Maso (2006) has proposed that psi phenomena may be explained by a collective mind theory grounded in panpsychism (the doctrine that all matter is imbued with consciousness. We will consider several of these theories in turn, beginning with that of Jung.

JUNG'S THEORY OF SYNCHRONICITY
AND THE COLLECTIVE UNCONSCIOUS

Carl G. Jung was one of Freud's most prominent disciples in the early psychoanalytic movement; indeed, he was regarded as Freud's "crown prince" until he broke with Freud to found his own school of Analytical Psychology. To account for similarities in the hallucinations and delusions of his psychotic patients (as well as the presence of apparent references to classical mythology in the delusional productions of apparently uneducated schizophrenic patients), Jung was led to postulate the existence of a "collective unconscious." Jung proposed that this collective unconscious existed at a deeper level of the psyche than the "personal unconscious" discovered by Freud. He also invoked the collective unconscious to explain the many similarities among the mythological and religious traditions of apparently unrelated peoples.

Jung also proposed the existence of an "acausal connecting principle," which he called the principle of "synchronicity." This principle acts to produce "meaningful coincidences." An example of a synchronistic occurrence is provided by the case of one of my friends in graduate school, who, not being prepared for the preliminary examination for his doctoral degree, postponed the examination after much soul-searching. That night, he went to eat in a Chinese restaurant. When he opened his fortune cookie, it said, "It is best to put off until tomorrow that which you may botch today."

Jung viewed the collective unconscious as being capable of extending its influence to the external physical world. In fact, he regarded all reality as being "psychoid" in nature (meaning that even seemingly inanimate objects have a psychic component). For instance, in one oft-discussed incident, Jung was in the middle of having an argument with Freud when loud raps were heard, seemingly coming from a nearby bookshelf. Jung attributed this coincidence to the "exteriorization" of an archetype (a doctrine that he also invoked to explain sightings of ghosts).

Several parapsychologists have objected to Jung's use of the term "acausal" to describe synchronistic occurrences. First of all, many of Jung's examples of synchronistic effects could be explained on the basis of ESP or PK. For instance, Jung might have unconsciously used his own psychokinetic powers to produce the raps in the bookcase (he described feeling intense symptoms of anger in his abdomen just preceding the incident). Also, it seems that Jung implicitly assumed that synchronistic events are in some sense caused by factors in the collective unconscious. As Beloff (1978) has noted, Jung seems to confuse causation with mechanical causation. What Jung probably wanted to deny was the existence of ordinary physical causes for synchronistic effects. Beloff (1974) has also argued that it is difficult to explain the movement of large objects in poltergeist cases as being due to a "meaningful coincidence" as the events are virtually impossible in the first place. However, it should be noted that Jung himself and the German parapsychologist Hans Bender (1980) have invoked Jung's notion of reality as psychoid and his concept of the collective unconscious to account for certain types of poltergeist and other macroscopic PK effects.

It would, however, seem as though these explanations are causal rather than acasual in nature. Although no direct causal chain may link, say, the anger in a poltergeist agent and the inexplicable movement of a filing cabinet in Jung and Bender's interpretation, both events seem to be postulated to be caused by psychic events happening somewhere in the collective unconscious (hence the theory really is in fact a causal theory, despite Jung's protestations). Palmer (2004) notes that Jung's theory in fact is a causal theory, with the archetypes of the collective unconscious acting as causal agents. As both Beloff and Palmer point out, the confusion over the causation issue is linked to Jung's equation of causation with mechanical "billiard ball" causation. To the extent that Jung abandons causation altogether, he is throwing out the baby with the bathwater and rendering his theory unfalsifiable, as it may be difficult to derive empirical predictions unless it is assumed that one set of circumstances will give rise to (cause?) another set of circumstance.

It was, incidentally, Jung's abandonment of the principle of mechanical causation that made his theory so attractive to Arthur Koestler, who saw similarities between Jung's principle of synchronicity and the mysterious interconnections between apparently mutually isolated physical events involved in quantum nonlocality, as well as Mach's principle and the Pauli exclusion principle in physics (Koestler, 1978). As Palmer (2004) notes, in Koestler's view the principle of synchronicity encompassed "meaningful coincidences" between two physical events, whereas Palmer interprets Jung as restricting the principle to pairs of events in which at least one of the events is psychically "inner" or subjective.

TYRRELL'S THEORY OF SUBLIMINAL SELVES

The parapsychologist G. N. M. Tyrrell (1953) proposed a theory of the collective unconscious that bears a certain resemblance to Jung's theory.

According to Tyrrell, the human personality consists of a hierarchy of selves. Essentially, Tyrrell believed that people share regions of their minds at a deep unconscious level. He asserted that, at the unconscious level, the "midlevel centers [of the personality] possess in some degree *both* the qualities of selfhood *and* of otherness from self" (p. 119, italics in original). It is in these regions that our dreams and hallucinations are constructed, which is why witnesses are consistent in their descriptions of collectively perceived apparitions. Also, as this deep region of the unconscious has no organization in space or time according to Tyrrell, it enables telepathic exchanges to take place.

JAMES' "COSMIC CONSCIOUSNESS"

William James, one of the pioneers of both American psychology and American psychical research, postulated the existence of a "cosmic consciousness" into which individual minds merge during mystical experiences. James (1909/1960) saw the everyday, normal state of consciousness as being a circumscribed form of awareness designed for adaptation to the "external earthly environment." James' vision of a cosmic consciousness corresponds closely to Rao's depiction of an implicate order bearing a resemblance to the World Mind or Brahman of Hinduism.

MYERS' METETHERIAL WORLD

F. W. H. Myers (1903), one of the discoverers of the unconscious mind and a leader in the early psychical research movement, also postulated the existence of a deep region of the unconscious or "subliminal self" capable of accounting for paranormal events (although he was somewhat vague as to the mechanism underlying psi). He also proposed the existence of a "metetherial world," which he conceived to be a world of images lying beyond the normal world of ether (the substance once thought to be the medium in which light waves propagated, but which is now generally regarded as nonexistent by physicists). On the basis of the fact that apparitions are frequently seen by more than one observer, Myers was led to conjecture that apparitions are not mere hallucinations but have a real existence in the metetherial world. He called such apparitions "metetherial presences" and conjectured that they represented modifications in regions of physical space, thus implying some sort of coextension between normal physical space and the metetherial world. Myers compared the metetherial world to a dream world, noting that phantoms often appear to behave in a dreamlike manner. Thus, Myers' metetherial world might be considered to be a form of collective unconscious.

Myers' view that apparitions occupied regions of physical space and were external to the minds of the percipients of the apparition was opposed by his contemporary Edmund Gurney (e.g., Gurney, Myers & Podmore, 1886a, 1886b), who believed that collectively perceived apparitions could be accounted for on the basis of the telepathic spreading of a hallucination from one percipient to the others.

PRICE'S DREAM WORLD

The philosopher H. H. Price (1939, 1940, 1948, 1953, 1959, 1961) also argued for the existence of a collective unconscious, noting that the possible existence of continuous telepathic rapport between minds makes it foolish to argue for a total separation of minds. Like the philosopher Henri Bergson (1914), he assumed that a repressive mechanism acts to prevent biologically irrelevant telepathic information from entering consciousness while the person is awake. He suggested that this suppressive mechanism may be relaxed in the dream state and in the states of dissociation associated with mediumship, making these states particularly conducive to the occurrence of psi phenomena.

Price proposed that one survives death in a dreamlike afterlife, whose characteristics are determined in part by a person's wishes and beliefs (and in part by telepathic impulses from other minds). Price assumed, like Myers, that the images persisting in the psychic "ether" may acquire a life of their own and may be responsible for experiences of hauntings and apparitions. In particular, Price argued that cases in which persons undergoing out-of-body experiences have been perceived at the locations to which they have projected (that is, "reciprocal hallucinations") provide evidence that apparitions serve as "vehicles of consciousness." Noyes (1998) has also proposed that an afterlife realm such as Price's world of images could be in some sense coextensive with, and have effects in, the physical world, producing phenomena such as apparitions and materializations.

In an extension of Price's theory, Michael Grosso (1979) suggests that the ego may become fragmented in the afterlife and that, when one's wishes and desires are played out, one may eventually achieve the sort of transpersonal state experienced by mystics. Grosso attributes the repetitive, rudimentary forms of behavior frequently exhibited by ghostly apparitions to such fragmentation of the personality.

More recently, Patterson (1995) also proposed a form of afterlife equivalent to a collective dream. Patterson notes that such a world would be an intersubjective, but not purely objective, realm. Of course our current dreams depend on the activity of a neural substrate (our brains), and it is not clear that dreams of an discarnate soul lacking such a substrate could be qualitatively similar to the dreams of a human with an intact brain.

CARINGTON'S ASSOCIATION THEORY

The noted psychical researcher Whately Carington (1949) proposed a variety of "neutral monism" in which the universe is considered to consist exclusively of "cognita," atomistic mental events related by the laws of association. If an agent (i.e. sender in a telepathy experiment) happens to be thinking of cognitum A at the same time that he is exposed to cognitum B (the target), an associative link will be established between A and B. Thus, when a percipient thinks of A, this will tend to call up the association B, and he will become aware of the agent's experience. The more cognita or K-ideas (connecting ideas) that are shared between the agent and percipient, the higher the likelihood of the telepathic transfer of information between the two will be, which explains the frequency of telepathy between closely related persons (who presumably share many cognita and associations).

At least one attempt to test Carington's theory by providing the percipient with a detailed picture of the agent and the agent's room (in an attempt to increase the number of K-ideas linking the two) failed to produce any evidence of psi (Soal & Bateman, 1954). However, the notion of using K-ideas to bolster psi is not dead by any means. Although they do not mention K-ideas or Carington by name, Murray, Simmonds and Fox (2005) have presented a new research design in which both sender and receiver will be immersed in similar virtual realities in an attempt to facilitate telepathy.

Carington's theory has the distinctively negative feature of abandoning the assumption of the existence of the physical world without replacing the powerful predictive value of physical theories with any comparable predictive value of its own. A further difficulty with Carington's theory is its assumption of a single value for the associative strength between two cognita A and B. Surely, the strength of the association between A and B will vary from mind to mind, as a large amount of empirical evidence will attest.

Murphy's Theory of the Interpersonal Field

The well-known American psychologist (and parapsychologist) Gardner Murphy proposed a theory of the collective mind type, in which every psychological event is hypothesized to leave a trace in the "interpersonal field" or "paranormal matrix" (Murphy, 1945). Murphy further contended that the normal concepts of space and time do not apply to the paranormal matrix, thus allowing psi.

Rao (1966) has challenged Murphy's explanation of psi phenomena in terms of the paranormal matrix, observing that the evidence for pure clairvoyance is difficult to account for on the basis of this theory, unless one postulates the existence of a psychic aspect to all objects. Rao also asks if the interpersonal field contains traces of all psychological events, past, present and future. If not, the paranormal matrix theory may be unable to account for precognition. If so, Rao asks, is it not a contradiction to talk about events "leaving a trace?"

Murphy (1973) proposed that the mind might survive death in a fragmentary state in a type of collective consciousness. However, Murphy noted that the idea that the individual mind will survive death in an intact condition presupposes that the individual mind is a rigid, encapsulated entity. Instead, Murphy argued, the individual mind, being merely an aspect of a larger field of consciousness, may take on new qualities and form new structural relationships, no longer clinging to its narrow, biologically-oriented form of organization. He quotes Nietzsche's remark that the ego is a "grammatical illusion," and notes that the Buddhists deny the existence of a personal soul. William Roll (1982a, 1984) has cited instances involving the apparent fusion of memories from different people in mediumistic communications and in past-life memories reported by children as giving further support to Murphy's contention that personalities may undergo fragmentation, fusion and reorganization after death.

Murphy's views of the collective mind and possible afterlives are similar to those proposed by Price, Grosso and Carington. To further wed his theory to Carington's theory, Murphy suggests that the localization of apparitions in haunting cases may be due to K-ideas provided by the physical location.

Hardy's "SeCo Theory"

Hardy (1998) proposed a theory that is similar to that of Carrington and Murphy, in which the mind is seen as composed of interacting and somewhat autonomous "semantic constellations" (or "SeCos" in her terminology).

Palmer's "Psiad" Theory

Palmer (1995) proposed that patterns of brain activity can give rise to integrate packet of psychic content called "psiads." Once formed, the psiads can exert psychokinetic effects on the brains that gave birth to them. The psiads may drift free of the "mother brain" and exert psychokinetic effects on other host brains with activity or mental content similar to that occurring in the "mother brain" at the time of the psiad's development. Meanwhile, the original mother brain is giving birth to new psiads. This provides a mechanism to explain telepathy. Palmer asserts that telepathy should be most common between individuals who are genetically related. However, a great many spontaneous cases on record involve telepathy between spouses. Perhaps, a lifetime of common experiences provide an additional basis for psiads to "glom onto" a new host brain. Palmer attributes collectively perceived apparitions and similar experience to psiads simultaneously interacting with multiple percipients' brains. He also explains mediumship and cases in which children report memories related to previous lives (as discussed more fully in Chapter 6) to interactions with psiads. Gauld (1996) has noted that psiads would not provide a mechanism for personal survival, but only for the survival of a fragment of one's experiences that would bear a tenuous relationship with the original self or person. Gauld further notes that it is different to see how an experimental test could distinguish between Palmer's theory and, say, the association theories proposed by Carington and Murphy.

ROLL'S THEORY OF "PSI FIELDS" AND THE "LONG BODY"

Another version of the collective mind theory has been proposed by William Roll (1961, 1964, 1966, 1979, 1981, 1982a, 1982b, 1983). Roll contends that physical objects contain "psi fields," or localized memory traces of events happening in their vicinity. This quasi-physical memory trace may then interact with the memory system or psi field of an observer, such as in the form of ESP known as psychometry or object reading, in which a psychic uses physical contact with an object to facilitate extrasensory contact with a person or place associated with the object.

Roll has suggested that normal memory may consist of nothing more than psychometry of the brain. He further postulates that the system of psi fields constitutes a type of collective mind he calls a "psi structure." He suggests that individual minds are not entirely separate entities but a merely parts of this psi structure. Even mind and matter may not constitute separate domains in Roll's theory. He asserts that people remain psi-contiguous with people and places with whom they have interacted in the past, and he compares such "psi-contiguity to quantum entanglement. He predicts little or no success in an ESP task unless the subject has been in close physical proximity to the target, due to a lack of psi contiguity in such a case. Roll asserts that a person may "survive" in the form of the traces he or she leaves in the psi fields of objects.

He explains place-related effects, such as hauntings in which a ghost is seen performing some repetitive act in a particular location in a house, as being due to the activation of the psi fields associated with a particular location or object. He notes that apparitions, like memory traces, dissipate over time, thus the form of survival of death Roll is postulating is a time-limited one.

Roll incidentally, denies the existence of backward causation. In the case of an ostensibly precognitive dream, Roll suggests that either an event in the "psi structure" is responsible for causing both the dream and the confirming event or that the dreamer leaves a "charge" in the psi structure, which later causes the confirming event. Thus, under Roll's theory, psi fields are capable of influencing or causing physical events and thus may account for PK as well as ESP.

In recent years, Roll (1988, 1989, 2005) has reformulated his theory in terms of the Iroquois' concept of the "long body." The long body encompasses one's tribe, its physical environment and other material objects associated with the self or tribe. As Williams (2005) points out, the idea of the long body bears a similarity to the beliefs of many the southwestern United States tribes as well, including the Hopi, Navajo, Laguna and Zuni. Williams also notes that the concept of the long body was first introduced to parapsychology by Aanstoos (1986) before it was adopted and extended by Roll. Under the concept of the long body, close friends and relatives as well as tribal objects and lands are considered part of the self. Thus, the concept of the long body supports the existence of psi phenomena.

"ORTHODOX" COLLECTIVE MIND THEORIES

It should be noted that several more "orthodox" theories of a collective have been proposed. For instance, Midgley (2006) has asserted that some mental states may be shared between two persons (as in experiences of religious communion or falling in love). He also proposes that, just like the collection of neurons in a human brain, insect colonies might be said to possess a collective consciousness despite the fact that its members may be spatially discrete from one another. He further proposes that the entire human species might be said to share a collective consciousness, with its members perhaps playing a role akin to that neurons in a human brain. This conscious entity would, he asserts, "far exceed in complexity and subtlety the capacity of an individual human being" (p. 108). He even suggests that all life on the planet might be said to share a collective consciousness in view of their intimate dependencies and interactions.

SUMMARY OF COLLECTIVE MIND THEORIES

Obviously, if telepathy exists, human minds can no longer be thought of as entirely separate objects and one person's mind may be thought of as part of the unconscious mind of another person. Thus, the existence of some sort of collective mind is trivially true if psi exists. The similarities among the various versions of the collective mind theory are obvious, and it would be difficult in most instances to find ways of testing between them. The extent to which psi is to be attributed to a collective unconscious or to interactions between separate minds may to a large extent be a matter of emphasis, although some empirical evidence, such as collectively perceived apparitions, would seem to favor the collective mind theory over the separate minds theory. As argued both at the outset of this book and in later chapters, it is doubtful that the self, conceived as a center of pure consciousness could be identified with the memory systems, associational links and Jungian archetypes postulated to inhabit the collective mind.

The "Shin" Theory

The parapsychologists Robert Thouless and B. P. Wiesner proposed an "internal psi" model of mind-brain interaction (Thouless & Wiesner, 1948). In referring to the mind, they use the Hebrew letter "Shin" (ש) in order to avoid the metaphysical baggage involved in the use of the word "soul." They propose that the mind becomes aware of brain states by "clairvoyantly" monitoring neural activity. They propose that volitional activity is accomplished through the "psychokinetic" influence of neural events. They see psi phenomena such as ESP and PK as rare, externalized forms of the mind's normal interactions with the brain. In fact, they hypothesize two types of telepathy: γ-telepathy, in which a Shin clairvoyantly monitors the activity of a brain other than its own (which might correspond to the Rhines' theory that percipients use their psi powers in an active manner to monitor the external situation for relevant information), and κ-telepathy, in which a Shin psychokinetically influences a brain other than its own.

Obviously, in Thouless and Wiesner's theory, there must be some force restricting the vast majority of the Shin's interactions to the brain, corresponding in some sense to the philosopher Henri Bergson's (1914) suggestion that the brain acts as a filter, admitting primarily need-relevant information to the mind. After all, it would not be evolutionarily advantageous to be a clairvoyant spectator of a basketball game in progress as one drives one's car at 80 miles an hour on the freeway past the stadium. Such considerations led the psychoanalyst Jan Ehrenwald (1977, 1978) to suggest that the reason for the weakness of most psi effects in the laboratory is that they must make use of "flaws" in the Bergsonian filter, whereas psi phenomena in real life tend to be need-relevant and adaptive.

Ehrenwald hypothesized that the psi-filter resides in the reticular activating system (RAS) of the brain stem, presumably because this area acts as a filter for many sensory processes, although he conceded that areas of the midbrain, limbic system, and the frontal and temporal lobes may be involved in the filtering process. Of course, much filtering of normal afferent sensory impulses occurs before these impulses even reach the central portion of the brain, suggesting that filtering may occur on whatever afferent pathway underlies ESP (which may not even be a physical pathway based on our current understanding of what is "physical"). Ehrenwald provided little in the way of hard evidence that the psi-filter is located in the RAS, so this hypothesis is really a conjecture on his part.

Ehrenwald compared percipients' sketches in successful telepathy experiments involving the attempted transmission of line drawings to the drawings of brain-damaged patients, and he suggested that like brain-damaged patients (as least those with primarily left hemisphere involvement), the telepathic subject may be relying on the right hemisphere of the brain. However, this hypothesis would seem to be contradicted by the often-reported phenomenon of dissociation (the breaking up of the target picture into its components) in the early telepathic drawing experiments, such as those reported by Warcollier (1948/1963). Such dissociation would seem to more akin to that produced by damage to the spatially- and holistically-oriented right hemisphere than by damage to the more verbally-oriented and "linear" left hemisphere.

Ehrenwald suggested that one should expect higher psi scoring among brain-damaged patients (due to disruption of the psi filter) than among normal subjects. In support of this contention, he cites successful psi experiments with retarded patients and patients suffering from concussions. He also hypothesized that some schizophrenic patients may be suffering from "psi pollution" due to damage to the filter. However, Rogo (1975) reported finding no higher psi-scoring among psychotics than among normal subjects in a review of the experimental literature.

There is a smattering of parapsychological evidence that has some relevance to Thouless and Wiesner's theory. Honorton and Tremmel (1979), for instance, conducted a study in which they found that success in a PK task was positively correlated with the subject's ability to control his own brain waves. They interpret their finding as providing support for Thouless and Wiesner's internal psi model of mind-brain interaction. On the other hand, if it is assumed that the Shin has a limited attentional capacity, one might anticipate that subjects would be successful in a PK task precisely when their attention was not devoted to controlling their brain waves, and that therefore a negative correlation would be expected. Just such a prediction was in fact made by Rogo (1980), citing Roll's finding of a high incidence of epilepsy among presumed poltergeist agents (Roll, 1978) in support of the view that successful PK is accompanied by the disruption of normal brain processes. It should also be noted that a study by Varvoglis and McCarthy (1982) failed to replicate Honorton and Tremmel's results. Indeed, Varvoglis and McCarthy found that significant PK effects occurred only during trials in which the subjects performed poorly on the brain-wave control task.

Other evidence that the mind might be capable of influencing brain activity is provided by Baumann, Stewart and Roll's (1986) finding that humans could psychokinetically influence the firing rate of the pacemaker neuron of the marine snail *Aplysia* and Rein's (1986) finding that activity of monoamine oxidase, an enzyme regulating neurotransmitter concentrations, could be influenced through psychokinesis. Neither of these studies was methodologically perfect, however.

Evidence from telepathy experiments that percipients perceive specific neurological events in the brains of the senders would give support to Thouless and Wiesner's theory of telepathy. As discussed briefly above, Rene Warcollier (1948/1963) reported evidence of what he called "dissociation" in his experiments on the telepathic reception of drawings. This dissociation consisted of the percipient's drawing fragments of the target (such as isolated corners of a line drawing), suggesting that the percipient may have been responding to individual eye fixations on the part of the sender or even to "feature analyzers" in the sender's brain.

John Beloff (1980) has expressed doubt that someone could read the idiosyncratic "neurological code" employed by someone else's brain. Beloff's objection would suggest that telepathic interaction must take place at a higher, mental level, rather than involving the direct reading of another person's brain state. Incidentally, Beloff himself has proposed a model of mind-brain interaction very similar to that of Thouless and Wiesner, except that Beloff further conjectures that the mind or Shin might survive the death of the brain with some of its memories intact (Beloff, 1990).

Some further support for Thouless and Wiesner's theory, in particular for the concept of kappa-telepathy, is provided by the rather voluminous literature reporting successful attempts to influence the behavior of living organisms using psi (which is sometimes interpreted as evidence of psychokinesis and sometimes as evidence of telepathy).

IMPLICATIONS OF SPLIT-BRAIN RESEARCH

The results of research with split-brain patients pose severe difficulties for a naïve interpretation of any theory in which a single immaterial mind is assumed to interact in a global manner with large areas of the brain, as in Thouless and Wiesner's Shin theory. As discussed in Chapter 1, in some cases of intractable epilepsy, a drastic surgical procedure involving the severing of the neural connections between the two cerebral hemispheres may be performed in order to stop electrical seizures of the brain from spreading from one hemisphere to the other. This procedure involves cutting the fibers of the corpus callosum, a bundle of nerves directly connecting the two hemispheres of the brain. This operation is called a commisurotomy or callosectomy. The act of severing the corpus callosum seems to result in a person with two separate spheres of consciousness, one residing in the right hemisphere and one residing in the left hemisphere. If one were to have such a patient visually fixate a point on a movie screen and then flash a picture of a hammer in his left visual field and a picture of a pencil in his right visual field, the two hemispheres would have different ideas about what was shown on the screen. If you asked the patient what he saw, he would usually say "a pencil," because the brain structures involved in the production of language generally reside in the left cerebral hemisphere and information from the right visual field is funneled into the left hemisphere. On the other hand, if you asked the patient to pick up the object that he saw on the screen with his left hand (which strangely enough is controlled by his right hemisphere), he would pick up the hammer. (His right hand may very well be reaching out and trying to guide the left hand to the pencil, however.) Similarly, if you blindfolded him and gave him a chess piece to hold in his left hand, he would not be able to describe verbally what object he had been holding (as the sensory information from the left hand is fed to the right hemisphere and linguistic ability is located in the left). He would, however, be able to identify the chess piece by using his left hand to pick it out from an array of objects on a table.

These findings pose grave difficulties for a naïve theory of mind-brain interaction of the Thouless and Wiesner type. Under Thouless and Wiesner's theory, the patient's Shin should be able to overcome the above communication gap. Through clairvoyant perception of the sensory information in the right hemisphere and psychokinetic influence of the language centers in the left hemisphere, a split-brain patient should be able to give a verbal description of an object held in the left hand. That such an effect is not observed would seem to constitute devastating evidence against Thouless and Wiesner's theory. Two means of saving the theory are apparent, however. First, it could be assumed that the mind's influence on the brain is restricted to the facilitation and inhibition of the transmission of information across synapses. (Synapses are microscopic gaps between neurons. When a neuron fires, it releases chemicals called neurotransmitters that travel across the synapse. When the neurotransmitters reach the postsynaptic neuron, they may bind to receptors on its surface. These neurotransmitters may either increase or decrease the probability that the postsynaptic neuron will fire.) Under this version of Thouless and Wiesner's theory, the mind would be unable to integrate the activity of the brain in the absence of the corpus callosum and might be assumed to experience two alternating or parallel, but independent, streams of consciousness.

Further discussion of the notion of multiple selves in split-brain patients will be postponed until Chapter 7, in which we consider the notion of the "self" and its relation to brain activity.

Psi and Evolution

In recent years, an increasing amount of attention has been paid to the possible role of psi in the evolution of biological organisms. Levin (1996, 2000) notes that one argument against the reality of psi is that such abilities would have been vastly improved over the course of evolution and should by now be stronger than they appear to be. They should also be in widespread use among organisms. Levin, however, observes that psi is likely a feature of the mind rather than the brain. Thus, it is only indirectly affected by the genes and therefore may be uncoupled from improvement via biophysical evolution. He suggests that the lack of improvement of psi abilities over the course of biological evolution speaks against mechanistic explanations of psi phenomena.

Taylor (2003) responds to Levin's assertion that because psi abilities are weak, they may not be subject to normal evolutionary processes. He notes that the following assumptions must be met in order for there to be an evolutionary explanation of psi:

- Psi has a genetic basis.
- Psi ability is variable among the population.
- Possession of a certain amount of psychic ability confers biological fitness on an individual.

Taylor notes that the evolution of well-controlled psi may involve huge changes in the makeup of an organism rather than a gradual change as one might expect on the basis of evolution, and he compares the evolution of psi abilities to the evolution of a wheeled organism. He suggests that psi abilities may operate unconsciously due to the competing information-processing demands of monitoring one's physical environment and that psi-scanning may be intermittent because of such demands. He proposes that psi abilities may provide warnings of impending disasters as well as providing a means of monitoring the behavior and welfare of close biological relatives. He notes that psi ability in laboratory situations is correlated with the psychological trait of vigilance (ability to see a threat in a degraded sensory image), citing the work of Watt and her co-workers in this regard (Watt & Gissurarson, 1995; Watt & Morris, 1995). He also cites Radin's research on pre-cognitive "presentiment" responses to emotional targets (e.g., Radin 1997b, 2003). As to the question of why people do not use psi more often to avoid disasters, Taylor replies that people often do not avoid disasters even when provided with compelling sensory information.

Beloff (2002) notes that if researchers can detect psi abilities in "lower" species, this may offer clues as to when, in the course of evolution, consciousness first appeared. This of course implicitly links psi abilities to consciousness. The evolution of consciousness in supposedly insensate matter is of course one of the deepest (and as yet unanswered) questions facing not only neuroscience, but perhaps physics itself.

Finally, McClenon (2004) hypothesizes that the ability to enter dissociative states on the part of some members of tribal organizations may have been passed on due to the psi-mediated success of such persons when acting as shamans. McClenon notes that shamanism, in which the practitioner enters into a trance-like state to contact spirit helpers, is universal among hunter-gatherer societies. He notes that cave art suggests that shamanism has been practiced for over 30,000 years and has provided the basis for all later religions. He hypothesizes that the capacity to enter dissociative/hypnotic states could not increase indefinitely because such traits have negative consequences (for instance, fantasy-prone individuals often suffer from psychosomatic illness as well as other forms of dissociative disorder). To some extent, McClenon's remarks echo Henri Bergson's observation about the need for a psychic filter to screen out competing psi information and keep the organism's focus on stimuli that are directly pertinent to the organism's biological survival.

Conclusions

One of the major developments in the past half-century has been the growing realization that psi phenomena need not be in conflict with established laws of science. The past two decades have seen the experimental confirmation of the principle of nonlocality in quantum mechanics and the growing realization of the importance of that principle for a theory of psi phenomena. At present, theorizing in parapsychology is held back by the lack of a reliable database and repeatable psi effects upon which a powerful theory of psi might be constructed and refined. Thus, many of the theories in this chapter represent mere presentations of "theoretical environments," within which more specific theories yielding more powerful experimental predictions might be constructed.

This chapter has been concerned primarily with theories aimed at explaining how psi information might be transmitted and with the implications of psi phenomena for our understanding of the nature of mind, matter, space and time.

Now we turn inwards to the examination of the nature of the conscious self and its possible survival of the death of the physical body. Chapter 6 concludes our study of parapsychology by examining the evidence that the personality or a portion thereof may survive death. The evidence for such survival will include ghosts and apparitions, dreams, out-of-body and near-death experience, the evidence from mediumship and the evidence for reincarnation. As noted in the Introduction, survival of the mind with major portions of the human personality intact is improbable in view of the fact that human emotions, memories and beliefs appear to be intimately dependent on brain processes in light of modern neuropsychological research. In Chapter 7, we will revisit the nature of the self and examine the possibility that the true self, in the form of a center of pure consciousness, may survive death and may in fact be only temporarily associated with any given physical body.

6

Death and the Mind

Who are we? What are we? We emerge, seemingly from nothingness, into the physical world. Is it to nothingness that we return? Are we our physical bodies? Our personalities? Or is each of us a field of pure consciousness through which thoughts, sensations and emotions flutter like so many butterflies?

Much of the parapsychological evidence for the survival of death, including that from mediumship and reincarnation cases, suggests that the mind is able to survive death with large portions of its memories, skills and personality intact. There is, however, an overwhelming amount of evidence that one's emotions, patterns of behavior and cognitive skills are intimately tied to the state of one's brain. For instance, damage to the right hemisphere of the brain can turn a depressed musician into a happy-go-lucky, tone-deaf individual. Damage to the frontal lobes of the brain can turn a law-abiding citizen into a raincoat-opening exhibitionist. Surely the removal of one's entire brain at death would change one's state of consciousness profoundly!

Memory also appears to be intimately dependent on brain structures. There is an abundance of evidence that damage to the hippocampal and thalamic areas of the brain can destroy one's ability to store new long-term memories. People with such a condition live in a kind of dream state. They will not recognize the nurse who has been taking care of them daily for years, but will greet him each time as if meeting someone new. There is also an increasing amount of evidence that some memories may be stored in localized regions of the brain and may be erased when these areas are damaged. For instance, in a bilingual patient who speaks, say, English and Greek, it is possible to interfere with his inability to speak Greek by electrically disrupting one area of his brain and to interfere with his ability to speak English by disrupting another area. (Ojemann, 1983).

Michael Gazzaniga (1989) describes a case in which a localized brain lesion rendered a woman incapable of naming the color of red fruits, although she could name the color of non-red fruits such as bananas as well as of red objects such as fire engines. Kinsbourne & Warrington (1964) report a case in which a very circumscribed brain lesion rendered a patient unable to name colors altogether. Localized memory traces have also been demonstrated in nonhuman subjects. Memory for a conditioned eyeblink response has, for instance, been shown to reside in the cerebellum of the rabbit (see Squire, 1987; and Krupa, Thompson & Thompson, 1993). There is also a considerable body of evidence that the storage of memories is dependent on changes in the synaptic connections among the neurons of the brain (see Squire, 1987; Baringa, 1990; Zhong & Wu, 1991; Rose, 1992; and Fanselow, 1993).

Even the avowed dualist Sir John Eccles believed that long-term memories are stored as changes in synaptic connections between neurons. Eccles did, however, feel compelled to postulate the existence of a second, nonphysical memory system in which "recognition memory" (which monitors the correctness of recalled information) resides, even though he maintained that memories of the details of the events in one's life are physically stored in the brain and hence lost at death (Eccles, 1979; Eccles & Robinson, 1984). The prominent reincarnation researcher Ian Stevenson (1981) likewise proposes that there are two memory stores, one physical and one nonphysical. He suggests that, although brain mechanisms may control access to all memories before death, this does not prove that the memory traces themselves are physical.

The parapsychologist Alan Gauld (1982) has also questioned whether memories are stored as physical traces in the brain, noting that memories are sometimes gradually recovered after brain damage. David Lund (1985) makes the argument that the brain may be the transmitter rather than the generator of consciousness, a view that goes back to William James (1898/1992). Under this analogy, a damaged brain may simply be unable to receive the signal from an intact consciousness. On the other hand, Barry Beyerstein (1987) has argued that a nonphysical mind should be able to compensate for the effects of brain damage. Why, he asks, can the mind allegedly separate from the body in an out-of-body experience and perceive the environment if it cannot overcome perceptual deficits caused by brain damage (such as blindness arising from damage to the visual cortex)?

What Could Survive?

Obviously, the physical body does not survive the death of the physical body. As we have just seen, it appears unlikely that our memories and personalities could survive the dissolution of our physical brains. What, however, constitutes our essential selves? Are we our bodies? Our personalities and memories? Or are we in fact pure centers of consciousness with the remaining aspects of our personalities just so much baggage to be checked (and inevitably lost) as we board the celestial starship for yet another ride?

Many philosophers see the physical body as an essential part of one's self. In Terence Penelhum's view, for instance, it makes no sense to talk about people surviving their deaths in some sort of disembodied state. If such a disembodied ghost were to communicate through a medium and relate memories of the person's life, this would prove nothing according to Penelhum, as memories might be illusory. He thinks that people can only be identified on the basis of their physical bodies and that therefore it makes no sense to talk about people surviving the deaths of those bodies (Penelhum, 1987). Of course, physical appearances can also be deceptive. Persons can disguise themselves as someone else, for instance. Thus, it is not clear that physical appearance is a foolproof means of identifying a person either.

Peter Geach (1987) is another philosopher who maintains that personality traits and memories are not a sufficient basis to identify a person. He compares the transfer of personality traits and memories from one body to another, such as might occur in one of Stevenson's reincarnation cases, to the spreading of a disease.

The noted philosopher Antony Flew (1987, 1991) also contends that immaterial souls would not be identifiable. In Flew's opinion, the idea that a person survives death can only be made intelligible if you assume that people possess some sort of quasi-physical astral body, on the basis of which they could be identified. Flew views the ideas of disembodied survival and incorporeal souls as incoherent notions. He maintains that the word "person" refers to a flesh and blood creature and that it therefore makes no sense to talk of a person surviving the death of his physical body.

All of these writers contend that some sort of physical body is necessary in order to establish the continuity of personal identity. It is not clear why we should put so much more stock in physical appearance than in mental appearance. If we are in fact our physical bodies, then what survives in the long run is a fossilized skeleton, seemingly devoid of consciousness (although the panpsychists may give us an argument on this point) and a dispersed collection of elementary particles, some of them "reincarnated" in animals, plants and other living things and some of them finding lodging in inanimate objects, also seemingly devoid of consciousness (but again, as the panpsychists may argue, perhaps associated with a rudimentary form of "protoconsciousness").

We now turn to an examination of the evidence amassed by psychical researchers that the human personality or some portion thereof survives the death of the physical body. Such survival is a central tenet of many major religions such as Islam and Christianity as well as the mythological and shamanistic traditions. As already noted, the findings of neuroscientific research in the past half-century have established an intimate dependence of the personality, including one's memories, thoughts and emotions, on the physical state of the brain. This body of research makes the survival of the personality of the death and dissolution of the brain a much more improbable prospect that it was in the days of the early physical researchers such as Frederic W. H. Myers and William James. Nevertheless these researchers and their "descendants," including a significant minority of the parapsychological community today, have amassed a considerable body of evidence that the human personality, or some portion thereof, may survive the death of the physical body. This evidence includes: out-of-body and near-death experiences; hauntings; apparitions; dreams; some poltergeist cases; evidence provided by mediums and "psychics;" cases suggestive of "obsession" and reincarnation, in which people report memories of past lives or are seemingly influenced by discarnate spirits; and miscellaneous attempts to photograph, weigh, record or otherwise physically measure and detect souls or spirits.

In Chapter 7, we will turn to an examination of the nature of the self and explore the possibility that the self, construed as a center of pure consciousness, could survive the death of the physical body.

Out-of-Body Experiences

We begin our study with possible glimpses of the afterlife that occur prior to the actual death of the physical body, that is with out-of-body experiences (OBEs) and near-death experiences (NDEs). NDEs often incorporate OBEs as well as apparent visions of another realm and its inhabitants.

In OBEs, people are apparently able to separate from their physical bodies and travel to near and distant locations. OBErs often report that they experience themselves encased in some sort of "astral body," usually resembling the physical one (often even wearing "astral clothes") during these wanderings.

Some people experience but one OBE in their lifetimes, whereas others experience OBEs repeatedly. In some cases, the OBE occurs without any conscious effort to induce it; in others, the OBE occurs as a result of a deliberate induction or incubation process. The following is an example of the former type of OBE and is taken from the collection of Susan Blackmore, an unusual researcher who is at once one of parapsychology's harshest critics and at the same time a prominent investigator of OBEs:

> I crossed the road and went into a well-lit wood. My distant vision began to blur and within five or ten seconds I could only see a distance of a few feet, the rest was "fog."
>
> Suddenly my sight cleared and I was looking at the back of myself and the dogs from a position eight or ten feet behind myself and about a foot higher than my height. My physical self had no sight or other senses and it was exactly as if I was simply walking along behind some-one, except that some-one was me ... [Blackmore, 1982a, p. 9].

The following case is provided by Hornell Hart:

> Sometime before 1907, a well-known physician in New York City ... was on a river steamer.... He had been having some curious sensations of numbness and of psychological detachment for some days. During the night on the steamer he found that his feet and legs were becoming cold and sensationless. He then 'seemed to be walking in air'.... In this state he thought of a friend who was more than 1000 miles distant. Within a minute he was conscious of standing in a room ... and his friend was standing with his back to him. The friend turned, saw him and said: 'what in the world are you doing here? I thought you were in Florida,' and he started to come toward the appearer. The appearer heard the words distinctly but was unable to answer.
>
> Then he re-entered his physical body.
>
> On the next day he wrote a letter to the distant friend whom he had perceived in this excursion. A letter from the friend crossed his in the mail, stating that he had been distinctly conscious of the appearer's presence, and had made the exclamation which the appearer heard [Hart, 1954, p. 133; as cited by Steinkamp, 2002, p.72].

Such cases, in which the OBEr's presence is felt or seen by witnesses at the remote location are sometimes called "reciprocal hallucinations" (a term that is perhaps somewhat prejudicial as to the explanation of the phenomenon).

Involuntarily experienced OBEs can occur for no apparent reason, as in the first case above, or they can be the result of fatigue, drug intoxication, sensory deprivation, and psychological or physical stress, as in the second case. A most dramatic form of out-of-body experience occurs when a person is rendered nearly unconscious and near death but is able to witness attempts to revive or resuscitate her physical body from a perspective well above the body. Often such a person feels herself being pulled back into the body at the moment of successful resuscitation. Such cases may be regarded as one form of the near-death experience. Near-death experiences will be discussed in greater detail in the next section.

Obviously, there may be nothing paranormal about OBEs in and of themselves. They may simply be a kind of delusion, hallucination or dream in which one experiences oneself outside of one's body. OBEs have been of interest to parapsychologists for at least two reasons. First, they suggest the existence of a mind or soul that is capable of traveling beyond the confines of the physical body in ways that are not explainable by current theories of physical science. Also, many people experience themselves as being encased in a secondary body while in the OBE state. Often this secondary body takes the form of a duplicate of the person's ordinary physical body. This has suggested to some researchers that there may exist a nonphysical or quasi-physical "astral body" in which the soul or mind may be housed during its extrasomatic sojourns. If so, this body would be of a type unknown to current theories of science. Of course, the fact that people experience themselves as possessing astral bodies could be explained in terms of hallucination and fantasy, unless some means of detecting such astral bodies with physical instruments could be devised.

Several parapsychologists have in fact attempted to use some sort of physical measuring device to detect astral bodies, as will be discussed in greater detail below. Most parapsychologists remain skeptical about the reality of astral bodies due to the fact that people generally perceive themselves as being clothed while in the astral state. This would seem to indicate that astral bodies are merely hallucinations (at least as literally perceived), unless one wishes to assume that clothes have astral bodies too!

A second reason parapsychologists have become interested in OBEs is that there are many anecdotal reports of persons becoming aware of information during out-of-body travel to remote locations that would have been inaccessible to them at the location of their physical bodies during the OBE. For instance, the well known psychiatrist and consciousness researcher Stanislav Grof (1990) describes a case in which a woman who was undergoing cardiac arrest felt herself leaving her body and exiting from her hospital room. She then seemed to travel in the out-of-body state to a point outside of the hospital, and she felt herself rise to a point near a tennis shoe that was sitting on a ledge near a third floor window. A subsequent search revealed that there really was such a shoe on the ledge. (A determined skeptic, could of course always argue that the patient might have caught a glimpse of the shoe when she was admitted or when entering the hospital on a previous occasion, as her admission took place at night.) Incidentally, Roach (2005) reports two similar cases involving a red shoe and a plaid shoe (the latter being understandably noticeable even to one in a comatose state). Roach observes that the "OBE traveler's affinity for foot wear must remain a mystery" (Roach, 2005, p. 277).

The following case, taken from the journal of a British army officer (Ogston, 1920), is cited by Cook, Greyson and Stevenson (1998):

> In my delirium night and day made little difference to me. In the four-bedded ward where they first placed me I lay, as it seemed, in a constant stupor which excluded the existence of any hopes or fears. Mind and body seemed to be dual, and to some extent separate. I was conscious of the body as an inert, tumbled mass near a door; it belongs to me but it was not *I*. I was conscious that my mental self used regularly to leave the body ... until something produced a consciousness that the chilly mass, which I then recalled was my body, was being stirred as it lay by the door. I was then drawn rapidly back to it, joined it with disgust, and it became *I*, and was fed, spoken to, and cared for. When it was left again I seemed to wander off as before....
>
> In my wanderings there was a strange consciousness that I could see through the walls of my building, though I was aware that they were there, and that everything was transparent to my senses. I saw plainly, for instance a poor R. A. M. C. [Royal Army Medical Corps] surgeon, of whose existence I had not known before, and who was in quite another part of the hospital, grow very ill and scream and die; I saw them cover his corpse and carry him softly out on shoeless feet, quietly and surreptitiously, lest we should know that he had died, and the next night—I thought—take him away to the cemetery. Afterwards, when I told these things to the sisters [senior nurses], they informed me that all this had happened.... [Cook, Greyson and Stevenson, 1998, p. 383].

Cases such as these have led parapsychologists to perform experiments in which people have tried to travel to a remote location in the out-of-body state in order to identify target materials placed at that location. These experiments will be discussed later in this section. Of course, if these experiments are no more successful than ordinary ESP experiments, it would not be necessary to assume that the subjects literally traveled out of their bodies; instead, one could simply assume that the subjects used their ESP abilities to identify the target.

On rare occasions, witnesses present at the location to which an OBEr has traveled in the out-of-body state may experience an apparition of the OBEr or otherwise become aware of the OBEr's presence. Such cases are sometimes given the (somewhat prejudicial) label "reciprocal hallucinations," because both the OBEr and the witness have mutually consistent experiences, as in case of the physician on the steamer presented earlier in this section.

Perhaps the most famous instance of reciprocal hallucination in the annals of psychical research is the Wilmot case, reported in Myers (1903). It has in fact become almost obligatory to cite the Wilmot case in an introductory work on parapsychology. The events in this case occurred in the 1860s, so it is a very old case indeed. A Mr. S. R. Wilmot was sailing from Liverpool to New York when his boat passed through a severe storm. During the storm, he had a dream in which he saw his wife come into the door of his stateroom, hesitate and then bend down to kiss and caress him. Upon awakening, his fellow passenger William Tait said to him, "You're a pretty fellow to have a lady come and visit you in this way." When Wilmot pressed him for an explanation, Tait said that, as he lay awake in the upper bunk, he saw a woman enter, hesitate and then kiss Mr. Wilmot.

When Mrs. Wilmot greeted him upon his arrival in Watertown, Connecticut, she almost immediately asked him if he had received a visit from her on the night in question. She said that she had been anxious about the severity of the weather and the reported loss of another vessel. She had lain awake for a long time and at about 4:00 A.M. she had the sensation of leaving her physical self and traveling across the stormy sea until she reached her husband's stateroom. She said she saw a man in the upper berth looking right at her and so for a moment she was afraid to go in. But she did enter, kissed and embraced her husband and then departed.

One major drawback to this case is that the principal informants did not give their testimony until about twenty years after the events in question.

Alan Gauld (1982, pp. 222–223) provides a more recent case of reciprocal hallucination. He quotes from a statement sent to the American Society for Psychical Research by a 26-year-old woman from Plains, Illinois. This woman experienced a dream on the morning of January 27, 1957, in which she seemed to travel to the home of her mother in northern Minnesota, 926 miles away:

> After a little while I seemed to be alone going through a great blackness. Then all at once way down below me, as though I were at a great height, I could see a small bright oasis of light in the vast sea of darkness. I started on an incline towards it as I knew it was the teacherage (a small house by the school) where my mother lives.... After I entered, I leaned up against the dish cupboard with folded arms, a pose I often assume. I looked at my Mother who was bending over something white and doing something with her hands. She did not appear to see me at first, but she finally looked up. I had sort of a pleased feeling and then after standing a second more, I turned and walked about four steps.

Gauld also quotes a letter the woman received from her mother:

> I believe it was Saturday night, 1.10, 26 January, or maybe the 27th. If would have been 10 after two your time. I was pressing a blouse here in the kitchen.... I looked up and there you were by the cupboard just smiling at me. I started to speak and you were gone. I forgot for a minute where I was. I think the dogs saw you too. They got so excited and wanted out—just like they thought you were by the door—sniffed and were so tickled.
> Your hair was combed nice—just back in a pony tail with the pretty roll in front. Your blouse was neat and light—seemed almost white. [Miss Johnson confirmed in correspondence that this was an accurate description of her subjective appearance during the OBE.]

It is difficult to decide whether to classify this experience as a dream or as an OBE.

Philosopher Michael Grosso (1976) suggests that the OBE is just one in a continuum of states of consciousness encompassing schizophrenic, meditative, drug, reverie and dream states. He further argues that ESP, "traveling clairvoyance" (in which a person seems to project his mind to a distant location and to become aware of events happening at that location), and the OBE may merely represent three aspects of the same process.

There are a few other states of consciousness that also bear a resemblance to the OBE. Psychiatrists use the term "depersonalization state" to refer to instances in which a person feels himself to be detached from his emotions, actions and even his body. A person undergoing feelings of depersonalization may describe himself as hovering over his body and watching his body perform actions without really being a part of them himself. Janet Mitchell (1981) argues that depersonalization states differ from OBEs in that depersonalization states, unlike OBEs, may involve feelings of derealization (in which one's environment is felt to be unreal). It should also be noted that the flattening of affect (that is, diminished emotional reactions) that is often a characteristic of depersonalization states is not usually reported by people undergoing OBEs.

Irwin (1996) notes that the reporting of OBEs is correlated with the reporting of childhood traumas, and he suggests that a tendency toward dissociation and the experiencing of OBEs may a type of defense mechanism. Irwin (2000) also reports evidence of elevated somatoform dissociation in persons reporting OBEs. In addition, he found that OBErs scored more highly on the trait of psychological absorption (e.g., the ability to "lose" oneself in a book one is reading).

RELATED EXPERIENCES

Autoscopy. In some cases one perceives a double or apparition of oneself in the external environment, such as across the street. This is known as autoscopy, which differs from the OBE in that the person's location of consciousness seems to remain located in the physical body rather than in the double. Tyrrell (1953, p. 144) reports the case of Archbishop Frederic, who saw an apparition of himself after awakening from a deep sleep. He stated that the apparition was "luminous, vaporous and wonderfully real" and that the apparition was looking at him. This state lasted for a few seconds, after which the apparition disappeared. A few seconds later, the specter reappeared, only to vanish once again after a few more seconds.

Doppelgangers. Closely related to autoscopy is the experience of the "doppelganger." "Doppelganger" is a German word used to refer to the apparition of a living person who is not present. In many reported cases, the doppelganger presages the arrival of the person and is often reported to perform acts later performed by the real person. Andrew MacKenzie cites the case of Canon J. B. Phillips, whose wife had gone with an ambulance to the hospital to see after an injured person. Phillips reported hearing a car driving up the road to his chalet. He then heard his wife's voice saying "Thank you very much, goodnight," and he said he then "distinctly" heard the slamming of the car door. He ran out to welcome his wife, but there was no one there at all. About an hour later, these auditory events were replayed, but this time for real (MacKenzie 1971, p. 82). Like autoscopy, the doppelganger experience differs from the OBE in that the person's consciousness remains in the physical body, not in the appearing double.

Bilocation. The phenomenon that will perhaps most strain the reader's credulity is that of bilocation, in which a person, often a Christian, Hindu or Buddhist saint, is experienced as being physically present at two distinct physical locations at the same time. For example, on one night in 1774, the monk Alphonso de Liguori was reported to have been seen simultaneously in his cell and at the bedside of the dying Pope Clement XIV about 100 miles away. (Mitchell, 1981, p. 106). Susan Blackmore relates the case of a schoolteacher in the 1840s who evidently frequently appeared in duplicate (Blackmore, 1982a, p. 12). The students would see two copies of her standing side by side at the blackboard and also at dinner. Two copies of her would also be seen performing activities at different locations around the school. Blackmore reports that this teacher was fired from her job. One would have thought the administration was getting quite a bargain! Finally, Osis and Haraldsson (1977c) report on two Indian swamis, Sai Baba and Dadajai, who have been reported to bilocate in more recent times.

Bilocation is a very infrequently reported phenomenon and few parapsychologists would put much credence in it. Bilocation appears to differ from the OBE in that the double appears to be a solid physical object that does not vanish into thin air and that is capable of physical interaction with its environment. Also, as both copies of the self are reported to be capable of performing complex acts, bilocation would seem to involve a duplication of consciousness as well as of the body. It might of course be possible to explain such phenomena by assuming that the person's mind is at least temporarily split into two distinct subpersonalities. This would be a type of mental, as well as physical bilocation that is not usually reported in OBE cases.

EXPLANATIONS OF THE OBE

Theories concocted to explain OBEs may be divided into roughly two types. Theories of the first type postulate that the OBE involves an "exteriorization" or projection of some (possibly nonphysical) aspect of the person outside of the physical body. This projected aspect is variously conceptualized as the mind, the soul, or some form of quasi-physical "astral body." Theories of this type date back to at least 5000 B.C., the time of the creation of portions of the *Egyptian Book of the Dead* (Mitchell, 1981). The ancient Egyptians postulated the existence of a *ka*, a form of astral body inhabited by the *ba*, or soul, after death. Likewise, the *Tibetan Book of the Dead* postulates the existence of a Bardo-body to house the soul after death. Some Mahayana Buddhists subscribe to the doctrine of *kayatraya*, postulating three bodies. This multiple body principle was later adopted by the religion of Theosophy, which has its roots in Buddhism. Non-Western shamanistic traditions also incorporate the notion of out-of-body travel, as in the case of the Australian aborigines, whose "clever men" are alleged to be able to project themselves at will.

Based on his analysis of a large number of reported out-of-body experiences, Robert Crookall (1970) was led to propose that the astral separation takes place in two stages. In the first stage, the soul or "soul body" is housed in a quasi-physical "vehicle of vitality." When in this state, the OBEr experiences a gloomy Hell-like environment. The second stage, which occurs after the soul body is successful in shedding the vehicle of vitality, is characterized by a great sense of peace, beauty and tranquility. Several writers in the early days of OBE research (e.g., Muldoon & Carrington, 1929) were led, based on anecdotal reports, to postulate the existence of a "silver cord," or sometimes cords, connecting the astral and physical bodies, often through the head or solar plexus. Modern OBErs are much less likely to see such cords, however.

The OBE has been taken by many to suggest that some portion of the human personality may be capable of surviving outside of the physical body and hence capable of surviving the death of that body. Indeed, Thomas Metzinger (2005) has argued that the very concept of the soul derives from OBEs, which he notes is a widely experienced, transcultural phenomenon.

William Roll (1982b) has warned that survival in the form of an astral body may be sharply limited in time, as the number of reported crisis apparitions declines steeply with the time interval since the death of the appearing person (assuming that such apparitions are perceptions of astral bodies). Rodger Anderson (1981) observes that the OBE does not constitute unequivocal evidence for the mind's survival after death, as the site of consciousness might occasionally extend beyond the body yet still perish with the body. He also notes that the silver cord need not be thought of as a means of animating the physical body, as some advocates of astral projection believe, but may instead be a means of animating the astral body by serving as a conduit for the delivery of energy from the physical body.

Perhaps the most devastating argument against the interpretation of the OBE as the literal projection of an astral body is that people are generally unable to identify stimuli placed at locations to which they have supposedly traveled in the out-of-body state in experimental situations, as will be discussed in greater detail below. Attempts to detect a quasiphysical astral body at its projected location through the use of physical instruments will also be discussed below.

The second category of theories includes those that propose a largely psychological explanation for the OBE, several of which have already been discussed. The psychiatrist Jan Ehrenwald (1974) viewed the OBE as an attempt to assert the reality and autonomous existence of the soul and as a psychological defense against the threat of extinction at death. Russell Noyes (1972) likewise sees the OBE as a form of psychological "negation of death." On the other hand, the existing evidence indicates little relationship between anxiety about death and the reporting of OBEs (e.g., Myers, Austrin, Grisso & Nickeson, 1983; Smith & Irwin, 1981).

D. Scott Rogo (1978), Carl Sagan (1977), and Barbara Honegger (1983) have each suggested that the OBE (and the closely related phenomenon of the near-death experience or NDE) may be based on a rebirth fantasy or a reliving of the birth process. Some of the evidence they cite in support of this hypothesis includes the experiencing of tunnel-like passageways during OBEs and NDEs, as well as the cord-like connection between the physical body and the astral body reported by some OBErs (this cord being taken as reminiscent of an umbilical cord). There is some reason to be skeptical of this hypothesis. First, there is considerable doubt in the scientific community that the process of birth can be remembered in any detail, due to the incomplete myelinization of the neonatal brain. Second, Susan Blackmore (1983a) has attempted to test the hypothesis that persons born by Cesarean section (and hence who have not experienced a classical birth process to relive) will report fewer OBEs than persons born by vaginal delivery. She found no relationship between the reporting of OBEs and type of birth in her survey. It remains possible of course that OBEs may be related to fantasies or archetypal ideas about birth even if they do not involve a literal reliving of the birth process.

John Palmer (1978, 1986) has proposed that OBEs may be triggered by changes in the body concept arising from altered patterns of feedback from nerves monitoring the positions of muscles and limbs. Such altered proprioceptive feedback might occur in sleep, in conditions involving physical trauma, or following the administration of anesthetics. In Palmer's view, these changes in body concept may threaten the normal concept of the self or sense of individual identity. As a result, the person's unconscious defenses are activated in order to reestablish a sense of identity, and this reestablishment may take the form of an OBE. When the normal body concept is reestablished, the OBE ends.

Susan Blackmore (1984b) proposes a psychological model of the OBE that is quite similar to that proposed by Palmer. Like Palmer, she suggests that the OBE represents a mental model of the world that is constructed in response to a breakdown in the usual body-centered model of the world. This breakdown may be due to reduced sensory input or to a diminishment of proprioceptive feedback under conditions of reduced bodily movement. This secondary model of the world is often constructed from a "bird's eye view," suggesting to the person that he or she is located in the air above the physical body. Blackmore contends that such a bird's eye view is frequently adopted when remembering a scene from one's past and is thus a characteristic of mental models of the world constructed on the basis of memory. While it is true that in her own research she found that OBErs (that is, people who claim to have had an OBE) were no more likely than non–OBErs to recall scenes from an overhead vantage point, she did find that OBErs were able to switch viewpoints in such imagined scenes more easily than were non–OBErs. Blackmore further conjectures that if a dreaming person becomes aware that he is sleeping, he may construct a model of himself lying in bed and thus come to see himself as located outside of his body. In her view, this might explain why the reporting of OBEs tends to go hand-in-hand with the reporting of lucid dreams (a term used to denote dreams in which one becomes aware that one is dreaming).

Murray and Fox (2004) report evidence that persons reporting OBEs have body images that differ from those of persons not reporting OBEs. Among several other measures examined, they found that OBErs had higher levels of somatoform dissociation (psychological dissociation from one's body), reduced self-confidence and reduced confidence in self-presentation. These findings lend support to the psychological theories of OBE proposed by Palmer, Blackmore, Irwin and others.

Blanke and his coworkers have linked the generation of OBEs to a site in the right angular gurus of the brain (Blanke, Ortigue, Landis, & Seek, 2002; Blanke, Landis, Spinelli & Seeck, 2004). However, Neppe (2003) disputes this claim that an OBE-generating site exists in the right angular gyrus, pointing out that Blanke et al.'s findings are based on a single subject who had temporal lobe epilepsy with a site near the purported OBE center. Neppe further observes that this subject's OBEs were brief and atypical. Neppe also points out that the existence of such a brain site does not rule out the possibility that OBEs involve paranormal processes.

RESEARCH FINDINGS RELATING TO THE OBE

Incidence rates. A great many surveys have been conducted to determine how frequently people in the general population report OBEs (e.g., Hart, 1954; Green, 1967; Blackmore, 1978, 1982b, 1982c, 1984a; Palmer, 1979; Myers, Austrin, Grisso & Nickeson, 1983; Irwin 1980; Tart, 1971). The estimates of the incidence rate vary widely, from a low of 8 percent reported by Haraldsson et al. (1977) to a high of 54 percent reported by Kohr (1980). Most surveys, however, indicate that somewhere between 10 percent and 20 percent of the general population report having had an OBE at some time in the past.

Blackmore (1984a) found that 85 percent of the people who reported any OBE said that they had experienced out-of-body travel on more than one occasion. She also found that 85 percent experienced some sort of strange sensation before entering the OBE state. These sensations included vivid imagery, disorientation, shaking and vibrations, and the seeing of tunnels and doorways.

Carlos Alvarado (1984) asked college students reporting OBEs whether they experienced themselves as being housed in any sort of second body during the OBE. Thirty-five percent said they experienced themselves as not having any sort of body, 23 percent experienced themselves as located in a second body similar to the physical body, 13 percent experienced themselves as a cloud, mist, ball of light or point in space, 8 percent had no recollection, and 20 percent reported some other form of existence. Alvarado found that 81 percent of the students who reported having an OBE claimed to have had more than one OBE, a figure similar to Blackmore's.

Psychological factors. A large number of studies have been conducted to see if there is any relation between the reporting of OBEs and mental imagery ability (e.g., Palmer & Vassar, 1974; Irwin, 1979, 1980, 1986; Cook & Irwin, 1983; Blackmore, 1982c, 1983b, 1986b). Such a positive relationship might be taken as support for the idea that the OBE is largely a fantasy experience. The net result of these studies is that there is little evidence for a relationship between the reporting of OBEs and the experienced vividness of mental images, a person's ability to control her mental imagery, or the tendency to adopt any particular perspective when recalling or imaging a visual scene. There is, however, a fairly consistent body of evidence indicating that OBErs have a greater ability to switch perspectives when viewing imagined scenes than do persons not reporting OBEs (Cook & Irwin, 1983; Blackmore, 1983b, 1986b). There is also a fairly consistent body of evidence indicating that persons who report OBEs tend to fit the profile of a "fantasy-prone" personality (Irwin 1980, 1981; Myers, Austrin, Grisson & Nickeson, 1983; Wilson & Barber, 1982; Stanford, 1987; but see also Gabbard, Jones & Twemlow, 1980). This would lend some support to the view that OBEs may simply be the product of an overactive imagination.

One fairly consistent finding is that OBErs tend to report having lucid dreams more often than do non–OBErs (Blackmore, 1982b, 1982c, 1983a, 1984a, 1986a, 1986b; Irwin, 1986; Stanford, 1990b). Rex Stanford (1990b) has interpreted this to mean that people tend to confuse OBEs with lucid dreams. (Lucid dreams, it will be recalled, are dreams in which the dreamer is aware of the fact that he or she is dreaming.) Another possibility is suggested by the fact that some people have reported that they are able to deliberately launch OBEs from the lucid dream state. One such person was the late D. Scott Rogo. Rogo trained himself to control his hypnagogic imagery (the imagery one has when first falling asleep) in order to enter a state of lucid dreaming. While in the lucid dream state, Rogo like many other lucid dreamers was able to manipulate his dream imagery. He used this ability to "order up" a car, which he then drove and crashed, producing an OBE. Perhaps other lucid dreamers have learned similar techniques (Mitchell, 1981).

EXPERIMENTAL STUDIES OF THE OBE

There have been several attempts to determine whether people can identify target items placed at a location to which they have allegedly projected during an OBE. Of necessity, these experiments have focused on deliberately produced OBEs, sometimes using special subjects who claim to be able to enter an OBE at will and sometimes using ordinary people as subjects. In the latter case, the subjects typically undergo some sort of training procedure that supposedly will allow them to experience an OBE in the experimental situation. Such induction techniques usually involve the subject entering a state of relaxation, possibly through the use of auditory tapes. Occasionally visual input is restricted by placing ping-pong balls over the subject's eyes, producing a "ganzfeld," or blank field of homogeneous visual stimulation. John Palmer and his colleagues used such techniques in an attempt to induce OBEs in a group of ordinary citizens, who were then asked to travel to another room in the OBE state and to identify an ESP target placed there. While 45 percent of the subjects claimed to experience literal separation from their bodies, they were not successful in identifying the target (Palmer & Vassar, 1974). A second experiment was a little more successful, with the subjects reporting OBEs having greater success in identifying the target than subjects not reporting OBEs (Palmer & Lieberman, 1975). In a similar experiment, Smith and Irwin (1981) found a positive relationship between degree of experienced out-of-body separation and success in identifying a target. One problem with their experiment is that the same materials, a small sheep skull and potted palm, served as targets for all the subjects. Thus, their results could be due to a tendency for people who claim to experience OBEs to also report death-related or plant-like imagery.

Several studies have been made of special subjects who claim to be able to produce OBEs at will. One of the most famous of these is Charles Tart's study of the subject he refers to as Miss Z (Tart, 1968). In the one reported trial with Miss Z, she was asked to identify a five digit number that had been placed on a shelf above her while she lay on a cot with EEG electrodes affixed to her scalp. She was able to identify all five digits successfully, a feat which would occur by chance only one time in one hundred thousand. Unfortunately, no one was in the room observing her at the time. Tart conceded that it might be possible that Miss Z could have seen a reflection of the number in a clock that was present in the experimental chamber. Susan Blackmore (1982c) has pointed out that Tart placed the number on the shelf when Miss Z was already in the room, so that it is possible that she was able to get a glimpse of it then. Thus, this experiment was far from perfect. Unfortunately, Miss Z moved away from Tart's area and was not available for further testing (although one might have thought that, given her level of success, Tart would have moved his lab to her new location!). Tart (1967, 1969) attempted a similar experiment with Robert Monroe, a well-known OBEr who has written several books on the subject, but without success.

Janet Mitchell (1981) conducted a very similar experiment with another prominent OBEr, the artist Ingo Swann. Swann did have some success identifying the target materials, but once again he was allowed to be in the room with the target materials with no one observing him. While his movements were restricted by the EEG electrodes attached to his head, it is conceivable that he could have used a device such as an extensible mirror to identify the targets, which were placed on a platform near the ceiling of the room.

Osis and McCormick (1980) conducted an experiment in which the special subject Alex Tanous attempted to identify a target displayed in an "Optical Image Device" (OID) while in the OBE state. Although Tanous had little overall success in identifying the target, a strain gauge placed in the vicinity of the OID showed greater activity when Tanous correctly identified the target than when he did not.

There have been several other attempts to detect some sort of physical effect at the site to which a person has allegedly projected during an OBE, using both animate observers and physical instruments as detection devices. Such physical effects could be interpreted as signs of an astral body. Perhaps the most elaborate such attempt was conducted with the special subject Keith Harary at the Psychical Research Foundation in Durham, North Carolina (Morris, 1974; Morris, Harary, Janis, Hartwell & Roll, 1978). In this study, Harary attempted to project himself from the experimental room to an adjacent building during a voluntarily produced OBE. He was unable to identify target materials placed in the second building. No behavioral changes were observed in a snake or small rodents located in the second building during Harary's projection, although a kitten was less active and cried less during Harary's OBE than during control time periods.

This effect was not, however, obtained in two follow-up studies. No consistent responses from human detectors were observed, although one witness claimed to have seen Harary on a video monitor during one of his projections. Several instruments were used to measure physical effects in the area to which Harary had projected. These included devices to measure several electromagnetic effects and a delicate thermistor to measure temperature changes. No physical effects related to Harary's OBEs were observed with these devices.

There have been many attempts to detect the astral body by weighing or photographing the soul as it leaves the physical body upon death or by photographing the human aura, which is sometimes identified with the astral body. However, these attempts have not been performed with the subject explicitly in an OBE state. Thus, they are not directly relevant to OBEs as such.

Conclusions

Most people are unable to identify target materials while claiming to be located in the vicinity of those target materials during an OBE. In fact, the overall results from these types of OBE experiments are in general no more impressive than the fairly weak effects obtained in ESP experiments, and thus it is plausible that even these minimal successes are due to simple ESP. This failure to reliably identify target material during OBEs constitutes fairly strong evidence against the view that some aspect of the person has literally projected from the body and is perceiving the remote location. This body of evidence would thus support the view that OBEs are simply the product of fantasy or hallucination.

Near-Death Experiences

Some people who have come close to dying, such as in cases of cardiac arrest or being knocked unconscious during an automobile accident, but who have been revived after a period of apparent unconsciousness, report an encounter with an apparently nonphysical or postmortem realm.

Such experiences are called "near-death experiences" (NDEs) and were brought to the attention of the general public through the publication in 1975 of Raymond Moody's best-selling book *Life after Life* (Moody, 1975). Moody lists the following characteristics of the NDE:

- Loud ringing or buzzing noises,
- Sensations of traveling down a tunnel-like passage,
- Out-of-body experiences,
- Viewing the physical body from an external vantage point,
- Emotional upheavals,
- Sensations that one possesses a quasi-physical astral body,
- Encounters with the apparitions of deceased relatives and friends,
- An encounter with a "being of light," who serves as a spiritual guide (frequently interpreted as a Christ-like being in the West),
- Undergoing an evaluation of one's life,
- Experiencing a panoramic review of one's life,
- Approaching a barrier or border,
- Being told that one must go back (that is, return to one's physical body and rejoin the realm of the living),
- Not wishing to return,
- Experiencing deep feelings of joy and peace,
- Experiencing a reunion with the physical body, and
- Having experiences of an ineffable nature (e.g., sensations of color or mystical union that cannot be described in words).

Of the fifteen elements listed above, Moody notes that usually eight or more are reported by a typical NDEr, although no single case in his collection included more than 12 of the above 15 characteristics. He further notes that no single item of the 15 is included in every single NDE account.

Cook, Greyson, and Stevenson (1998) cite the following case from the May 26, 1935 (London) *Sunday Express*, which contains everything one could ask for in a spontaneous case of psi. Not only does it involve an NDE, but also multiple incidents of crisis psi as well as an attempted reincarnation.

> In 1911, at the age of sixteen, I was staying about twelve miles from my own home when a high wall was blown down by a sudden gust of wind as I was passing.
>
> A huge coping stone hit me on top of the head.
>
> It then seemed as if I could see myself lying on the ground, huddled up, with one corner of the stone resting on my head and quite a number of people rushing toward me.
>
> I watched one of them move the stone and some one took off his coat and put it under my head, and I heard all their comments: "Fetch a doctor." "His neck is broken." "Skull smashed like an eggshell."
>
> He [apparently a doctor] then wanted to know if anyone knew where I lived, and on

being told that I was lodging just around the corner he instructed them to carry me there.

Now all this time it appeared as though I was disembodied from the form lying on the ground and suspended in mid-air in the center of the group, and could hear everything that was said.

As they started to carry me it was remarked that it would come as a blow to my people, and I was immediately aware of a desire to be with my mother.

Instantly I was at home, and father and mother were just sitting down to their midday meal. On my entrance mother sat bolt upright in her chair and said, "Bert something has happened to our boy."

"Nonsense," he said, "whatever has put such an idea in your head?"

There followed an argument, but mother refused to be pacified, and said that if she caught the 2 p.m. train she could be with me before three and satisfy herself.

She had hardly left the room when there came a knock on the front door. It was a porter from the railway station with a telegram saying that I was badly hurt.

Then suddenly I was again transported—this time it seemed to be against my wish—to a bed-room, where a woman whom I recognized was in bed, and two other women were quietly bustling around, and a doctor was leaning over the bed.

Then the doctor has a baby in his hands.

As once I became aware of an almost irresistible impulse to press my face through the back of the baby's head so that my face would come into the same place as the child's.

The doctor said, "It looks as though we have lost them both." And again I felt the urge to take the baby's place in order to show him we was wrong, but the thought of my mother crying turned my thoughts in her direction, when straightaway I was in a railroad carriage with both her and father.

He [Mr. Martin's father] was looking at his watch, and she [Mr. Martin's mother] was saying that the train was right on time.

I was still with them when they arrived at my lodgings and were shown into my room where I had been put to bed.

Mother sat beside the bed and I longed to comfort her, and the realization came that I ought to do the same things as I felt impelled to do in the case of the baby and climbed into the body in the bed.

At last I succeeded, and the effort caused me to sit up in bed fully conscious. Mother made me lie down again, but said I was alright, and remarked that if was odd she knew something was wrong before the porter had brought the telegram.

Both she and dad were amazed were amazed at my knowledge. Their astonishment further increased when I repeated almost word for word some of the conversation they had at home and in the train.

Mother remarked that she supposed that when some people came close to death they were gifted with second sight.

I replied by saying that I had also been close to birth as well, and told then that Mrs. Wilson, who lived close to us at home, had a baby that day, but it was dead because I could not get into its body.

We subsequently learned that Mrs. Wilson died on the same day at 2:05, delivering a stillborn girl.

I am convinced that if I had willed myself into that baby's body, today I would be a Miss Wilson, instead of being—W. Martin, 107 Grove Streed, Liverpool. [Quotation taken from Cook, Greyson and Stevenson (1998, pp. 387–388).]

Several surveys relating to NDEs have been carried out (e.g., Sabom, 1982; Pasricha, 1993, 1995; Ring, 1980; Long, 2003; Britton & Bootzin, 2004). The data indicate that somewhere around one half of the people who have been revived from a state of clinical death claim to have experienced an NDE, a remarkably high figure (see Sabom, 1982; Pasricha, 1993, 1995; and Ring, 1980); although Baruss (2003) reports an incidence rate of 9 percent to 18 percent

Kenneth Ring (1979, 1980) conducted a study of 102 persons who had experienced

NDEs in order to determine how frequently various elements of the NDE, as described by Moody, occurred. He found that 60 percent of his respondents reported feelings of peace and contentment during their NDEs, 33 percent reported an out-of-body experience, 23 percent reported sensations of entering a region of darkness or traveling down a tunnel, 20 percent sensed a (typically benevolent) presence who aided them in reviewing and evaluating their lives, 17 percent reported seeing a light to which they were drawn, and 10 percent experienced seeing a world of "preternatural beauty."

The skeptical view of NDEs is of course that they simply represent hallucinations, dreams and fantasies constructed by the mind under conditions of physical trauma or stress. Various neurophysiological causes for such hallucinations have been proposed, including seizures in the temporal lobes of the brain, (e.g., Thorton, 1984; Wilson, 1928; Carr, 1982; Persinger, 1983), lack of oxygen to the brain (e.g., Rodin,1980; Schnaper, 1986), the release of endorphins in the brain (e.g., Shaver, 1986; Blackmore, 1993), and the random firing of cells in the visual cortex of the brain (e.g., Blackmore 1991b, 1992; Siegel, 1980). Ronald Siegel (1977) has also noted that tunnel-like imagery is one of the eight common "form constants" of hallucinations induced by LSD.

Britton and Bootzin (2004) found that persons reporting NDEs are characterized by elevated temporal lobe epileptiform EEG activity relative to control subjects and also report significantly more temporal lobe epileptic syndromes. The elevated epileptiform activity is almost completely lateralized to the left hemisphere in such subjects. Britton and Bootzin found that NDEs were not associated with dysfunctional stress reactions, such as dissociation, post-traumatic stress disorders and substance abuse. Instead, they found NDEs to be associated with positive coping styles.

Theories attributing the out-of-body component of the NDE to states of depersonalization, a denial of death, and a reliving of the birth trauma were discussed in the previous section.

As with the other categories of evidence for survival of the personality of death to be discussed below, the primary evidence that NDEs are not simply fantasies or hallucinations is provided by cases in which patients become anomalously aware of information during an NDE when they apparently had no normal means of acquiring such information. In many cases, this information pertains to events at the scene of an accident or during a surgical procedure that the patient witnesses from a vantage point above the body, while the body itself is apparently unconscious. For instance, a patient undergoing cardiac arrest may describe events occurring during the resuscitation procedure. If the procedure itself is simply described, it is possible that the patient is merely demonstrating knowledge of resuscitation procedures she has gleaned from watching television shows, etc. If specific idiosyncratic events in the vicinity of the patient's body are described, it is quite possible that the patient, despite her apparent unconsciousness, retained enough awareness and sensory ability to perceive the described events. Indeed, there is a wide body of evidence that patients retain some sensory capacity even under conditions of deep surgical anesthesia (e.g., Bennett, Davis & Giannini, 1985; Goldmann, Shah & Hebden, 1987; Evans & Richardson, 1988; Furlong, 1990; Pearson, 1961; Kihlstrom, Schachter, Cork, Hurt & Behr, 1990; Millar & Watkinson, 1983).

It is less easy to explain cases in which the patient reports awareness of events occurring at locations remote from the body during the NDE, such as the case of the woman who saw a tennis shoe on a window ledge in the hospital during an NDE, which was discussed in the previous section. Such cases are exceedingly rare, however. There are some data indicating that NDErs tend to have fantasy-prone personalities (see for instance Twemlow & Gabbard, 1984; and Council, Greyson & Huff, 1986), which would give further support to the theory that NDEs simply represent fantasies and hallucinations.

Deathbed Visions

Closely related to the near-death experience is the phenomenon of deathbed visions, in which dying patients apparently see apparitions of deceased relatives and friends, who appear at their bedside for the seeming purpose of conducting the dying person into the afterlife. In fact, out-of-body experiences and deathbed visions could conceivably be regarded as unusual NDEs in which only one component of the NDE occurs. One feature that distinguishes deathbed visions from typical NDEs is that the patient is not generally in a state of unconsciousness or "clinical death" at the time of the experience. Deathbed visions have been studied by William Barrett in the 1920s and the team of Karlis Osis and Erlendur Haraldsson in the 1960s and 1970s (Barrett, 1926; Osis (1961; Osis & Haraldsson, 1977a, 1977b). Osis and Haraldsson collected their data from surveys of doctors and nurses in the United States and India regarding their recollections of any visions reported by dying patients. In the United States, hallucinated figures were primarily of deceased persons (70 percent), the rest being split between living persons (17 percent) and religious figures (13 percent). In India, a much higher percentage of religious figures was reported (50 percent), with deceased persons representing only 29 percent of the hallucinations, and living persons 21 percent. In approximately three-fourths of the cases in both countries, the purpose for the apparitional figure's appearance was interpreted to be to escort the dying person into the afterlife. In both countries, the percentage of patients reporting such apparitions declined as the clarity of consciousness, as measured by the drugs administered and the presence of fever, declined. Osis and Haraldsson take this as evidence that such apparitions do not represent mere hallucinations engendered by psychopathological states; on the other hand, it could equally well be argued that persons in an impaired state of consciousness may be less able to communicate coherently about such an apparitional experience.

One type of deathbed vision case that is a little more difficult to attribute to a simple hallucinatory process occurs when a deceased person appears to a dying patient who had no knowledge that the appearing person had died. Karlis Osis quotes the following case from William Barrett's investigations:

> On Jan. 12, 1924, a Mrs. B. was dying in a hospital in England. Her sister Vida had died on Dec. 25, 1923, but her illness and death had been carefully kept from Mrs. B because of her own serious illness. As Mrs. B. was sinking, she said: 'It is all so dark, I cannot see.' A moment later her face brightened and she exclaimed: 'Oh it is lovely and bright; you cannot see as I can.' A little later she said: 'I can see father, he wants me, he is so lonely.' then with a rather puzzled expression: 'He has Vida with him,' turning to her mother—'Vida is with him!' A few moments later she died [Osis, 1961, p. 16].

On the other hand, Michael Grosso (1981) has noted that such "Peak in Darien" cases (as they are called) are extremely rare.

Stevenson (1995) describes a case that is very unusual in that a second witness perceived the deathbed visitor. This case involved a girl whose grandfather, who was dying of leukemia, was living with her family. She reports:

> Granddaddy called to me to give him a drink of water. I failed in my attempts to lift him enough to wet his lips. The disease had reduced his once tall, strong stature to [that of] a frail, weak invalid. I called mom at work to ask for help, but she told me it would have to wait until dad ... returned from work at noon.
>
> Shortly thereafter I heard granddaddy calling out to his wife Hazel. Grandmom had died nine years prior, ... so I thought he must be losing his mind. I ran down the hall to make another attempt to help him. I was amazed to find him sitting up, smiling with his arms reaching out. The room was filled with a warm, bright light. He spoke to grandmom, who was standing at the foot of the bed. Neither of them acknowledged my presence. She was there for a brief moment, and when granddaddy laid back down, his soul escaped with her. He died with a smile on his face [Stevenson, 1995, p. 360].

Dreams

Occasionally, deceased persons appear in dreams. Usually, of course, such figures can be dismissed as images constructed by the dreamer's subconscious mind (or spontaneously firing neurons). On rare occasions, however, such deceased persons may communicate information to the dreamer that neither the dreamer nor any other living person had any apparent normal means of knowing. In one famous and oft-cited case, known as the Chaffin will case (described in Myers, 1903), a father communicated the existence of an alternative will to one of his sons in a dream. Under the original will, one of the dreamer's brothers had inherited the father's farm and the rest of the family had inherited nothing. Based on information given to him in his dream, the son was able to locate a second will in his father's handwriting, in which the property was distributed more equally. This will was admitted to probate. A cynic could dismiss this case as fraud combined with forgery, especially as the dreamer had much to gain by perpetrating such a fraud. In fact, Ian Wilson (1987) has noted that most of the witnesses in the Chaffin will case were family members who stood to profit from the new will. Less cynically, one might assume that the dreamer learned of the will's existence and location through clairvoyance or that he had picked up cues as to the will's existence from his father's behavior before death.

George Zorab (1962) has compiled a collection of cases of the "Chaffin will type." In one such case, a bookkeeper in Holland had been accused of embezzling approximately 1,800 guilders and died before his name could be cleared. After the bookkeeper's death, his son had a dream in which a white figure appeared to him and said, "Look in the ledger at the dates." Upon checking, it was found that his father had included the date at the top of a column in one of his additions. It is quite possible that the son may have unconsciously noted the identity between the disputed amount and the date and that this fact entered his conscious awareness in the form of the dream in question. There are many examples on record of such problem-solving activity in dreams, a notable one being Elias Howe's invention of the sewing machine, which was based in part on a dream Howe had in which a group of cannibals were about to eat him. In this dream some of the cannibals thrust spears at Howe. These spears had holes in them near their tips, which suggested to Howe that he should put the hole near the point of the needle in his sewing machine rather than at the base of the needle. Another example of such problem-solving activity in dreams is provided by August Kekule's discovery of the ringlike structure of the benzene molecule, which was presented to him in the form of a dream in which benzene molecules were transformed into a group of dancing snakes that suddenly took their tails into their own mouths.

Because of the existence of such counterexplanations as those discussed above, the existing evidence from dreams cannot be taken as definitive evidence of the survival of the human personality of death.

Apparitions

Another category of spontaneous psi experiences that are often taken as evidence for the survival of human personality of death consists of apparitional experiences. The sighting of apparitions or "ghosts" is not as uncommon as one might think. In John Palmer's mail survey of the greater Charlottesville, Virginia, area, 17 percent of the respondents reported having seen an apparition (Palmer, 1979). A Gallup poll indicated that about 9 percent of the population of Britain believe that they have seen a ghost (Gallup, 1982).

The following case, taken from Wright (1999), involves an auditory crisis "apparition."

> I was always very close to my grandfather. He had a wonderful sense of humor and he always related to me as though I were a little kid. And he'd tease me. He'd say very affectionately in this real deep voice, "Mary-Minn, you're a baddie, a real baddie." He said that from the time I was about four or five and he still said it when I was in my twenties. Well, he went into a coma for a week or two. I wasn't talking to most people in my family—we had had some horrible feud. But I'd been keeping up with my grandmother and I knew he was in a coma and would probably die, so I was sitting in the office one rainy afternoon, typing up a disbursement voucher, and suddenly this deep voice came out and said, "Mary-Minn, you're a baddie, a real baddie." And that was it. I knew it was him and I knew that nobody else heard it. I mean I knew that he had died, he had just expired. Well, the phone rang about two minutes later and he had [Wright, 1999, p. 262].

Of course, a determined skeptic could attribute this case to the fact that the grandfather's death was not unexpected, which may have triggered auditory memories sufficiently vivid to be classed as hallucinatory.

A more classic, visual ghost experience is reported by Stevenson (1995):

> [O]n the morning of May 29, 1975, E. W. [the percipient in Stevenson's case] went to the outside door of her house (which faces the main road) in order to bring inside the delivered bottles of milk that had been left on her doorstep. She later thought she had done this between 10:00 and 10:30 a.m. She looked across the road and saw her neighbor Ronald McKay walking out of the driveway of his house and then along the road or drive as if going to the nearby factory of which he was the manager. E. W. and her husband had known that the McKays had been away on vacation and believed that they were still away. When E. W. went back inside her house, she said casually to her husband: "I see the McKays are back." Her husband asked her when they had come back. E. W. replied: "I don't know, but I saw Ron go down the drive." About a half hour or perhaps an hour later, a senior employee of Ronald McKay's factory came to the house and spoke with E. W.'s husband. He then asked her when she had seen Ron McKay, and she repeated what she had said earlier. Her husband then said that the factory employee had information that Ronald KcKay had died that morning while on vacation in England about 150 miles away from Dunfermline [Stevenson, 1995, p. 358].

Stevenson estimates that the time interval between E. W.'s apparitional experience and McKay's death could not have been more than 3–4 hours. He also estimates that she watched the apparition for at least ten seconds from a distance of 50 feet, reducing the chances of misidentification.

Stevenson cites several survey sources indicating that somewhere between 10 percent and 27 percent of the general population have had apparitional experiences.

Erlendur Haraldsson (1981) conducted a detailed survey relating to apparitional experiences in Iceland. Of the 902 respondents in Haraldsson's survey, 31 percent affirmed having experienced the presence of a deceased person. Detailed interviews with 100 of the respondents who reported such experiences indicated that 16 percent of the experiences involved the mere feeling of the deceased person's presence, 70 percent involved a visual hallucination, 24 percent included an auditory experience, 7 percent a tactile experience, and 5 percent an olfactory sensation. One-third of the cases occurred when the percipient was falling asleep, which indicated to Haraldsson that hypnagogic imagery was frequently involved in the experience. In 23 percent of the cases the appearing person had died violently, which Haraldsson notes is a disproportionately high number. In 43 percent of the cases, more than one person was present at the time of the apparition, and in one-third of these cases it was claimed that the apparition was collectively perceived.

A survey modeled after the early "Census of Hallucinations" conducted by the British Society for Psychical Research (Sidgwick et al., 1894) has been reported by D. J. West (1990). As in the original census, volunteers interviewed their acquaintances regarding apparitional experiences. Of 1,129 distributed questionnaires, 840 were returned, with 14.6 percent of the respondents reporting an experience with hallucination of a human figure. Discounting dubious cases, West concludes that 11.3 percent of the respondents reported "genuine" hallucinations, which he notes compares favorably to the figure of 10 percent obtained by the early Society for Psychical Research. Only 9 of the 840 respondents reported detailed, apparently psi-related hallucinations, a figure that is also comparable to the proportion obtained in the earlier survey.

It is very common for people to experience the presence of a deceased spouse. A study in Wales indicated that 43 percent of widows and widowers had seen an apparition of their dead spouses (Rees, 1971), and a second survey indicated that nearly 60 percent of the widows in the greater Los Angeles area had experienced the presence of their deceased spouse (Kalish and Reynolds, 1974). Of course, the fact that a bereaved widow has a vision of her deceased husband does not imply that she has accurately perceived the presence of her husband's now disembodied spirit. The vision could simply be a grief-induced hallucination.

Occasionally, however, such postmortem apparitions transmit information to the percipient which the percipient had no apparent normal means of knowing. In the case of crisis apparitions, the information transmitted is usually simply that the appearing person has died or been injured. As we have previously remarked, such apparitions could be simply ESP-induced hallucinations, and therefore they cannot be taken as providing definitive evidence that the spirit of the appearing person has survived death.

On the other hand, not all cases involving information transmission fit into the crisis apparition category. For instance, Stanislav Grof (1990) describes two cases in which participants in LSD sessions apparently received accurate information from the dead. The first case involved an LSD session in America, in which the participant "saw" a deceased person who gave him the name and address of his parents in Moravia. When the parents were contacted at the address in Moravia, they stated that they had a son who had died three weeks prior to the LSD session.

In Grof's second case, the wife of Grof's colleague Walter Pahnke, who had died in a scuba diving accident, experienced an LSD-induced vision of her deceased husband. The apparition requested her to return a borrowed book located in the attic of her house. She claimed to have had no prior knowledge of the book or its location, but she was able to find it and return it.

Of course, neither of these cases constitute definitive evidence of survival. In fact, both could be due to cryptomnesia, or hidden memory. Possibly the first percipient may have read an obituary notice for the dead Moravian youth, but had forgotten that he had read it. Similarly, Mrs. Pahnke may have had a subconscious memory of the borrowed book. Counterexplanations in terms of ESP are also possible.

One apparitional experience that is frequently cited as providing evidence of survival is that of the "Red Scratch" case, reported in Myers (1903). The percipient in this case was a traveling salesman, who was staying in a hotel room. At one point he looked up from recording his orders and saw an apparition of his sister, who had died nine years previously, sitting beside him at the table. As he addressed her and moved toward her, she disappeared. Later, telling his parents about the apparition, he mentioned a red scratch that he had seen on the side of the girl's face. At that point his mother nearly fainted, then arose trembling and stated her belief in the survival of her daughter's spirit, as she had in fact made such a scratch on her daughter's face at her funeral while attending to the body. She covered up the scratch with makeup and had told no one about it. It is, however, easily imaginable that the makeup job was not perfect and that the son may have noticed the scratch at the time of the funeral. Alternatively, he may have subconsciously overheard his mother talking in her sleep about the incident soon after the funeral (or, possibly, derived the information telepathically from her). Once again, this case does not provide conclusive evidence of survival.

Hauntings

Haunting cases involve repeated anomalous events, usually associated with a particular location or object. Very often, apparitions or "ghosts" are sighted. Sometimes several witnesses will claim to have seen apparitions at the location over a period of time. Some of the apparitions may be collectively perceived. Occasionally anomalous sounds are heard, including raps, footsteps and voices. Sensations of cold and strange odors are sometimes reported. Occasionally, anomalous movements of objects are associated with hauntings, although cases in which this feature is prominent are usually classified as poltergeist cases. As mentioned in Chapter 3, Gauld and Cornell (1979) found hauntings and poltergeist cases to constitute two fairly distinctive "clusters" of phenomena in their statistical analysis of such cases. Among their findings, they found that cases involving apparitions were more likely to involve the rattling and opening/shutting of windows and doors as well as experiences of unseen but felt hands.

Hauntings have been recorded throughout the ages. The Roman writer Pliny the Younger, for instance, reported a haunting case in the first century A.D.

Certain types of haunting phenomena may be due to the effects of suggestion and to the misattribution of normal sounds to paranormal causes. A frightened person alone in a house with a reputation for being haunted may misinterpret a normal settling noise as a paranormal rap or a ghostly footstep. The resulting shivers of fear may be responsible for sensations of cold.

The repeated sighting of apparitions by multiple witnesses is of course less easy to explain as the misinterpretation of normal stimuli or as due to psychopathology on the part of the percipient. There is thus a greater temptation in such cases to attribute the recurring vision to the surviving spirit of a deceased person.

Let us examine a fairly typical haunting case that was investigated by Teresa Cameron and William Roll (Cameron & Roll, 1983). This case involved repeated sightings of an apparition of a male figure, who was usually described as about six feet tall, weighing 190 pounds, and typically wearing a brown suit, in a radio station in Virginia over a time period from October of 1980 through April of 1981. The figure was usually seen in a standing position, and the sightings occurred in a hallway near the women's restroom or in the doors leading off the hallway. Five employees witnessed the apparition. Three of the employees had heard stories about ghosts in the station, but had treated these stories in a joking manner. Evidently, a former employee had reported many sightings of apparitions, both inside and outside the building. This employee reportedly had severe psychological problems and left her employment under strained circumstances. She did not respond to Cameron and Roll's inquiries or grant an interview.

The first sighting during the time period in question was by William Morrison, an engineer and carpenter. After an initial fleeting glance, Morrison saw a male figure wearing a brown suit from a distance of about twenty feet. He said the figure appeared to take a few steps while he was looking at it, although he did not recall seeing any legs or feet.

Carolyn McDougall, a 30-year-old continuity director at the station, heard papers "riffling" as she came out of the ladies' room. She then saw a male figure wearing a brown jacket standing in a doorway. She stated that she saw only "down to the start of his pants." She did not recall seeing any face, legs or feet on the figure. Although her experience occurred a day or two after Morrison's sighting, she did not hear of Morrison's experience until after her own vision. Both of these sightings occurred in October of 1980.

In April of 1981, Gloria Johnson, a receptionist at the station, was coming out of the ladies' room when she saw a transparent male figure wearing a dark suit moving (but neither walking nor "gliding") down the hallway. She had heard nothing about prior sightings at the station before she had her experience, and she had begun her employment in December of 1980.

A 30-year-old engineer named Henry Eaton saw a strange male seated at a fellow employee's desk. He turned to reach for his own chair in order to sit down, and by the time he redirected his attention to the unknown figure it had vanished. This sighting occurred on the same day as the vision of Gloria Johnson, but he did not mention it until Miss Johnson burst into the room to describe her own sighting. He had previously heard stories about ghosts in the building.

Jack Sneider, a 21-year-old announcer on the evening shift, twice saw a strange male figure when no one else was presumably in the building, these sightings taking place in November and December of 1980.

Cameron and Roll had the witnesses take Wilson and Barber's Inventory of Childhood Memories and Imaginings (ICMI). Based on these scores and interview data,

Cameron and Roll conclude that three of the witnesses may have been psychologically pre-disposed to having apparitional experiences. Carolyn McDougall obtained a very high score on the ICMI, indicative of a fantasy-prone personality. She is also a self-described psychic who has had other apparitional experiences and has reported seeing UFOs. Gloria Johnson had previously seen an apparition of her grandfather and had experienced a recurrent apparition in her childhood. Henry Eaton obtained a high score on the ICMI and has been diagnosed as manic-depressive. Thus, these three witnesses may have had various forms of psychopathology, or at least fantasy-prone personalities, that may have rendered them prone to having apparitional experiences.

Cameron and Roll note that Eaton and Morrison both had visual problems and that Morrison and Sneider saw the visions at night and in poorly lit areas. Morrison also reported feeling quite fatigued on the night of his sighting. Having previously heard stories of ghosts in the station, these witnesses might have been primed to interpret ambiguous stimuli experienced under poor observational conditions as ghostly phenomena. (While Sneider had reportedly not heard such stories prior to his experiences, these stories may have colored his retrospective interpretation of ambiguous events.)

One piece of evidence supporting the paranormality hypothesis, Cameron and Roll conclude, is the tight clustering in time of Morrison's and McDougall's experiences as well as of Johnson's and Eaton's experiences. As to agency, McDougall and Morrison thought that the apparitions resembled Charles Michaux, a former employee of the station who had died in 1978. Michaux had been fired under stressful conditions before Christmas of 1977, causing a fight to break out among the remaining employees during the annual Christmas party. Michaux died of a heart attack shortly thereafter. Obviously, however, the evidence from this case, like the evidence from most hauntings, does not constitute a clear cut case for any type of paranormal process, much less the survival of a discarnate spirit.

Even animals can sometimes appear as ghosts. My next-door neighbor during my teenage years had the experience of repeatedly seeing a cocker spaniel lying on a particular step in her stairway or under a desk built into the wall. When she mentioned this to the former owner of the house, he told her that at the time he lived in the house he had a pet cocker spaniel that used to like to sleep in precisely those locations.

There have been a few attempts to study hauntings scientifically. One method, used by Michaeleen Maher and her coworkers (Maher & Schmeidler, (1975; Maher & Hansen, 1992a, 1992b, 1995; Roll, Maher & Brown, 1992), involves dividing up a house into many different zones. A number of psychics, or "sensitives," then state which zones they feel are associated with ghostly phenomena and attempt to describe any apparitions that might have been seen. A set of control subjects or skeptics then do the same. While the results have been mixed, in some cases the psychics' descriptions of the ghostly phenomena corresponded more closely to the witnesses' accounts than did the skeptics' descriptions. This, however, proves nothing, as certain locations in the house may naturally suggest ghostly presences, thus accounting for the fact that both the psychics and the actual witnesses assumed that ghosts would be present at these locations. Similarly, certain houses may suggest certain types of ghosts. Thus, correspondences between witnesses' and outsiders' descriptions of the location and nature of ghosts cannot be taken as proving anything about the paranormality of the phenomena. Similarly, if the psychics were to provide descriptions that corresponded more closely to witnesses' accounts than the control subjects or skeptics did, this would again prove nothing. Psychics and people who see ghosts may merely tend to think alike. Also, self-proclaimed sensitives who frequently investigate hauntings may have gathered a great deal of knowledge relating to where people will report seeing ghosts.

There have been a few attempts to detect physical anomalies at haunting locations, but these have generally failed to yield any sort of consistent effect. One intriguing finding was reported by Dean Radin and William Roll (1994). They found the activity of a Geiger counter to be significantly increased when placed in an area of space said by a psychic to be currently occupied by a ghost, suggesting that this ghost may have been in some sense "radioactive." They speculate that the psychic may have been able to sense local regions of increased radioactivity, such as pockets of radon gas, or that she may have influenced the results by moving a radioactive piece of jewelry closer to the Geiger counter during the tests. Two of the investigators also witnessed a luminous blob in a room that the psychic claimed was occupied by a ghost, further suggesting the existence of some sort of physical anomaly in the environment.

Maher and Hansen (1995) found curious artifacts in Polaroid and video recording tests performed at sites of reported haunting phenomena.

Tandy (2000) found elevated infrasound levels at a frequency of 18.9 Hz in a reputedly haunted 14th century cellar beneath a tourist Information Center in Coventry, England. These infrasound waves were especially pronounced at sites where apparitions have been experienced. Tandy and Lawrence (1998) had previously proposed that apparitions and sensations of a "presence" might be caused by 19 Hz standing waves.

Braithwaite, Perez-Aquino and Townsend (2004) found evidence of heightened magnetic activity in the area of a pillow in a haunted castle. They theorize that the increased magnetic fields may have triggered a hallucinatory experience on the part of witnesses to haunting phenomena in the castle who slept in this bed.

Hornell Hart (1959) has noted that the fragmentary, repetitive nature of most apparitions' behavior does not seem consistent with the hypothesis that apparitions are indications of the fully surviving consciousness of the deceased. Several other theories of haunting apparitions, including those of Myers, Tyrrell and Roll, have already been discussed in Chapters 3 and 5, and so we will not repeat those discussions here.

The evidence for survival provided by haunting cases, while suggestive, is not particularly strong. In many cases, a skeptic could maintain that the apparitional figures are simply hallucinations, perhaps caused by fatigue or some sort of pathological state in the witnesses. Also, normal settling noises and other sounds may be misinterpreted as ghostly phenomena in a house with a reputation for being haunted. It should also be realized that haunting cases, in the narrow sense of the repeated sighting of apparitions in a single location by several witnesses, are much more rarely reported than are spontaneous psi experiences. Thus, hauntings might more easily be attributed to psychopathology or fraud than spontaneous psi cases could be.

Mediumship

The belief that it is possible to contact the dead through the intermediary of a living person forms a part of many formal and informal religious traditions. Ian Wilson (1987) notes that rites for contacting the dead existed in ancient Greece and observes that the Biblical tradition has Saul contacting the deceased Samuel through the mediumship of the witch of Endor. Spiritualistic séances go back at least as far as 1000 A.D. in the Norse tradition, and mediumship was intimately associated with the phenomenon of animal magnetism or mesmerism (now called hypnosis) in the first half of the nineteenth century (Leahey and Leahey, 1983). Mediumship has of course always been associated with shamanistic religions, possibly even into prehistoric times. Nevertheless, in most people's minds, mediumship is most clearly associated with the Spiritualist tradition that began to flourish in America and England during the second half of the nineteenth century and which is still alive in a somewhat muted form today.

The birth of the modern Spiritualist movement is usually traced to the Fox sisters, who claimed to be able to communicate with the spirits of the deceased through mysteriously produced rapping sounds. The Fox sisters' phenomena began with a series of raps that occurred over a time period beginning in 1847 in their childhood home in Hydesville, New York. The raps appeared to answer questions, and, when an alphabetic code was worked out, claimed to originate from the spirit of a peddler who was murdered in the house. A body was found buried in the cellar of the house, and the Fox sisters became celebrities. They subsequently developed a stage act in which they produced rapping messages from the deceased in front of large audiences. The sisters later became alcoholics, and one of them confessed that she had fraudulently produced the rapping noises by popping the joint of her big toe (although she later retracted this confession). By this time, mediumship had become a growth industry, and Spiritualism developed as a religious movement centered around mediumistic phenomena. The heyday of Spiritualism is past, although the recent mania for "channeled" advice from the beyond and the success of television psychics such as Jonathan Edward clearly has its roots in the mediumistic tradition.

PHYSICAL MEDIUMSHIP

When anomalous physical phenomena seemingly connected with the spirits of the dead are manifested in the presence of a human intermediary or medium, one is said to be dealing with "physical mediumship." Such phenomena are typically obtained in the context of a séance, in which a group of people seeking contact with the dead, called "sitters," gather in the presence of a medium. Frequently, but not invariably, the medium enters a trance state as part of the ritual of contacting the dead. The phenomena obtained may include materializations or "apports" of objects (that is, the seeming appearance of objects out of thin air), the production of ectoplasm (an alleged wispy or ghostlike substance which may form the material for the physical reconstruction of the body of an appearing dead person), the production of strange sounds, including raps, the anomalous movement of objects, including the tilting of the séance table, and the anomalous appearance of written messages, such as chalk-writing on a board of slate. This list is not meant to be exhaustive, and many other types of phenomena may be manifested.

Many physical mediums have been detected in fraud. The medium Mina Crandon, for instance, was allegedly able to obtain many physical phenomena, among them the production of wax fingerprints of her dead brother Walter. Fraud was revealed when E. E.

Dudley was able to ascertain that a sample of such fingerprints were actually those of the medium's very much alive dentist (Hansel 1980, p. 77).

In another celebrated case, a medium named Florence Cook was allegedly able to produce a materialization of the highly attractive body of a spirit named Katie King while Cook herself was tied to a chair inside a "cabinet." On one occasion (and in violation of the etiquette of séance behavior), a sitter named George Sitwell grabbed the materialized form of Katie King. The cabinet was then thrown open, and the medium's chair was found to be empty, the ropes slipped, and the medium's clothes to be lying in disarray about the cabinet. Cook had herself portrayed Katie King (see Oppenheim, 1985, for more details).

While the above two exposures of fraudulent mediums took place in the nineteenth century, fraudulent physical mediums continue to be exposed in recent times. In an incident similar to the Katie King fiasco, several spirits at the Facet of Divinity Church (endorsed by death and dying expert Elizabeth Kübler-Ross) were found to be very much alive and kicking after they had taken the extraordinary step of having sexual relations with worshipers in need of "comfort" from the beyond (see Randi, 1980, p. 9). Melvin Harris (1986) describes the exposure of the medium Paul McElhaney. One of the features of McElhaney's act was the apparent materialization of carnations; however, inspection of his possessions revealed that he had hidden the carnations to be materialized inside a tape recorder prior to the séance.

Because of the high incidence of fraud, most parapsychologists today cast a wary eye at physical mediumship. There continues to be debate about the genuineness of some phenomena, but in general the observational conditions for physical mediumship have been quite poor. Ectoplasm, for instance, was conveniently asserted to be sensitive to light, necessitating a darkened room in order to avoid injury to the medium (or, more likely, the medium's reputation). The apparent levitation of the medium D. D. Home outside of an upper story window is one incident that is still argued to be genuine by some psychical researchers; however, this alleged levitation took place under very poor observational conditions, including total darkness (Jenkins, 1982).

MENTAL MEDIUMSHIP

In mental mediumship, messages are purportedly received from the dead through the agency of a medium. In some cases, these messages may be relayed through the process of automatic writing, whereby the medium's hand writes messages of which the medium claims no knowledge and for which she claims no responsibility. Occasionally, a device such as a Ouija board or planchette is used to facilitate the production of such unconsciously received messages. Alternatively, the medium may be "possessed" by the spirits of the dead, who then communicate directly through the vocal apparatus of the medium. Such possession is often produced by the medium's entering a trance state. More rarely, the voice of the postmortem personality is heard to emanate from a point in space unoccupied by any person. This form of mediumship is called "direct voice." One of the lesser-known projects of Thomas Edison was the development of an ideal megaphone or "trumpet" through which the dead could speak in this manner.

In trance mediumship, the medium is often possessed by a "control" spirit, who acts as "master of ceremonies" during the séance. Such control spirits may introduce new discarnate personalities, who then may displace the control in terms of possession of the medium's body. In many instances, the control is a childlike figure, such as Feda, the little Indian girl who served as the control for the medium Gladys Osborne Leonard. In some cases, such as that of Mrs. Leonora Piper's control Phinuit, who claimed to be a French physician serving royalty, the control spirit appears to be a totally fictional character. Most psychical researchers have come to view such control spirits as little more than secondary personalities of the mediums.

Sometimes information is provided by such ostensible deceased communicators which is accurate and which the medium would have no normal means of knowing. For a period of time the spirit of the deceased psychical researcher Richard Hodgson served as Mrs. Piper's control. As reported by William James (1910), on one occasion "Hodgson" reminded a sitter of an anecdote Hodgson had related via letter to the sitter before his death. The anecdote involved a starving couple who were praying for food. The couple's prayers were overheard by a passing atheist. The atheist dropped some bread down a chimney and heard the couple thanking God. When the atheist revealed himself as the couple's benefactor, the wife replied, "Well the Lord sent it even if the devil brought it."

During the sitting with Mrs. Piper, the Hodgson control asked, "Do you remember a story I told you and how you laughed about the man and woman praying?"

The sitter replied, "Oh and the devil was in it. Of course I do."

"Hodgson" then added, "Yes the devil, they told him it was the Lord who sent it even if the devil brought it…. About the food that was given them…. I want you to know who is speaking."

The provision of such seemingly accurate messages by alleged deceased communicators has rendered some psychical researchers more favorably disposed toward mental mediumship than they are toward physical mediumship. There are, however, ways in which a medium can gain information about deceased persons without directly communicating with the spirits of the dead. Some fraudulent mediums may conduct research on the lives of persons likely to consult them. The medium Arthur Ford, for instance, was discovered to have kept elaborate files on prospective sitters. Ray Hyman (1977) has described techniques whereby a medium or psychic can give a "cold reading" for a client he does not know by deliberately using vague statements, which are then progressively refined based on feedback from the client until an apparently accurate body of information has been communicated.

Mediumistic communications may also include information that is derived from obituary notices and other written records. Sometimes such information is apparently used unconsciously by a seemingly honest medium, through a process known as cryptomnesia. In a case of cryptomnesia, a person may read an obituary notice in a newspaper and then later "receive" this information from the apparent surviving spirit of the deceased while playing with a Ouija board. In such cases, the medium or Ouija board operator may have forgotten having ever seen the obituary notice, although this information has presumably been retained at an unconscious level and is being used subconsciously to construct the "communication" from the deceased. Ian Stevenson and John Beloff have described several cases in which all the information provided by a "drop in" communicator (a spirit who emerges uninvited during a séance) had previously been published in an obituary notice or other single written source (Stevenson, 1978; Stevenson & Beloff, 1980). In one case, Stevenson was able to demonstrate that the obituary notice was on the same page of the newspaper as the crossword puzzle that the Ouija board operator worked daily.

Another possibility, if one is willing to grant the existence of psi, is that mediums may be able to use their ESP faculties to gather information about the deceased from the minds of the sitters present or from other persons or written records scattered throughout the world. In its extreme form, this has become known as the "super-ESP" hypothesis. (Of course, if one extends this hypothesis to include direct retrocognitive telepathy with the previously existing mind of the deceased, the super-ESP hypothesis begins to merge with the survival hypothesis. If one grants that the minds of deceased persons can be accessed telepathically after their death, then those minds in at least some sense can be said to exist after death, inasmuch as their contents continue to be accessible through retrocognitive telepathy.)

In one amusing application of the super-ESP theory, the psychologist G. Stanley Hall constructed a biography for a fictional niece named Bessie Beals. He then received communications from Bessie Beals through the prominent medium Mrs. Piper that related some of the information in the fictional biography. It is surprising that Mrs. Piper could acquire this information through ESP but remain unaware of its fraudulent nature. In this context, it should be noted that E. E. McAdams and Raymond Bayless (1981) have argued that a real person named Bessie Beals may have existed.

Finally, recent evidence indicates that some séance records have been fraudulently altered. Melvin Harris (1986) has charged that the British researcher S .G. Soal, who is known to have altered some of the data in his experimental work in parapsychology, altered transcripts of at least one séance in which he participated. The case in question involved a communication from the supposedly deceased spirit of Gordon Davis, a friend of Soal's, who turned out to be very much alive at the time of the communication. The medium involved was Blanche Cooper. Through Cooper, "Davis" provided an accurate description of a house that the real Gordon Davis would move into well after the séance was held. Harris notes that Davis' future house was located near Soal's own residence. He charges that Soal may have looked in the window of the house to gain information as to its appearance, which he then inserted into the transcript of the prior séance. One of these details was that of a statue of a black bird sitting on Davis's piano. However, a duplicate copy of the séance in question, in Soal's own handwriting, had been sent to the Reverend A. T. Fryer, a fact that Soal had apparently forgotten when he altered his copy of the document. The duplicate transcript held by Fryer showed no references either to Davis or to a statue of a black bird. While obviously not proof of survival, the Gordon Davis case had stood for years as a prominent example of psi phenomena occurring in the context of mediumship.

There have been a few recent attempts to apply statistical tests to determine whether the accuracy of statements made by mental mediums exceeds that which would be expected by chance. Robertson and Roy (2004) report the results of eight experiments designed to eliminate cues such as body language of the part of sitters and expectancy effects. However, McCue (2004) has raised the point that Robertson and Roy's statistical analysis used the individual statement as the unit of analysis, whereas statements cannot be treated as independent events (such as statements that the target person has an injured leg and that he uses a cane or crutch). Also, Robertson and Roy's evidence could be interpreted as evidence of psi powers on the part of the medium rather than as evidence for a survival discarnate personality.

Several studies of mental mediumship have been recently conducted by Gary Schwartz and Linda Russek (which are summarized in Schwartz, 2002). Schwartz' experiments involved a medium (often a prominent medium such as Jon Edward) giving a reading for a sitter over the phone. The statements made by the medium are then compared to the answers supplied by a control group of college students. However, as both Wiseman and O'Keefe (2001) and Stokes (2002a) have pointed out, the medium and the students are in much different situations. Whereas the medium is free to throw out "Barnum" statements (statements which many people might agree with) such as "your father felt kindly toward poor people," the college students were given a much different task in which they had to answer the question of "who felt kindly toward poor people?" For instance, Wiseman and O'Keefe note that one such statement was "your son was good with his hands" which was affirmed by 82 percent of the subjects when posed as a "Barnum" statement, but only 36 percent of a control group "correctly" answered "the son" when posed with the question "who was good with his hands?" Also, the sitters rated the readings given for them against readings for other sitters. However, in most instances, the sitters heard portions of the reading given for them, so this rating was not conducted blindly.

In view of the fact that in many of Schwartz et al.'s experimental trials the sitter provided "yes/no" answers to questions and statements posed by the medium, the medium could use these answers to refine his of her statements, using the "cold reading" technique described by Hyman (1977). As pointed out by both Wiseman and O'Keefe (2001) and Stokes (2002a), other sensory cues were provided by the subject's breathing, movements, etc., in those trials in which the sitter was in the same room with the medium or in phone contact with the sitter with the latter's phone unmuted. Also, in most trials the experimenter interacting with the medium knew the sitter's identity and thus was in a position to provide inadvertent cues through body language and facial expressions.

Finally, the statistical calculations performed by Schwartz et al., in which they found astronomical odds against their mediums' doing as well as they did by chance, were inappropriate (see Stokes, 2002a, for more details).

Due to the counterexplanations of fraud, "cold reading" techniques, and the possible ability of mediums to gather information about deceased persons through psi, few parapsychologists today would be willing to conclude that the survival of death of the human personality has been demonstrated through the study of mediumship.

We now turn to the evidence for reincarnation, which constitutes perhaps the strongest form of parapsychological evidence for survival.

Reincarnation

There is a body of parapsychological evidence that suggests that a process of reincarnation may take place, in which a mind or soul may survive the death of the physical body and be reborn in a new physical body, with at least some elements of its former personality (e.g., memories, emotions, or possibly "karmic debt") intact. As noted in the Introduction and elsewhere, in view of the intimate dependence of the personalities and its memories on the physical state of the brain, there are good *a posteriori* reasons to be skeptical that such a process could take place. While it will be argued that the notion of reincarnation in the sense of continually recycling fields of consciousness makes sense and is even to a large extent compatible with the currently prevailing worldview of modern science, the notion that the personality, with its associated memories, emotions and beliefs could survive the dissolution of the physical brain (without being first down loaded into a computer, etc.) is fairly incompatible with the worldview of modern neuroscience.

However, some parapsychological researchers have amassed evidence that, at least in some instances, some human personalities, or portions thereof, have survived death and have been transferred to, or reborn in, new human bodies.

This evidence is roughly of three kinds. The first category of evidence consists of "readings" by psychics and other spiritual advisers, who are allegedly able to use their psychic abilities to gather information about the past lives or former incarnations of their clients. Perhaps the best known of such psychics was the psychic diagnostician Edgar Cayce, who frequently described the past lives of patients who consulted him for medical advice. Past lives as described by Cayce often involved such exotic locales as the lost continent of Atlantis and other planets. A second line of evidence arises from the technique of hypnotic age regression, in which a hypnotized subject is led backward in time to his or her childhood and then regressed even further backward in time to previous lives. Psychological and medical problems are often ascribed by past-life hypnotherapists to events that occurred in the patient's previous incarnations as revealed in such past-life hypnotic regression techniques. A third form of evidence for reincarnation consists of spontaneous reports by young children of memories relating to previous lives. In such cases, which occur primarily in cultures having a strong religious belief in reincarnation, the child typically claims to be the reincarnation of a person who had died within the past few years. The child may exhibit knowledge of that previous life which is difficult to explain on the basis of the child's experiences in his or her present life. The child may also manifest personality traits and behaviors consistent with those of the claimed former personality. These behaviors are sometimes at variance with the behavioral norms of the culture in which the child is being raised. There also may be birthmarks or other defects on the child's body that seem to be related to events in the claimed previous life (often the manner of death). As we shall see, this type of case provides the strongest evidence for reincarnation of any of the three categories of evidence discussed above.

PHILOSOPHICAL BACKGROUND

Many cultures around the world subscribe to a belief in reincarnation. A partial list of such cultures would include the ancient Egyptians, Hindus, Buddhists, Jains, large numbers of Druse and Shiite Moslems, and several shamanistic traditions, including those of the native tribes of northwestern North America, the Trobriand Islanders, Australian aborigines, and the Ainu of northern Japan. Many prominent thinkers in the Western tradition have also been reincarnationists, among them Pythagorus, Plato, Walt Whitman, Henry David Thoreau, Ralph Waldo Emerson, Henry Ford, Charles Lindbergh and Tom Cruise. The French philosopher Voltaire is responsible for the memorable quote "It is no more surprising to be born twice than it is to be born once."

Within the Judeo-Christian-Islamic tradition, a different view has held, namely that we live but one life. Some sects adhere to the doctrine that the bodies of everyone who ever lived will be physically resurrected on the Day of Judgment. Many sects within the Judeo-Christian-Islamic tradition hold that eternal damnation or salvation is dependent on acts committed within this one physical incarnation, a stern doctrine indeed.

It is interesting to note that the early Christian Gnostics, including such figures as Origen in the third century A.D., taught the doctrine of reincarnation. Reincarnationist beliefs within the Christian tradition were finally suppressed, however, by an ecumenical council held in 553 A.D. Despite the banning of reincarnation as heresy, many people within the Western culture continue to believe in reincarnation. A Gallup poll of American adults indicated that 21 percent believed in reincarnation, with another 22 percent indicating that they were "not sure" whether reincarnation occurs or not (Gallup & Newport, 1992). A similar result was obtained in a recent poll by Farha and Steward (2006), who found that 25 percent college students professed a belief in reincarnation.

It is perhaps not surprising that the belief in reincarnation is so widespread. The reincarnationist cycle of birth, death and rebirth bears many similarities to other naturally occurring cycles, such as the annual changes of the seasons, the daily cycle of light and darkness, and the chemical recycling of atoms in photosynthesis and respiration. Just as our bodies incorporate atoms that were once parts of the bodies of other people, so it might not be too surprising if our bodies also harbored souls (or Shins) that once resided in the bodies of other persons.

Another advantage of the reincarnation process is that it renders our present incarnate state less puzzling. Under the official Judeo-Christian-Islamic view, one lives but one human lifetime, which is but a flicker of an eyelash when compared to the 13.7 billion years or so that have elapsed since the creation of our current universe in the Big Bang as well as the eons that lie ahead before the universe's quiet end in a "heat death" (or, less probably in view of recent findings by astrophysicists, its eventual recollapse at the time of the "Big Crunch"). Because our lives are such infinitesimal spans when compared to the age of the universe, each conscious person must marvel at the fact that this present moment in time just happens to be one of the moments when he or she (construed as the conjunction of a physical body and personality, as in the Western religious tradition) exists. If a moment were to be chosen at random from the history of the universe, the probability that any person would exist at that time would be essentially zero. The fact that the moment that has somehow mysteriously been selected to be "now" is also a moment at which the reader is conscious must surely seem like a miracle if the single life hypothesis is true (and the Western construal of the self as consisting one's physical body and personality is appropriate). The fact that "now" happens to be a moment when you are conscious would become much less surprising under the hypothesis of reincarnation, as "now" would only have to correspond to any moment in a potentially endless succession of lives rather than a single life. If one were to allow the possibility of incarnation in nonhuman life forms, or even on other planets or in other universes, it becomes more and more probable that a particular person (construed as a center of consciousness, soul or Shin) would be conscious "now."

Several objections have been raised to the idea of reincarnation. One, which was raised by the third century Christian philosopher Tertullian and has been reiterated by the philosopher Paul Edwards, is based on the population explosion (Edwards, 1997; Tertullian, 1997). There are many more human beings alive today than have lived at any time in the past. Thus, it is claimed, there would not be enough souls to animate each new human body, as the number of bodies must surely outrun the number of reincarnating souls. This objection could easily be met by assuming that souls or Shins that were once housed in nonhuman beings could reincarnate in humans. (It might not be surprising that kids like dinosaurs so much if you assume they spent one hundred million years incarnated in their bodies.) If the terrestrial animal population is not large enough, it may be that souls can be drawn from other planets (assuming that interstellar travel would not constitute any great difficulty for a soul existing outside of physical spacetime) or even from other decaying universes. (One of the explanations for the anthropic principle, the fact that the laws and conditions of our universe seem to be very delicately balanced to support the existence of life, is that many universes are created and we of necessity exist in a universe capable of supporting life. The anthropic principle will be discussed in greater detail in Chapter 8.)

It is also conceivable that Shins or souls might spend considerable amounts of time not housed in biological bodies. As noted in Chapter 2, some physicists, such as Evan Harris Walker, have postulated the existence of "proto-consciousnesses" responsible for the collapse of quantum mechanical state vectors governing events that are remote in space and time from human (or other biological) observers (Walker, 2000). Hill (2005) has observed that, if the universe has been designed, it appears to be devised for creatures or consciousnesses that inhabit the vast, inhabitable regions of outer space. The design of such a vast cosmos for the mere purpose of entertaining a few randomly evolved, ephemeral sacks of protoplasm (such as ourselves) crawling about on a minor planet of a second rate star would be most uneconomical indeed. Perhaps proto-consciousnesses (or souls or Shins) are as common as electrons or quarks. If such is the case, then Edwards' population-based argument against reincarnation carries as much force as the argument that human bodies cannot be inhabited by electrons, insofar as due to population growth, the number of human bodies must surely outrun the number of available electrons. Indeed, later in this book, it will be argued that our essential selves are likely fields of pure consciousness akin to Walker's hypothesized "proto-consciousnesses" and that there may be a great many such selves (mini-Shins) inhabiting a single human brain at any given time. It is likely that these mini-Shins are, like electrons and other elementary particles, only temporarily associated with a particular brain and are being constantly recycled through a succession of biological and nonbiological host systems. Against this view, Edward's objection based on the growth of the human population carries no weight.

A second objection to reincarnation is that we have no memory of our previous lives. Actually, that may not always be the case. Much of the parapsychological evidence for reincarnation, to be discussed below, consists of instances in which persons have in fact claimed to remember details of their previous lives. Reincarnation could of course occur without any transfer of memory from one incarnation to another. As discussed elsewhere in this book, a considerable body of evidence exists that memories are either physically stored in the brain or at least intimately dependent on certain brain structures. It would be difficult therefore to imagine that memories could in general survive the dissolution of the physical brain at death. In fact, we do not remember the events of many previous days of our lives, although we did in fact live through them. Our system of memories changes over time, with some memories decaying and new ones being formed. Our essential selves, on the other hand, seem to remain unchanged over time. We are not identical with any particular set of memories. Thus, it would be easily conceivable that one's self could be reincarnated in a new body, while retaining no memory of one's previous life. Several writers, including Ken Wilber (1990) and the author (Stokes, 1982, 1987, 2002b), have in fact suggested that reincarnation might occur in just such a memory-less manner.

The parapsychologist D. F. Lawden (1989) has suggested that minds or consciousnesses experience the passage of time only when incarnated in a physical body. After death, Lawden proposes, the mind would exist in a timeless, mystical state of identification with the entire spacetime continuum. This mystical state of union with the cosmos as a whole is unstable according to Lawden, and so the mind's attention once again contracts to a single stream of consciousness and one is reborn into a new physical body. In Lawden's view, the order among successive rebirths may not correspond to their order in physical time due to the timeless nature of the state between incarnations. Thus, one's "next life" may be in the Middle Ages, or one might be born again in the twentieth century and encounter one's present self as a friend. If one were to extend Lawden's theory to encompass the alternate universes inherent in Hugh Everett's "many worlds" interpretation of quantum mechanics, one could even imagine being reborn as one's present self, but eventually experiencing a different life history as one travels up a different branch of the tree of possible futures!

A somewhat similar view has been proposed by Carroll Nash (1995). Nash postulates the existence of a postmortem condition in which one's mind exists in a timeless state and is capable of seeing all the events of one's life (one's "worldline") at once. He proposes that this experience may form the basis of the "life reviews" frequently reported by persons undergoing near-death experiences. He further suggests that one might become bored with one's own worldline and thus might be drawn to experience other worldlines as well. In Nash's opinion, this common sharing of pain and pleasures would resolve some of the inequities of our earthly lives and would unify all minds in a single consciousness.

Writing in *The Skeptical Inquirer*, a journal notably skeptical of the claims of parapsychology in general and of reincarnation in particular, Greta Christina (2005) proposes that each human being achieves a kind of immortality insofar as the worldline that comprises a human life enjoys a timeless status in the spacetime of general relativity. As will be recalled from Chapters 2 and 5, the theory of relativity denies the existence of a unique present moment and the concept of time flow. Thus, the continued existence of one's worldline in spacetime, when viewed from a "timeless" perspective, confers an immortality of sorts on all human beings. Christina's observations bear a certain similarity to Nash's theory, but omit Nash's proposal that one may experience one's own worldline repeatedly (as in the philosopher Friedrich Nietzsche's doctrine of the "eternal return") or experience the world lines of other creatures (much like a visitor to a four-dimensional art gallery).

Both Lawden's and Nash's hypotheses are of course purely speculative. Lawden explicitly notes the similarity of some of his views to those of the Hindu-Buddhist tradition. In the Indian Vedic tradition, God or Brahman (the one Self of the universe) becomes bored with his solitary existence and splits himself into all the creatures of the earth. The Hindu tradition has it that one's progression from incarnation to incarnation depends on one's level of moral development. Persons of high spiritual development are rewarded by being reborn into more favorable conditions, while miscreants may be punished for their misdeeds in the circumstances of their next lives through a process known as karma. According to Hindu philosophy, the goal of spiritual development is to realize the identity between one's individual self (atman) and the universal Self of the cosmos (Brahman). In Buddhism, the goal of spiritual development is to reduce one's own suffering (and that of others) through the extinction of the cravings and desires that give rise to suffering (to the extent that they are invariably unfulfilled). The final aim is to achieve a state of total extinction of desire known as nirvana. Nirvana is essentially a state of extinction of the self. Despite Buddhists' belief in reincarnation, the Buddhist doctrine of *anatta* is essentially a denial of the existence of a permanent self. Ken Wilber (1990) notes that while Buddhism denies a permanent existence to the individual soul or self, it does grant a "relative existence" to the soul. Indeed, the doctrine of *anatta* seems directed primarily against the idea that personality patterns and traits have a permanent existence. Thus, seekers of enlightenment should not cling to their present mental states. Rather, each such seeker should see himself or herself as pure consciousness and awareness, something separate from the personality traits, memories, feelings and sensations that may form the source or objects of desire or clinging, preventing one from reaching a state of enlightenment. The similarities between Eastern views regarding the extinction of self and union with a World Soul and Lawden's and Nash's views discussed above should be apparent (indeed, Lawden explicitly comments on these similarities).

An interesting element of Hindu and Buddhist doctrine is the concept of the *kalpa*, the great cycle beginning with the creation of the world through the splitting of Brahman and ending with the annihilation of the world (which is then created anew). One *kalpa* is thought to last 4.3 billion years, which is extraordinarily close to the 13.7 billion years modern physicists believe have elapsed since the creation of the universe in the Big Bang.

The parapsychological evidence is equivocal regarding the existence of the Hindu and Buddhist principle of karma, wherein one is rewarded or punished for the deeds of one's past lives in the circumstances of one's present life. As will be seen, the evidence from psychic readings and hypnotic regression suggests the existence of such a principle, but these cases do not provide the strongest evidence for reincarnation. The more compelling evidence from the spontaneous recall of past life memories does not in general suggest the existence of any moral karmic principle governing the assignment of incarnations.

PARAPSYCHOLOGICAL EVIDENCE FOR REINCARNATION

Psychic Readings. One form of evidence for reincarnation consists of instances in which a professional psychic describes details of the alleged past lives of a client who has consulted the psychic for spiritual or medical advice. If the psychic has displayed evidence of paranormal ability by accurately describing details of the client's life that the psychic had no apparent normal means of knowing, then the client and other observers may be inclined to accept the psychic's description of the client's past lives as accurate knowledge obtained through the same extrasensory abilities the psychic employed in describing the more mundane (yet at the same time more verifiable) details of the client's present life.

By far the most famous collection of such past life readings was provided by the psychic diagnostician Edgar Cayce, who has been discussed earlier in connection with psychic healing. Cayce, it will be recalled, was allegedly able to enter a trance and diagnose people's illnesses, given only their names and addresses. What is of interest in the present context is that Cayce frequently traced the cause of the illness to events occurring in a previous life of the patient. Often the illness seemed to be a means of paying a karmic debt. After entering his trance, Cayce would describe consulting the "akashic records," in which the details of everyone's past lives are recorded. Cayce was initially surprised at the Hinduistic nature of his readings, which indicated the operation of a karmic principle governing reincarnation that was quite at variance with Cayce's own fundamentalist Christian upbringing. Cayce's past life readings have been popularized in many books (e.g., Cermina, 1967; Stearn, 1967; Woodward, 1971), and form the basis for many people's belief in reincarnation.

The following is a typical Cayce reading. This particular reading was given for a client who was suffering from a bone cancer in her hip. Cayce traces this condition to the client's having laughed at the suffering of the Christian gladiators in a past life during Nero's reign in Rome. In reading the text of Cayce's remarks, the reader should bear in mind that Cayce typically used the phrase "the entity" in referring to the client, or more precisely, the client's soul. The reading is as follows:

> During the period in Nero's reign in Rome, in the latter portion of the same, the entity was then in the household of Parthesias—and one in whose company many became followers of, adherents to, those called Christians in the period, and during those persecutions in the arena when there were physical combats. The entity was as a spectator of such combats, and under the influence of those who made light of them; though the entity felt in self that there was more to that held by such individuals, as exhibited in the arena, but the entity—to carry that which was held as necessary with the companionship of those about the same— laughed at the injury received by one of the girls in the arena, and suffered in mental anguish when she later—or became cognizant of—the physical suffering brought to the body of that individual during the rest of the sojourn [Woodward, 1971, p. 61].

As the reader can gauge from the above passage, Cayce's readings are not primarily remembered for the literary value of their prose. The main shortcoming of Cayce's readings, and of psychics' past-life readings in general, as evidence for reincarnation is that there has typically been little or no attempt to verify that the persons who formed the described past incarnations ever existed. Such attempts as have been made have been largely futile due to the extreme scarcity of records pertaining to the lives of most people who lived even as recently as one century ago. Thus, there is little reason to believe that such readings represent anything more than the psychic's fantasies. In the case of Cayce, this is doubly true insofar as Cayce frequently described past lives on the lost continent of Atlantis, the existence of which would contradict a vast body of geophysical evidence, as well as on such planets as Mercury and Jupiter, which are not likely to support life. At least some of what Cayce said about past lives has to be erroneous; possibly all of it is.

Hypnotic age regression. A great deal of interest in reincarnation was stirred up in the 1950s with the publication of the "Bridey Murphy" case by Morey Bernstein, a businessman and amateur hypnotist (Bernstein, 1956). Bernstein's subject was a Colorado housewife named Virginia Tighe. Bernstein used the technique of hypnotic age regression to take Tighe back to the time of her early childhood. Then he suggested that she could go even further back in time, beyond her birth, where she would find herself in "some other scene, in some other place, [and] in some other time." At this point Tighe began to describe another life as Bridget (Bridey) Murphy, an Irish girl living in Cork and Belfast during the early part of the nineteenth century. While in the Bridey Murphy persona, Tighe used several Irish expressions, such as "lough" to refer to a lake, "linen" to refer to a handkerchief and "flat" to refer to a platter. At one point, she even danced an Irish jig. She also correctly named two Belfast grocery stores and accurately stated that a big rope company and a tobacco house were operating in Belfast at the time in question.

The details of her life as Bridey Murphy were not verifiable due to the scarcity of records. Two of her statements were challenged. She had stated that Bridey's husband,

Brian McCarthy, had taught law at Queen's University in Belfast. *Life* magazine charged that there was no such institution, but the existence of Queen's University was later proven. "Bridey" also asserted that she had a metal bed. *Life* charged that such beds were not introduced until at least 1850, but the psychical researcher Eric Dingwall was able to locate an advertisement for metal beds in Bridey's home town of Cork in 1830, and the philosopher C. J. Ducasse was able to show that iron beds existed even in the eighteenth century (Ducasse, 1961).

A more devastating criticism was delivered by the *Chicago American*. That newspaper asserted that a woman named Bridey Murphy Corkell had lived across the street from Virginia Tighe when she was a little girl and suggested that an unconscious memory of this woman formed the underpinnings of Tighe's construction of the Bridey Murphy persona under hypnosis. Curiously, Mrs. Corkell was the mother of the editor of the Sunday edition of the *Chicago American*. There proved to be some difficulty in verifying that her maiden name was Murphy, so this detail may be questionable. In any event, the Bridey Murphy case, despite its powerful role in creating a reincarnation "flap," is surprisingly weak in terms of detailed statements made by Tighe that were subsequently verified. This weakness will prove to be a characteristic of the hypnotic regression evidence in general, as we shall see.

Hypnotic regression to past lives has become a growth industry at least in certain facets of American culture. Several versions of "past lives therapy" have flourished, in which it is claimed that patients' medical and psychological problems can be alleviated when the patients discharge pent-up emotions by reexperiencing traumatic events they suffered through in their prior incarnations (see Goldberg, 1982; Wambaugh, 1978; and Weiss, 1988, for instance). Many other people have undergone hypnotic regression to past lives outside of any therapeutic context.

The main problem with the body of evidence that has emerged from hypnotic regression is that there has generally been little or no attempt on the part of the investigators involved in these cases to verify any of the details contained in these descriptions of past lives. Usually, there is not even an attempt to ascertain that the person described as a former incarnation of the subject actually existed! Thus, for the bulk of these cases, there is no compelling reason to regard these descriptions of past lives as anything other than the product of the subjects' imaginations.

In a few rare cases, some details contained in past life descriptions obtained through hypnotic regression have been verified. Linda Tazari (1990), for instance, reports a case in which a woman recounted a life in Spain during the sixteenth century. The woman provided the names of several members of the Inquisition and their victims. She also accurately described buildings used by the Inquisitors and gave the correct dates of publication of several documents. Several obscure English documents and Spanish language sources had to be consulted in order to verify this information, so it is unlikely that the subject would have had easy access to this information.

In most such cases, however, it is difficult to rule out the possibility that the subject could have acquired the information given in a past-life description through normal channels. In fact, in several instances, it has been shown that all the details provided in a past-life description were contained in a single written source, which makes it appear plausible that the subject's knowledge of these details could be explained by the phenomenon of cryptomnesia, or unconscious memory of reading the source in question. Melvin Harris

(1986) describes two such cases. In the first, a woman described a previous life in Britain during the third century. Every detail in her description was found to be contained in Louis de Wohl's novel *The Living Wood*. In the second case, hypnosis was used to regress the subject back to the times when she first learned of the details given in her past life descriptions. Under hypnosis, she was in fact able to recall reading the books that provided the material from which she constructed her past life accounts. Jonathan Venn (1986) cites a case in which a hypnotically regressed subject gave the date of a witchcraft trial as 1556, whereas the real date was 1566. The erroneous date had appeared in several books, one of which may have been the source of the subject's material. Venn also provides a statistical analysis of a single case, in which he found that statements that related to commonly available records were more likely to be true than those that related to less accessible records.

Also, memories of past lives recovered through hypnotic regression bear a striking similarity to false memories of sexual abuse created through leading questions (and sometimes hypnosis) on the part of interviewer and therapists. The veracity of such "recovered memories" has been strongly questioned by memory researchers such as Elizabeth Loftus (1995).

For all these reasons, hypnotic regression cases provide less than compelling evidence for reincarnation.

Spontaneous recall. The strongest evidence for reincarnation is provided, at least at the present time, by cases in which young children spontaneously report memories of previous lives. The most prolific investigator of such cases has been Ian Stevenson, a professor of psychiatry at the University of Virginia, who, together with his coworkers and intellectual descendants, have generated a prodigious number of publications on the subject (Akolkar, 1992; Cook, Pasricha, Samararatne, Maung & Stevenson, 1983; Haraldsson, 2000a, 2000b; Haraldsson & Abu-Izzedin, 2002; Keil, 1991, 2005; Mills, 1989, 2004; Mills, Haraldsson & Keil, 1994; Pasricha, 1978, 1992a, 1992b, 1998; Pasricha & Barker, 1981; Pasricha, Keil, Tucker & Stevenson, 2005; Pasricha & Stevenson, 1979; Stevenson, 1960a, 1960b, 1966, 1970a, 1972, 1973, 1974a, 1974b, 1974c, 1975, 1977a, 1977b, 1977c, 1980, 1983a, 1983, 1986, 1987, 1988a, 1988b, 1989, 1990, 1992, 1993, 1997a, 1997b, 2003; Stevenson & Chadha, 1988; Stevenson & Keil, 2000; Stevenson & Pasricha, 1979, 1980; Stevenson, Pasricha & Samararatne, 1988).

To give an example of a case involving the spontaneous recall of a past life, Haraldsson and Abu-Izzeddin (2002) report the case of Nazih Al-Danaf, a boy living in Baalchmay, Lebanon. At the age of one and a half years, Nazih began to speak about a former life of a man who was fatally shot by a group of armed people in Beirut. Nazih's family were Druze Muslims, a secretive sect that affirms the doctrine of reincarnation. Nazih's older sister had also spoken of a previous life.

Nazih was born in 1992 and was eight years old when he was first interviewed by Haraldsson and Abu-Izzedin. His initial statements about a previous life included a denial that he was a child ("I am not small, I am big"), and that he carried two pistols as well as hand grenades. According to his sister Sabrine, he stated that his first name was Fuad prior to the identification of the family in the ostensible previous life. Although Nazih's mother initially confirmed Sabrine's statement, she later thought that perhaps Nazih had not uttered the name "Fuad" until after Nazih's present and "previous" families met.

Nazih told his mother that: "My wife is prettier than you. Her eyes and mouth are more beautiful." This statement may have been the first that made her think that Nazih was speaking of a past life. Nazih made similar statements to most of his six sisters.

Nazih stated that he had a friend who was mute and had only one hand. He said that this friend could hold a gun in one hand and work it, getting it ready for firing. He described how he had been killed in a shootout in which he was able to kill one of his armed opponents.

Nahiz also manifested behaviors more typical for an adult than a child, such as requesting cigarettes and whiskey, particularly during the period in which he spoke most about his previous life.

By the age of eight, Nazih had stopped talking about this previous life and his memories of this life seem to have faded. This is a common feature of cases involving the spontaneous recall of previous lives.

Beginning at the age of two and a half, Nazih began insisting that his parents take him to village in which he lived in his prior life. When Nazih was six years old, his father and mother agreed to drive him to this village, following his directions. Nazih led them to a village named Qaberchamoun, about 17 kilometers from their home village of Baalchmay. Nazih's father stated that Nazih had mentioned the name Qaberchamoun prior to this trip, although his mother and siblings do not remember him making such a statement.

After leading his family to a particular neighborhood in Qaberchamoun, Nazih got out the car and he and his father began asking people if anyone knew of a neighbor who had been recently martyred. They learned of one person who had died in a bomb blast, but this did not seem to fit with Nazih's memories of being shot. However, Nazih's mother and sisters met a man named Kamal Khaddage at the house next to where they had parked the car. He stated that Nazih's memories seemed to correspond to events in the life of his father, Fuad Khaddage. At this point, Kamal's mother was summoned, and Nazih indicated that she was his wife in the previous life.

The Khaddages then interrogated Nazih regarding events in the life of Fuad Khaddage. When asked who had built a particular gate to the house, Nazih correctly replied: "A man from the Faraj family." He stated correctly that he kept his pistol and other weapons in a particular cupboard in the house. Kamal's mother (Najdijay Khaddage) then asked Nazih if she had had any accident when they were living at the house in Ainab. (The Khaddages were living in Ainab while the present house was under construction. That house was not fully completed at the time of Fuad's death.) Nazih correctly stated that she had skidded on plastic nylon and fallen while picking pinecones and had dislocated her shoulder. When asked about an illness experienced by Fuad's young daughter Fairuz, Nazih correctly stated that she eaten Fuad's medication pills and had become poisoned. Nazih also recollected an incident in which their car had stalled and was started up again by Israeli soldiers, who recharged the battery.

Nazih also recalled a night in which (as Fuad) he had come home drunk and found that Najdijay had locked the door and was forced to sleep outside on a rocking sofa. He also stated that there had been a barrel in the garden that he used as a target when teaching Najdijay how to shoot. When asked to find the barrel in questions he went to garden and pointed to it.

In a later visit to the house of Fuad's younger brother Sheik Addeb, he correctly recalled giving a handgun as a gift to his younger brother. When asked the brand, Nazih correctly replied that it was a Checki 16. When presented with another handgun and asked if it was the one, Nazih correctly denied that it was. This incident convinced Sheik Addeb that Nazih was truly Fuad reincarnated, as no one else would have known about this gift (except possibly for Addeb's wife). When asked where Fuad's original house was (where he first lived with his wife), Nazih walked down the street and correctly pointed to that house as well as the house of Fuad's father. Nazih also correctly stated that (as Fuad) he had built a wooden ladder that was still standing in the house. Nazih also correctly identified his first wife and several family member in photographs.

Haraldsson and Abu-Izzedin (2002) present a table listing 23 statements that Nazih made prior to the initial meeting between the two families at Qaberchamoun as confirmed by witnesses. Of these 17 were correct, including the fact that Fuad had a mute friend and that there was a cave near his former house. Haraldsson and Abu-Izzedin present this as evidence that Nazih made several correct statements about the life of Fuad Khaddage that were not the result of leading questions, physical cues and other sources of information provided by the Khaddage family and their physical surroundings.

One of the weaknesses of the above case, as pointed out by one of its investigators, David Barker, is that no written records of Nazih's statements were made prior to his visit to Qaberchamoun, and that therefore one has to rely on the memory of various witnesses as to what Nazih actually said. Mills (2004) reports that 1.3 percent of the cases on record in 2004 involved written records of the child's statement prior to the case being "solved" (i.e., the former personality identified).

FEATURES OF REINCARNATION CASE REPORTS

Birthmarks. Stevenson (1993) notes that in 35 percent of his reincarnation cases, the child is born with a birthmark or birth defect that seems significantly related to events in the life of the claimed previous personality, with similar percentages reported by other investigators (Keil, 2005; Pasricha, 1998). Frequently such birthmarks correspond to wounds incurred at the time of a violent death. In one such case, the subject was born with a long birthmark around his neck that seemed to correspond to the wounds received by the person whose life the subject claimed to remember; that person had died of a slit throat (Stevenson, 1974c). Pasricha, Keil, Tucker and Stevenson (2005) report a case in which a child was born with a large nevus (wrinkled skin of unusual roughness) in his scalp. This child claimed to be a man who was murdered by an axe blow to the head in a previous life. Finally, Haraldsson (2000a) reports a case in which a child who had made several accurate statements about a previous personality had a large birthmark on her abdomen that seemed to correspond to marks made by the tires of the bus that had run over the previous personality abdomen, killing him.

Stevenson (1988a, 1989, 1992, 1997a, 1997b) suggests that such birth defects may be psychologically induced. He presents evidence that some birthmarks and birth defects may be caused by maternal fright or otherwise generated by maternal sensory impressions. In several anecdotal reports, a woman who had seen an injury or a deformity later gave birth to a child with a similar mark or deformity. Stevenson also cites a case in which in which a man murdered another man and then cut off his limbs with a sword. The victim's mother cursed the murderer's wife. Her child was subsequently born without arms and with deformities of the feet. Based on this evidence, Stevenson suggests that birthmarks and birth defects may be psychically induced. Stevenson (1997a) notes that birthmarks found in reincarnation cases often differ from run-of-the-mill birthmarks in that they consist of hairless, puckered tissue, are often raised or depressed, and that some are oozing or bleeding at the time that the baby is born.

Announcing dreams. Another feature of reincarnation cases is the announcing dream, in which a pregnant woman may dream of a deceased relative or acquaintance who informs her of his intention to be reborn as her child. Of the twenty-four cases that Stevenson (1977c) investigated among the Haida Indians of British Columbia, fourteen were characterized by announcing dreams. In one of Stevenson's Haida cases, a tribal elder had said that he wished to be born with only one hand so that he could avoid manual labor. After his death, his grandchild was born without a hand on his right arm.

Unusual interests and skills. Many of Stevenson's subjects displayed skills and interests that seem to represent a continuation of skills and interests developed in the claimed previous life. Nazih Al-Danaf's interest in guns is an example of this phenomenon. Also, many subjects display phobias that seem related to their past life memories. One of Stevenson's cases involved a boy who recalled a past life in which he had been killed when a van crashed into the abutment of a bridge. The child displayed a fear of that particular bridge and of automobiles in general (Stevenson, 1990). Stevenson notes that such phobias, which occur in about one third of his cases (Cook et al., 1983), seem in most instances to relate to the manner of death of the previous personality. He has even gone so far as to contend that unusual phobias, talents, and interests in general (including transsexualism) may have their roots in past life experiences, whether they are remembered or not.

Cases in which a person manifests a skill that he or she had no opportunity to acquire in the present life provides further evidence for reincarnation. The same holds true for mediumship. If a medium with no apparent mathematical skills is possessed by the spirit of a deceased mathematician and is able to solve randomly chosen partial differential equations, this would constitute a strong case for survival, as it is unlikely that a medium could acquire such a complex skill through telepathy. However, Braude (2002) has noted that prodigies and savants often manifest complex skills, such as piano-playing and mathematical calculations that that seem inexplicable on the part of the prodigy's training and prior experience. In view of this fact, Braude suggests that it is premature to assume that such a manifestation of a complex skill must have been acquired in a different lifetime or through the exercise of some "superpsi" ability capable of acquiring complex skills from other living persons.

Xenoglossy. In a handful of cases, a medium or person remembering a past life has been able to speak in a language that he or she had no opportunity to learn normally, a phenomenon known as xenoglossy. The principal investigator of the phenomenon of xenoglossy has been Ian Stevenson (Stevenson, 1974d, 1976, 1984; Stevenson & Pasricha, 1979, 1980). In one of Stevenson's cases, a woman who had been hypnotically regressed to a previous life spoke in German, a language that she did not know in her normal waking state (Stevenson, 1976). Some skepticism was expressed by German-speaking observers as to whether the subject really understood what she was saying in this case. D. Scott Rogo (1987) also contended that this subject attempted on at least one occasion to fake knowledge of German by consulting a dictionary. In any event, Rogo asserts, her knowledge of German was rudimentary and she was unable to keep track of long speeches and complex phrases.

Another case, investigated by Stevenson and Pasricha (1980), is quite unusual in that it resembles a case of possession more than a typical reincarnation case. In this case, an Indian woman first spoke of memories of a previous life when she was in her thirties. Her body was apparently completely taken over by the personality of the previous incarnation. Her primary personality had amnesia for events occurring when the previous personality was in control of the body, and the previous personality had amnesia for events occurring when the primary personality was in control of the body, although this mutual amnesia was not entirely complete. When the previous personality was manifesting, the subject spoke Bengali, a language Stevenson and Pasricha claim she had no opportunity to learn. Six native speakers verified that she was fluent in Bengali while in the previous personality state. In an independent investigation of the case, V. V. Akolkar (1992) was able to determine that this subject did in fact have some training in Bengali, which of course diminishes the evidence for xenoglossy considerably.

Sarah Thomason (1987) has argued that two of Stevenson's cases fail to provide evidence for true responsive xenoglossy (in which a subject can hold a two-way conversation in the language) as opposed to recitative xenoglossy (in which the subject may simply recite a phrase or word he may have previously memorized or may simply parrot back words presented to him by the questioner). Thomason claims that Stevenson's subjects show an extremely limited vocabulary, that they provide only short answers, which often consist of mere repetition of phrases, when questions are posed to them, and that they make simple mistakes that are probably due to the fact that the subject understands only one or two words in a sentence.

A new case of xenoglossy has been presented by Barrington, Mulacz and Rivas (2005), with a minor correction published in Barrington (2005). In this case, in 1933 a fifteen-year-old Hungarian girl, Iris Farczady, who had dabbled in mediumship, underwent a complete personality change, claiming to be Lucinda, a 41-year-old Spanish woman who had died earlier that year. After the transformation, "Lucinda" spoke only in Spanish, a language that Barrington, Mulacz and Rivas claim Iris had never learned nor had to opportunity to acquire. Still in control in at age 86 in 1998 (the time of Barrington et al.'s investigation), Lucinda has remained in existence and considers Iris to be another person, who ceased to exist in 1933.

In general, the evidence for xenoglossy is quite fragmentary. Xenoglossy cases are extremely rare, and only four cases have received thorough investigation, three of them by Stevenson. At least two of Stevenson's cases are extremely weak, and in any event it would seem to be an impossible task to demonstrate conclusively that an adult subject never had enough exposure to a given foreign language to enable him or her to produce a few simple phrases (or demonstrate increasing fluency over 70 years of practice in the case of Iris Farczady).

Prevalence of violent deaths. In an extraordinarily large number of cases involving the spontaneous recall of past lives, the previous life ended in a violent death. Such deaths occur in well over half of Stevenson's cases (Stevenson, 1987). James Matlock (1990) observes that this represents a substantial elevation over the rate of violent deaths in the general population, which stands at five percent. Stevenson observes that the details of a violent death are frequently the most prominent memories in such cases. In instances of homicide, the murderer's name is frequently recalled, and occasionally events that the previous personality would have no way of knowing are nevertheless recalled (such as the process whereby an object came to fall on one's head, resulting in death). Stevenson further notes that even cases in which the death of the previous personality was nonviolent frequently involve sudden death or unfinished business (such as when a mother of young children dies or when the subject reports dying as a child in the previous life). Stevenson believes that such unfinished business can result in past life memories being more likely to emerge in the next incarnation and can also lead to a shorter time interval before reincarnation than might otherwise be the case. In fact, he presents evidence that cases involving a violent death involve a shorter time interval before rebirth than cases involving a nonviolent death (Stevenson & Chadha, 1988). The average time interval between lives is, incidentally, only 15 months in Stevenson's cases.

Stevenson offers a few speculations regarding the process of reincarnation based on his research (Stevenson, 1987). He suggests that between lives the personality exists as a discarnate trace called a "psychophore." The psychophore retains images relating to the previous life. These images are then capable of being described once the child whose body becomes associated with the psychophore develops the ability to speak. Stevenson further notes that his cases provide little support for the hypothesis that a moral principle of karma guides the reincarnation process.

CRITICISMS OF REPORTED EVIDENCE

Critics have attacked the evidence for reincarnation based on spontaneous recall on several fronts. First and foremost among these criticisms is the possibility that the child may have acquired the information about the previous life through normal means and consciously or unconsciously used this information to construct a past-life fantasy or hoax. Certainly, in cases in which the recalled past life is that of a deceased member of the subject's family, the possibility for sensory transmission of information is enormous. In other cases, the subject's present family may have had contact with or knowledge of the family of his claimed former incarnation. In fact, in only about one-quarter of such cases are the two families unknown to each other (Stevenson, 1986; Cook, 1986).

The high proportion of cases involving violent death in Stevenson's collection raises the suspicion that the death of the prior personality may have received much formal and informal publicity, rendering it even more likely that the subject could have been exposed to information relating to the death through normal channels.

Keil (2005) reports that the median distance between the subject and the residence of the claimed prior personality in a sample of 1200 coded cases from Stevenson's collection is only 14 kilometers and only a handful of cases involve distances of more than 500 kilometers. This close proximity would be consistent with the sensory leakage theory. On the other hand, it could be interpreted as evidence that "souls" or "psychophores" may be somehow confined in spacetime or constrained by spacetime in such a way as to not travel great distances between incarnations. A third hypothesis would be that being born in close proximity to one's home in the former life provides cues that trigger memories of a past life, cues that may not be available if one is reborn in a remote location.

For a parapsychologist willing to admit the existence of psi, ESP constitutes another channel whereby the subject may have acquired information relating to the claimed past life. In such a scenario, the subject would then use the information consciously or unconsciously to impersonate the prior personality or to construct a past life fantasy (which a confused subject might actually believe). Stevenson counters this charge by noting that his subjects evidence no extraordinary extrasensory abilities apart from the reincarnation memories themselves. He also points to the behavioral and emotional components of such cases (such as the manifestation of skills or phobias relating to a past life), which he claims are not so easily explainable on the basis of ESP (Stevenson, 1987). In this context, it is interesting to note that in one of three cases extensively investigated by Antonia Mills (1989), the subject did in fact display extrasensory awareness (including precognitive awareness) of events happening to the family of the previous personality after the case had developed.

Another possibility is that reincarnation cases may be consciously perpetrated hoaxes. Stevenson himself has detected several such cases (Stevenson, Pasricha & Samararatne, 1988). Ian Wilson (1987, 1988) has argued that a disproportionately large number of Stevenson's cases consist of poor children remembering wealthy lives. He contends that these cases may represent a scheme to bilk money from the family of the claimed former incarnation. In fact, however, the evidence does not indicate any great tendency for subjects to recall past lives under better conditions than their present one (Matlock, 1990; Mills, 1989; Pasricha, 1978).

One weakness of most reincarnation cases is that no written record is made of the child's statements regarding his alleged past life prior to the attempted verification of those statements. This allows the possibility that the child and his family may mingle their memories of what the child said with what they have subsequently learned about the previous personality through meeting and interviewing the family, consulting records, and so forth. Stevenson has introduced the term "paramnesia" to describe such memory distortion, and he himself thinks that the easiest way to attack his research would be on the basis of the unreliability of witnesses' memories (Stevenson, 1977b, 1987). In fact, in only about 1.3 percent of Stevenson's cases were written records made of the child's statements prior to attempts to verify them (Keil, 2005). On the other hand, some of these cases, such as the case of Bishen Chand (Stevenson, 1972), are fairly impressive in terms of the number of accurate details contained in the child's statements. Keil (2005) notes that there are on average 25.5 documented statements made by the child claimant in cases with a written record of the child's statements (with 76.7 percent of these statements verified as accurate descriptions of the life and circumstances of the claimed former incarnation). There are an average of 18.5 statements in cases without written records, with 78.4 percent of the statements corroborated. Keil takes these results as evidence against the "social contamination" hypothesis. Also, an examination of the evidence by Stevenson and Keil (2000) found that the child claimants provided fewer details regarding their claimed past lives when there were delays in investigating the case. Stevenson and Keil take this as evidence against the hypothesis that the stories are being embellished over time; rather, details are being forgotten and lost. Of course, it may be possible that investigators are quicker to respond to cases in which the child has provided a lot of detailed information about the past life rather than just a few vague statements.

One concern regarding Stevenson's reincarnation cases is that such cases may be manufactured as a result of parental or cultural encouragement. Certainly, the vast majority of Stevenson's cases arise in cultures that already subscribe to a belief in reincarnation, such as the Hindu population of India, Druse Moslems, or the Tlinget Indians of Alaska. Also, the features of such cases may vary across cultures. For instance, announcing dreams and rebirth within the same family are far more common among the Native American tribes of the Northwest than among the Hindus of India (Stevenson, 1987, 1990). Stevenson suggests that nascent cases may be suppressed in cultures hostile to reincarnation (Stevenson, 1974b). He further notes that such cultures provide no cognitive framework in which such memories could be made intelligible.

PREVALENCE OF CASES

Reincarnation cases are not as rare as one might expect. As of 1990, Ian Stevenson's collection included approximately 2,500 such cases. In a systematic survey of Northern India, Barker and Pasricha (1979) found an incidence rate of nineteen reincarnation cases per thousand inhabitants. In a mail survey of the population of the greater Charlottesville area, Palmer (1979) found that somewhere between eight and nine percent of the respondents claimed to have memories of a past life, although Palmer did not attempt to verify the details of these memories.

POSSESSION AND OBSESSION

Closely related to reincarnation cases are cases in which a person's normal personality is apparently temporarily or (much more rarely) permanently displaced by the personality of a deceased human being (or other entity). This phenomenon is known as possession. A milder form of this syndrome occurs when a person merely seems to be under the influence or partial control of a discarnate personality, without the person's primary personality being displaced. Such cases are commonly termed instances of "obsession."

Several of Ian Stevenson's reincarnation cases might be better interpreted as cases of possession, including the xenoglossy case discussed above. Stevenson's collection also contains several cases in which a child's normal personality seemed to be supplanted by the personality of a deceased person well after the child's birth. In fact, Stevenson himself has suggested that cases of this type might be better explained in terms of possession rather than reincarnation (Stevenson, 1987, p. 124).

CONCLUSIONS

The strongest evidence for reincarnation or possession are Ian Stevenson's reincarnation cases. Even those cases have their shortcomings. As noted elsewhere in this book, given the findings of modern neuroscience, which has convincingly established that mental activity is at least intimately dependent on, if not identical with, brain activity, it is extremely unlikely that you could leave your physical brain behind and still retain all the memories, thoughts and feelings that have plagued you through this life. Reincarnation need not involve memory. As the ancient Greeks thought, we may drink of the river of Lethe and remember no more. Like the elementary particles that compose our physical body, our souls or selves (construed as centers of pure consciousness) may be constantly recycled through a succession of living organisms and non-biological structures (some such structures perhaps being beyond our ken at the present time). Memory, like a telephone number scrolled on a note pad, may reside in the structure, not the soul. This present life (or, as we shall presently see, perhaps a small portion thereof) may be but a brief interlude in continuing journey through spacetime (and perhaps through other realms beyond our present understanding).

Attempts to Physically Detect the Soul

There have been attempts to measure and record the activities of discarnate spirits with physical devices. These include attempts to weigh the soul, to photograph ghosts, and to record the voices of the deceased. Space considerations prohibit the detailing of this type of evidence here. The interested reader may find my thoughts regarding this type of evidence in Stokes (1997). Suffice it to say here that these lines of investigation have provided little in the way of compelling evidence for the physical detection of discarnate entities.

Conclusions and Perspectives

We here conclude our examination of the evidence for the survival of the personality, or at least some aspect thereof, of the death of the physical body as well as our examination of the evidence for psi phenomena. As stated at the outset of this book, in view of the findings of modern cognitive neuroscience, it is doubtful that major portions of the "person" (defined as the concatenation of one's memories, beliefs, emotions and habits) could survive the death of the physical body. By the end of the second millennium, it had been amply demonstrated that one's cognitive and affective life is intimately dependent on brain activity. A twist of a scalpel in one's hippocampus, and one loses the ability to store new episodic memories. How then, with their hippocampi long since decomposed, can the dead regale us with tales of their adventures in the afterlife? Remove his amygdale, and a violent maniac is turned into a docile creature. How then can a restless spirit, torn not only from its amygdala but its entire brain, terrorize us from beyond the grave to avenge some past injury? It is simply no longer possible to maintain that the personality is independent of the brain or that the brain is simply the conduit through which the soul speaks, rather than the generator of the personality, if not the soul. How, if a mind cannot maintain its memories once the brain has entered the ravages of Alzheimer's, could it remember its adventures on earth when the entire cerebrum has been reabsorbed into the dust?

Psi powers, if they exist, would be strong evidence against the physicalist view that the universe is solely composed of physical particles already known to science, or minor modifications thereof. Also, should such faculties as retrocognitive telepathy exist, the dead would be granted a trans-temporal form of survival. If through retrocognitive telepathy one can "converse" with a lost friend, then somehow that friend's mind (and personality) can in some sense be said to exist "now." However, the current body of evidence, while suggestive of the paranormal, compels neither the belief in psi nor the belief in continued existence of the personality after the death of the brain.

In the next chapter, we will take up the question of the nature of the self, construed as a field of pure consciousness. It will be proposed that the self should not be identified with the patterns of memories, emotions, thoughts and sensations swirling through the physical brains which we are mysteriously (and perhaps only momentarily) trapped. Our memories, emotions, thoughts and sensations are fleeting and change from moment, whereas our conscious selves seem to persist (at least through macroscopic time intervals, if not through periods of sleep or a Sunday afternoon's "microsleep" during the huddle in a televised football game).

The contents (sensations, emotions, memories etc.) of the greatest entertainment center we know, our brains, may separate and scatter into different corners of the mindscape or leave our conscious minds altogether. However, those minds, conceived as centers of pure consciousness, appear intuitively to be unitary and not divisible into components. If we are something like the proto-consciousnesses proposed by Walker (2000), or "mini-Shins," then we likely share the same ontological privileges awarded to fundamental particles or fields, including conservation over time. Perhaps we are even identical with particles or fields already known to physics (much like a proton responding to a complex quantum-mechanical field, which connects it to the rest of the universe, thus rendering it in some sense aware of that universe). On the other hand we may be a fundamental entity yet to be identified by modern science. In either event, our association with any given brain or other physical system is likely to be more temporary than we think (the illusion of decades of continuous inhabitation of a particular brain arising from the memories stored in that brain and our construction of that social entity known as the "person"). The illusion of being the person, in the sense of the conjunction of our physical bodies and personality traits such as memories and desires, likely arises in part from a false identification with the physical body and its needs, which may serve our biological imperatives but perhaps not our spiritual needs.

This universe is one of conservation, of matter-energy, and baryon number and angular momentum. It is a universe of rearrangement, not destruction. If, as a centers of pure consciousness, we are granted at least some form of parity with such seemingly (to us) mindless and insignificant entities such as quarks and electrons, then it is likely that we like they, are recycled from system to system, continually falling into the murky depths of one system of primitive awareness after another, but perhaps from time to time becoming united in a "supersystem," from which vantage point our present human consciousness will appear like that of an ameba.

If the materialists are correct in their view that we are nothing but matter-energy and our intuition is correct that we are unitary, much more like a quark on an electron than a temporary conglomeration of atoms, then the prosurvivalist may rejoice. The universe conserves mass-energy, recycling it from one part of the cosmic show to another. Uncountable beauties and terrors may await us as we are torn free of our human form and the illusion created by our stories of the self and our identification with the Person.

In the chapters to come, these ideas will be explored further, beginning with the nature of the self and its relation to the physical brain.

7

The Nature of the Self

In this chapter we will examine the nature of the self, its relationship with the physical brain, and the issue of whether the self, or some portion thereof, could survive the dissolution of the brain at death.

The question of whether the human mind or spirit survives the death of the physical body is one of the oldest and least tractable problems to confront human (and other hominid) philosophers, scientists and theologians. As we have just seen, in more recent times, it was a central occupation of investigators in the early days of psychical research, the field that gave rise to parapsychology, and continues to be the central concern of a minority contingent of parapsychologists today.

This problem has, however, receded into the murky background, due to its intractability, to the existence of alternative explanations of the evidence for survival, and to advances in modern cognitive neuroscience that have revealed the intimate dependence of the human personality on the state of the physical brain. Writers such as Patricia Churchland (2002) have suggested that such dependence is so complete as to rule out the possibility that any souls or other nonphysical aspects of the mind exist. This would seem to shut the door on the case for survival; however, I will argue below that any such door slamming is at best premature.

In this chapter, I will be arguing for the existence of a persisting self (or more likely a myriad of persisting selves) in each person. However, such persisting selves may not in fact persist in the commonly understood sense of lifelong and continuous association with one particular physical body, yet may persist long beyond the deaths of the bodies they currently inhabit. This seemingly paradoxical position will hopefully become clearer as the chapter goes on. It will also be argued that such persisting fields of consciousness enjoy an ontological status that is not inferior to that of elementary particles such as electrons and quarks, as is commonly supposed, but may play a fundamental role in determining the outcomes of quantum processes and, as will be discussed in the next chapter, possibly even in the design and creation of the universe itself.

The Persisting Self

Most of us (at least most of us who are not professional philosophers) believe that we have some sort of continuing self, a field of consciousness that persists from our birth to our death. While this self may be thought to lapse during deep sleep and under conditions such as surgical anesthesia, most of us generally believe that the self that wakes up after each lapse is the same as the self that preceded the lapse. There is perhaps no rational basis for such belief. The self that wakes could be an entirely different entity from the self that inhabited the body prior to the loss of consciousness. After all, if a self can somehow become "stuck" in a human body sometime after conception and released somehow at death, it stands to reason that such a self could also become stuck in the body well after the body's birth and to depart long before its death.

However, if the self that wakes is only able to access memories stored in the current brain, it would naturally come to believe that it experienced the events corresponding to these memories and hence is the same self that inhabited the body prior to the lapse in consciousness. Meanwhile, the prior self (field of consciousness) might be waking up in a new body and quickly forming the belief that it had inhabited the (new) body all along. In view of the occasional experience in which one is unsure of one's location or even one's identity for a few brief moments after waking, this "realization" (or possibly this delusion) may not be so sudden after all.

The Denial of the Self

However, as noted in the Introduction, there are those, such as Daniel Dennett (1991), Susan Blackmore (1991a, 1993, 2002), Galen Strawson (1997), Patricia Churchland (2002) and Thomas Metzinger (2003), among others, who deny the very existence of any continuing self, or "Cartesian theater," as Dennett calls it, even over a limited time period. They assert that the self is merely a cognitive construct, a convenient "story" we tell ourselves in an attempt to render our experiences coherent and consistent. As such, the self enjoys only a fictional existence. Under this view, "we" (our illusory selves) are nothing more than the scattered contents (fleeting sensations, thoughts, and emotions) of "our" minds. As Metzinger (2003, p. 397) puts it, "no such things as selves exist in the world," only mental models of the self.

Stephen Priest (1991) has countered Descartes' argument that "I think therefore I am" by asserting that thoughts do not imply the existence of a thinker. Even William James (1890/1992) argued that there may be no substantial soul, but only an ongoing stream of consciousness. James' view has been echoed by Thomas Clark (1995), who contends that a person is simply an assemblage of "qualia" or experiences and denies the existence of a self separate from the experiences themselves.

The basic problem with this denial of the existence of the self is that one cannot have a stream of consciousness without a riverbed for it to flow through. One of the foremost modern deniers of the self is the philosopher Derek Parfit. In Parfit's opinion, in each person there is only a continuing series of thoughts, sensations, memories and feelings, with no continuing self to experience them. But in order to explain the unity and continuity of experience, Parfit (1987) is forced to assert that these thoughts, sensations and memories are experienced by the same "state of awareness." But this state of awareness is nothing more nor less than the self or soul, assuming one is willing to equate the self with a field of pure consciousness.

Most people, following Descartes, find the existence of a continuing self to be immediately given and obviously true. It is an integral part of our essential existence as commonly understood.

Certain Eastern religious traditions, including Zen Buddhism, also deny the existence of a continuing self. Motoyama (2002) traces the differences between the Eastern and Western concepts of the self to the fact that food was abundant and agricultural conditions were favorable in the Far East, whereas food was scarce and agricultural conditions unpredictable in the ancient Middle East, the birthplace of the three major Western religions. One consequence of this unpredictable environment, Motoyama asserts, is that the Western religious traditions are characterized by a belief in a personal afterlife in which one's present personality would experience a less uncertain and painful form of existence. Motoyama notes that the Western religious traditions have often led to inter-religious wars, whereas there are no such wars in the Buddhist-dominated cultural spheres in Asia. He notes that self-denial and submissiveness to nature and God are principal features of Asian cultures and lifestyles, whereas self-affirmation is a prominent feature of Semitic and European culture and lifestyles.

The Buddhist denial seems more directed at the concept of the self as one's personality, comprising one's aspirations, motivations, cravings for material possessions, lusts, pride, and so forth, rather than at the existence of a field of pure consciousness. Buddhist meditative practices are designed to distance oneself from these transitory elements and to attain an inner state of peace and tranquility. In order to achieve such a state, the Buddhists teach that one must suppress and eliminate one's cravings and greed, as such unfulfilled desires lie at the root of all human misery and suffering.

Most branches of Buddhism and Hinduism teach that the true self is pure consciousness, not the contents or objects of consciousness, such as the swirl of memories, emotions, gleeful pride in our achievements, and the fears and hopes for the future that are continually swirling through the dark (perhaps Cartesian) theaters of our minds. The Eastern philosophies teach that our personalities are transitory and not our true selves. One's true self in this view is the pure consciousness that in Hindu philosophy is taken to be identical with all consciousness, including that of the World Soul or Brahman. It is thus not clear that these Eastern philosophies deny the reality of a persisting self in the sense of a field of consciousness, as opposed to the contents of one's consciousness or one's personality or motives (which obviously do not persist unchanged even from moment to moment).

Timothy Sprigge (2002) has several observations to make regarding the self and the mind. First, he notes that the mere existence of consciousness falsifies materialism, as materialistic science neither predicts nor is able to explain the presence of conscious experiences. Sprigge sees no real difference between regarding a stream of events with a certain degree of connectedness as the successive states of an enduring individual (i.e., conscious mind or "Cartesian theater") and talking only of the stream. Thus, Sprigge asserts that it makes no sense to talk only of the stream of consciousness (as "self-less" philosophers such as Dennett and Blackmore do) without reference to an enduring individual (or "stream-bed" if you will). To this, I would add that in Descartes' experience and my own, the existence of a self in the form of a field of consciousness is immediately given (i.e., thoughts, sensations, longings and pain flow through me, or past me, therefore I am). I would affirm Descartes' intuition that the (at least temporary) existence of my field of consciousness is one of the few facts of which one can be certain, whereas even the existence of the material universe may be cast into doubt as a potential dream or illusion.

Sprigge notes that the opposition between an "event ontology" such as that advocated by Blackmore and Dennett (in which there are only, say sensations, with no conscious self to do the sensing) and an ontology of "enduring substances or individuals" (read fields of consciousness) may be more one of language than of substance. He suggests that consciousness may turn out to be identified with a physical field pervading the brain. In an even more speculative vein, Sprigge postulates that conscious selves are "higher-order monads" that are in turn contained in a Divine Mind or "Absolute." Sprigge does not see how the physical world could subsume conscious experience in that part of it called the brain, without doing so more generally. He asserts that the only two viable philosophical options are a mind-brain dualism or a form of panpsychistic idealism (in which all physical entities are assumed to have experiential components).

As observed earlier in this book, during the past few decades it has been amply demonstrated that one's sensations, feelings, thoughts, emotions, ideas, and even personality can be radically altered through electromagnetic, surgical, chemical, and accidental interventions in the brain. If relatively minor modifications of brain states can substantially alter the nature of one's experience and personality, how could your personality and experiences manage to continue on in a more or less an uninterrupted fashion after the far more drastic event of the destruction of the entire brain? Also, many of the concerns that drive the structure of your personality have to do with the preservation of your own physical body and those of people who are closely related to you. Perhaps, as Dawkins (1989) would have it, these concerns are primarily directed at the propagation of your "selfish genes." What would be the point of the continuance of these concerns once your physical body has been returned to dust and your ability to intervene in the physical world perhaps radically curtailed?

"Downloaded" into Heaven

Some philosophical functionalists, such as Hans Moravec (1988), Grant Fjermedal (1987), and Frank Tipler (1994) among others, have suggested that one's thoughts, memories and personality could be "downloaded" into a computer or robot, allowing one's essential self to survive after death in a cybernetic world or as a cybernetic simulacrum operating in the physical world. Of course, it would be just as easy to create multiple simulacra of oneself rather than just one. It is counterintuitive to think that one's "self" could really inhabit all the copies simultaneously, providing another indication that one's self cannot be identified with one's emotions, thoughts, memories and personality.

In fact, a persisting self not only cannot be identified with the fleeting and ever-changing contents of consciousness, it also cannot be identified with the particular configuration of material particles that constitute one's physical body or brain, as these too are continually undergoing change and replacement. Due to the constant exchange of material substance with your environment, your present physical body shares few if any molecules with your body of 20 years ago. You have already survived the death and dissolution of that earlier body. Thus, any self or field of consciousness associated with the physical body that persists unchanged from birth to death (or even from hour to hour) cannot be identified with any particular physical body (configuration of material particles) or conglomeration of mental contents such as thoughts, feelings and personality traits, as neither of these (the body or the contents of consciousness) persists unchanged from moment to moment.

The fact that you have apparently survived the dissolution of your body of several years ago suggests that you may likewise survive the ultimate death and dissolution of your present body as well. It is, however, unlikely that you would survive death with your personality traits and memories intact as suggested in the Western religious traditions (and by much of the research on survival conducted by psychical researchers), due to the dissolution of the brain activity and neural structures underlying your current personality traits and memories. It is conceivable, however, that a field of pure consciousness might survive the ultimate death of the physical body much as it seems to have survived the "death" of the prior bodies that have been "shed" through a process of molecular replacement and recycling.

Modern Dualists

The postulation of a continuing contentless field of consciousness brings us perilously close to Cartesian dualism, a once dominant philosophical position that has become increasingly out of favor in the current intellectual climate, which is dominated by several remarkably successful scientific disciplines that largely adopt a materialistic or reductionist stance toward the realm of mental events. The postulation of a self or field of consciousness that is in some sense independent of, or external to, the brain, immediately raises the question of how such a self and brain could interact.

One of the last holdouts for a dualistic position during the latter half of the twentieth century was the Nobel laureate neurophysiologist Sir John Eccles. (Eccles, 1979, 1980, 1983, 1987, 1989; Eccles & Robinson, 1984; Popper & Eccles, 1977), who proposed the existence of a conscious self lying outside (in a nonspatial sense) of the physical brain. Eccles viewed this conscious self as being capable of receiving information from the brain and acting upon the brain. At one point, Eccles (1977) used the term "psychokinesis" to describe the mediating vehicle whereby the mind or self influenced the brain.

Modern science is generally at a loss to explain how a nonphysical mind could interact with a physical brain, hence its general denial of the existence of the former. Thus, the terms "internal psychokinesis" and "internal clairvoyance" may be as good as any to describe such mind-brain interaction (assuming the existence of a nonphysical mind). The use of the terms "internal psychokinesis" and "internal clairvoyance" in this context does not necessarily commit one to affirming the existence of psi phenomena as usually defined, which involve anomalous interconnections between internal and *external* events. The provisional use of the terms "internal psychokinesis" and "internal clairvoyance" in the present context is intended merely as a way of recognizing our current state of bafflement as to how a nonphysical mind could interact with a physical brain.

THE "SHIN" MODEL

As noted in Chapter 5, two writers to take Eccles' suggestion that mind-brain interaction may be mediated by "internal psychokinesis" literally (albeit nearly three decades before Eccles got around to making the suggestion) were Thouless and Wiesner (1948). They proposed that each brain has associated with it an entity they termed the "Shin." They proposed that the Shin becomes aware of brain states through a type of "internal clairvoyance" and that this awareness manifests itself in consciousness as various forms of "cognita," to borrow a term from Carington (1949), such as sensations, emotions, memories, and impulses. Conversely, the Shin controls the physical body and brain activity through internal psychokinesis. Thouless and Wiesner postulated that psi phenomena as traditionally defined correspond to an "externalization" of the mind's usual relation with the brain.

Clearly, under the view that physical bodies are associated with immaterial minds that are conceived as fields of "contentless consciousness," with virtually all of the activity underlying cognition and motor activity being embodied by material brain processes, some sort of theory analogous to that proposed by Thouless and Wiesner commends itself, if one wishes to adhere to a dualistic model in which consciousness is conceived as a component of the world that is in some sense "external to" (i.e., not identical with any part of) the physical brain.

Of course, such dualistic terminology may only be provisional. Should a "Shin-o-scope" be invented that would allow the physical location and activity of Shins to be measured, it is likely that Shins would come to be viewed as physical components of brains. We are, however, a long way from a complete, partial, or even minimal understanding of consciousness, and "Shin-o-scopes" do not appear to be in the immediate offing. To the extent that such hypothetical Shins cannot at present be identified with any particular component of the physical world, it may be appropriate to continue to use the word "nonmaterial" to describe them, recognizing that such attribution of nonphysicality is provisional and may need to be withdrawn in the light of subsequent scientific discoveries. Indeed, the fact that Shins seem to get "stuck," however temporarily, in physical brains suggests that they exist in spacetime and therefore correspond to some sort of quasimaterial objects. At the same time, if psi phenomena exist, this is an indication that minds may have nonlocal aspects and direct access to a "higher dimension" or at least a wider region of spacetime than is encompassed by the brain. But the same could be said of all quantum objects and hence all matter.

The Thouless and Wiesner Shin theory does carry one advantage over classical Cartesian dualism in that the apparatus of thought and cognition may be ascribed largely to the physical brain, whereas under many interpretations of Cartesian dualism, much cognitive activity is carried out in the nonphysical realm. Descartes' "I think, therefore I am" may need to be replaced by "I am aware of my thoughts from time to time, therefore, I am." This is perhaps not as catchy a phrase, but does recognize the implications of modern research in cognitive neuropsychology showing the intimate connections between mental events, such as thoughts, emotions and perceptions, and brain processes. If such research has not yet established the identity of mental events with physical events, it has certainly revealed the intimate dependence of the former on the latter.

NAÏVE DUALISM AND SPLIT BRAINS

As noted in Chapter 5, the results of research on split-brain patients (which was largely conducted after the publication of Thouless and Wiesner's paper in which they developed the concept of the Shin, but is now well emblazoned in the brains of all veterans of introductory psychology courses) pose devastating problems for any naïve version of the Shin theory. As discussed in Chapter 5, a split-brain patient may be unable to verbally describe an object held in his left hand, but will be able to point to a picture of the object with his left hand when later requested to do so. This is a result of the fact that the sensory input from the left hand is fed into the right hemisphere of the brain. However, the right hemisphere has no means to transfer this information to the language centers in the left hemisphere in the brain due to the fact that the corpus callosum, the main neural fibers connecting the two hemispheres, has been disconnected. Under the naïve version of Thouless and Wiesner's theory, a single Shin should be able, through "clairvoyant" perception of the right hemisphere, to gain knowledge of the object held in the left hand and then be able to describe the object through "psychokinetic" influence of the language centers in the left hemisphere. Thus, the findings of split-brain research would seem to directly refute the single Shin theory. In fact, these findings are precisely the evidence Patricia Churchland uses to refute the existence of a nonphysical self or soul (Churchland, 2002, pp. 46–47).

Thalbourne (2004) has responded to this argument by Churchland by proposing that "a callosectomy causes one portion of the self to become *unconscious* to the main center" (p. 17, emphasis in original). He then goes on to propose that one portion of the brain is controlled by the conscious aspect of the self and that the other portion is controlled by the unconscious self. Thalbourne asserts that in such cases, "the self would maintain an overall unity, but be divided with respect to consciousness or unconsciousness of process" (p. 17). However, instances of conflict between the hemispheres and the ability of the right, presumably unconscious, hemisphere to respond to verbal commands and to communicate itself (sometimes through such devices as a Scrabble set) makes it seem unreasonable to deny consciousness to that hemisphere. Indeed, in the following sections it will be argued that many spheres of consciousness may somehow reside within a single human brain. Thalbourne further suggests that the single self or Shin might be able through practice to reacquire the ability to "clairvoyantly" acquire information from one hemisphere and "psychokinetically" influence the other. However, if such reacquisition occurs, it is likely only partial, as a full functional recovery from a severed corpus callosum would be nothing short of miraculous and would be widely reported in the scientific literature. In view of the evidence for psi phenomena, a partial reacquisition might be possible (indeed, a partial reacquisition might be achieved in the absence of psi through the remaining subcortical neural channels connecting the hemispheres). However, the existing neurological evidence suggests that inter-hemispheric information transfer likely depends primarily on neural pathways. Also the instances of motivational conflict between the hemispheres alluded to above, as well the "minor" hemisphere's ability to communicate messages sometimes at odds with its partner's motivations, strongly suggest that there are multiple selves or Shins in split-brain patients that are likely to be, to use Morton Prince's term, co-conscious. Indeed, as argued below, it may be that there are multitudinous Shins lurking in a single brain, with many or most of them "buying into" the delusion that they are the Person and the sole center of consciousness residing in the body. If in fact they are transient residents in the brain, as suggested below, it would not do from an evolutionary perspective for this fact to be widely recognized among the Shins. The service of the genes may require that the Shins fall into the delusion that they are the Person (i.e., the body, memories, personality, etc.).

In fact, the scientific and philosophical community has found it difficult agree on a clear line of demarcation between conscious and nonconscious beings. Some (e.g.,

Descartes) would draw the line at humans and deny consciousness to animals. This seems to me to involve a retreat to the pre-Copernican view that humankind stands at the center of the universe. Others (e.g., the panpsychists) would extend consciousness all the way "down" the evolutionary chain to amobae or even to plants and elementary particles, as discussed in more detail below.

We are complex organisms; each of our brains is composed of billions of amoeba-like neurons, much like a "Woodstock" for single-celled creatures. Perhaps, as argued below, our brains may harbor multiple, perhaps countless "selves" (i.e., fields of consciousness), with the majority of them identifying with the body as whole and quickly falling under the pre-Copernican delusion that each of them is the sole "self" or consciousness inhabiting the body. This identification of our "selves" with the body or the personality (the "Person") is natural but, as we have seen above, a false identification. To identify our true "selves" with our bodies and personalities is to fall into the same delusion that the Buddhists (and to some extent Blackmore and Dennett) have warned us against. Our selves (conceived as centers of pure consciousness) seemingly persist unchanged, while our bodies (and our personalities) grow, blossom, metamorphose, wither and die. From an introspectionist perspective, it seems clear that we are centers of consciousness that persist over macroscopic time intervals (contra Blackmore and Dennett). If the self as a center of consciousness does not even exist, the problem of survival does not arise—there is simply nothing left to survive (or die). However, it is more plausible that, like the physical particles that make up our bodies, these centers of consciousness are continually entering and exiting the brain. If memories are stored in the brain, a newly entering Shin would quickly come to believe that it had been there all along, its memories of its former incarnations lost like a misplaced scrap of paper on which an important phone number was scrawled. The view that we are a single self that persists in the same body from day to day and year to year likely arises from the false identification of one's self with one's body and personality. We may be constantly recycled, awakening in a new body in each morning with no memories of our real adventures the day before. This view may be depressing to many, in that it does not involve the survival of the Person. However, despite the fact this process may be random and "meaningless," like so much else in this universe, it is "fair" in the sense that we all may share the experiences of being deformed and poor or handsome and wealthy. Despite their centering in seemingly moral Agents and Principles, the "will of God" of the Judeo-Christian-Islamic tradition and the karmic principle of Hinduism (responsible in part for the "caste wars" in India) seem much less fair than the purely random and frequent reassortment being proposed here. The latter view may also promote the values of kindness and altruism (if only out of egoism), as you may find yourself housed in (or stuck to) the other's body tomorrow. The main downside is that such a view may promote a "seize the day" form of hedonism in which one would elect to maximize's one's pleasure now, with no thought of the consequences to the body or the "Person" the next day.

TWO HEMISPHERES, TWO SHINS?

As intimated above, one way around the difficulty posed by split-brain patients would be to propose that the right and left hemispheres are associated with separate Shins or selves. It could be postulated that the two Shins were present prior to the callosectomy or that a second Shin was acquired during or shortly after the callosectomy. Each Shin would be restricted to interaction with its own hemisphere. As Eccles (1980) notes, many prominent split-brain researchers, including Puccetti, Sperry, Bogen and Gazzaniga, have postulated the existence of two spheres of consciousness in split-brain patients, although Gazzaniga has since modified this view (Gazzaniga, 1992). As noted in Chapter 1, Libet (1994) has postulated the existence of "conscious mind fields" (CMFs), which he sees as being produced by brain activity. CMFs are capable of causal action upon brain activity and provide the means whereby diverse neural activity is synthesized into unified perceptions and experiences. He notes that the existence of CMFs would be compatible with a variety of philosophical positions on the mind-body problem. Following the lead of the above researchers, Libet speculates that there may be two CMFs in split-brain patients. Libet asserts that CMFs are not describable in terms of any externally observable physical events or of any the currently constructed theories of physics.

Incidentally, not all may be sweetness and light between the selves of the two hemispheres. Mark (1996) describes a 33-year-old female split-brain patient who displayed oppositional behavior between her two hands. She also gave contradictory verbal responses to questions (she had previously been demonstrated to have language centers in both hemispheres via the Wada test). Spence and Frith (1999) report on two cases of "alien hands" in which the left hands of patients who exhibited lesions or pathology in the corpus callosum actually attempted to strangle the patient. They also report instances of motivational conflict between the hands of such patients, such as when the one hand fastens a button, which is then immediately unfastened by the other hand.

Perhaps the most convincing line of evidence for the existence of separate selves in the two cerebral hemispheres comes not from research on humans but rather from research on our cetacean friends. As pointed out by Patricia Churchland (1986, p. 181), dolphins sleep one hemisphere at a time.

A Proliferation of Selves

Two conscious selves may, however, not be enough, as there are more ways to divide up (or dissociate) a brain than are dreamt of in the classical split-brain paradigm. Take for instance the phenomenon of blindsight. "Blindsight" is a term coined by Lawrence Weiskrantz to describe a syndrome in which cortically blind subjects respond appropriately to visually presented stimuli even though they report no conscious awareness of such stimuli (Sanders et al., 1974; Weiskrantz, 1986; Marcel, 1988; Rafal et al., 1990). Cortical blindness refers to blindness that is a result of damage to the visual cortex in the occipital lobes of the brain. Even though the eyes of such patients may be normal, they may be blind in part of their visual field because of such damage to their visual cortex. If you present a small dot of light to such patients in the blind areas of their visual fields, they will say that they saw nothing. However, if you ask them to just take a guess by pointing to where the dot of light might have been, they frequently point at the exact location that the dot occupied. If you present erotic pictures to such a patient in the blind area of the visual field, the patient may blush or giggle or say things such as "That's quite a machine you've got there, Doc!" They will still, however, deny having consciously seen anything. Interpretations of words may be biased by information presented in the blind area of the visual field, and eye movements may be altered by such stimuli (Rafal et al., 1990). Many researchers have speculated that blindsight is mediated by a secondary visual center in a subcortical area of the brain known as the superior colliculus, although some researchers have challenged this view. Francis Crick (1994) has noted that other areas must be involved as well, in that blindsight sometimes involves responsiveness to color differences, and there are no color-sensitive neurons in the superior colliculus.

The phenomenon of blindsight might lead one to postulate the existence of a secondary center of consciousness, perhaps located subcortically in the superior colliculus. However, some writers, such as Flanagan (1992) and Marcel (1988), have argued against any attribution of full consciousness to this secondary center, insofar as information acquired through blindsight is not generally acted upon. For instance, the patient may be thirsty, but will not respond to the sight of a water fountain presented to the blind area of the visual field. It would be possible to argue that this secondary center cannot move the patient's body of its own accord as it is a subordinate "module." (Actually, most researchers feel that the primary function of this secondary center is to guide eye movements, and perhaps this is not a role that one would want to associate with consciousness.) Young (2006) suggests that phenomenal consciousness is required for the initiation of action and that Marcel's thirsty subject failed to reach for the water because the information gained through blindsight does not reach conscious awareness. In a commentary on Young's article, Spence (2006) cites evidence that intentions are subject to electrical disruption for up to 200 msec after the motor act has occurred. Thus, he argues, conscious intentions are slow to cohere and are not responsible for the initiation of motor acts.

In addition to the superior colliculus, many other regions of the brain have been nominated as "centers of consciousness." Indeed, it would almost seem that no region of the brain has been omitted from the list of brain regions that form the primary center of consciousness according to one researcher or another. As noted in Chapter 1, these proposed centers of consciousness or mind/brain interaction have included the "liaison" brain (the "liaison" being between mind and brain) predominately located in the cerebral cortex of the left hemisphere (Eccles), the higher brain stem, or diencephalon (Penfield, 1975), the frontal lobes of the brain (Ramachandran, 1980), the linguistic apparatus of the brain (Ledoux, 1985), the septohippocampal region involved in mental representations of the world and memory formation (O'Keefe, 1985), the hippocampus and neocortex (Oakley, 1985a, 1985b), the supplementary motor area of the cerebral cortex (Libet, 1989, 1991a), the thalamus (Cotterill, 1995), more specifically the intralaminar nucleus of the thalamus (Churchland, 1995), the right parietal lobe (Damasio, 1994), the temporal lobes (Ramachandran & Hirstein, 1997), patterns of synchronous firings of neurons (Burns, 1993, Crick, 1994), nonrandom, coherent deviations of the brain's electromagnetic field from its resting state (John, 2003), the anterior cingulate gyrus, amygdala, and temporal lobes (Ramachandran & Blakeslee, 1998) and, last but not least, water in the microtubules composing the cytoskeletons of neurons (Penrose, 1994; Hameroff, 1994). Each of these authors presents a cogent argument in favor of their candidate for the area of the brain (or brain process) that is the center of consciousness (or of the interaction between consciousness and mind).

With this many candidates for the *primary* center of consciousness (or of interaction between the conscious mind and brain), it may begin to seem that no center is primary and that many different brain centers and processes may be associated with their own conscious activity, and that these centers of consciousness may not be mutually accessible to one another, at least in a direct sense.

A HIERARCHY OF SELVES

The notion that the human mind may be composed of an assembly of interacting centers of consciousness is an old one. It may be traced as far back as Aristotle, who postulated the existence of "vegetative soul," a "sensitive soul" and a "rational soul" in each person. F. W. H. Myers (1903) hypothesized the existence of several independent selves within the unconscious or "subliminal" mind. William McDougall (1926) proposed that the normal human mind is composed of a hierarchy of "coconscious personalities," each carrying out its own separate function. McDougall used Morton Prince's term "coconscious" rather than the usual terms "subconscious" or "unconscious" to describe such secondary personalities in order to emphasize their self-awareness. Ostensible cases of multiple personality (if genuine) may represent instances in which one or more of these subordinate personalities has rebelled against the primary, executive personality. In support of McDougall's view, many lines of psychological research, including studies of subliminal perception, posthypnotic suggestion, preattentive filters, and automatic motor performance suggest that the human mind is capable of conducting a great deal of sophisticated mental activity outside of the field of awareness of the primary personality.

For instance, his investigations into hypnotic phenomena led Ernst Hilgard (1977) to propose what he called the "neodissociation" theory of hypnosis. Hilgard asserted that the hypnotized person was associated with a subconscious "hidden observer" that was aware of events for which the primary, conscious personality had no knowledge because of hypnotically induced amnesia, anesthesia, or negative hallucinations (e.g., when a hypnotized subject is instructed *not* to see a particular person or object). Hilgard was able to hold conversations with such "hidden observers," and the latter frequently reported awareness of events (posthypnotic suggestions, pain, etc.) for which the primary personality claimed no knowledge. However, many scientists have asserted that Hilgard's "hidden observers" were the result of suggestions; thus, they were created by Hilgard's hypnotic suggestions rather than being autonomous entities that were "discovered" by Hilgard. Spanos and Hewitt (1980), for instance, were able to evoke a hidden observer that felt less rather than more pain than the primary subject. They hypothesize that this "hidden observer" was an artifact manufactured through their own hypnotic suggestions.

Ramachandran and Blakeslee (1998) cite dreams in which another character tells an unexpected joke to the dreaming self as further evidence of the existence of multiple centers of consciousness within a single brain.

In the decades since the "cognitive revolution" in psychology, research into the "cognitive unconscious" has led to the creation of many hierarchical models of the mind, such as the "Massachusetts modularism" proposed by Jerry Fodor (1983), in which the mind is seen as being split into modular "computational" components.

Michael Gazzaniga (1985, 1989) likewise rejects the notion of a unitary consciousness in favor of the view that the mind is composed of a collection of independently-functioning modules that he, following William McDougall, describes as "coconscious." As evidence for this modular view of the mind, Gazzaniga cites post-hypnotic suggestions, apparent unconscious (or coconscious) problem-solving activity (in which the solution to a complex problem suddenly emerges full-blown into consciousness), blindsight, the existence of separate procedural and episodic memory systems, and split-brain research. Gazzaniga tends to identify the "conscious self" with the module that is in control of the language centers of the brain, and he refers to this module as the "executive module." He cites many instances in which the executive module uses confabulation to explain behavior that was in fact generated by other modules. For instance, a person who acts under a posthypnotic suggestion to close a window may claim that he was cold. Gazzaniga also cites several instances of confabulation by the left hemisphere to explain actions performed in response to directions given to the right hemisphere in split-brain patients. It might not be far-fetched to suppose that all or most modules might likewise maintain the illusion that they were the sole center of consciousness or in sole control of the body. For instance, modules hearing the mouth issue verbal utterances may be under the illusion that they were primarily responsible for producing those utterances. They might naturally identify with the body as a whole rather than with the particular brain region in which they are located.

In particular, Gazzaniga and Roser (2004) contend that the "left-hemisphere interpreter" may be responsible for one's feelings that one's consciousness is unified. Gazzaniga and Roser suggest that either consciousness may have a "graded relationship" to brain activity or possibly that consciousness results whenever brain activity exceeds a particular threshold. They note that brain activations correlated with consciously perceived stimuli and those associated with unseen stimuli display differences in intensity and spatial extent.

Daniel Wegner (2002) notes that the well-known brain researcher Jose Delgado (1969) found that movements produced by direct electrical stimulation of the motor areas of the brain were experienced as voluntarily produced, thus supporting the hypothesis that "free will" may in many cases be an illusion. Wegner does however affirm the existence of the self, which he defines in terms of a continuous memory structure. He asserts that in cases of fugue, multiple personality or apparent "possession," a new self exists if the person has amnesia for the prior self.

The Perceived Unity of Consciousness

As discussed in Chapter 1, Francis Crick (1994) has ascribed the unity of consciousness to global 40 Hz (cycles per second) waves of coordinated neural activity. Farber (2005) has suggested that if consciousness corresponds to such 40 Hz synchronous oscillations, the conscious experience should "quantize" into discrete moments of awareness. Farber notes that such quantization of brain activity was originally proposed by Rudolfo Llinas. He notes that Llanis and his coworkers found that people were able to distinguish auditory clicks that are separated by at least 13 milliseconds. However, when the time interval separating the clicks was 12 milliseconds or less, then the clicks were perceived as one single click, in support of Llinas' quantization hypothesis (Joliot, Rubary, & Llinas, 1994).

Koch (1996) proposes that visual awareness arises from the firing of coordinated sets of neurons for 100 to 200 milliseconds. He notes that stimuli presented within shorter periods are not perceived as separate stimuli. For instance, a red light presented for 20 milliseconds followed by a green light presented for 20 milliseconds is typically reported as a yellow light. This finding supports Llinas' notion of a "quantization" of consciousness. Koch asserts that the vast majority of neurons are not associated with awareness but rather with unconscious processing. He conjectures that unless a group of neurons projects to prefrontal "planning" areas of the cerebral cortex, their activity is probably not consciously perceived.

Clark (2005b) asserts that the role of consciousness is to make information available over time in the absence of direct stimulation. In Clark's view, conscious states permit the organism to engage in novel, non-automatized behavior and allow thus allow spontaneous, goal-directed behavior. He proposes that phenomenal (conscious) experience is associated with widely distributed, but highly integrated neural processes, involving communication between multiple subsystems in the brain. One of Clark's central theses is that that the brain produces representations of the world, but that there is no conscious observer of such representations over and above the representations themselves. He asserts that qualia (i.e., "raw feels' such as red patches and sharp pains) are merely nonconceptual representations of the world.

The Location of Consciousness

In general it seems that fields of consciousness are blissfully ignorant of their physical location and sphere of activity. After all, Aristotle and many other ancient philosophers located the seat of consciousness in the heart rather than the brain. Also instructive is a short science fiction story entitled "Where am I?" by Daniel Dennett (1981). In Dennett's "story," sensory information is transmitted to a human brain from a robot or decerebrated human body, and the brain's motor commands are in turn relayed to the remote body or robot, thus controlling its activity. Dennett's story leaves no doubt that the brain would locate its center of consciousness in the remote body or robot under these circumstances and not in its "real" location in the physical brain.

Ramachandran and Blakeslee (1998) describe an experiment in which a subject held his hand under a table while it and the table top were simultaneously stroked. Subsequently, the subject exhibited a large galvanic skin response when the table was hit by a hammer. Ramachandran interprets this as suggesting that the table's surface had been incorporated into the subject's body image.

Thus, our centers of consciousness may thus not be located where we think they are.

Each "module" or center of consciousness may subscribe to a "unitararian" philosophy of the self or soul, in which it believes itself to be unitary and indivisible and in sole control of the body. If such modules in fact correspond to centers of contentless consciousness that are fundamental constituents of the universe existing prior to the evolution of complex organisms, they may be correct in regarding themselves as unitary and indivisible but sadly mistaken in the view that they are in sole control of the body.

Thus, one means of addressing the problems posed by split-brain research and other neurological findings (e.g., blindslight) would be to propose that each person is composed of an aggregation of selves or fields of consciousness associated with local brain regions. This raises the question of what characteristics are necessary for a brain region to "host" (or comprise) a field of consciousness. Must the region be large (an assembly of thousands of neurons)? Or could it be "medium-sized" (a single neuron) or small (a single quark)? Perhaps, as some writers (e.g., Bohr, 1958; Eddington, 1935; Hodgson, 1991; Leggett,

1987a, 1987b; Margenau, 1984; Squires, 1990; Stapp, 1992; 1996; Beck, 1994; Penrose, 1994; Hameroff, 1994; Walker, 2000) have suggested, consciousness may reside in the "hidden variables" that govern the collapse of quantum mechanical state vectors in the brain.

It should be noted, however that contrary views have been expressed by Mohrhoff (1999) and Wilson (1999), who have argued that any action of a nonphysical mind on the brain would entail the violation of physical laws, such as the conservation of energy and momentum and the requirement that the outcomes of quantum processes be randomly determined. However, conscious selves might turn out to be physical or quasi-physical entities possessing physical energy. Also, it might turn out that the outcomes of quantum processes inside complex systems such as brains are not randomly determined but are governed by fields of consciousness, whereas those in simpler systems are not so governed. In fact, many parapsychological researchers, going back to Schmidt (1970), have produced evidence that conscious minds may be capable of determining, or at least biasing, the outcomes of quantum processes.

PANPSYCHISM

How small a brain region could be represented by a center of consciousness? Many of the writers listed above have suggested that a relatively large "suborgan" of the brain (such as the cortex of the left hemisphere or the thalamus) is the center of consciousness. However, David Skrbina (2003, 2005) has recently provided a comprehensive and brilliant defense of the philosophical tradition known as "panpsychism." Under this doctrine, all matter is imbued with consciousness. Skrbina argues for instance that an electron must somehow sense the presence of a proton in order to respond to its attractive force. An electron may even enjoy a certain degree of freedom of action due to quantum indeterminacy and may be able to sense a quantum field that is highly complex and global in nature. As Srkbina notes, the ancient Greek philosopher Epicurus contended that atoms have a form of free will, and can initiate contact from other atoms in order to deviate from a "predetermined" course.

Skribina observes that the eighteenth century mechanist Julien LaMettrie, who was a staunch materialist who denied the existence of a nonphysical soul, opposed Descartes in denying conscious to animals (although he did extend Descartes' view that animals were essentially machines to humans). In Skrbina's view, LaMattrie's position is basically that of a panpsychist, granting consciousness to all matter, although LaMattrie never explicitly developed this position in detail.

Skribina also points out that the prominent eighteenth century philosopher Arthur Schopenhauer also viewed all matter (including magnets and thrown rocks) as possessing will. Skribina notes that the German philosopher Eduard von Hartmann further developed Schopenhauer's thesis, postulating that each living cell has a form of consciousness. Von Hartmann postulated that the unity of consciousness in the brain was achieved via neural connections.

THE NEURON AS THE SELF

Recently Jonathan C. W. Edwards (2005), a physician and cell biologist, has "gone von Hartmann one better," proposing that a conscious self resides in each neuron, with each person thus housing billions of selves. He notes that the hypothesis that the single neuron is the center of consciousness solves the "binding problem," which is how to account for the fact that that a single unified conscious experience can arise from an array of diverse neurons. For instance, when one looks at an apple one has a single, unified experience of the apple, despite the fact that the neurons that fire in response to the apple's color and shape reside in different areas of the brain. Edwards asserts that the idea that there is a single "soul" in each person is simply a confabulation by the brain, with each neuron under the delusion that it is the sole self.

Edwards compares his view with the "polyzooism" of William James, as propounded in James (1890/1983). However, as Edwards notes, James later abandoned this position in favor of the hypothesis that there is a single pontifical cell in the brain that comprises the center of consciousness.

Edwards notes that each neuron in the brain has thousands of synapses, each of which can receive tens of messages per second. To Edwards, this may be sufficient to account for the complexity of conscious experience. He observes that "we think we are aware of hundreds of things at once, but it may be much fewer" (Edwards, 2005, p. 69).

Edwards also postulates that a limited form of consciousness may reside in other cells of the body. As noted before, the bodies of humans and other multicellular creatures are really just armies (in some cases platoons) of one-cell amoeba-like creatures. On the panpsychist view, even a single amoeba is thought to be associated with a center of awareness.

Edwards notes that all cells may fall under the illusion that the human body is "me." He notes that while each neuron may be aware of a wide range of stimuli, it is likely that 99 percent of volitional acts by the "Person" are "decided upon" elsewhere in the brain. In his view, most of our decisions and thoughts are "unconscious" (i.e., carried out by other cells). However, each neuron has access to the "story of the self" concocted by neurons in the left hemisphere and falls under the delusion that it is this self (i.e., the Person).

Edwards suggests that "me" cells may not be located in the cerebral cortex, as is the prevailing belief among neurophilosophers, but rather in the thalamus or the brain stem. He notes that the thalamus is richly supplied with sensory input and that areas of the brain stem are involved in maintaining and "turning off" consciousness.

He also proposes the alternative (or perhaps qualifying) hypothesis that consciousness resides in the electrical waves of the cell membrane. He notes that many physical systems are nonlocal, and observes that a single photon passing through a 1000-hole "micro-colander" is somehow aware of all 1000 holes.

One difficulty with Edward's proposal that the neuron corresponds to the conscious self is the intuition that the self is a unified, single persisting entity and thus (to reiterate the introspective conclusions of Descartes and others) cannot be identified with an aggregate (entity composed of numerous and changing parts, such as a cell). This problem might be avoidable if one assumed that the self corresponds to an "elementary" particle such as an electron, which is conserved over time (give or take an identity change from time to time) or to some field or entity yet to be discovered by physicists. Such a field or entity (such as a mini-Shin) would perhaps qualify as "nonphysical," at least in the context of current theories of physics. However, it may "become physical" if incorporated in physical theories yet to be developed.

Willard Miranker (2005) has also proposed that the individual neuron can sense synaptic activity and thus acts as a center of awareness. Miranker notes that this view should not be construed as meaning that individual neurons are homunculi, only that they have a primitive psychic capacity. He notes the similarity of his ideas with panpsychism. He proposes that the psychic activity of the neuron is causally effective in changing the strengths of the synapses with other neurons; thus this psychic activity is not epiphenomenal in Miranker's view. He proposes that there is a hierarchy of fields of awareness, with higher-level fields guiding the activities of assemblages of neurons, and still higher-level fields of awareness governing more macroscopic brain systems. Miranker proposes that sensory awareness becomes more magnified as one ascends the levels of the hierarchy.

AGGREGATES AND THE SELF

As we have seen, the panpsychists argue for a form of consciousness (perhaps rudimentary) in all physical matter. Elementary particles that are not incorporated into larger, more complex aggregations would be associated with a rudimentary consciousness. Skrbina (2005) notes that Ernst Haeckel, one of first major philosophers to embrace Darwin's theory of evolution, proposed that in order to account for the attraction of molecules, the molecules must somehow "feel each other" (Haeckel, 1899/1929). More complex forms of consciousness may be associated with aggregates of matter, such as single neurons, or large assemblies of neurons such as hippocampi and cerebral hemispheres. (However, it should be noted that such aggregates of matter, much like one's personality and physical body do not persist over time and thus cannot form the basis of a continuing self. Also, fields of consciousness appear to be unitary and indivisible, much more like a quark than like a molecule or a neuron.)

Skribina notes that Nagel (2002) extends consciousnesses to subsystems of aggregates such as cell assemblies, neurons and even possibly atoms and elementary particles. The problem confronting Nagel is how to account for the merger of these consciousnesses into a single point of view. He notes that Seager (1995) asserts this problem of combination was a "showstopper to any viable reading of panpsychism" (Skribina, 2005, p. 243), but observes that Seager himself offers quantum nonlocality and quantum superposition as one way around this stumbling block.

Nonlocality: Quantum "Hidden Variables"

For many writers, such as Walker (2000), who equate consciousness with the "hidden variables" that govern the collapse of the quantum mechanical state vector, the physical arena over which consciousness works is often assumed to be restricted to local areas of the brain (such as Eccles's "liaison brain") or specific networks of entities within the brain (e.g., quantumly-entangled water molecules in microtubules, as proposed by Penrose, 1994). If the area is deemed to be a wide region, encompassing virtually the entire brain, such a theory might be based on the influence of nondeterministic events governing synaptic transmission, as proposed by Eccles, Walker and others. In this case, the conscious mind (if assumed to be single and unitary) would be unable to overcome the effects of a severed corpus callosum in split brain-patients and might be supposed to experience a field of consciousness fluctuating between awareness of one hemisphere and the other.

As is by now well known to any consumer of the literature on "new age" physics (or

Chapter 2 in this book, for that matter), quantum systems exhibit nonlocality. For instance, the quantum state of a proton may be instantaneously influenced by measurements made on another proton light years away from it, if their quantum states are entangled. It might be thought that local areas of the brain might be "connected" of "entangled" with larger areas of the brain though such nonlocal quantum interconnections and thus local regions might in some sense be "aware of" or have "knowledge" of a wide array of brain activity. If the quantum wave governing its activity is presumed to be sufficiently complex and to contain substantial nonlocal information, perhaps even a single proton could be said to possess awareness of large portions of brain activity. Thus, even a proton could constitute one of a myriad of selves, each under the illusion that it is was the sole self associated with the body. However, it should be noted that Penrose (1994) has proposed that the collapse of quantum state vectors may require a minimal amount of mass-energy or gravitational potential that would likely exceed that of a single proton.

Panexperientialism

What could form the physical basis of a "self," conceived as a field of consciousness that seems to persist despite rapid turnover in the contents of consciousness, such as sensations, thoughts and feelings, and despite the constant turnover of physical matter in the underlying brain region? If the self is a proton or a quark, it would be expected to survive the physical death of the body and thus to constitute a "soul-like" entity (although it would likely retain no memory of its previous life once it became disentangled from the brain state).

The self might instead be an aggregate self or "compound individual" of the sort proposed in the "panexperientialism" of David Ray Griffin (1988a, 1988b, 1994, 1997). Such compound individuals are composed of, or arise from, a hierarchical collection of more primitive selves or "individuals." For instance, a neuron would be a compound individual in relation to its individual constituents such as molecules, and a "suborgan" such as the hippocampus that is composed of neurons would be a compound individual somewhat further up the hierarchy. All such "individuals" would have both mental and physical aspects under the panexperientialist view, although only hierarchically-ordered structures would be assumed to have a highly organized and structured consciousness. Less well-organized structures, such as rocks, would be ascribed only vague "feeling responses" according to Griffin's panexperientialist theory. Again, it is doubtful that conscious selves can be identified with aggregates of matter in that selves seem to persist through time periods in which the configuration and composition of such aggregates change and the fact that fields of consciousness seem to be unitary and indivisible whereas such aggregates are not.

Mini-Shins

A compound individual (in the panexperientialist sense) would only be able to survive death (of the body or its associated neural structure) if its identity is not dependent on the aggregate structure that supports it remaining intact (e.g., if it is a field of consciousness associated with or acquired by the structure rather one emerging from the structure and depending on the latter's exact composition for its existence). Such a view would be analogous to postulating mini-Shins (in the sense of Thouless and Wiesner) associated with localized brain regions. Such mini-Shins could be thought to possess global awareness of brain activity both through entanglement with complex and global quantum states as well as through classical (neural) connections. If its awareness of brain activity were sufficiently global, each such mini-Shin might develop the delusion that it was the supreme executive module governing the activity of the body (as it is likely that its primary identification would be with the entire body rather than with the local brain region with which it was directly associated). For instance in Libet's famous experiment (see Libet, 1991a), subjects believed that their "will" spontaneously controlled the flexing of their hands, even though the neurological record showed a "readiness potential" building in their brains for 350 milliseconds prior to the time the subject's "will" decided to act. Thus, the subjects' "fields of consciousness" in Libet's experiment may only have thought they were in control of the entire body and could move it at will, when really their "wills" were at least in part the result of prior brain activity outside of their knowledge or control. However, it should be noted that as Metzinger (2003) points out, Haggard and Eimer (1999) found that when subjects were asked to report when they "first felt the urge to move," the reported time was on average 296 milliseconds *prior* to the onset of electromyographic movement, although the standard verbal reports regarding the moment of decision replicated the finding of Libet.

Levy (2005) has also challenged Libet's identification of this unconscious brain activity with the intention or decision to act rather than with a growth of the urge or desire to act. Thus, Levy asserts, Libet's experiments do not challenge the doctrine of "free will." In Levy's view, Libet's subjects may have delegated the motor task to their unconscious minds. Levy further observes that the "controller" cannot control the control system, as this notion would lead to an infinite regress.

Young (2006) argues that the awareness of the moment of conscious decision is a second-order introspection and therefore it is not surprising that Libet found the reporting of the awareness of the decision to come 350 msec after the initiation of the readiness potential, as the awareness of the decision must follow upon the decision itself.

Other recent findings that suggest multiple consciousnesses may be associated with a single human brain include Alvarez and Cavanagh's (2005) finding that people can track twice as many objects when the objects are presented to both the right and left hemispheres of the brain that when they are presented to only one hemisphere, which Alvarez and Cavanagh interpret as evidence for two attentional foci in the brain.

Also, Massimini et al. (2005) found that, as sleep sets in, the communication between the different parts of the cerebral cortex breaks down (i.e., induced activity in one subsystem of the brain no longer spreads to other subsystems). Mashour (2005) notes that such cognitive "unbinding" also occurs in anesthesia. Massimini et al. conjecture that such communication among subsystems may be a prerequisite for consciousness. Massimini et al.'s results also suggest a central role for consciousness in integrating brain activity. Their findings suggest that the role of consciousness may be somehow tied to the integration of brain activity, which might imply that we may be more akin to mini-Shins or Walker's quantumly-nonlocal "protoconsciousnesses" than to Edwards' conception of the individual neuron as the basis of the self. However, there may be many surprises for us lurking in future theories of physics and consciousness. Our conscious selves may prove to correspond to a type of particle, field or entity that is quite far beyond our current understanding of the world.

Thus, it is likely that each "person" is composed of a multitude of fields of consciousness, with many of them under the illusion that they are the "executive module" controlling the entire body. Should these fields of consciousness be comprised of elementary particles, such as quarks, mini-Shins in the sense of Thouless and Wiesner (1948) or particles, fields or other entities that are yet to be discovered, they might be supposed capable of surviving the death of the body. Indeed, such mini-Shins may frequently transit in and out of the body during its physical lifetime.

The idea that one's self or soul becomes attached to one's body shortly after conception and remains attached until death is likely the result of the false identification of one's self with one's body and one's personality (i.e. ongoing saga of brain states). This self is, perhaps as Blackmore and Dennett insist, likely to be a story that we tell ourselves. The "purpose" of such a story in an evolutionary sense might well be to preserve the physical body and combination of one's genes. Such stories and the fear of death they engender would serve to preserve the organism and thus may be the result of evolutionary processes. However, our true selves (fields of pure consciousness) should not be confused with these "heroes" of our own personal fables. One source of the fear of death is precisely the identification of selves with "persons" in the sense of physical bodies conjoined with personalities. The "person" is not likely to survive the death of the physical brain. But we are at once much more and much less than persons.

Note that the identification of the self with the quantum mechanical wave function governing the brain or with some other sort of field surrounding the brain is also likely to be a false one, just as is the identification of the self with the physical body and personality. Such functions and fields undergo constant change and are in essence divisible into parts, unlike fields of pure consciousness, which appear to be changeless and unitary. Even Edwards' identification of the self with a single neuron runs into the same trouble, in that the constituents of neurons change over time and in that neurons, like physical bodies are aggregates, whereas the self, interpreted as a pure "point of view," appears intuitively to be indivisible and persisting over macroscopic time intervals.

The mini-consciousnesses or "proto-consciousnesses" proposed by Walker (2000) to govern the collapse of state vectors corresponding to events that are remote from human observers might be thought to correspond to mini-Shins in the sense of Thouless and Wiesner, if such mini-Shins are viewed as corresponding to, or containing, some of the "hidden variables" that determine the outcomes of quantum processes (whether in a human brain or elsewhere).

Mini-Shins so construed may persist after the death of the physical body. However, it is unlikely that they would retain much in the way of memory for events occurring during their association with their former bodies, traces of former personalities, or other contingent psychological characteristics.

One main feature of the universe appears to be conservation, whether of mass-energy, momentum, spin or baryon number. Things and quantities are not thrown away in such a universe; they are conserved and constantly rearranged. It is likely that the universe is at least as fond of mini-Shins as it is of, say, total quantum spin and might be expected to go to great lengths to conserve both items.

Indeed, physical bodies may continually be acquiring and expelling such mini-Shins, much as they do material particles. Such mini-Shins might then be reacquired by new bodies or incorporated into new "compound individuals" in Griffin's sense. Thus, each of us, if a mini-Shin, may be "dead" long before we suspect we will and possibly even long before the death of our current physical bodies, the good news being that we won't in fact suspect our deaths or remember our lives for that matter, having no access to the memories stored in our former brains and being completely absorbed in new cognitive tasks. Thus, life and death may equally be illusions.

The Riddle of the "Now"

If centers of consciousness are indeed fundamental components of the universe, whether being identified with elementary physical particles, the "hidden variables" that determine the outcomes of quantum processes, or mini-Shins à la Thouless and Wiesner (these possibilities not being necessarily mutually exclusive), one fundamental mystery would be solved. As noted in the Introduction, if each of us is identical with his or her physical body (or a component thereof), it is most surprising that we would find ourselves conscious at the present moment of time. A human lifespan is but the flicker of an eyelash in comparison to the age of the universe. But somehow, the one moment in time that has, in some mysterious fashion (hitherto unexplained by science), been selected from the vast history of the universe to be the "now" just happens to be a moment in your lifetime. The probability that the particular set of genes that make up your body would ever have come together is also practically zero. Thus, on the view that you are your physical body, it is virtually impossible that you exist now. But here you are.

If, however, fields of consciousness or mini-Shins are fundamental constituents of the universe, it is conceivable that they may be somehow "breathed out" and "breathed in" by physical bodies in much the same way as those bodies acquire and expel material particles. Under this view, the probability that your conscious self would exist now may be something approaching one.

The Self as "Recyclable"

In the oft-quoted words of Voltaire, it is no more surprising to be born twice than it is to be born once. On the view advocated here, it may not even be surprising to be born (and die) every several hours, as one's center of consciousness is acquired by and expelled from various physical bodies and other material systems. (During its association with a particular brain, the field of consciousness might even be under the illusion that it is in sole control of the body, as discussed above, not realizing that a "team effort" is likely involved.) One would of course have no memory of one's former (possibly fleetingly brief) "lives," as such memories (and former personality traits for that matter) are presumed to be located in, or at the very least highly dependent on, the activity and structure of brains to which one no longer has access. Of course, many such lives may consist of associations with animal brains, quantum computers, and possibly even plants or other material or nonmaterial systems deemed to possess consciousness (such as Walker's "proto-consciousnesses" that govern the collapse of state vectors remote from physical observers). Such survival of consciousness after dissociation from a particular human brain would thus not correspond to the sort of afterlife proposed in traditional Western religious traditions, in which memories and personalities are presumed to survive relatively intact (or perhaps only partially intact, as in the shades that inhabited the realm of Hades in ancient Greek mythology). But it would go a long way toward explaining the amazing fact that one finds oneself conscious "now" (which is highly improbable on the basis of the standard materialistic view as noted above). Just because we cannot explain consciousness does not imply that consciousness plays any less fundamental a role or enjoys less of a permanent status in the universe than do material particles. We may not be ontologically inferior to protons after all. (Indeed, we might even be quite proton-like ourselves, in light of the above discussion. Or perhaps we might be much more, as discussed in the ensuing chapter.)

Ian Stevenson's research into children who report memories of past lives (see Stevenson, 1987) has uncovered little in that way of evidence of the operation that a moral principle such as karma governs the process of reincarnation (even assuming for the moment the unlikely possibility that memories can be transferred from life to life). However, the idea that we are mini-Shins housed only temporarily in our present bodies does, as noted above, introduces an element of fairness. We may not be trapped for long in suffering bodies and may not for long enjoy the pleasure of bodies born into luxuriant circumstances. We each may sample many (and possibly all) of the human and nonhuman lives open to us, thus spreading around not only the suffering but the pleasure. Also, we should treat others well, if only out of self-interest. It might not be long before we find ourselves guests in their "body hotels."

Indeed, it may well be that such "human hotels" would not earn a "four star" status from such rating boards as may exist beyond our ken. A human body may not be the ideal place to be.

Next we turn to ultimate questions regarding the role of consciousness in the physical world as we examine the possibility that the world may in fact have been designed, however poorly, to house and "entertain" conscious observers.

8

The Self Writ Large

Several writers have suggested that conscious minds may play a truly grand role in the universe, perhaps even being responsible for the creation and design of living beings and the creation and design of the very physical universe itself. Strangely enough, the evidence is most compelling for the most grandiose of these claims, namely that the universe may have been designed by a conscious agent or agents. Let us begin, however, by examining the less cosmological assertion that minds may have played a role in the emergence of life and in directing the course of evolution.

The Creation of Life

According to currently accepted scientific wisdom, life emerged from random chemical reactions in the early stages of the Earth's development. Several prominent scientists have, however, expressed skepticism that the random mixing of chemicals could produce the complex, self-replicating entities we call living beings. Among these scientists are two British knights, Sir Francis Crick, a co-winner of the Nobel prize for the discovery of the structure of DNA molecules, and Sir Fred Hoyle, a noted astronomer. Both Crick (1981) and Hoyle (Hoyle, 1983; Hoyle & Wickramasinghe, 1981, 1988) have proposed that life evolved in outer space and then migrated to Earth. Outer space is considerably more spacious than the Earth and consequently affords life more opportunity to evolve randomly. Given the vast reaches of space and innumerable planetary systems, even the most improbable events, such as the creation of living beings from the random mixing of chemicals, are bound to occur.

Hoyle (1983) has even suggested that certain disease epidemics are caused by viruses descending to Earth from outer space. In some cases, Hoyle contends, these viruses may insert their genes into the genomes of terrestrial animals, altering the course of biological evolution.

Both Michael Hart (1990) and Richard Dawkins (1986) have also argued that it is extremely improbable that life will evolve in any given planetary system. However, because of the large number of planetary systems in the universe, they argue, life is bound to emerge in some of them. In fact, Hart argues that the existing evidence indicates that our universe is spatially infinite, so that all possible forms of life will emerge. Dawkins and Hart agree that because of the extremely low probability that life will emerge randomly in any given planetary system, life would be expected to be extremely sparsely distributed in the universe. Perhaps this is why we see so little evidence of extraterrestrial civilizations in our local area of the universe (discounting the reports in such second-tier scientific journals as the supermarket tabloid the *Weekly World News*).

John Casti (1989) has observed that life depends crucially on the accurate self-replication of molecular systems. He further observes that one cannot have reliable replication without large RNA molecules and that one cannot get large RNA molecules without a reliable replication system, thus producing a "Catch-22" situation, rendering it implausible that life could evolve randomly. Sidney Fox (1988), on the other hand, has proposed that the first life forms consisted of microspheres composed of spontaneously forming thermal proteins. In Fox's view, DNA and RNA molecules emerged later in the course of evolution. However, Julius Rebek and his coworkers at M.I.T. succeeded in synthesizing very simple self-replicating molecules, showing that self-replication need not involve RNA or DNA and may be achieved by quite simple molecules that are likely to arise randomly in a "prebiotic soup" on the early Earth (see Pool, 1990; Amato, 1994; and Feng, Park & Rebek, 1992).

Thus, it seems by no means impossible that life could have emerged from random chemical reactions either on Earth or in outer space, and so we are not compelled to assume that conscious minds must have played a role in the creation of the first self-replicating life forms. Later in this chapter, however, we will see that the physical universe itself seems to be delicately designed to allow the possibility of life's emerging in it. Perhaps a conscious agent or agents had a hand in designing the very laws of nature and in setting the initial conditions of our universe.

Directed Evolution

As was discussed in Chapter 1, until fairly recent times, even orthodox biologists assumed that some sort of psychical energy or vital force animated living creatures. We have already traced the retreat of this doctrine of vitalism in the face of scientific advances such as the synthesis of the biological molecules urea and glucose in the laboratory. Still, the philosophy of vitalism is not dead and retains some adherents today. For instance, in the early 1960s, the philosopher C. J. Ducasse of Brown University proposed a solution to the mind-body problem that he called "hypophenomenalism," in which the mind is viewed as animating the body (Ducasse, 1961). Under this doctrine, the mind is responsible for maintaining the life of the body.

The Australian biologist Charles Birch (1988) has contended that the mind cannot be reduced to brain activity and that mental events such as ideas and emotions may influence physical events in the body, such as the behavior of molecules. He further proposes that minds may be able to influence the outcome of seemingly "random events" in the process of biological evolution.

As we have already seen, Carroll Nash (1984b) reported evidence that human subjects could use their psychokinetic powers to influence the rate at which bacterial genes mutate.

Sir John Eccles (1989) went so far as to maintain that there exists a divine guidance over the course of evolution. The physicist O. Costa de Beauregard (1979) has postulated that biological evolution is directed from the future through the emission of advanced waves that travel backward in time. Another modern vitalist is consciousness researcher Willis Harman, who contends that there exists a "self-organizing" force governing living beings that cannot be explained on the basis of the principles of physics (Harman, 1993).

One of the most enthusiastic proponents of the doctrine that purposive influences guide the course of biological evolution in recent years was the popular science writer Arthur Koestler (1967, 1972, 1978). Koestler provided several examples of evolutionary development that he felt could not be accounted for by the neo–Darwinian theory that evolution proceeds through random mutations in genes. One of these examples was that of the sixth finger of the giant panda. Koestler argued that the finger would have been useless unless it was equipped with its own nerves, blood supply and system of muscles. Koestler felt that this confluence of events was unlikely to occur by chance. Koestler's view appears to be based on the assumption that a separate mutation would be required for each system. When one considers how frequently domestic cats are born with extra toes, Koestler's argument seems to fall apart. Evidently, viable supernumerary digits can arise without the divine coordination of a host of separate mutations.

Similarly, Koestler argued that the evolution of birds required the "simultaneous transformation of scales into feathers, solid bones into hollow tubes, the outgrowth of air sacs into various parts of the body, the development of shoulder muscles and bones to athletic proportions, and so forth" (Koestler 1978, p. 175). Once again it is only Koestler's assumption that these transformations had to be simultaneous and discrete rather than nonsimultaneous and gradual. That Koestler's assumption is in fact false is readily apparent upon an examination of the Jurassic bird Archeopteryx, which represents a transitional form between the reptiles and birds in the course of evolution. Archeopteryx had small wings (which were used mainly for gliding), clawed fingers (which were presumably used for climbing), teeth and feathers, but no hollow bones.

Koestler asserted that mutations are almost always trivial or harmful and thus could not serve to further the course of evolution. He cited the example of mutations that change the color of a plant, contending that such mutations were so trivial that they could not have any evolutionary significance. However, such a mutation could increase a plant's fertility by making it more attractive to bees or could increase the plant's longevity if the color change resulted in the plant's resembling a poisonous species. Similar mutations affecting the color of an animal might confer camouflage benefits or increased attractiveness to the opposite sex.

As further evidence that evolution is guided by some sort of purposeful force rather than being the result of random mutations, Koestler cited the example of mutant eyeless flies, which, when inbred, gave rise to several flies with normal eyes after a few generations. An advocate of neo–Darwinism can readily cope with this finding, however. The neo–Darwinist can simply assert that the mutation responsible for the eyeless condition was unstable and that the gene backmutated to its normal form. Also, as William Day (1984) points out, the emergence of a gene having a new function in the course of evolution is usually preceded by the duplication of the old gene, so that copies of the old gene are preserved in the animal's DNA should something go awry with the new gene.

Another piece of evidence for a purposive influence guiding the course of evolution educed by Koestler was the fact that the isolated marsupial animals of Australia evolved into similar types of animals as did the placental animals elsewhere on the Earth. The neo–Darwinist can, however, readily retort that similar environmental "niches" will tend to favor the evolution of similar types of animals.

Koestler argued for a modified form of Lamarck's theory of the inheritance of acquired characteristics. As evidence in favor of his theory, he cited the fact that the skin on the

soles of the feet of the human embryo is thickened, which he thought reflected the acqui-
sition of calluses by prior generations of walking humans. On the other hand, it would be
quite easy for the neo–Darwinist to cope with this observation by pointing out that mutations favoring thick skins on the soles of the feet will be favored by natural selection, as
thin-soled children may not be able to flee from predators over long distances. In summary, Koestler did not provide much in the way of compelling evidence to challenge the
neo–Darwinian position.

Ken Wilber (1996) also argues that a purposive force guides the course of evolution,
in a manner similar to Koestler. He assert that hundreds of mutations would be need to
occur simultaneously to produce, say, a wing in a wingless creature. He asserts that "half
a wing" will confer no biological advantage to an organism. However, contra Wilber, half
a wing might indeed confer superior gliding ability on an arboreal creature jumping from
tree limb to tree limb. Also single mutations, especially those producing dominant alle-
les of gene, can produce striking changes in an animal's phenotype (e.g., body design);
such changes do not require hundreds of simultaneous mutations as Wilber asserts.

There is a smattering of evidence supporting the view that some forms of directed
mutation exist. The team of Cairns, Overbaugh and Miller found that a mutant form of
the *E. coli* bacterium that is unable to metabolize lactose mutated back to the normal form
when placed on a medium containing high concentrations of lactose, suggesting that the
mutations tended to occur in a direction favorable to the organism. Similarly, B. G. Hall
found that bacteria that are unable to synthesize the amino acids tryptophan and cysteine
mutate in such a way as to be able to synthesize these amino acids when they are unavail-
able in the environment. Recent findings suggest that starvation does indeed affect the
types of mutation that occur, although it has yet to be determined that the mutations occur
in a purposeful rather than random manner. See Stahl (1990), Thaler (1994), and Culotta
(1994) for a more detailed discussion of this line of research.

Morphic Resonance

Another recent writer to challenge the neo–Darwinian theory is biochemist Rupert
Sheldrake (1981, 1983a, 1983b, 1988a, 1988b, 1990), who proposes that embryological
development is guided through a process he terms "morphic resonance." Sheldrake's ideas
and the evidence supporting them have already been discussed in Chapter 5. As noted
there, Sheldrake proposes that, for instance, a flamingo embryo will be guided in its development through "resonating" with the "morphic fields" of all the flamingos that have preceded it into the world. Susan Blackmore (1985) has pointed out that Sheldrake's theory
is circular insofar as Sheldrake explains the similarity of two creatures in terms of resonance and the resonance between two creatures on the basis of their similarity. Similarly,
it is difficult to see how morphic resonance could account for the process of evolution and
the emergence of novel forms of life, as morphic resonance would confine creatures to
repeating previous patterns of biological development. Also, as discussed in more detail
in Chapter 5, most if not all of Shledrake's experimental evidence for the existence of morphic resonance is based on studies with numerous design flaws, allowing for the possibility of experimental artifacts.

Biologists have been quick to condemn Sheldrake's theory as being baseless and have pointed out that orthodox biological and physical processes can account for most of the biological effects Sheldrake ascribes to morphic resonance.

Intelligent Design

Recently, there has been a movement to promote the idea that life shows evidence of intelligent design in American public schools. To the dismay of many scientists, belief in Biblical creationism (i.e., the literal the truth of the account of creation in chapter of Genesis in the bible) is widespread at the present time in America (although much less so in Europe and elsewhere). A recent CBS poll indicates that a slight majority of Americans believe that humans and other animals were created in their present forms and did not evolve from earlier life forms (www.cbsnews.com/stories/2005/10/22/opinion/polls/main 965223.shtml, accessed December 12, 2005).

There have been attempts in several American states to mandate the teaching of creationism alongside Darwin's theory of evolution in the public schools, with the theories being presented as equally plausible alternatives. Creationism in the form of a literal interpretation of the Biblical book of Genesis, with its implied recent creation of the Earth, the coexistence of human and dinosaurs, etc., is contradicted by a such a wide body of scientific evidence that space considerations prohibit a detailed overview in this book. However, a newer and more sophisticated version of a teleological alternative to Darwinism (at least to theory of Darwinian evolution based on the notion that genetic mutations occur randomly) has been proposed and goes by the moniker of "intelligent design." In most states, the battle for the public school curriculum in America is between those who wish the theory of intelligent design taught alongside with traditional Darwinism and those who wish to exclude it as unscientific (and possibly because they regard it as a front for those wishing to promote a literal Biblical creationism). Intelligent design presents a more sophisticated adversary for the latter, as it does not rely on the hypotheses of a recent creation of the Earth along with the present lifeforms presently inhabiting it (i.e. creation within the past few millennia). It is also more consistent with the formidable body of scientific evidence indicating that the Earth is several billion years old and the fossil record indicating the gradual development of life into the species existing at the present time.

One of the most prominent exponents of the intelligent design theory in recent years has been William A. Dembski, an associate research professor in the conceptual foundations of science at Baylor University. Dembski (2001) proposes that biological life shows evidence of having been designed by an intelligent agent or agents, rather than evolving solely through Darwinian processes involving purely "natural" causes. He considers the issue of whether intelligent agents themselves constitute natural causes. He concludes that they are not to be considered natural causes if they themselves are designed by an intelligent agency that is irreducible to natural causes. In such a case, he argues, the intelligent agents "cannot be reduced to natural causes without remainder" (Dembski, 2001, p. xiv). Dembski notes that the designers he is proposing are not equivalent to the Designer proposed by William Paley in his "natural theology," which was a thinly disguised version of the Christian god.

Dembski asserts that intelligent agents leave behind traces of "specified complexity" or "complex specified information" (which he abbreviates as CSI). According to his definition, a phenomenon must satisfy three conditions to be considered an instance of CSI. First, it must be contingent (i.e., not an inevitable result of deterministic natural laws). Second, it must be complex (i.e., improbable). Third, it must contain evidence of specification (i.e., must manifest some type of "meaningfulness"). As an example of CSI, he cites the message received by radio astronomers in Carl Sagan's novel *Contact*. This message consisted of an encoded sequential list of the prime numbers. He argues that such a message would be unlikely to have arisen by chance as the result of purely natural phenomena and manifests a high degree of meaningfulness.

Dembksi next considers the issue of how improbable an event must be in order to rule out the hypothesis that the event occurred merely by chance as a result of natural laws. Computing the number of possible transitions of each of the 10^{80} elementary particles in the observable universe during the entire history of the universe, he arrives at 10^{150} as an upper bound on the number of elementary events that could have occurred in the history of the (known) universe. Strangely, he uses 10^{-45} seconds as his estimate of the Planck time (the shortest possible meaningful temporal internal) rather than the more commonly accepted value of 10^{-43} seconds. However, this "error" only makes his treatment more conservative and only strengthens his argument (not to mention providing him with a very aesthetically pleasing value for the highest number of elementary events that could have occurred during the history of the observable universe). However, one way in which his treatment is not conservative is that he does not take into account the number of states each elementary particle could adopt in each transition. This would seem to require another multiplier in his expression for the possible number of states that could have occurred in the history of the universe.

Dembski argues that in computing the probability of an event occurring by chance, calculations must be restricted to states of the known universe. It is, he claims, an illegitimate tactic to assume a universe much larger than the observable universe or to assume that multiple universes exist, as in Hugh Everett's "Many Worlds" interpretation of quantum mechanics, as this inappropriately inflates probabilistic resources. However, it would seem to be a quite reasonable explanation of our improbable existence to assume that we naturally (i.e., by definition) inhabit a region of a greater universe (or one of many universes in a "multiverse") that is characterized by conditions that support human life. One argument Dembski offers in opposition to the multiple universe view is that there is no independent evidence for the existence of such multiple universes. He notes that if one were to see Arthur Rubenstein playing a piece by Liszt flawlessly, we would assume that his playing was due to skill, rather than that he is playing random notes and we just happen to inhabit a region of spacetime in which the random notes happen to replicate a piece by Liszt. In other worlds, one does not normally postulate unlimited probabilistic resources in explaining observed instances of CSI.

Dembski notes that deterministic natural laws merely take a given state of a physical system into one and only one subsequent state of the system, and thus cannot give rise to CSI unless CSI was already encoded in the initial state of the system. Similarly, he notes that deterministic natural laws combined with random processes such as those postulated in the theory of quantum mechanics cannot generate CSI in a system lacking CSI, due to the extreme improbability of any event yielding CSI from a system lacking CSI. (He assumes 10^{-150} as the upper bound on the probability of any system exhibiting CSI; thus, he argues that CSI subsumes events that are so improbable that they would never have arisen by chance during the history of the known universe.) He proposes a Fourth Law of Thermodynamics, which he terms the Law of Conservation of Information. Under this law, the amount of CSI can never increase (by chance) in a closed system.

Following this discussion, Dembski turns to the "evolutionary algorithms" proposed by Darwinists. He contends that the Darwinian mechanism of random variation followed by natural selection is inadequate to account for either the origin of life or the course of evolution (i.e., the emergence of complex species from the first rudimentary forms of life).

He debunks a particular instance of the evolution of CSI through random variation followed by natural selection offered by Richard Dawkins in his book *The Blind Watchmaker* (Dawkins, 1986). Dawkins considers a process whereby a random sequence of 28 characters evolves into the sentence "METHINKS IT IS LIKE A WEASEL." The process involves randomly varying each letter and then retaining each letter that matches the desired sequence on each iteration. Dawkins notes that the correct sequence was usually obtained after approximately forty iterations of this process of random variation followed by "natural selection." However, Dembski points out that this is not an instance of the generation of CSI, as under the rules of the game the probability that the correct sequence would emerge after a small number of iterations is approximately 1. He notes that in this game the design in fact came from the mind of Dawkins, who "frontloaded" the rules of selection to produce the desired result. Thus, the obtained sequence is in fact the result of intelligent design rather than being selected through true Darwinian mechanisms. He notes that when evolution proceeds by feedback, the rules governing the feedback themselves may manifest evidence of being intelligently designed, as many feedback algorithms are possible.

In particular, Dembski notes that the "fitness function," the function that determines the probability of survival and replication, may itself be intelligently designed (as in Dawkins' example). He argues that, when averaged across all possible fitness functions, evolutionary algorithms cannot outperform a blind search, which is extremely unlikely to result in an instance of specified complexity.

Dembski also considers the example of a computerized neural net model that learned how to play an expert game of checkers. He notes that this does not constitute an instance of spontaneously emerging CSI, as the neural net model was itself intelligently designed by its programmers to produce the desired result. (One feature of the program design was the inclusion of a "preprocessing layer" specifically designed to represent a two-dimensional checkerboard. Intelligent design was also involved in the comparison of win-loss records between programs, which determined which neural net would survive.)

Dembski briefly considers the wider topic of the anthropic principle, the notion that the fundamental constants of the universe seem specifically designed to support the existence of life and hence intelligent observers (to be discussed in more detail in the second half of this chapter). In particular, he argues that specifically Earth-like conditions had to exist in order for life to emerge. However, it is quite possible that radically different forms of life may emerge under different circumstances, and it may be "chauvinistic" to assume that all intelligent observers must be oxygen-breathing carbon-based life forms such as ourselves. Given such uncertainties, Dembski's definitive statements as to the probability of life emerging are unwarranted. Dembksi argues also that, even after the initial forms of life have emerged, Darwinian processes (increased replication driven by differential survival and reproduction) will favor simplicity over complexity (although one wonders how Dembksi knows this with such certitude). The emergence of complex forms, he asserts, is dependent on additional information in the fitness function, which itself may be intelligently designed.

Dembski asserts that the assumption that life emerged from purely physical causes imposes an arbitrary and unnecessary restriction on scientific inquiry and the types of scientific hypotheses that are deemed "politically correct." He notes that the origin of life is just one example of what he terms "emergence without causal specificity." He cites the emergence of consciousness from neurophysiological processes as another example of such emergence.

Dembski states that he specifically wishes to focus on the emergence of complex life and the diversity of life from simple life forms. He sees Darwinian mechanisms as being unable to account for such emergence, and he readily admits that Darwinian mechanisms may account for smaller changes, such as the evolution of antibiotic resistance in bacteria. Incidentally, he asserts that the process of lateral gene transfer in bacteria (the mechanism through which many bacteria acquire antibiotic resistance) is "thoroughly non-Darwinian" (Dembski, 2001, p. 287). Thoroughly non-Darwinian it may be, but it is nonetheless compatible with reductionism.

Dembski then introduces the notion of "irreducible complexity." A system is irreducibly complex if it is composed of many components, the removal of any one of which will prevent the system from functioning. As his central example of irreducible complexity, he cites the case of the bacterial flagellum, a whip-like tail that propels the organism. The flagellum is composed of many interlocking and interdependent parts, the loss of any one of which would prevent the flagellum from performing its function of propulsion. However, even in this case, one could imagine a more motionless flagellum serving the organism as a rudder or appendage. Parts of the system could have initially evolved for other purposes. Interestingly enough, Dembski only briefly mentions the eye, long the poster organ for irreducible complexity among design theorists, and that mention comes only at the end of the book. This omission is undoubtedly due to the fact that the eye has long since been demolished as an example of irreducible complexity by opponents of design theory. Rather compelling arguments have been made that this organ has emerged gradually and several times independently over the course of evolution.

Strangely, Dembski argues that whole organisms may not be irreducibly complex, citing the fact that the human body may continue to function even if its appendix is removed. (However, this observation considerably weakens Dembski's argument.)

Bower (2005) has noted that irreducible complexity, in which the removal of a single part destroys a system's function is evidence of poor design, not intelligent design. Perakh (2005) concurs with Bower that irreducible complexity in which the whole system fails if a single part fails is a sign of bad or even "stupid" design. In Perakh's view, an intelligent designer would include safeguards and redundancy into the system. Perakh notes that a pile of stones is less random than a brick (in Kolmogorov's sense of the shortest computer program needed to produce or describe the object or system). However, a brick is more likely to be intelligently designed than the rock.

Dembski notes that the theory of intelligent design may need to propose a positive research program in order to overthrow Darwinism as the primary research paradigm. He notes that design theory does indeed led to a new set of research questions, including:

- How did the designer(s) construct living organisms?
- How is the design process perturbed under changing circumstances?
- What are the intentions/goals of the designer(s)?
- Who were the designers?

He states that the last two questions are not proper questions for science. Here, he may be giving away his deistic leanings, as the last two questions are indeed considered questions for science these days when, say, the designers were prehistoric human beings. It is not clear why this situation would necessarily change if the designers were alien (or even immaterial) beings.

Other questions include the issue of how abiotically-generated information is transferred into organisms. Dembski notes that design could be achieved without violating any natural laws, but he implies that natural laws provide an incomplete description of the universe. (He notes that natural laws as presently understood provide an incomplete description of the universe, as they are, for instance, unable to account for the emergence of the conscious mind from the physical brain.)

Dembski next considers the question of how the theory of intelligent design should be integrated into the biology curriculum, a thorny issue indeed in these days of rancorous debate over creationism. He asserts that one need not discard the notion of evolution in biology curricula, but should rather abandon the position that Darwinian selection combined with random variation is the sole driving force in generating the diversity of life forms.

He does assert that the sudden explosion of life into a multitude of bodily designs in the Cambrian Era is difficult to square with the notion of common descent.

Dembski next turns to a discussion of the implications of the theory of quantum mechanics for design theory. He notes that quantum indeterminism provides the designer or designers with some "elbow room" to get their work done. (In a deterministic Newtonian framework, each subsequent state of the universe is uniquely determined by the initial state, eliminating any opportunity for a designer to intervene in the state of affairs. Of course, a physically-embodied designer would be able to act in such a universe, but Dembski is of the view that the designers are most likely not physically embodied.)

Dembski asserts that the prevailing view in modern quantum mechanics is the "Many Worlds" interpretation, in which the universe is seen as splitting into a myriad of alternative universes at each quantum decision point, with each universe corresponding to a particular outcome of the quantum process, noting that this view is advocated by such prominent theorists as Stephen Hawking and Murray Gell-Mann. However, it is my sense that most physicists see the Many Worlds theory as pathologically unparsimonious and still prefer the probabilistic interpretation of quantum mechanics over the Many Worlds interpretation. Dembski, of course objects to the Many Worlds interpretation because the plethora of universes it prescribes affords more probabilistic resources and hence makes it more likely that CSI could emerge by chance. Dembski raises the question of why, if there are so many worlds, is the world we happen to inhabit characterized by CSI. The answer of course is the same as that given by opponents of the anthropic principle: "Because we are here!" By definition we must exist in one of the universes characterized by a high degree of CSI. Dembski also argues that the probabilistic interpretation of quantum mechanics was put forth prior to the Many Worlds interpretation, and that indeed the latter is parasitic on the former.

Dembski objects to the "frontloaded" design hypothesis, in which it is postulated that CSI was infused in the initial state of the universe and that the designer or designers do not intervene in the world after its creation. He sees this as a form of kowtowing to the mechanistic model of the universe advocated by modern science and objects to the "hands-off" version of design theory on this basis. He asserts that there are no good reasons for preferring this view over a more interactionist model. In support of the idea of continued intervention, he cites the case of the sudden explosion of life into a diversity of life forms in the Cambrian Era.

He next considers Richard Dawkins' objection that if one postulates a Designer, then one must in turn explain the origin of (i.e., design of) the Designer. Thus, design arguments involve an infinite regress in Dawkins' view. Dembski, however, states that he "declines" the regress. He asserts that the principal question is whether design theory is useful as a scientific hypothesis in generating and answering questions. He asserts that the designer or designers are not part of nature as presently understood by the scientific community. Thus, he claims, there is no "marker" attached to the designer to indicate that the designer itself must be designed. However, this argument may fail in a causal sense, as one may ask what caused the designer (even granting that the designer has no known features that would suggest deliberate design). Dembksi, on the other hand, argues that the design hypothesis is intended to provide "local" or "proximate" explanations rather than ultimate explanations.

Dembski next considers the objection put forward by Eugenie Scott (2001), a prominent critic of intelligent design theory (IDT) and creationism, that IDT is unfalsifiable. Dembski counters that it is in fact Darwinism that is unfalsifiable (a charge not uncommonly directed at Darwinism), whereas IDT is not. (Actually, although IDT predicts the existence of CSI, this is an existential claim, which may be verified but not falsified. In fact, Dembski argues that the existence of CSI falsifies Darwinism, showing that Darwinism is indeed falsifiable after all.)

Dembski notes that IDT does not repudiate Darwinism entirely, but incorporates Darwinian selection as one of the principles driving biological evolution. He observes that the objections to IDT seem to have their root in a fear of the reemergence of occult and religious entities in scientific explanations, which may lead to the destruction of modern science, at least in the eyes of orthodox scientists.

He notes that the British natural philosophers embraced a world governed by mechanistic laws with all design being of the "frontloaded" variety. This stance did much to undermine the design theory, in Dembski's view. He argues, however, that the nonmechanistic aspects of modern quantum theory imply that design need not only be of the frontloaded variety and that interactionistic versions of IDT no longer violate the established principles of science (which of course continue to change and evolve with new discoveries).

In the final analysis, Dembski's case rests on his probabilistic arguments for the presence of CSI. Given the present state of our knowledge, it is unlikely that these probabilities can be computed with any degree of certainty (e.g., the probability of bacterial flagellum proteins emerging by chance from some prior adaptation). For this reason, it cannot be said that Dembski has definitively established a case for intelligent design.

There is thus no compelling evidence for an influence of mind on the creation of life or the direction of biological evolution. A God or Designer who pushes macromolecules about with Her Divine Finger seems no more credible than Newton's God, whom Newton called upon to continually reestablish the harmony of the planetary movements.

There is a bit more of a suggestion of a role for the mind in the creation of the universe itself, however, as we shall now see.

Mind as Deity

The universe we inhabit seems very delicately designed to support the existence of living creatures and hence of conscious minds. This suggests that the universe may have been created by a conscious Being or beings to serve as some sort of cosmic amusement park. The fact that the universe seems designed to support the existence of intelligent beings has been commented on by many physicists, who have coined the term "anthropic principle" to denote this element of apparent design in the universe.

As the physicist Paul Davies (1983) points out, if the rate of expansion of the universe immediately after its creation in the Big Bang had differed even slightly from its actual value, life as we know it could not exist. Had the rate of expansion been infinitesimally slower, all matter would have collapsed into black holes shortly after the creation of the universe. Had the rate been slightly faster, the matter density would have been too small to allow galaxies to form. Davies also points out that matter seems to be very uniformly distributed throughout the galaxy. If the mass distribution had been less homogeneous, the gaseous clouds needed to form stars, planetary systems and living beings would not have existed, and most of the mass in the universe would have been consumed in black holes.

Roger Penrose (1986) has pointed out that the universe was created in a very highly ordered state that would not be expected to occur by chance.

The laws of physics themselves seem to be delicately contrived to allow for the emergence of life. In their book *The Anthropic Cosmological Principle*, John Barrow and Frank Tipler (1986) note that even minuscule variations from the existing ratios of the strength of the nuclear force to the electromagnetic force, of the total number of photons to the total number of protons in the universe, and of the mass of the electron to the mass of the proton would have rendered the universe incapable of supporting life. They further contend that the existing abundances and properties of the chemical elements seem to be designed to facilitate the emergence of life, noting in particular that the most abundant chemicals, such as water and carbon dioxide, appear to be optimally suited to supporting life. John Gribbin and Martin Rees (1989) point out that the so-called "weak force" that governs radioactive decay must be extremely fine-tuned in order for stars to shed matter in great quantities during supernova explosions. (Our bodies are composed of elements that were forged in the interior of stars and then released in supernova explosions. As Carl Sagan was fond of saying, we are all "starfolk.") George Greenstein (1988) has observed that even a difference of one part in 100 billion in the electrical charges of the electron and the proton would cause physical objects to fly apart due to electrical repulsion among their parts. Greenstein further notes that if the ratio of the masses of the proton and the neutron were reversed, protons would decay into neutrons and even simple elements such as hydrogen would not exist (and hence neither would life).

In a recent review of the evidence for the anthropic principle, Mario Livio and Martin Rees (2005) consider all possible universes with the same natural laws and the same value of all physical constants as our own but one, the cosmological constant $\wedge$, which describes the "pressure " of the physical vacuum. They assert that the value $\wedge$ we observe in our universe seems fine-tuned to support life. If $\wedge$ were higher by an order of magnitude, the universe would have expanded so quickly that no galaxies could have formed, and thus life (or more precisely the carbon-based life forms with which we are familiar) would not have arisen. Livio and Rees cite three other cosmic "coincidences" that seem necessary:

- The presence of baryons (particles such as protons and neutrons).
- The fact that the universe is not infinitely smooth, allowing for the possibility of structure.
- The fact that the force of gravitation is weaker than the forces that act within atoms and molecules by a factor of 10^{40}.

Even the number of dimensions of space seems uniquely suited to supporting the existence of life. Planetary orbits would be unstable if space had more than three dimensions (see Barrow & Tipler, 1986; Gribbin & Rees, 1989; and Greenstein, 1988), and Greenstein (1988) has pointed out that a universe of at least three dimensions may be required in order that brains with highly complex connections among their neurons can exist (which may be necessary for consciousness).

On the contrary side, physicist Steven Weinberg (2001) has argued that the fine-tuning of the universe may not be that fine after all. He notes that the ratio of the energy of a beryllium 8 nucleus to that of a hydrogen nucleus is 20 percent higher than the optimum ratio for carbon production. He suggests that there may be room for substantial "errors" in such ratios.

Bernard Carr (2004) notes that the universe needs to be about 10^{10} years old in order to support life, but that after this epoch all matter will be in stellar remnants. This may be part of the reason why the moment in time that has been somehow selected as the "now" is within the range of ages of the universe that will support life. As biologically based conscious observers, we could exist at no other time. A discussed in Chapter 2, many physicists (e.g., Walker, 2000) have proposed that quantum processes do not give rise to a definite outcome unless such outcomes are witnessed by a conscious observer. Indeed, some physicists (e.g., Wheeler, 1983) have suggested that the universe itself, conceived as a quantum process, could not have come into existence without some conscious observer to collapse state vectors and thus to give rise to a definite history of the universe. Wheeler terms this view the "participatory universe." Wheeler notes that this view may explain the "anthropic principle," the fact that the initial state and physical laws of the universe seem finely tuned to support the existence of conscious observers. Potential universes that do not support the presence of conscious observers could not become actualized in Wheeler's view, as there would be no conscious observers to collapse their state vectors in the proper "direction" to create such a history.

The physicist Edward Tryon (1973) has proposed that the creation of the universe may actually have been a quantum fluctuation. He further observes that the total energy of the universe may be equal to zero, as negative gravitational potential energies may balance out the positive energies of physical particles. If the total energy of the universe is zero, then there is no limit on how long the universe might exist under the Heisenberg Uncertainty Principle of quantum mechanics. Thus, the universe may be the ultimate "free lunch."

If the universe is a quantum fluctuation that can only become real through being observed, as Wheeler thinks, then the creation of the universe might have been the ultimate act of retroactive PK! (Wheeler himself would abhor this particular interpretation of his theory, as he is an ardent opponent of parapsychology.)

Hill (2005) notes that the vast emptiness of space is totally hostile to the existence of humanity. Thus, he suggests that the if the universe is designed to support the presence of conscious observers, the evidence would suggest that the universe was "designed" for beings that exist in the vacuum of space, not beings that are confined to rarely occurring spongelike brains found on one tiny speck of matter in one remote corner of a cold and desolate universe (or more likely a number of such tiny specks sparsely populating a virtually empty spacetime continuum). Indeed recent scientific photography has uncovered the startling beauty of the inanimate physical world, from the microscopic domains such as electromagnetic fields to the haunting beauty of the cloudlike nurseries of infant stars. The mini-Shins discussed in Chapter 7 might in fact correspond to the empty-space-dwelling beings postulated by Hill. Such beings may be lost in an artwork universe of their own creation. Alternatively, if the Eastern tradition's view that all consciousness is One is correct, the One may be wandering through Its creation one lifetime at a time, contemplating it from all angles, lost in its beauty and drama. The noted physicist Richard Feynman observed that a positron (the antimatter analogue of the electron) may regarded as an electron traveling backwards in time. He once joked that the reasons all electrons look identical to one another is that they are in fact the same particle zig-zagging its way backward and forward in time. Perhaps, the conscious self is much like Feynman's electron/positron.

The Universe

As noted in the Introduction, the physicist James Jeans (1937) once remarked that the universe resembled a "a great thought" more than it did a "great machine" and another great physicist, Arthur Eddington (1920/1959), called the fabric of the cosmos "mindstuff." More recently, another prominent physicist, Henry Stapp (2005a), has observed that under the *Weltanschauung* of quantum mechanics, the world has "an essentially 'idea-like' structure." In a recent essay in *Nature*, the flagship journal of materialist science, Richard Conn Henry proclaimed that:

> One benefit of switching humanity to a correct perception of the world is the resulting joy of discovering the mental nature of the Universe. We have no idea what this mental nature implies, but—the great thing is—it is true. Beyond the acquisition of this perception, physics can no longer help. You may descend into solipsism, expand to deism, or something else if you can justify it—just don't ask physics for help....
> The Universe is immaterial—mental and spiritual. Live and enjoy [Henry, 2005, p.25].

Indeed, the base reality of the world appears to be one of quantum probability waves inhabiting an abstract, multidimensional mathematical space rather than the solid, marble-like electron and protons zipping around in the four-dimensional spacetime continuum that we imagine to be the firm underpinnings of our material existence. The mathematical complexity and beauty of the laws of the quantum mechanics are remarkable. It does indeed seem as though the Creator is, as both Jeans and Einstein thought, a great mathematician.

Of course it could well be that the creation of the universe was a group effort, a kind of Manhattan Project involving trillions of mini-Shins embedded in an unimaginably complex "computer" made out of whatever passes for matter (if anything) in the "preuniverse." Given that we are embedded in organisms only a few genes removed from a chimpanzee (and possessing fewer genes than many seemingly simple plants such as rice), it may be no wonder that our brains are unable to unravel the real mysteries of the cosmos, including the origin and role of consciousness. Perhaps Colin McGinn (1999) is correct in his view that our present brains, with their mere 100 billion cells apiece, will never be able to penetrate these mysteries. There may, however, be nothing preventing us from one day in the distant future building a device that is capable of hosting a staggeringly large number of mini-Shins (in view of the fact that the American national debt now exceeds $8 trillion, we no longer stagger at the thought of our brain's mere 100 billion nerve cells). Such a device/superorganism might not only be capable of grasping such mysteries, but may have the intellectual wherewithal to create new Big Bangs, giving rise to new universes (perhaps even with "improved" or at least more entertaining laws of physics). Such a device/superorganism might be considered God under the definition of the deity as the creating force/intelligence. However, whatever "gods" may have lurked in the preuniverse were perhaps just as puzzled by the mystery of their own existence as we by ours. This is why recourse to any explanation of Creation in terms of a Creating Intelligence (CI) leads to an infinite regress, as one then is confronted with the task of explaining the CI's existence.

But if the universe is a thought as Jeans, Eddington and Stapp contend, whose thought is it anyway? Was the universe created as a vast cosmic amusement park or "art gallery" for the entertainment of mini-Shins (perhaps even those embedded in the CI)? Why go to trouble of designing such an elaborate version of "Disney World for mini-Shins") unless One intended to enjoy it Oneself, if only vicariously? Are our individual consciousnesses just aspects (or perhaps former components) of the CI, embedded in the myriad creatures the CI has managed to generate from Its mathematical inventions, much as a future teenage spree killer may become absorbed in the adventures of a homodical misogynic hero in his favorite virtual reality video game?

Of course, the anthropic principle is based on the observation that the laws and initial conditions of the universe must be extremely fine-tuned to support life *as we know* it (i.e. carbon-based life forms). However, perhaps there are other forms of life (e.g., nucleon-based) that might arise under different initial conditions or laws.

There are ways of accounting for the evidence for the anthropic principle without assuming that the universe was designed by a creative intelligence. Barrow and Tipler (1986) note that if one accepts Tryon's view that the creation of the universe was a quantum fluctuation, then Hugh Everett's Many Worlds interpretation of quantum mechanics would imply that all possible universes must be created.

Both Guth and Kaiser (2005) and Livio and Rees (2005), for instance, note that cos-

mic inflation (the currently favored model of cosmogenesis) may produce "pocket universes" in each of which the fundamental laws of physics might be different. Each universe might have its own set of initial conditions, and the laws of physics might crystallize
out into different forms in each universe. As conscious observers, we must of course be
living in one of the universes that is capable of hosting conscious beings. But this does
not mean that a conscious agent designed the universe, as all possible universes must occur.

M. A. Markov (1985) has hypothesized that universes may spawn "daughter universes" which become separate from the "mother universe." Indeed, there has been spec-
ulation that it might be possible for a mad scientist to create such a universe in his own
basement. This would lead to another version of the many universes theory.

Another possibility, which has been extensively discussed by George Gale (1990), is
that of an oscillating universe. If the amount of matter of our universe is sufficiently large,
then we are living in what is known as a "closed universe," that is a universe that is des-
tined to recollapse in a "Big Crunch." The Big Crunch is a time-reversed version of the
Big Bang, in which all the matter of the universe becomes compressed in a spacetime singularity, or black hole. Because the known laws of physics break down in a singularity,
several physicists have proposed that the universe will be reborn after the Big Crunch in
a process known as the "Big Bounce." The new version of the universe will have different
initial conditions and possibly even different laws of physics from the previous universe.
During many of these cycles, the universe may be incapable of supporting life as we know
it, but we by definition inhabit a cycle that is conducive to our existence. Thus, it seems
to us that the universe has been especially designed to support life, whereas in fact it has
not. In passing, we should note that this model of an oscillating universe bears a certain
resemblance to the cyclic views of time held by the ancient Greeks, such as Plato, Aristotle and Pythagoras, as well as to the great cosmological cycles called kalpas in Hindu
philosophy.

A spatial rather than temporal version of the many worlds hypothesis is offered by
A. D. Linde (1985). He suggests that the laws of physics may have assumed different forms
in different regions of our own universe. We of course live in a region where the laws of
physics are conducive to our existence.

Again, we of necessity inhabit a pocket universe that is capable of support the existence of conscious observers.

Also, as remarked above, given that the vast realms of empty space are hostile to life
as we know it, the primary observers may well be drifting "naked" mini-Shins that just
happen to become stuck in physical bodies from time to time. And still one is confronted
with the task of explaining the laws and initial conditions that gave rise to cosmic inflation
in the first place, which may again produce an infinite regress of questions and explanations.

Mind, viewed as the creator of the physical world, is literally deified. If the intelligence that created the physical world is somehow to be identified with the souls (read "mini-
Shins') that now inhabit it, then that intelligence is unlike the post–Newtonian Christian
God who stands remote from his creation once it is complete. It resembles much more the
Vedic view of the Universal Self that divides into the minds of the myriad creatures of the
world, which derives from the *Brhadaranyaka Upanisad*. The philosopher Alan Watts was
fond of comparing this Indian view of creation to God playing hide-and-seek with himself in the physical world.

Consciousness and Cosmos

One's true self in the Eastern view is the pure consciousness that in Hindu philosophy is taken to be identical with all consciousness, including that of the World Soul or Brahman. Under the Vedantic worldview, there is only one pure consciousness, and we are all the Universe looking at itself from different perspectives. Thus, when persons temporarily abandon their individual identities and perceive themselves as merging with the Cosmos or as being in perfect union with God, as in the mystical experiences described by James (1902), they are seeing directly into their true selves, according to this view. All consciousness is the one Consciousness that underlies this and all other worlds. In this view, we are fragments of the World Soul, our selves at once separate from, and yet identical to, one another. Sufism, a branch of Islam, proclaims the doctrine of *marifa*, that there is no me, there is no you, but all is God (Frager, 2002).

W. T. Stace (1960) has argued that the pure ego of each individual being (atman) must be identical to the universal ego (Brahman), as both are simply fields of pure consciousness. He suggests that this identity is intuitively recognized in mystical experiences in which a person feels herself to be at one with the World and with God. He notes that scientific and mathematical concepts are based on dissection of the world into atomistic concepts, and he proposes that the reason why mystical experiences are "ineffable," or impossible to describe in words, lies in the inability of scientific language to describe a nonatomistic or holistic reality.

Astrophysicist David Darling (1995) contends that our individual, encapsulated egos are illusions and that, when a person dies, this illusory self is dissolved and the person's consciousness merges with the world consciousness.

Larry Dossey (1996), a well-known writer on spiritual healing, also argues that the mind is nonlocal in nature. He cites the physicist Erwin Schrödinger's remark that "the overall number of minds is just one" and proposes that the resistance to the view of the mind as unbounded and infinite derives from a deep-seated fear of this view of the world. In Dossey's opinion, people feel safer in a closed-in and finite identity.

Walker (2000) too proposes that all observers are in fact one and that this single observer is responsible for the collapse of all quantum mechanical state vectors, although the activity of this single observer may be manifested as multiple "proto-consciousnesses" acting to collapse quantum mechanical state vectors into definite outcomes.

The philosopher Colin McGinn (1995) has observed that the mind is frequently conceived as being nonspatial in nature and that some type of nonspatial order must have preceded the creation of space in the Big Bang. He suggests that this nonspatial order may still persist and may form the basis of consciousness.

Of course, a creative intelligence need not be benign. The early Christian Gnostics viewed the creator of the world as a malevolent demiurge who wished to trap spirits in matter and to prevent their return to a state of disembodied divine being. Also, as Joseph Campbell (1964) pointed out, the second century Christian philosopher Marcion viewed the God of the Old Testament as an evil being responsible for imprisoning spirits in matter.

The anthropic principle seems to strike a note of euphoria in many people. Certainly, if the universe has been designed to support conscious observers (or if those observers created the universe themselves), a certain elation may be experienced at the idea that one's existence is not as precarious and fragile as one might have thought and that one may be a great deal more powerful than appearances would indicate. However, if the universe is designed to house conscious beings, one could easily argue that, from the existing evidence, the universe appears more likely to be designed as a torture chamber than as a playground for the gods. (Perhaps if this universe was indeed a construction project carried out by quadrillions of Shins united in some sort of colossal quantum computer or superorganism, we should make a note to use more mini-Shins in order to get it right next time. Even superorganisms/computers may make stupid blunders from time to time and might not be able to anticipate all possible design errors in their cosmogenic projects).

The moral implications of the above views are less clear than many would suppose. The conception that we are all parts of one Universal Self could just as easily lead us to mistreat others ("I'm only hurting myself—a victimless crime") or to commit murder ("he'll just get reincarnated anyway") or to treat all humans as siblings (an attempted nonsexist translation of "all men are brothers"). Also, as noted above, if conscious observers created the universe, the question then arises as to who or what created them as well as any "pre-universe" they may have inhabited. One thus arrives at the usual intractable infinite regress that accompanies explanations of the Creation in terms of a Creator. Certainly at this stage of our inquiry, a more manageable question, and one perhaps more amenable to scientific investigation, is that of the relationship of the conscious mind to the physical brain. Given the current state of our knowledge, this is as (or more) profound and exciting a question as that of the role of conscious agents in creating the universe itself.

9

A Summing Up

We began this journey with an awakening from dreams. The first awakening was from the Dream of Matter. The existence of mental events is undeniable. Also the arguments against epiphenomenalism show that mental events do not simply exist, they are able to exert causal influence on physical events. This may indicate that the dualist interactionism is the only viable solution to the mind-body problem, or it may suggest that some form of panpsychism is true, in which all matter-energy is viewed as having a psychic aspect. If the latter, orthodox scientists would not need to abandon their beloved principle of the causal closure of the physical world. Of course, if scientists ever do develop testable hypotheses regarding the influence of "souls," or for that matter mini-Shins, these "new" entities could be incorporated into the body of physics, and the physical world might become causally closed once again (through an act of definitional fiat).

It should be noted that many of the scientists who most vehemently defend the tenet of the closure of the physical world seem to subscribe to an outmoded deterministic Newtonian view of the physical world that has been overthrown by development of modern theories of quantum mechanics. Other scientists, not so mired in Newtonian determinism still fall victim to the psychological pressure for closure, the need to believe that one's worldview does not leave out essential facts. Such scientists, while affirming quantum indeterminism, steadfastly adhere to the principle that all quantum events are randomly determined and are not subject to influences from outside of the physical world as described in current theories of physics. However, a substantial minority of physicists and neuroscientists contend that the macroscopic behavior of the brain is governed by the outcome of quantum processes that may be influenced by a self or field of consciousness that is not described within the theory of quantum mechanics itself. Henry Stapp (2005b), for instance, notes that quantum mechanical laws must be used to describe the process of exocytosis (the emission of neurotransmitters into the synaptic cleft between neurons). He suggests that conscious attention may stabilize the quantum state of the brain, thus biasing it toward a particular outcome. The results of several lines of parapsychological investigation also suggest that conscious minds may be able to bias the outcomes of such quantum events.

The existence of psi phenomena, with their apparent spacetime independence, suggest that existing theories of physics are woefully incomplete and that there may be nonlocal influences between physical and mental events that cannot be explained on the basis of current theories of physics. The evidence for psi phenomena was reviewed in Chapters 3 through 5. As yet, laboratory investigations of psi have not succeeding in producing an effect that can be readily replicated by the vast majority of experimenters. Also a determined skeptic can construct counterexplanations of most apparent cases of spontaneous psi, such as apparently precognitive dreams, on the basis of sensory cues, unconscious inference, false memories and confabulation. For these reasons, the existing body of evidence for psi phenomena, while suggestive, does not compel belief in such phenomena.

Psi phenomena are, in any case, not needed as an alarm clock to wake us from our second dream, the Dream of the Person. We are not our thoughts, our memories, our beliefs or our emotions. These cognita are ephemeral and fleet away the moment we try to grasp them. From an introspective standpoint, it appears clear that we are a center of pure consciousness that feels our feelings, that senses our sensation. In short, our essential selves seem to be akin to the "Cartesian theaters" so abhorred by Daniel Dennett and other modern deniers of the self such as Susan Blackmore and Thomas Metzinger. What is less clear from an intuitive point of view is that we may be one among many such centers somehow attached to our present brain (and possibly even inhabiting cells elsewhere in our bodies). This realization is what is needed to wake from the Dream of Atman and Brahman.

We have already shed countless emotions and several "personalities" and in fact innumerable physical bodies on our journeys from womb to tomb. Likely too, our bodies have already shed many "souls" or mini-Shins. Such "naked fields of consciousness" may prove to be identical with physical particles or fields already known to science. Alternatively, they may prove to be sufficiently similar to such fields and particles to earn the rubric "physical" under some future extended theory of physics. On the other hand, they may prove to be so dissimilar to physical matter and fields that, when eventually characterized, they will be regarded as "nonphysical" or "immaterial." If so, dualism will once again rear its ugly head, but this time with sharpened teeth.

As the present time, it is not exactly clear how such mini-Shins or "souls" might be empirically studied. Experimental methodologies may evolve that will allow scientists to distinguish between the hypothesis that human brains are associated with only a few mini-Shins and the hypothesis that millions of mini-Shins are at work in a single brain. With a little creativity, the mini-Shin hypothesis may be rendered testable. Certainly the hypothesis that there is only a single Shin in each brain can be falsified in experimental tests and indeed has been falsified in split-brain research and other lines of neuropsychological investigation, as argued by Patricia Churchland.

We are not our physical bodies. Each of us has already shed several such bodies the way a snake sheds its skin, if our memories are correct. Of course, our memories may not be correct. Most likely, our memories of past years are just our present decoding of records stored in the vast array of synaptic connections in the brains we temporarily call home. If we can somehow become attached to a particular brain at some time shortly after conception and detached at the moment of death, what would prevent us from "glomming on" to our full-grown brains yesterday and "checking out" of them tomorrow, in much the same was as the physical particles that make up our bodies do? In the meantime, mired in our present brains, we generally fall victim to the network of memories, hopes and aspirations embedded in our temporary housing and fall once again under the Dream of the Person. Perhaps, having lost our memories of our previous existences at the time we departed from the physical (or nonphysical) systems that formerly held us, we quickly fall under the delusion that we are our physical bodies, that our essential selves are the patterns of memories and feeling that we are presently experiencing (however temporarily), and that we have been present in our current brains through the spacetime history of the ever changing bags of molecules that we call our physical bodies.

We likely play a role in the world that is at least as fundamental as the roles played by electrons and quarks and probably more fundamental than the temporary agglutinations of material particles that comprise our physical "selves" under the Dream of the Person. Unlike the prevailing view in modern science, we are, under the view fostered here, not ontologically inferior to elementary physical particles after all. If physics has taught us anything about the universe, it is that it loves to conserve quantities (including for example baryon number, mass-energy, electrical charge, momentum, and angular momentum). Mini-shin number may well be another example of a conserved quantity. Mini-Shins leaving our bodies may be no more likely to wink out of existence than are oxygen atoms expelled through our nostrils.

This universe appears to be a place of transformation rather than a place of de novo creation and ultimate destruction. It is likely just as enamored of mini-Shins as it is, say, of up quarks, and thus may preserve the former as it does the latter.

Consciousness may even be, as Colin McGinn (1995) has argued, prior to space and time themselves. For the time being, however, we might as well lie back and enjoy the show. Somebody (possibly we ourselves embedded in an unimaginably complex and long forgotten system) went to a lot of trouble to put it on for us, although it admittedly suffers from design flaws that may need to be corrected on the next Iteration.

One might imagine that a conscious system so complex and vast as to be able to create (perhaps literally to dream up) such a startlingly wonderful (and frightening) world as this one might well become bored with its omniscience and may wish to lose itself in its creation, if only temporarily. It may need to fragment itself and temporarily shed much of its omniscience to accomplish this. Then it may begin the task of solving the puzzle of the universe once again. We too might well begin to stagnate and become bored if we were to somehow become immortal and become trapped in our present bodies and mired in our present personalities and situation for all eternity. Death may be the rope thrown to free us from the quicksand of our current identities.

If these thoughts are correct, each of us, as centers of consciousness, will be around for a long time to come. But the lengths of our associations with our present personalities may be much shorter than we think. Our true selves, however, may be both much less than and much greater than we think.

The musings in this book are but hints of what shape the answers to our Ultimate Questions may take. Given the present state of our knowledge (and the facts that our brains are not that far removed from those of chimpanzees and our bodies contain only a small number of genes when compared to many plants), it is not possible to do more than sketch a fuzzy outline of what the Ultimate Answers may be.

Bibliography

Aanstoos, C. (1986). Psi and the phenomenology of the long body. *Theta*, *13–14*, 49–51.

Ader, R. (1981). *Psychoimmunology*. New York: Academic Press.

Akolkar, V. V. (1992). Search for Sharada: Report of a case and its investigation. *Journal of the American Society for Psychical Research*, *86*, 206–247.

Alvarado, C. S. (1984). Phenomenological aspects of out-of body experiences: A report of three studies. *Journal of the American Society for Psychical Research*, *78*, 219–240.

Alvarez, G. A., and Cavanagh, P. (2005). Independent resources for attentional tracking in the left and right visual hemifields. *Psychological Science*, *16*, 637–643.

Amato, I. (1992). Capturing chemical evolution in a jar. *Science*, *255*, 800.

Anderson, R. I. (1981). Contemporary survival research: A critical review. *Parapsychology Review*, *12(5)*, 8–13.

Aspect, A. J., Dalibard, J., and Roger, G. (1982). Experimental test of Bell's inequalities using time varying analyzers. *Physical Review Letters*, *49*, 1804–1807.

Azuma, N., and Stevenson, I. (1987). Difficulties confronting investigators of "psychic surgery" in the Philippines. *Parapsychology Review*, *18(2)*, 6–8.

Baringa, M. (1990). The tide of memory, turning. *Science*, *248*, 1603–1605.

Barker, D. R., and Pasricha, S. (1979). Reincarnation cases in Fatehabad: A systematic survey in North India. *Journal of Asian and African Studies*, *14*, 231–240.

Barrett, W. (1926). *Death-bed visions*. London: Methuen.

Barrington, M. R. (2005). Correction [Letter to the Editor]. *Journal of the Society for Psychical Research*, *69*, 232.

_____, Mulacz, P., and Rivas, T. (2005). The case of Iris Farczady—A stolen life. *Journal of the Society for Psychical Research*, *69*, 49–77.

Barrow, J. D., and Tipler, F. S. (1986). *The anthropic cosmological principle*. New York: Oxford University Press.

Barry, J. (1968a). General and comparative study of the psychokinetic effect on fungus culture. *Journal of Parapsychology*, *32*, 237–243.

_____. (1968b). PK on fungus growth. *Journal of Parapsychology*, *32*, 55. (Abstract.)

Baruss, I. (2003). *Alterations of consciousness*. New York: American Psychological Association.

Baumann, S., Stewart, J. L., and Roll, W. G. (1986). Preliminary results from the use of two novel detectors for psychokinesis. In D. H. Weiner and D. I. Radin (Eds.), *Research in parapsychology, 1985* (pp. 59–62). Metuchen, NJ: Scarecrow Press.

Beck, F. (1994). Quantum mechanics and consciousness. *Journal of Consciousness Studies*, *1(2)*, 153–255.

Becker, R. O. (1990). The relationship between bioelectromagnetics and psychic phenomena. *ASPR Newsletter*, *XVI*, 11–14.

_____. (1992). Electromagnetism and psi phenomena. *Journal of the American Society for Psychical Research*, *86*, 1–17.

Bell, J. S. (1964). On the Einstein-Podolsky-Rosen paradox. *Physics*, *1*, 195–200.

Bell, M. (1956). A pioneer in parapsychology. *Journal of Parapsychology*, *20*, 257–62.

Beloff, J. (1974). [Review of *The challenge of chance*]. *Journal of the Society for Psychical Research*, *47*, 319–326.

_____. (1978). Explaining the paranormal with epilogue—1977. In J. Ludwig (Ed.), *Philosophy and parapsychology* (pp. 353–370). Buffalo, NY: Prometheus Books.

_____. (1980). Could there be a physical explanation of psi? *Journal of the Society for Psychical Research*, *50*, 263–272.

_____. (1990). *The relentless question: Reflections on the paranormal*. Jefferson, NC: McFarland.

_____. (2002). Psychical research and the case for dualism. In V. G. Rammohan (Ed.), *New frontiers of human science* (pp. 60–64). Jefferson, NC: McFarland.

Bem, D. J. (2003). Precognitive habituation: Replicable evidence for a process of anomalous cognition. Paper presented at the 46th annual convention of the Parapsychological Association, Vancouver, Canada.

Bender, H. (1980). Transcultural uniformity of poltergeist patterns as suggestive of an "archetypal arrangement." In W. G. Roll (Ed.), *Research in parapsychology, 1979* (pp. 23–25). Metuchen, NJ: Scarecrow Press.

Bengston, W. F., and Krinsley, D. (2000). The effect of "laying on of hands" on transplanted breast cancer in mice. *Journal of Scientific Exploration, 14*, 353–364.

Bennett, H. L., Davis, H. S., and Giannini, J. A. (1985). Non verbal response to intraoperative conversation. *British Journal of Anaesthesia, 57*, 174–179.

Berger, H. (1940). *Psyche*. Jena: Verlag Gustav Fischer.

Bergson, H. (1914). Presidential address to the Society for Psychical Research (1913). *Proceedings of the Society for Psychical Research, 27*, 157–175.

Bernstein, M. (1956). *The search for Bridey Murphy*. Garden City, NY: Doubleday.

Beyerstein, B. L. (1987). The brain and consciousness: Implications for psi phenomena. *Skeptical Inquirer, 12*, 163–173.

Bierman, D. J. (1996). Exploring correlations between local emotional and global emotions events and the behavior of a random number generator. *Journal of Scientific Exploration, 10*, 363–373.

_____, and Walker, E. H. (2003). Conscious collapse of the state vector as support for the quantum observational theory. Paper presented at the 46th annual convention of the Parapsychological Association, Vancouver, Canada.

Bigu, J. (1979). A biophysical approach to paranormal phenomena. In B. Shapin and L. Coly (Eds.), *Brain/mind and parapsychology* (pp. 52–98). New York: Parapsychology Foundation.

Birch, C. (1988). The postmodern challenge to biology. In D. R. Griffith (Ed.), *The reenchantment of science* (pp. 69–78). Albany, NY: State University of New York Press.

Bisaha, J., and Dunne, B. J. (1979). Multiple subject and long-distance precognitive remote viewing of geographical locations. In C. T. Tart, H. E. Puthoff, and R. Targ (Eds.), *Mind at large* (pp. 107–124). New York: Praeger.

Blackmore, S. J. (1978). *Parapsychology and out-of-body experiences*. London: Society for Psychical Research.

_____. (1982a). *Beyond the body*. London: Heinemann.

_____. (1982b). Have you ever had an OBE: The wording of the question. *Journal of the Society for Psychical Research, 51*, 292–302.

_____. (1982c). Out-of-body experiences, lucid dreams and imagery: Two surveys. *Journal of the American Society for Psychical Research, 76*, 301–317.

_____. (1983a). Birth and the OBE: An unhelpful analogy. *Journal of the American Society for Psychical Research, 77*, 229–238.

_____. (1983b). Imagery and the OBE. In W. G. Roll and R. A. White (Eds.), *Research in parapsychology, 1982* (pp. 231–232). Metuchen, NJ: Scarecrow Press.

_____. (1984a). A postal survey of OBEs and other experiences. In R. A. White and R. S. Broughton (Eds.), *Research in parapsychology, 1983* (pp. 57–61). Metuchen, NJ: Scarecrow Press.

_____. (1984b). A psychological theory of the out-of-body experience. Journal of Parapsychology, 48, 201–218.

_____. (1985). Rupert Sheldrake's new science of life: Science, parascience or pseudoscience? *Parapsychology Review, 16(3)*, 6–8.

_____. (1986a). Spontaneous and deliberate OBEs: A questionnaire survey. *Journal of the Society for Psychical Research, 53*, 218–224.

_____. (1986b). Where am I: Perspectives in imagery, memory and the OBE. In D. H. Weiner and D. I. Radin (Eds.), *Research in parapsychology, 1987* (pp. 108–111). Metuchen, NJ: Scarecrow Press.

_____. (1991a). Beyond the self: The escape in reincarnation in Buddhism and psychology. In A. S. Berger and J. Berger (Eds.), *Reincarnation: fact or fable?* (pp. 117–129). London: Aquarian.

_____. (1991b). Near-death experiences: In or out of the body? *Skeptical Inquirer, 16*, 33–45.

_____. (1992). Glimpse of an afterlife or just the dying brain? *Psi Researcher*, No. 6, 2–3.

_____. (1993). *Dying to Live*. Buffalo, NY: Prometheus.

_____. (2002). There is no stream of consciousness. *Journal of Consciousness Studies, 9(5/6)*, 17–28.

Blanke, O., Landis, T., Spinelli, L., and Seeck, M. (2004). Out-of-body-experiences and autoscopy of neurological origin. *Brain, 127*, 243–258.

_____, Ortigue, S., Landis, T., and Seeck, M. (2002). Stimulating illusory own-body perceptions. *Nature, 419(6904)*, 269–270.

Bohm, D. (1980). *Wholeness and the implicate order*. London: Routledge and Kegan Paul.

_____, and Peat, F. D. (1987). *Science, order and creativity*. New York: Bantam.

Bohr, N. (1958). *Atomic physics and human knowledge*. New York: Wiley and Sons.

Bösch, H. (2004). Reanalyzing a meta-analysis of extra-sensory perception dating from 1940, the first comprehensive meta-analysis in the history of science. Paper presented at the 47th annual convention of the Parapsychological Association. Vienna University, Austria.

Bower, B. (2005). Irreplaceable perplexity 101. *Science News*, *168*, 414–415.

Braithwaite, J. J., Perez-Aquino, K., and Townsend, M. (2004). In search of magnetic anomalies associated with haunt-type experiences: Pulse and patterns in dual time synchronized measurements. *Journal of Parapsychology*, *68*, 255–288.

Braud, W. G. (1985). The two faces of psi: Psi revealed and psi observed. In B. Shapin and L. Coly (Eds.), *The repeatability problem in parapsychology* (pp. 150–182). New York: Parapsychology Foundation.

_____, and Davis, G., and Wood, R. (1979). Experiments with Matthew Manning. *Journal of the Society for Psychical Research*, *50*, 199–223.

_____, and Schlitz, M. J. (1983). Psychokinetic influence on electrodermal activity. *Journal of Parapsychology*, *47*, 95–117.

_____, and _____. (1989). Rule of possible intuitive data sorting in electrodermal biological psychokinesis (bio-PK). *Journal of the American Society for Psychical Research*, *83*, 289–302.

_____, Schlitz, M. J., Collins, J., and Klitch, H. (1985) Further studies of the bio-PK effect: Feedback, blocking, generality/specificity. In R. A. White and J. Solfvin (Eds.), *Research in parapsychology, 1984* (pp. 45–48). Metuchen, NJ: Scarecrow Press.

_____, _____, and Schmidt, H. (1990). Remote mental influence of animate and inanimate target systems: A method of comparison and preliminary findings. In L. A. Henkel and J. Palmer (Eds.), *Research in parapsychology, 1989* (pp. 42–47). Metuchen, NJ: Scarecrow Press.

Braude, S. E. (2002). The problem of super-psi. In F. Steinkamp (Ed.), *Parapsychology, philosophy and the mind. Essays honoring John Beloff* (pp. 91–111). Jefferson, NC: McFarland.

Britton, W. B., and Bootzin, R. R. (2004). Near-death experiences and the temporal lobe. *Psychological Science*, *15*, 254–258.

Broughton, R. S. (1991). *Parapsychology: The controversial science*. New York: Random House.

_____. (2004). Exploring the reliability of the "presentiment" effect. Paper presented as the 47th annual convention of the Parapsychological Association, Vienna University, Austria.

Bunnel, T. (1999). The effect of "healing with intent" on pepsin enzyme activity. *Journal of the Society for Psychical Research*, *13*, 139–148.

Burns, J. E. (1993). Current hypotheses about the nature of the mind-brain relationship and their relationship to findings in parapsychology. In K. R. Rao (Ed.), *Cultivating consciousness: Enhancing human potential, wellness and healing* (pp. 139–148). Westport, CT: Praeger.

Burruss, R. P. (2006). A metric clock—calendar for the second cosmic year. *Free Inquiry*, *26(4)*, 47–49.

Butterfield, H. (1957). *The origins of modern science*. New York: Macmillan.

Cameron, T., and Roll, W. G. (1983). An investigation of apparitional experiences. *Theta*, *11*, 74–78.

Campbell, J. (1964). *The masks of God: Oriental philosophy*. New York: Penguin Books.

Carington, W. (1949). *Mind, matter and meaning*. New Haven: Yale University Press.

Carr, B. (2004). Mind and the cosmos. In D. Lorimer (Ed.), *Science, consciousness and ultimate reality* (pp. 33–64). Exeter, UK: Imprint Academic.

Carr, D. (1982). Pathophysiology of stress-induced limbic lobe dysfunction: A hypothesis for NDEs. *Anabiosis*, *2*, 75–89.

Casti, J. (1984). *Paradigms lost*. New York: William Morrow.

Cermina, G. (1967). *Many mansions*. New York: Signet.

Cha, K. Y., Wirth, D. P., and Lobo, R. A. (2001). Does prayer influence the success of in vitro fertilization–embryo transfer? *Journal of Reproductive Medicine*, *46*, 781–787.

Christina, G (2005). Comforting thoughts about death that have nothing to do with God. *Skeptical Inquirer*, *29(2)*, 50–51.

Churchland, P. M. (1989). *A neurocomputational perspective*. Cambridge, MA: MIT Press.

_____. (1995). *The engine of reason, the seat of the soul: A philosophical journey into the brain*. Cambridge, MA: MIT Press.

Churchland, P. S. (1986). *Neurophilosophy*. Cambridge, MA: MIT Press.

_____. (2002). *Brain-wise: Studies in neurophilosophy*. Cambridge, MA: MIT Press.

Clark, T. W. (1995). Function and phenomenology: Closing the explanatory gap. *Journal of Consciousness Studies*, *2*, 241–254.

_____. (2005a). Hodgson's black box. *Journal of Consciousness Studies*, *12(1)*, 38–59.

_____. (2005b). Killing the observer. *Journal of Consciousness Studies*, *12(4–5)*, 23–32.

Clarke, C. (2004). Quantum mechanics, consciousness and the self. In D. Lorimer (Ed.), *Science, consciousness and ultimate reality* (pp. 65–92). Exeter, UK: Imprint Academic.

Cook, A. M., and Irwin, H. J. (1983). Visuospatial skills and the out-of-body experience. *Journal of Parapsychology*, *47*, 23–35.

Cook, E. W. (1986). Research on reincarnation type cases: Present status and suggestions for future research. In K. R. Rao (Ed.), *Case studies in parapsychology* (pp. 87–96). Jefferson, NC: McFarland.

_____, Greyson, B., and Stevenson, I (1998). Do

any near-death experiences provide evidence for the survival of the human personality after death? Relevant features and illustrative case reports. *Journal of Scientific Exploration, 12,* 377–400.

_____, Pasricha, S., Samararatne, G., Maung, U. W., and Stevenson, I. (1983). A review and analysis of "unsolved" cases of the reincarnation type. II. Comparison of features of solved and unsolved cases. *Journal of the American Society for Psychical Research, 77,* 115–135.

Coover, J. E. (1917). Experiments in psychical research at Leland Stanford Junior University. *Psychical Research Monograph No 1.* Stanford, CA: Leland Stanford Junior University Publications.

Cotterill, R. M. J. (1995). On the unity of conscious experience. *Journal of Consciousness Studies, 2(4),* 290–312.

Council, J. R., Greyson, B., and Huff, K. D. (1986). Fantasy-proneness, hypnotizability, and reports of paranormal experiences. Paper presented at the annual convention of the American Psychological Association. San Francisco, California.

Cox, W. E. (1956). Precognition: An analysis, II. *Journal of the Society for Psychical Research, 50,* 99–109.

Crick, F. (1981). *Life itself.* New York: Simon and Schuster.

_____. (1994). *The astonishing hypothesis: The scientific search for the soul.* New York: Charles Scribner's Sons.

Crookall, R. J. (1970). *Out-of-the-body experiences.* Hyde Park, NY: University Books.

Culotta, E. (1994). A boost for "adaptive" mutation. *Science, 265,* 318–319.

Damasio, A. (1994). *Descartes' error: Emotion, reason and the human brain.* New York: G. P. Putnam's Sons.

Darling, D. (1995). *Soul search.* New York: Villard Books.

Davies, P. (1983). *God and the new physics.* New York: Simon and Schuster.

Dawkins, R. (1986). *The blind watchmaker.* New York: Norton.

_____. (1989). *The selfish gene.* Oxford: Oxford University Press.

Dean, D. (1983a). An examination of infra-red and ultra-violet technique to test for changes in water following the laying on of hands. Unpublished doctoral dissertation. Humanistic Psychology Institute, San Francisco.

_____. (1983b). Infrared measurements of healer-treated water. In W. G. Roll, J. Beloff and R. A. White (Eds.), *Research in parapsychology, 1982* (pp. 100–101). Metuchen, NJ: Scarecrow Press.

_____, and Brame, E. (1975). Physical changes in water by laying-on-of-hands. *Proceedings of the Second International Congress of Psychotronic Research.* Paris: Institute Metapsychique International.

de Beauregard, O. C. (1979). Quantum paradoxes and Aristotle's twofold information concept. In C. T. Tart, H. E. Puthoff and R. Targ (Eds.), *Mind at large* (pp. 175–187). New York: Praeger.

Delgado, J. M. R. (1969). *Physical control of the mind: Toward a psychocivilized society.* New York: Harper and Row.

Dembski, W. A. (2002). *No free lunch: Why specified complexity cannot be purchased without intelligence.* New York: Rowman and Littlefield. 2002.

Denbigh, K. (1981). *Three concepts of time.* New York: Springer-Verlag.

Dennett, D. C. (1981). Where am I? In D. R. Hofstadter and D. C. Dennett (Eds.), *The mind's I: Fantasies and reflections on self and soul* (pp. 217–231). New York: Basic Books.

_____. (1988). 'Quining qualia.' In A. J. Marcel and E. Bisiach (Eds.), *Consciousness in contemporary science* (pp. 42–77). Oxford, England: Oxford University Press.

_____. (1991). *Consciousness explained.* Boston: Little, Brown.

de Pablos, F. (1998). Spontaneous precognition during dreams: Analysis of a one-year naturalistic study. *Journal of the Society for Psychical Research, 62,* 423–433.

D'Espagnat, B. (1979) The quantum theory and reality. *Scientific American, 241(5),* 158–181.

Diaconis, P. (1978). Statistical problems in ESP research. *Science, 201,* 131–136.

Dobbs, H. (1967). The feasibility of a physical theory of ESP. In J. Smythies (Ed.), *Science and ESP* (pp. 225–254). New York: Humanities Press.

Dolin, Y. S., Davydov, V. A., Morzova, E. V., and Shumov, D. V. (1993). Studies of a remote mental effect on plants with electrophysiological recording. Paper presented at the 36th annual convention of the Parapsychological Association. Toronto, Canada.

_____, Dymov, V. I., and Khatchenkov, N. N. (1993). Preliminary study of a human operator's effect on the psycho-physiological state of another individual with EEG recording. Paper presented at the 36th annual convention of the Parapsychological Association. Toronto, Canada.

Don, N. S., Warren, C. A., McDonough, B. E., and Collura, T. F. (1988). Event-related brain potential and a phenomenological model of psi-conducive states. In D. H. Weiner and R. L. Morris (Eds.), *Research in parapsychology, 1987* (pp. 72–76). Metuchen, NJ: Scarecrow Press.

Dossey, L. (1996). Guest column: Distance, time and nonlocal mind: Dare we speak of the implications? *Journal of Scientific Exploration, 10*, 401–409.

Ducasse, C. J. (1961). *The belief in a life after death.* Springfield, IL: Thomas.

Eccles, J. C. (1953). *The neurophysiological basis of mind.* Oxford: Clarendon.

_____. (1970). *Facing reality.* New York: Springer-Verlag.

_____. (1977). The human person in its two-way relationship to the brain. In J. D. Morris, W. G. Roll and R. L Morris (Eds.), *Research in parapsychology, 1976* (pp. 251 262). Metuchen, NJ: Scarecrow Press.

_____. (1979). *The human mystery.* New York: Springer International.

_____. (1980). *The human psyche.* New York: Springer International.

_____. (1983). Voluntary movement, freedom of the will, moral responsibility. *Perkins Journal, 36(4),* 40–48.

_____. (1987). Brain and mind, two or one? In C. Blakemore and S. Greenfield (Eds.), *Mindwaves: Thoughts on intelligence, identity and consciousness* (pp. 293–304). New York: Basil Blackwell.

_____. (1989) *Evolution of the brain: Creation of the self.* New York: Routledge.

_____, and Robinson, D. (1984). *The wonder of being human.* New York: The Free Press.

Eddington, A. S. (1920/1959). *Space, time and gravitation: An outline of the general relativity theory.* New York: Harper and Row.

_____. (1935). New pathways in science. Cambridge, England: Cambridge University Press.

Edelman, G. M., and Jononi, G. (1995). Neural darwinism: The brain as a selectional system. In J. Cornwall (Ed.), *Nature's imagination* (pp. 78–100). New York: Oxford University Press.

Edge, H. L. (1980b). The effect of laying-on-of-hands on an enzyme: An attempted replication. In W. G. Roll (Ed.), *Research in parapsychology, 1979* (pp. 137–139). Metuchen, NJ: Scarecrow Press.

_____. (2002a). Dualism and the self: A cross-cultural perspective. In F. Steinkamp (Ed.), *Parapsychology, philosophy and the mind: Essays honoring John Beloff* (pp. 33–56). Jefferson, NC: McFarland.

_____. (2002b). Parapsychology and the philosophy of mind. In V. G. Rammohan (Ed.), *New Frontiers of Human Science* (pp. 30–45). Jefferson, NC: McFarland.

_____, Morris, R. L., Palmer, J., and Rush, J. H. (1986). *Foundations of parapsychology.* Boston, MA: Routledge and Kegan Paul.

Edwards, J. C. W. (2005). Is consciousness only a property of individual cells? *Journal of Consciousness Studies, 12(4/5),* 60–76.

Edwards, P. (1997). Introduction. In P. Edwards (Ed.), *Immortality* (pp. 1–70). Amherst, NY: Prometheus Books.

Ehm, W. (2005). Meta-analysis of mind-matter experiments: A statistical modeling perspective. *Mind and Matter, 3(1),* 85–132.

Ehrenwald, J. (1974). Out-of-body experiences and the denial of death. *Journal of Nervous and Mental Disease, 159,* 227–233.

_____. (1977). Psi phenomena and brain research. In B. B. Wolman (Ed.), *Handbook of parapsychology* (pp. 716–729). New York: Van Nostrand Reinhold.

_____. (1978). *The ESP experience.* New York: Basic Books.

Einstein, A., Podolsky, B., and Rosen, N. (1935). Can quantum mechanical description of reality really be considered complete? *Physical Review, 47,* 777–780.

Estabrooks, G. H. (1927). *A contribution to experimental telepathy.* Boston: Boston Society for Psychical Research.

Evans, C., and Richardson, P. H. (1988). Improved recovery and reduced postoperative stay after therapeutic suggestions, during general anesthesia. *Lancet, 8609,* 491–493.

Everett, H. (1957). 'Relative state' formulation of quantum mechanics. *Reviews of Modern Physics, 39,* 454–462.

Fanselow, M. S. (1993). Associations and memories: The role of NMDA receptors and long-term potentiation. *Current Directions in Psychological Science, 2,* 152–156.

Farber, I. (2005). How a neural correlate can function as an explanation of consciousness. *Journal of Consciousness Studies, 12(4–5),* 77–95.

Farha, B., and Stewart, G. (2006). Paranormal beliefs: An analysis of college students. *Skeptical Inquirer, 30(1),* 8–9.

Feng, Q., Park, T. K., and Rebek, J. (1992). Crossover reaction between synthetic replicators yields active and inactive recombinants. *Science, 256,* 1179–1180.

Fenwick, P., and Hopkins, R. (1986). An examination of the effects of healing on water. *Journal of the Society for Psychical Research, 53,* 387–390.

Feuer, L. (1974). *Einstein and the generations of science.* New York: Basic Books.

Fjermedal, G. (1987). *The tomorrow makers.* New York: Macmillan.

Flamm, B. L. (2004). The Columbia University "miracle" study: flawed and fraud. *Skeptical Inquirer, 28(5),* 25–30).

_____. (2005). The bizarre Columbia University "miracle" saga continues. *Skeptical Inquirer, 29(2),* 52–53.

Flanagan, O. (1992). *Consciousness reconsidered.* Cambridge, MA: MIT Press.

Flew, A. (1987). Is there a case for bodied survival? In A. Flew (Ed.), *Readings in the philosophical problems of parapsychology* (pp. 347–361). Buffalo, NY: Prometheus Books.

_____. (1991). Transmigration and reincarnation. In A. S. Berger and J. Berger (Eds.), *Reincarnation: Fact or fable?* (pp. 101–116). London: The Aquarian Press.

Fodor, J. (1983). *The modularity of mind.* Cambridge, MA: MIT Press/Bradford Books.

Fox, S. (1988). *The emergence of life.* New York: Basic Books.

Frager, R. (2002). *The wisdom of Islam.* Hauppauga, NY: Godsfield Press.

Frazier, K. (1995). 'Columbus poltergeist' Tina Resch imprisoned in daughter's murder. *Skeptical Inquirer, 19(2),* 3.

Freeman, A. (2005). The sense of being glared at: What is it like to be a heretic? *Journal of Consciousness Studies, 12(6),* 4–9.

Friedman-Hill, S. R., Robertson, L. C., and Triesman, A. (1995). Parietal contributions to visual feature binding: Evidence from a patient with bilateral lesions. *Science, 269,* 853–855.

Fuller, J. G. (1974). *Arigo: Surgeon of the rusty knife.* New York: Thomas Crowell.

Furlong, M. W. (1990). A randomized double blind study of positive suggestions presented during anesthesia. In B. Bonke, W. Fitch, and K. Millar (Eds.), *Memory and awareness in anesthesia* (pp. 170–175). Lisse and Amsterdam: Swetzs and Zeitlinger.

Gabbard, G., Jones, F., Twemlow, S. (1980). The out-of-body experience. iii. Differential diagnosis. Paper presented at the 1980 annual meeting of the American Psychiatric Association. San Francisco, CA.

Gale, G. (1990). Cosmological fecundity: Theories of multiple universes. In J. Leslie (ed.), *Physical cosmology and philosophy* (pp. 189–206). New York: MacMillan.

Gallup, G. H. (1982). Among British people belief in the paranormal increasing. *Emerging Trends* (Princeton Religion Research Center), *4,* 5.

_____, and Newport, F. (1992). Belief in paranormal phenomena among adult Americans. *Skeptical Inquirer, 15,* 137–146.

Gardner, M. (1986). Magicians in the psi lab: Many misconceptions. In K. Frazier (Ed.), *Science confronts the paranormal* (pp. 170–175). Buffalo, NY: Prometheus Books.

Gauld, A. (1982). *Mediumship and survival.* London: Paladin Books.

_____. (1996). [Review of *Parapsychology and thanatology*]. *European Journal of Parapsychology, 12,* 100–106.

_____, and Cornell, A. D. (1979). *Poltergeists.* London: Routledge and Kegan Paul.

Gazzaniga, M. S. (1985). *The social brain: Discovering the networks of the mind.* New York: Basic Books.

_____. (1989). Organization of the human brain. *Science, 245,* 947–952.

_____. (1992). *Nature's mind.* New York: HarperCollins.

_____, and Roser, M. (2004). Automatic brains—interpretive minds. *Current Directions in Psychological Science, 13,* 56–59.

Geach, P. (1987). Reincarnation. In A. Flew (Ed.), *Readings in the philosophical problems of parapsychology* (pp. 327–337). Buffalo, NY: Prometheus Books.

Giroldini, W. (1986). A physical theory for paranormal phenomena. *European Journal of Parapsychology, 6,* 151–165.

Goldberg, B. (1982). *Past lives, future lives.* New York: Random House.

Goldberg, G. (1985). Supplementary motor area structure and function: Review and hypothesis. *Behavioral and Brain Sciences, 8,* 189–230.

Goldmann, L., Shah, M., and Hebden, M. (1987). Memory and cardiac anesthesia. *Anaesthesia, 42,* 596–603.

Goswami, A. (1993). *The self-aware universe: How consciousness creates the material world.* New York: Tarcher/Putnam.

Gould, S. J. (1999). *Rocks of ages: Science and religion in the fullness of life.* New York: Ballantine.

Grad, B. (1963). A telekinetic effect on plant growth. *International Journal of Parapsychology, 5,* 117–133.

_____. (1964). A telekinetic effect on plant growth. II. Experiments involving treatment of saline in stoppered bottles. *International Journal of Parapsychology, 6,* 473–498.

_____. (1965). Laying on of hands: A review of experiments with plants and animals. *Journal of the American Society for Psychical Research, 59,* 95–129.

_____. (1977). Laboratory evidence of "laying-on-of hands." In N. M. Regush (Ed.), *Frontiers of healing* (pp. 203–213). New York: Avon Books.

_____, Cadoret, R. J., and Paul, G. I. (1961). The influence of an unorthodox method of treatment of wound healing in mice. *International Journal of Parapsychology, 3(2),* 5–24.

_____, and Dean, D. (1984). Independent confirmation of infrared healer effects. In R. A. White and R. S. Broughton (Eds.), *Research in parapsychology, 1983* (pp. 81–83). Metuchen, NJ: Scarecrow Press.

Granone, F. (1972). Guaritorie chirurghi-medium filippini. *Rassegna d. Ipnosie Medicina Psicosomatica, 8,* 99–119.

Green, C. E. (1967). Ecsomatic experiences and related phenomena. *Journal of the Society for Psychical Research, 44*, 111–130.

Greenstein, G. (1988). *The symbiotic universe.* New York: William Morrow.

Gribbin, J., and Rees, M. (1989). *Cosmic coincidences.* New York: Bantam Books.

Griffin, D. R. (1988a). Introduction: The reenchantment of science. In D. R. Griffin (Ed.), *The reenchantment of science* (pp. 1–46). Albany: State University of New York Press.

_____. (1988b). Of minds and molecules: Postmodern medicine in a psychosomatic universe. In D. R. Griffin (Ed.), *The reenchantment of science* (pp. 141–163). Albany, New York: State University of New York Press.

_____. (1994). Dualism, materialism, idealism and psi. *Journal of the American Society for Research, 88*, 23–29.

_____. (1997). Panexperientialist physicalism and the mind-body problem. *Journal of Consciousness Studies, 4(3)*, 248–268.

Grof, S. (1990). Survival after death: Observations from modern consciousness research. In G. Doore (Ed.), *What survives? Contemporary explorations of life after death* (pp. 22–33). Los Angeles: Tarcher.

Grosso, M. (1976). Some variations of out-body experiences. *Journal of the American Society for Psychical Research, 70*, 179–193.

_____. (1979). The survival of personality in a mind-dependent world. *Journal of the American Society for Psychical Research, 73*, 367–380.

_____. (1981). Toward an explanation of near-death phenomena. *Journal of the American Society for Psychical Research, 75*, 37–60.

Gruber, E. (1980). Conforming of pre-recorded group behavior with disposed observers. In W. G. Roll (Ed.), *Research in parapsychology, 1979* (pp. 134–136). Metuchen, NJ: Scarecrow Press.

Grünbaum, A. (1964). Time irreversible processes and the physical status of becoming. In J. Smart (Ed.), *Problems of space and time* (pp. 397–425). New York: Macmillan.

Gurney, E. (1888–1889). Note relating to some of the published experiments in thought-transference. *Proceedings of the Society for Psychical Research, 5*, 269–270.

_____, Myers, F. W. H., and Podmore, F. (1886a). *Phantasms of the living. Vol I.* London: Trubner.

_____, _____, and _____. (1886b). *Phantasms of the living. Vol II.* London: Trubner.

Guth, A. H., and Kaiser, D. I. (2005). Inflationary cosmology: Explaining the universe from the smallest to the largest scales. *Science, 307*, 884–890.

Haeckel, E. (1899/1929). *The riddle of the universe.* London: Watts.

Haggard, P., and Eimer, M. (1999). On the relationship between brain potentials and the awareness of voluntary movement. *Experimental Brain Research, 126*, 128–133.

Hall, D. F., McFeaters, S. J., and Loftus, E. F. (1987). Alterations in recollection of unusual and unexpected events. *Journal of Scientific Exploration, 1*, 3–10.

Hall, J., Kim, C., McElroy, K., and Shimoni, A. (1977). Wave packet reduction as a medium of communication. *Foundations of Physics, 7*, 759–767.

Hameroff, S. R. (1994). Quantum coherence in microtubules: A neural basis for emergent consciousness. *Journal of Consciousness Studies, 1*, 91–118.

Hansel, C. E. M. (1966). *ESP: A scientific evaluation.* New York: Charles Scribner's Sons.

_____. (1980). *ESP and parapsychology: A critical re-evaluation.* Buffalo, NY: Prometheus.

Haraldsson, E. (1981). Apparitions of the dead: A representative survey in Iceland. In W. G. Roll and J. Beloff (Eds.), *Research in parapsychology, 1980* (pp. 3–5). Metuchen, NJ: Scarecrow Press.

_____. (2000a). Birthmarks and claims of previous-life memories. I. The case of Purnima Ekanayake. *Journal of the Society for Psychical Research, 64*, 16–25.

_____. (2000b). Birthmarks and claims of previous-life memories. II. The case of Chatura Karunaratne. *Journal of the Society for Psychical Research, 64*, 82–92.

_____, and Abu-Izzeddin, M. (2002). Development of certainty about the correct deceased person in a case of the reincarnation type in Lebanon: The case of Nazih Al-Danaf. *Journal of Scientific Exploration, 16*, 363–380.

_____, and Houtkooper, J. M. (1994). Perceptual defensiveness, personality and belief. Meta-analysis, experimenter and decline effects. Paper presented at the 37th annual convention of the Parapsychological Association. Amsterdam, the Netherlands.

_____, and Olafsson, O. (1980). A survey of psychic healing in Iceland. *The Christian Parapsychologist, 3*, 276–279.

_____, Gudmundsdottir, A., Ragnarsson, J. L., and Johnsson, S. (1977). National survey of psychical experiences and attitudes toward the paranormal in Iceland. In J. D. Morris, W. G. Roll and R. L. Morris (Eds.), *Research in parapsychology, 1976* (pp. 182–186). Metuchen, NJ: Scarecrow Press.

Hardy, C. (1998). *Networks of meaning: A bridge between mind and matter.* Westport, CT: Praeger.

Harman, W. W. (1993). Does further progress in consciousness research await a reassessment of the metaphysical foundations of modern science? In K. R. Rao (Ed.), *Cultivating consciousness: Enhancing human potential wellness and healing* (pp. 11–23). Westport, CT: Praeger.

Harris, M. (1986). *Investigating the unexplained.* Buffalo, NY: Prometheus Books.

Hart, H. (1954). ESP projection: Spontaneous cases and the experimental method. *Journal of the American Society for Psychical Research, 48,* 121–146.

_____. (1958). To what extent can the issues with regard to survival be reconciled? *Journal of the Society for Psychical Research, 39,* 314–323.

_____. (1959). *The enigma of survival.* Springfield, IL: Charles C. Thomas.

Hart, M. H. (1990). Atmospheric evolution, the Drake equation, and DNA: Sparse life in an infinite universe. In J. Leslie (Ed.), *Physical cosmology and philosophy* (pp. 256–266). New York: Macmillan.

Hasted, J. B. (1981). *The metal benders.* London: Routledge and Kegan Paul.

Hearne, K. M. T. (1984). A survey of reported precognitions and of those who have them. *Journal of the Society for Psychical Research, 52,* 261–270.

Henry, R. C. (2005). The mental universe. *Nature, 436,* 29.

Hilgard, E. (1977). *Divided consciousness.* New York: Wiley.

Hill, T. (2005) [Letter to the Editor.] *Skeptical Inquirer, 29(1),* 61.

Hines, T. (2003). *Examining the Psychology of Belief.* Amherst, NY: Prometheus Books.

Hirukawa, T., and Ishikawa, M. (2002). Anomalous fluctuations of RNG data in Nebuta summer festival in northeast Japan. Paper presented at the 47th annual convention of the Parapsychological Association. Vienna University, Austria.

Hodgson, D. (1991). *The mind matters.* New York: Oxford University Press.

_____. (2005). Response to commentators. *Journal of Consciousness Studies, 12 (1),* 76–95.

Honegger, B. (1983). The OBE as a near-birth experience. In W. G. Roll, J. Beloff, and R. A. White (Eds.), *Research in parapsychology, 1982* (pp. 230–231). Metuchen, NJ: Scarecrow Press.

Honorton, C. (1977). Psi and internal attention states. In B. B. Wolman (Ed.), *Handbook of parapsychology* (pp. 435–472.) New York: Van Nostrand Reinhold.

_____. (1985). Meta-analysis of psi ganzfeld research: A response to Ray Hyman. *Journal of Parapsychology, 49,* 51–91.

_____, and Ferrari, D. C. (1989). Meta-analysis of forced-choice precognition experiments. *Journal of Parapsychology, 53,* 281–308.

_____, _____, and Bem, D. J. (1990). Extraversion and ESP performance: A meta-analysis and a new confirmation. Paper presented at the 33rd annual convention of the Parapsychological Association. Chevy Chase, MD.

_____, and Tremmel, L. (1979). Psi correlates of volition: A preliminary test of Eccles' "neurophysiological hypothesis" of mind-brain interaction. In W. G. Roll (Ed.), *Research in parapsychology, 1978* (pp. 36–38). Metuchen, NJ: Scarecrow Press.

Hoy, D. (1981). Psychic surgery: Hoax or hope? *Zetetic Scholar, 8,* 37–46.

Hoyle, F. (1983). *The intelligent universe.* New York: Holt, Rhinehart and Winston.

_____, and Wickramasinghe, C. (1981). *Evolution from space.* New York: Simon and Schuster.

_____, and _____. (1988). *Cosmic life-force.* New York: Paragon House.

Huxley, T. H. (1874). On the hypothesis that animals are automata and its history. *Fortnightly Review, 22,* 555–580.

_____. (1877). *Collected essays.* New York: Appleton.

Hyman, R. (1977). "Cold reading": How to convince strangers that you know all about them. *Zetetic (Skeptical Inquirer), 1(2),* 18–37.

_____. (1985). The ganzfeld psi experiment: A critical appraisal. *Journal of Parapsychology, 49,* 3–49.

_____. (2005). Testing Natasha. *Skeptical Inquirer, 29(3),* 27–33.

Irwin, H. J. (1980). Out of the body down under: Some cognitive characteristics of Australian students reporting OBEs. *Journal of the Society for Psychical Research, 50,* 448–459.

_____. (1981). Some psychological dimensions of the out-of-body experience. *Parapsychology Review, 12(4),* 1–6.

_____. (1986). Perceptual perspective of visual imagery in OBEs, dreams and reminiscence. *Journal of the Society for Psychical Research, 53,* 210–217.

_____. (1996). Childhood antecedents of out-of-body and déjà vu experiences. *Journal of the American Society for Psychical Research, 90,* 157–170.

Jahn, R. G., and Dunne, B. J. (1987). *Margins of reality.* New York: Harcourt, Brace, Jovanovich.

_____, and _____. (2005). The PEAR proposition. *Journal of Scientific Exploration, 19,* 195–245.

Jaki, S. (1969). *Brain, mind and computers.* South Bend, IN: Gateway Editions.

James, W. (1890/1983). *The principles of psychology.* Cambridge, MA: Harvard University Press.

_____. (1890/1992). On the theory of the soul. In P. Edwards (Ed.), *Immortality* (pp. 177–183). New York: Macmillan.

_____. (1898/1992). Consciousness, the brain and immortality. In P. Edwards (Ed.), *Immortality* (pp. 282–291). New York: Macmillan.

_____. (1902). *The varieties of religious experience: A study in human nature.* New York: Longmans, Green.

_____. (1909/1960). The final impressions of a psychical researcher. In G. Murphy and R. O. Ballou (Eds.), *William James on psychical research* (pp. 309–325). New York: The Viking Press.

_____. (1910). Report on Mrs. Piper's Hodgson control. *Proceedings of the Society for Psychical Research, 23,* 2–121.

Jaswal, L. (2005). Isolating disparate challenges to Hodgson's account of free will. *Journal of Consciousness Studies, 12(1),* 43–46.

Jeans, J. (1937). *The mysterious universe.* Cambridge, England: Cambridge University Press.

Jenkins, E. (1982). *The shadow and the light.* North Pomfret, VT: Hamish Hamilton.

John, E. R. (2003). A theory of consciousness. *Current Directions in Psychological Science, 12,* 244–250.

Joliot, M., Rubary, U., and Llinas, R. (1994). Human oscillatory brain activity near 40 Hz coexists with cognitive temporal blinding. *Proceedings of the National Academy of Sciences, 91(24),* 11748–11751.

Jung, C. G. (1973). Synchronicity: An acasual connecting principle. Princeton, NJ: Princeton University Press.

Kalish, R. A., and Reynolds, D. K. (1974). Widows view death: A brief research note. *Omega, 5,* 187–192.

Kazhinsky, B. (1962). *Biologicheskaya Radio-svyaz.* Kizv: Ukranian Academy of Sciences.

Keil, H. H. J. (1991). New cases in Burma, Thailand and Turkey: A limited field study replication of some aspects of Ian Stevenson's research. *Journal of Scientific Exploration, 5,* 27–59.

_____. (2005). Children who claim to remember previous lives: Cases with written records made before the previous personality was identified. *Journal of Scientific Exploration, 19,* 91–101.

Kennedy, J. E. (2004). A proposal and challenge for proponents and skeptics of psi. *Journal of Parapsychology, 68,* 157–167.

Kihlstrom, J. F., Schachter, D. L., Cork, R. C., Hurt, C. A., and Behr, S. E. (1990). Implicit and explicit memory following surgical anesthesia. *Psychological Science, 1,* 303–306.

Kinsbourne, M., and Warrington, E. (1964). Observations on color agnosia. *Journal of Neurobiology, Neurosurgery and Psychiatry, 27,* 296–299.

Koch, C. (1996). Toward the neuronal substrate of visual consciousness. In S. R. Hameroff, A. W. Kaszniak, and A. C. Scott (Eds.), *Toward a science of consciousness. The first Tuscon discussions and debates* (pp. 247–257). Cambridge, MA: MIT Press.

_____, and Crick, F. (1991). Understanding awareness at the neuronal level. *Behavioral and Brain Sciences, 4,* 683–685.

Koestler, A. (1967). The ghost in the machine. New York: Macmillan.

_____. (1972). *The roots of coincidence.* New York: Random House.

_____. (1978). *Janus.* New York: Random House.

Kogan, I. M. (1968). Information theory analysis of telepathic communication experiments. *Radio Engineering, 23,* 122–130.

Kohr, R.L. (1980). A survey of psi experiments among members of a special population. *Journal of the American Society for Psychical Research, 74,* 395–411.

Kokubo, H., and Yamamoto, M. (2003). Case study—Tomika-cho incident—Analysis of electromagnetic data for a poltergeist incident in Japan. Paper presented at the 46th annual convention of the Parapsychological Association, Vancouver, Canada.

Krupa, D. J., Thompson, J. K., and Thompson, R. F. (1993). Localization of a memory trace in the mammalian brain. *Science, 260,* 989–991.

Lawden, D. F. (1989). Some thoughts on birth and death. *Journal of the Society for Psychical Research, 56,* 39–43.

Leahey, T. H., and Leahey, G. E. (1983). *Psychology's occult doubles.* Chicago: Nelson-Hall.

LeDoux, J. E. (1985). Brain, mind and language. In D. A. Oakley (Ed.), *Mind and brain* (pp. 197–216). New York: Methuen.

Lee, D. (1938). Conceptual implications of an Indian language. *Philosophy of Science, 5,* 89–102.

Leggett, A. J. (1987a). Reflection on the quantum measurement paradox. In B. J. Hiley and D. F. Peat (Eds.), *Quantum implications: Essays in honour of David Bohm* (pp. 85–104). London: Routledge and Kegan Paul.

_____. (1987b). *The problems of physics.* New York: Oxford University Press.

LeShan, L. (1969). *Toward a general theory of the paranormal.* New York: Parapsychology Foundation.

_____. (1976). *Alternate realities.* New York: Ballantine Books.

Levin, M. (1996). On the lack of evidence for the evolution of psi as an argument against the reality of the paranormal. *Journal of the American Society for Psychical Research, 90,* 221–230.

_____. (2000). What is the fundamental nature of consciousness? On the contribution of parapsychology to consciousness research. *International Journal of Parapsychology, 11,* 7–41.

Levy, N. (2005). Libet's impossible demand. *Journal of Consciousness Studies, 12(12),* 67–76.

Libet, B. (1989). Neural destiny: Does the brain have a mind of its own? *The Sciences, 29(2)*, 32–35.

_____. (1991a). Conscious functions and brain processes. *Behavioral and Brain Sciences, 14*, 685–686.

_____. (1991b). Conscious time vs. natural time. *Nature, 352*, 27.

_____. (1994). A testable field theory of mind-brain interaction. *Journal of Consciousness Studies, 1*, 119–126.

Lincoln, P. J., and Wood, N. J. (1979). Psychic surgery: A serological investigation. *The Lancet, i*, 1197–1198.

Linde, A. D. (1985). The universe: Inflation out of chaos. *New Scientist*, 105 (March 7), 11–18.

Lipkin, M. (2005). Fields in current models of consciousness: A tool for solving the hard problem? *Mind and Matter, 3(2)*, 29–85.

Livio, M., and Rees, M. J. (2005). Anthropic reasoning. *Science, 309*, 1022–1023.

Lobach, E., and Bierman, D. J. (2004a). The invisible gaze: Three attempts to replicate Sheldrake's staring effects. Paper presented at the 47th annual convention of the Parapsychological Association, Vienna University, Austria.

_____, and _____. (2004b). Who's calling at this hour? Local sidereal time and telephone telepathy. Paper presented at the 47th annual convention of the Parapsychological Association, Vienna University, Austria.

Lockwood, M. (1989). *Mind, brain and the quantum*. Cambridge, MA: Basil Blackwell.

Loftus, E. F. (1981). Mentalmorphosis: Alterations in memory produced by bonding of new information to old. In J. B. Long and A. J. Baddeley (Eds.), *Attention and performance. IX*. Hillsdale, NJ: Erlbaum.

_____. (1995) Remembering dangerously. *Skeptical Inquirer, 19(2)*, 20–29.

_____, and Greene, E. (1980). Warning: Even memory for faces may be contagious. *Law and Human Behavior, 4*, 323–334.

_____, Miller, D. G., and Burns, H. J. (1978). Semantic integration of verbal information into visual memory. *Journal of Experimental Psychology: Human Learning and Memory, 4*, 19–31.

Long, T. (2003). Dreams, near-death experiences and reality. Paper presented at the 45th annual convention of the Parapsychological Association. Vancouver, Canada.

Lund, D. H. (1985). *Death and consciousness*. Jefferson, NC: McFarland.

Lynn, S. J., Loftus, E. F., Llienfeld, S. O., and Lock, T. (2003). Memory recovery techniques in psychotherapy. *Skeptical Inquirer, 27(4)*, 40–46.

MacDonald, R. G., Hickman, J. L., and Dakin, H. S. (1977). Preliminary physical measurements of psychophysiological effects associated with three alleged psychic healers. In J. D. Morris, W. G. Roll, and R. L. Morris (Eds.), *Research in parapsychology, 1976* (pp. 74–76). Metuchen, NJ: Scarecrow Press.

MacKenzie, A. (1971). *Apparitions and ghosts*. New York: Popular Library.

_____. (1995). Precognition of a fatal fire. *Journal of the Society for Psychical Research, 60*, 258–260.

MacLellan, A. W. (1997). *Further speculations on the nature of ESP*. London: Regency Press.

Maher, M. C., and Hansen, G. P. (1992a). Quantitative investigation of a "haunted castle" in New Jersey. Paper presented at the 35th annual convention of the Parapsychological Association. Las Vegas, NV.

_____, and _____. (1992b). Quantitative investigation of a reported haunting using several detection techniques. *Journal of the American Society for Psychical Research, 86*, 347–374.

_____, and Schmeidler, G. R. (1975). Quantitative investigation of a recurrent apparition. *Journal of the American Society for Psychical Research, 69*, 341–352.

Marcel, A. J. (1988). Phenomenal experience and functionalism. In A. J. Marcel and E. Bisiach (Eds.), *Consciousness in contemporary science* (pp. 121–158). New York: Oxford University Press.

Margenau, H. (1984). *The miracle of existence*. Woodbridge, CT: Ox Bow Press.

Mark, V. (1996). Conflicting communicative behavior in a split-brain patient support for dual consciousness. In S. R. Hameroff, A. W. Kaszniak, and A. C. Scott (Eds.), *Toward a science of consciousness. The first Tuscon discussions and debates* (pp.189–196). Cambridge, MA: MIT Press.

Markov, M. A. (1985). Entropy in an oscillating universe in the assumption of universe 'splitting' into numerous smaller 'daughter universes.' In M. A. Markov, V. A. Berezin, and V. P. Frolov (Eds.), *Proceedings of the third seminar on quantum gravity*. Moscow: World Scientific.

Marks, D. F. (1986). Remote viewing revisited. In K. Frazier (Ed.), *Science confronts the paranormal* (pp. 110–121). Buffalo, NY: Prometheus Books.

_____, and Kammann, R. (1978). Information transmission in remote viewing experiments. *Nature, 274*, 680–681.

_____, and _____. (1980). *The psychology of the psychic*. Buffalo, NY: Prometheus Books.

_____, and Scott, C. (1986). Remote viewing exposed. *Nature, 319*, 444.

Markwick, B. (1978). The Soal-Goldney experiments with Basil Shackelton: New evidence of data manipulation. *Proceedings of the Society for Psychical Research, 56*, 250–277.

_____, and Beloff, J. (1983). Dream states and ESP: A distance experiment with a single subject. In W. G. Roll, J. Beloff, and R. A. White (Eds.) *Research in parapsychology, 1982* (pp. 228–230). Metuchen, NJ: Scarecrow Press.

Mashour, G. A. (2005). [Letter to the Editor.] *Science, 310*, 1768–1769.

Maso, I. (2006). Toward a panpsychistic foundation of paranormal phenomena. *European Journal of Parapsychology, 21.1*, pp. 3–26.

Mason, S. (1962). *A history of the sciences.* New York: Macmillan.

Massimini, M., Ferrarelli, F., Huber, R, Esser, S. K., Singh, H., and Tononi, G. (2005). Breakdown of cortical effective connectivity during sleep. *Science, 309*, 2228–2232.

Matlock, J. G. (1990). Past life memory case studies. In S. Krippner (Ed.), *Advances in parapsychological research, Volume 6* (pp. 184–267). Jefferson, NC: McFarland.

Mattuck, R. D. (1977). Random fluctuation theory of psychokinesis: Thermal noise model. In J. D. Morris, W. G. Roll, and R. L. Morris (Eds.), *Research in parapsychology, 1976* (pp. 191–195). Metuchen, NJ: Scarecrow Press.

_____. (1982). A model of the interaction between consciousness and matter using Bohm-Bub hidden variables. In W. G. Roll, R. L. Morris, and R. A. White (Eds.), *Research in parapsychology, 1981* (pp. 146–147). Metuchen, NJ: Scarecrow Press.

_____. (1984). A quantum mechanical theory of the interaction of consciousness with matter. In M. Cazenave (Ed.), *Science and consciousness* (pp. 45–65). New York: Pergamon Press.

May, E. C., and Spottiswoode, J. P. (2003). Skin conductance prestimulus response to future audio startle stimuli. Paper presented at the 46th annual convention of the Parapsychological Association, Vancouver, Canada.

McAdam, S. (2003). Bell's theorem and the demise of local reality. *American Mathematical Monthly, 110*, 800–811.

McAdams, E. E., and Bayless, R. (1981). *The case for life after death.* Chicago: Nelson Hall.

McClenon, J. (2004). What is to be done: Evaluating the ritual healing theory. Paper presented at the 47th annual convention of the Parapsychological Association, Vienna University, Austria.

McCue, P. (2004) Methodological problems with the 'Robertson-Roy' protocol. [Letter to the Editor.] *Journal of the Society for Psychical Research, 68*, 183–184.

McDonough, B. E., Don, N. S., and Warren, C. A. (2002). Differential event-related potentials to targets and decoys in a guessing task. *Journal of Scientific Exploration, 16*, 187–206.

McDougall, W. (1926). *An outline of abnormal psychology.* London: Methuen.

McGinn, C. (1995). Consciousness and space. *Journal of Consciousness Studies, 2*, 220–230.

_____. (1999) *Mysterious flame: Conscious minds in a material world.* New York: Basic Books.

Metzinger, T. (2003). *Being no one: The self-model theory of subjectivity.* Cambridge, MA: MIT Press.

_____. (2005). Out-of-body experience as the origin of the concept of a "soul." *Mind and Matter, 3(1)*, 57–89.

Midgley, D. (2006). Intersubjectivity and collective consciousness. *Journal of Consciousness Studies, 5*, 99–109.

Millar, B. (1975). [Review of *Superminds.*] *Journal of the Society for Psychical Research, 48*, 168–171.

Millar, K., and Watkinson, N. (1983). Recognition of words presented during general anesthesia. *Ergonomics, 6*, 585–594.

Mills, A. (1989). A replication study: Three cases of children in Northern India who are said to remember a previous life. *Journal of Scientific Exploration, 3*, 133–184.

_____. (2004). Inferences from the case of Ajandra Singh Chauhan: The effect of parental questioning of meeting the "previous life" family, an aborted attempt to quantify probability and the impact on his life as a young child. *Journal of Scientific Exploration, 18*, 609–641.

_____, Haraldsson, E., and Keil, H. H. J. (1994). Replication studies of cases suggestive of reincarnation by three independent investigators. *Journal of the American Society for Psychical Research, 88*, 207–219.

Milton, J. (1993). A meta-analysis of waking state of consciousness, free-response ESP studies. Paper presented at the 36th annual convention of the Parapsychological Association, Toronto, Canada.

Miranker, W. (2005). The Hebbian synapse: Progenitor of consciousness. *Mind and Matter, 3(2)*, 87–102.

Mitchell, J. L. (1981). *Out-of-body experiences: A handbook.* Jefferson, NC: McFarland.

Mohrhoff, U. (1999). The physics of interaction. In B. Libet, A. Freeman, and K. Sutherland (Eds.), *The volitional brain* (pp. 165–184). Thorverton, UK: Imprint Academic.

Moody, R. A. (1975). *Life after life.* New York: Bantam Books.

Moravec, H. (1988). *Mind children: The future of robot and human intelligence.* Cambridge, MA: Harvard University Press.

Morris, R. L. (1974). PRF research on out-of-body experiences. *Theta, No. 41*, 1–3.

_____, Harary, S. B., Janis, J., Hartwell, J., and Roll, W. G. (1978). Studies of communication during out-of-body experiences. *Journal of the American Society for Psychical Research, 72,* 1–21.

Motoyama, H. (2002). Humans and nature. In V. G. Rammohan (Ed.), *New frontiers of human science* (pp. 65–78). Jefferson, NC: McFarland.

Muldoon, S. J., and Carrington, H. (1929). *The projection of the astral body.* London: Rider and Co.

Murphy, G. (1945). Field theory and survival. *Journal of the American Society for Psychical Research, 39,* 181–209.

_____. (1973). A Caringtonian approach to Ian Stevenson's *Twenty cases suggestive of reincarnation. Journal of the American Society for Psychical Research, 67,* 117–129.

Murray, C. D., and Fox, J. (2004). Body image in respondents with and without out-of-body experiences. Paper presented at the 47th annual convention of the Parapsychological Association. Vienna University, Austria.

Murray, C.D., Sherwood, J., and Fox, J. (2005). Telepresence and telepathy in immersive video reality. Paper presented at the 48th annual convention of the Parapsychological Association. Petaluma, California.

Myers, F. H. W. (1903). Human personality and its survival of death. London: Longmans.

Myers, S. A., Austrin, H. R., Grisso, J. T., and Nickeson, R. C. (1983). Personality characteristics as related to the out-of-the-body experience. *Journal of Parapsychology, 47,* 131–144.

Nagel, T. (2002), *Concealment and exposure.* Oxford: Oxford University Press.

Nash, C. B. (1983). An extrasensory observational theory. *Journal of the Society for Psychical Research, 52,* 113–116.

_____. (1984a). Quantum physics and parapsychology. *Parapsychology Review, 15(3),* 4–6.

_____. (1984b). Test of psychokinetic control of bacterial mutation. *Journal of the American Society for Psychical Research, 78,* 145–152.

_____. (1995). Personal survival of death by worldlines. *Journal of the Society for Psychical Research, 60,* 317–321.

Nelson, R. D. (2002). Coherent consciousness and reduced randomness: Correlations on September 11, 2001. *Journal of Scientific Exploration, 16,* 549–570.

_____, Bradish, G. J., Dunne, B. J., Dobyns, Y. H., and Jahn, R. G. (1996). FieldREG anomalies in group situations. *Journal of Scientific Exploration, 10,* 111–141.

_____, _____, _____, and _____. (1996). Precognitive remote perception: Replication of remote viewing. *Journal of Scientific Exploration, 10,* 109–110.

_____, Jahn, R. G., Dunne, B. J., Dobyns, Y. H., and Bradish, G. J. (1998). FieldREG II: Conscious field effects: Replication and extensions. *Journal of Scientific Exploration, 12,* 425–454.

Neppe, V. (2003). Parapsychological approaches to interpreting anomalous brain function and subjective paranormal experience. Paper presented at the 46th annual convention of the Parapsychological Association, Vancouver, Canada.

Nickell, J. (2005b). Holy grilled cheese? *Skeptical Inquirer, 29(2),* 9.

Noyes, R. (1972). The experience of dying. *Psychiatry, 35,* 174–184.

Oakley, D. A. (1985a). Animal awareness, consciousness, and self-image. In D. A. Oakley (Ed.), *Mind and brain* (pp. 132–151). New York: Methuen.

_____. (1985b). Cognition and imagery in animals. In D. A. Oakley (Ed.), *Mind and brain* (pp. 99–131). New York: Methuen.

Ogston, A. (1920). *Reminiscences of three campaigns.* London: Hodder and Stoughton.

Ojemann, G. A. (1983). Brain organization for language from the perspective of electrical stimulation mapping. *Behavioral and Brain Sciences, 6,* 189–230.

O'Keefe, J. (1985). Is consciousness the gateway to the hippocampal cognitive map? A speculative essay on the neural basis of mind. In D. A. Oakley (Ed.), *Brain and mind* (pp. 59–98). New York: Methuen.

Oppenheim, J. (1985). *The other world: Spiritualism and psychical research in England, 1850–1914.* New York: Cambridge University Press.

Oppenheimer, P. (1986). [Letter to the Editor.] *The Sciences, 26(2),* 12.

Osis, K. (1961). Deathbed observations by physicians and nurses. *Parapsychological Monographs, No. 3.* New York: Parapsychology Foundation.

_____, and Haraldsson, E. (1977a). *At the hour of death.* New York: Avon.

_____, and _____. (1977b). Deathbed observations by physicians and nurses. *Journal of the American Society for Psychical Research, 71,* 237–259.

_____, and _____. (1977c). OBEs in Indian swamis: Sai Baba and Dadaji. In J. D. Morris, W. G. Roll, and R. L. Morris (Eds.), *Research in parapsychology, 1976* (pp. 147–150). Metuchen, NJ: Scarecrow Press.

_____, and McCormick, D. (1980). Kinetic effects at the ostensible location of an out-of-body projection during perceptual testing. *Journal of the American Society for Psychical Research, 74,* 319–329.

Pagels, H. (1988). *The dreams of reason.* New York: Simon and Schuster.

Pallikari, F. (2004) On the false hypothesis of psi-mediated shift of statistical average in tests with random event generators. Paper presented at the

47th annual convention of the Parapsychological Association, Vienna University, Austria.

Palmer, J. (1978). The out-of-body experience: A psychological theory. *Parapsychology Review, 9(5),* 19–22.

_____. (1979). A community mail survey of psychic experiences. *Journal of the American Society for Psychical Research, 73,* 221–251.

_____. (1986). [Review of *Flight of mind.*] *Parapsychology Review, 17(2),* 12–15.

_____. (1995). Toward a general theory of survival. In L. Coly and J. D. S. McMahon (Eds.), *Parapsychology and thanatology: Proceedings of an international conference held in Boston, Massachusetts, November 6–7, 1993* (pp. 1–32). New York: Parapsychology Foundation.

_____. (1997). The challenge of experimenter psi. *European Journal of Parapsychology, 13,* 110–125.

_____. (2004). Synchronicity and psi: How are they related? Paper presented at the 47th annual convention of the Parapsychological Association, Vienna University, Austria.

_____, and Lieberman, R. (1975). The influence of psychological set on ESP and out-of-body experiences. *Journal of the American Society for Psychical Research, 69,* 193–213.

_____, and _____. (1976). ESP and out-of-body experiences: A further study. In J. D. Morris, W. G. Roll, and R. L. Morris (Eds.), *Research in parapsychology, 1975* (pp. 102–106). Metuchen, NJ: Scarecrow Press.

_____, and Vassar, C. (1974). ESP and out-of-the-body experiences: An exploratory study. *Journal of the American Society for Psychical Research, 68,* 257–280.

Pamplin, B. and Collins, H. (1975). Spoon bending: An experimental approach. *Nature, 257,* 8.

Parfit, D. (1987). Divided minds and the nature of persons. In C. Blakemore and S. Greenfield (Eds.), *Mindwaves: Thoughts on intelligence, identity and consciousness* (pp. 19–26). New York: Basil Blackwell.

Parra, A. (2004). PK occurrences, epilepsy and repressed aggression: Analyses of Andres Vernier's case. *Paranormal Review, 32,* 23–27.

Pashler, H. (1998). *The psychology of attention.* Cambridge, MA: MIT Press.

Pasricha, S. K. (1978). An investigation into reported cases of persons who claimed to have reincarnated. Unpublished doctoral dissertation. Bangalore University, Bangalore, India.

_____. (1992a). Are reincarnation cases shaped by parental guidance? An empirical study concerning the limits of parents' influence on children. *Journal of Scientific Exploration, 6,* 167–180.

_____. (1992b). *Claims of reincarnation: An empirical study of cases in India.* New Delhi: Harman Publishing House.

_____. (1993). A systematic survey of near-death experiences in South India. *Journal of Scientific Exploration, 7,* 161–171.

_____. (1995). Near-death experiences in South India: A systematic survey. *Journal of Scientific Exploration, 9,* 79–85.

_____. (1998). Cases of the reincarnation type in Northern India with birthmarks and birth defects. *Journal of Scientific Exploration, 12,* 259–293.

_____, and Barker, D. R. (1981). A case of the reincarnation type in India: The case of Rakesh Gaur. *European Journal of Parapsychology, 3,* 381–408.

_____, Keil, J., Tucker, J. B., and Stevenson, I. (2005). Some bodily malformations attributed to previous lives. *Journal of Scientific Exploration, 19,* 359–383.

_____, and Stevenson, I. (1979). A partly independent replication of investigations of cases suggestive of reincarnation. *European Journal of Parapsychology, 3,* 51–65.

Patterson, R. W. K. (1995). *Philosophy and the belief in the survival of death.* London: Macmillan.

Pearce, J. C. (1973). *The crack in the cosmic egg.* New York: Washington Square Press.

Pearson, R. E. (1961). Response to suggestion given under general anesthesia. *American Journal of Clinical Hypnosis, 4,* 106–114.

Penelhum, T. (1987). Survival and disembodied existence. In A. Flew (Ed.), *Readings in the philosophical problems of parapsychology* (pp. 338–346). Buffalo, NY: Prometheus Books.

Penfield, W. (1975). *The mystery of the mind.* Princeton, NJ: Princeton University Press.

Penrose, R. (1986). Big bangs, black holes and 'time's arrow.' In R. Flood and M. Lockwood (Eds.), *The nature of time* (pp. 36–62). New York: Basil Blackwell.

_____. (1987). Quantum physics and conscious thought. In B. J. Hiley and F. D. Peat (Eds.), *Quantum implications: Essays in honour of David Bohm* (pp. 105–120). London: Routledge and Kegan Paul.

_____. (1994). *Shadows of the mind.* New York: Oxford University Press.

Perakh, M. (2005). Does irreducible complexity imply intelligent design? *Skeptical Inquirer, 29 (6),* 32–36.

Persinger, M. A. (1979). ELF field mediation in spontaneous psi events: Direct information transfer or conditional elicitation? In C. T. Tart, H. E. Puthoff, and R. Targ (Eds.), *Mind at large* (pp. 191–204). New York: Praeger.

_____. (1983). Religious and mystical experiences as artifacts of temporal lobe function: A general hypothesis. *Perceptual and Motor Skills, 57,* 1255–1262.

Pool, R. (1990). Closing the gap between proteins and DNA. *Science, 248,* 1609.

Popper, K., and Eccles, J. (1977). *The self and its brain.* New York: Springer International.

Price, H. H. (1939). Haunting and the "psychic ether" hypothesis: With some preliminary reflections on the present condition and possible future of psychical research. *Proceedings of the Society for Psychical Research, 45,* 307–374.

_____. (1940). Some philosophical questions about telepathy and clairvoyance. *Philosophy, 15,* 363–374.

_____. (1948). Psychical research and human personality. *Hibbert Journal,* 105–113.

_____. (1953). Survival and the idea of "another world." *Proceedings of the Society for Psychical Research, 50,* 1–125.

_____. (1959). Psychical research and human nature. *Journal of Parapsychology, 23,* 178–187.

_____. (1961). Apparitions: Two theories. *Journal of Parapsychology, 24,* 110–125.

Priest, S. (1991). *Theories of the mind.* New York: Houghton Mifflin.

Puthoff, H. E., and Targ, R. (1979). A perceptual channel for information transfer over kilometer distances: Historical perspectives and recent research. In C. T. Tart, H. E. Puthoff and R. Targ (Eds.), *Mind at large* (pp. 13–76). New York: Praeger.

_____, _____, and Tart, C. T. (1980). Resolution in remote-viewing studies: Mini-targets. In W. G. Roll (Ed.), *Research in parapsychology, 1979* (pp. 120–122). Metuchen, NJ: Scarecrow Press.

Radin, D. I. (1997a). *The conscious universe.* San Francisco: HarperEdge.

_____. (1997b). Unconscious perception of future emotions: An experiment in presentiment. *Journal of Scientific Exploration, 11,* 163–180.

_____. (2002). Exploring the relationship between random physical events and mass human attention: asking for whom the bell tolls. *Journal of Scientific Exploration, 16,* 533–547.

_____. (2003) Electrodermal presentiments of future emotions. Paper presented at the 46th annual convention of the Parapsychological Association, Vancouver, Canada.

_____. (2004). Electrodermal presentiments of future emotions. *Journal of Scientific Exploration, 18,* 253–273.

_____, and Ferrari, D. C. (1991). Effects of consciousness on the fall of dice: A meta-analysis. *Journal of Scientific Exploration, 5,* 61–83.

_____, and Roll, W. G. (1994). A radioactive ghost in a music hall. Paper presented at the 37th annual convention of the Parapsychological Association, Amsterdam, the Netherlands.

_____, May, E. C. and Thomson, M. J. (1986). Psi experiments with random number generators: Meta-analysis Part I. In D. H. Weiner and D.

I. Radin (Eds.), *Research in parapsychology, 1985* (pp. 14–17). Metuchen, NJ: Scarecrow Press.

_____, Rebman, J. M., and Mackwe, P. C. (1996). Anomalous organization of random events by group consciousness: Two exploratory experiments. *Journal of Scientific Exploration, 10,* 143–168.

_____, Taft, R., and Yount, G. (2003). Possible effects of healing intention on cell cultures and truly random events. Paper presented at the 46th annual convention of the Parapsychological Association, Vancouver, Canada.

_____, Taylor, R. K., and Braud, W. G. (1993). Remote mental influence of electrodermal activity: A preliminary replication. Paper presented at the 36th annual convention of the Parapsychological Association. Toronto, Canada.

Rafal, R., Smith, J., Krantz, S., Cohen, A., and Brennan, C. (1990). Extrageniculate vision in hemianopic humans: Saccade inhibition by signals in the blind field. *Science, 250,* 118–120.

Ramachandran, V. S. (1980). Twins, split brains and personal identity. In B. D. Josephson and V. S. Ramachandran (Eds.), *Consciousness and the physical world* (pp. 139–163). New York: Pergamon Press.

_____, and Blakeslee, S. (1998). *Phantoms in the brain.* New York: HarperCollins.

_____, and Hirstein, W. (1997). Three laws of qualia: What neurology tells us about the biological functions of consciousness. *Journal of Consciousness Studies, 4*(5/6), 429–457.

Randall, J. L. (1998). Physics, philosophy and precognition. *Journal of the Society for Psychical Research, 63,* 1–11.

Randi, J. (1979). Edgar Cayce: The slipping prophet. *Skeptical Inquirer, 4(1),* 51–57.

_____. (1980). *Flim-flam.* New York: Lippincott and Crowell.

_____. (1983a). The Project Alpha experiment: Part 1. The first two years. *Skeptical Inquirer, 7(4),* 24–33.

_____. (1983b). The Project Alpha experiment: Part 2. Beyond the laboratory. *Skeptical Inquirer, 8(1),* 36–45.

_____. (1985). The Columbus poltergeist case: Part I. *Skeptical Inquirer, 9,* 221–235.

_____. (1986). The Project Alpha experiment. In K. Frazier (Ed.), *Science confronts the paranormal* (pp. 158–165). Buffalo, NY: Prometheus Books.

_____. (1987). *The faith healers.* Buffalo, NY: Prometheus Books.

Rao, K. R. (1966). *Experimental parapsychology.* Springfield, IL: Thomas.

_____. (1978). Psi: Its place in nature. *Journal of Parapsychology, 42,* 276–303.

_____. (2002). *Consciousness studies: Cross-cultural perspectives.* Jefferson, NC: McFarland

Rees, W. D. (1971). The hallucinations of widows. *British Medical Journal, 4,* 37–41.

Rein, G. (1986) A psychokinetic effect on neurotransmitter metabolism: Alterations in the degradative enzyme monoamine oxidase. In D. H. Weiner and D. I. Radin (Eds.), *Research in parapsychology, 1985* (pp. 70–80). Metuchen, NJ: Scarecrow Press.

_____, and McCraty, R. (1994). Structural changes in water and DNA associated with new physiologically measurable states. Paper presented at the 13th annual meeting of the Society for Scientific Exploration, Austin, Texas.

Rhine, J. B. (1974). Telepathy and other untestable hypotheses. *Journal of Parapsychology, 38,* 215–225.

_____, and Pratt, J. G. (1954). A review of the Pearce-Pratt distance series of ESP tests. *Journal of Parapsychology, 18,* 165–177.

Rhine, L. E. (1951) Conviction and associated conditions in spontaneous cases. *Journal of Parapsychology, 15,* 164–191

_____. (1955). Precognition and intervention. *Journal of Parapsychology, 19,* 1–34.

_____. (1961). *Hidden channels of the mind.* New York: William Sloane.

_____. (1962a) Psychological processes in ESP experiences. Part I. Waking experiences. *Journal of Parapsychology, 26,* 88–111.

_____. (1962b). Psychological processes in ESP experiences. *Journal of Parapsychology, 26,* 172–199.

_____. (1963). Spontaneous physical effects and the psi process. *Journal of Parapsychology, 27,* 84–122.

_____. (1970). Dr. L. E. Rhine's reply to Dr. Stevenson. [Letter to the Editor.] *Journal of Parapsychology, 34,* 149–164.

_____. (1977). Research methods with spontaneous cases. In B. B. Wolman (Ed.), *Handbook of parapsychology* (pp. 59–80). New York: Van Nostrand Reinhold.

_____. (1978). The psi process in spontaneous cases. *Journal of Parapsychology, 42,* 20–32.

_____. (1981). *The invisible picture: A study of psychic experiences.* Jefferson, NC: McFarland.

Richet, C. (1884). La suggestion mentale et le calcul des probabilities. *Revue Philosophique, 18,* 609–674.

_____. (1888). Further experiments in hypnotic lucidity or clairvoyance. *Proceedings of the Society for Psychical Research, 6,* 66–83.

Rinaldi, G. M., and Piccinini, G. (1982). A survey of spontaneous cases in South Tyrol. Unpublished manuscript.

Ring, K. (1979). Further studies of the near death experience. *Theta, 7(2),* 1–3.

_____. (1980). *Life at death.* New York: Coward, McCann and Geoghegan.

Roach, M. (2005). *Spook.* New York: Norton.

Robertson, T. J., and Roy, A. E. (2004). Results of the application of the Robertson-Roy protocol to a series of experiments with mediums and participants. *Journal of the Society for Psychical Research, 68,* 18–34.

Rodin, E. A. (1980). The reality of near-death experiences: A perceptual perspective. *Journal of Nervous and Mental Diseases, 168,* 259–263.

Rogo, D. S. (1975). Psi and psychosis: A review of the experimental evidence. *Journal of Parapsychology, 39,* 120–128.

_____. (1978). *Mind beyond the body.* New York: Penguin Books.

_____. (1980). Theories about PK: A critical evaluation. *Journal of the Society for Psychical Research, 50,* 359–378.

Roll, W. G. (1961). The problem of precognition. *Journal of the Society for Psychical Research, 41,* 115–128.

_____. (1964). *The psi field. Proceedings of the Parapsychological Association, 1,* 32–65.

_____. (1966). ESP and memory. *International Journal of Parapsychology, 2,* 505–521.

_____. (1972). *The poltergeist.* New York: Signet.

_____. (1977). Experimenting with poltergeists? *European Journal of Parapsychology, 2,* 47–71.

_____. (1978). Towards a theory for the poltergeist. *European Journal of Parapsychology, 2,* 167–200.

_____. (1979). Psi structures. In W. G. Roll (Ed.), *Research in parapsychology, 1978* (pp. 16–17). Metuchen, NJ: Scarecrow Press.

_____. (1981). A memory theory for apparitions. In W. G. Roll and J. Beloff (Eds.), *Research in parapsychology, 1980* (pp. 5–7). Metuchen, NJ: Scarecrow Press.

_____. (1982a). Memory, mediumship and reincarnation. In W. G. Roll, R. L. Morris, and R. A. White (Eds.), *Research in parapsychology, 1981* (pp. 182–187). Metuchen, NJ: Scarecrow Press.

_____. (1982b). The changing perspective on life after death. In S. Krippner (Ed.), *Advances in parapsychological research, Volume 3* (pp. 147–291). New York: Plenum Press.

_____. (1983). The psi structure theory of survival. In W. G. Roll, J. Beloff, and R. A. White (Eds.), *Research in parapsychology, 1982* (pp. 155–120). Metuchen, NJ: Scarecrow Press.

_____. (1984). The psychopathological and psychophysiological theories of the RSPK agent. In R. A. White and R. S. Broughton (Eds.), *Research in parapsychology, 1983* (pp. 118–119).

_____. (1988). Psi and the phenomenology of memory. In D. H. Weiner and R. L. Morris

(Eds.), *Research in parapsychology, 1987* (pp. 131–134). Metuchen, NJ: Scarecrow Press.

_____. (1989). Memory and the long body. In L. A. Henkel and R. E. Berger (Eds.), *Research in parapsychology, 1988* (pp. 67–72). Methuchen, NJ: Scarecrow Press.

_____. (1993). The question of RSPK vs. fraud in the case of Tina Resch. Paper presented at the 36th annual convention of the Parapsychological Association, Toronto, Canada.

_____. (2005). Psi and the long body. Paper presented at the 48th annual convention of the Parapsychological Association, Petaluma, California.

_____, and Storey, V. (2004). *Unleashed: Of poltergeists and murder: The curious case of Tina Resch.* New York: Paraview.

_____, Maher, M. C., and Brown, B. (1992). An investigation of reported haunting occurrences in a Japanese restaurant in Georgia. Paper presented at the 35th annual convention of the Parapsychological Association. Las Vegas, Nevada.

Roney-Dougal, S. M., and Solfvin, G. F. (2004). Field study of an enhancement effect on lettuce seeds: Working in adverse conditions. Paper presented at the 47th annual convention of the Parapsychological Association, Vienna University, Austria.

Rose, S. (1992). *The making of memory.* New York: Anchor Books.

Sabom, M. B. (1982). *Recollections of death: A medical investigation.* New York: Harper and Row.

Sagan, C. (1977). *Broca's brain.* New York: Random House.

Saklani, A. (1988a). Preliminary test of PSI-ability in shamans of Garhwal Himalaya. *Journal of the Society for Psychical Research*, 55, 60–70.

_____. (1988b). Psi ability in shamans of Garhwal Himalaya. In D. H. Weiner and R. L. Morris (Eds.), *Research in parapsychology, 1987* (pp. 93–96).

_____. (1989). Psychokinetic effect on plant growth: Further studies. Paper presented at the 32nd annual convention of the Parapsychological Association, San Diego, California.

_____. (1990). Psychokinetic effects on plant growth: Further studies. In L. A. Henkel and J. Palmer (Eds.), *Research in parapsychology, 1989* (pp. 37–41). Metuchen, NJ: Scarecrow Press.

_____. (1991). Promising results in PK experiments with plants. Paper presented at the 34th annual convention of the Parapsychological Association, Heidelberg, Germany.

_____. (1992). Follow-up studies of PK effects on plant growth. *Journal of the Society for Psychical Research*, 58, 258–265.

Sanders, M. D., Warrington, E. K., Marshall, J., and

Weiskrantz, L. (1974). 'Blindsight:' Vision in a field defect. *Lancet* (April 20), *1(7860)*, 707–708.

Sarra, L., Child, R., and Smith, M. D. (2004). The precognitive habituation effect: An adaptation using spider stimuli. Paper presented at the 47th annual convention of the Parapsychological Association, Vienna University, Austria.

Satori, L., Massaccesi, S., Martinielli, M., and Tressoldi, P. E. (2004). Physiological correlates of ESP: Heart rate differences between targets and nontargets. *Journal of Parapsychology*, 68, 350–360.

Scargle, J. P. (2000). Publication bias: The "file drawer" problem in scientific inference. *Journal of Scientific Exploration*, 14, 91–106.

_____. (2002). Was there evidence of global consciousness on September 11, 2001? *Journal of Scientific Exploration*, 16, 571–577.

Schechter, E. I. (1984). Hypnotic inductions. Control conditions: Illustrating an approach to the evaluation of replicability in parapsychological data. In R. A. White and R. S. Broughton (Eds.), *Research in parapsychology, 1983* (pp. 49–52). Metuchen, NJ: Scarecrow Press.

Schlitz, M. J., and Gruber, E. R. (1980). Transcontinental remote viewing. *Journal of Parapsychology*, 44, 305–317.

_____, and _____. (1981). Trans-continental remote viewing. *Journal of Parapsychology*, 45, 233–237.

Schmidt, H. (1969). Precognition of a quantum process. *Journal of Parapsychology*, 33, 99–108.

_____. (1970). PK tests with animals as subjects. *Journal of Parapsychology*, 34, 255–261.

_____. (1975a). A logically consistent model of a world with psi interaction. In L. Oteri (Ed.), *Quantum physics and parapsychology* (pp. 205–228). New York: Parapsychology Foundation.

_____. (1975b). Toward a mathematical theory of psi. *Journal of the American Society for Psychical Research*, 69, 301–319.

_____. (1976). PK effect on pre-recorded targets. *Journal of the American Society for Psychical Research*, 70, 267–291.

_____. (1981). PK tests with pre-recorded and pre-inspected seed numbers. *Journal of Parapsychology*, 45, 87–98.

_____. (1984). Comparison of a teleological with a quantum mechanical theory of psi. *Journal of Parapsychology*, 48, 261–276.

_____. (1985). Addition effect for PK on prerecorded targets. *Journal of Parapsychology*, 49, 231–248.

_____. (1986). Human PK effort on prerecorded random events previously observed by goldfish. In D. H. Weiner and D. I. Radin (Eds.), *Research in parapsychology*, 1985 (pp. 18–21). Metuchen, NJ: Scarecrow Press.

_____. (1993). Observation of a psychokinetic effect under highly controlled conditions. *Journal of Parapsychology*, *57*, 357–372.

_____, Morris, R. L., and Rudolph, L. (1986). Channeling evidence for PK effects to independent observers. *Journal of Parapsychology*, *50*, 1–16.

_____, and Schlitz, M.J. (1988). A large scale pilot PK experiment with pre-recorded random events. Paper presented at the 31st annual convention of the Parapsychological Association, Montreal, Canada.

Schmidt, S., Muller, S., and Walach, H. (2004). Do you know who is on the phone? Replication of an experiment on telephone telepathy. Paper presented at the 47th annual convention of the Parapsychological Association, Vienna University, Austria.

_____, Schneider, R., Utts, J., and Walach, H. (2004). Distant intentionality and the feeling of being stared at: Two meta-analyses. *British Journal of Psychology*, *95*, 235–247.

Schnaper, N. (1980). Comments germane to the paper entitled "The reality of death experiences" by Ernst Rodin. *Journal of Nervous and Mental Disease*, *168*, 268–270.

Schouten, S. A. (1981). Analyzing spontaneous cases: A replication based on the Sannwald collection. *European Journal of Parapsychology*, *4*, 8–48.

Schriever, F. (1987). A 30-year "experiment with time." Evaluation of an individual case study of precognitive dreams. *European Journal of Parapsychology*, *7*, 49–72.

Schwartz, G. E. (2002). *The afterlife experiments: Breakthrough evidence of life after death*. New York: Pocket Books.

Schwartz, J., Stapp, H., and Beauregard, M. (2005). Quantum physics in neuroscience and psychology: A neurophysical model of mind/brain interaction. *Philosophical Transactions of the Royal Society, B 360(1458)*, 1309–1327.

Schwartz, S. A., De Mattei, R. J., Brame, E. G., and Spottiswoode, S. J. P. (1987). Infrared spectra alteration in water proximate to the palms of therapeutic practitioners. In D. H. Weiner and R. D. Nelson (Eds.), *Research in parapsychology, 1986* (pp. 24–29). Metuchen, NJ: Scarecrow Press.

Scofield, A. M., and Hodges, R. D. (1991). Demonstration of a healing effect in the laboratory using a simple plant. *Journal of the Society for Psychical Research*, *57*, 321–343.

Scott, C., and Haskell, P. (1974). Fresh light on the Shackleton experiments. *Proceedings of the Society for Psychical Research*, *56*, 43–72.

Scott, E. (2001). Icons of creationism: The new anti-evolutionism and science. Lecture presented at the University of California at Berkeley on January 18, 2001.

Seager, W. (1995). Consciousness, information and panpsychism. *Journal of Consciousness Studies*, *2*, 272–288.

Seife, C. (2003). Illuminating the dark universe. *Science*, *203*, 2038–2039.

Seligman, M. E. P. (1975). *Helplessness: On depression, development and death*. San Francisco: Freeman.

Shan, G. (2002). A primary quantum model of telepathy. Paper presented at the 47th annual convention of the Parapsychological Association, Vienna University, Austria.

Shaver, P. (1986). Consciousness without the body. [Review of *Flight of mind.*] *Contemporary Psychology*, *31*, 647.

Shear, J. (1995). Editor's introduction. *Journal of Consciousness Studies*, *2*, 194–199.

Sheldrake, R. C. (1981). *A new science of life*. Los Angeles: Tarcher.

_____. (1983a). Formative causation: The hypothesis supported. *New Scientist*, October 27, 279–280.

_____. (1983b). Morphic resonance, memory and psychical research. In W. G. Roll, J. Beloff, and R. A. White (Eds.), *Research in parapsychology, 1982* (pp. 81–85). Metuchen, NJ: Scarecrow Press.

_____. (1988a). The laws of nature as habits: A postmodern basis for science. In D. R. Griffin (Ed.), *The reenchantment of science* (pp. 79–86). Albany: State University of New York Press.

_____. (1988b). *The presence of the past*. New York: Times Books.

_____. (1990). Can our memories survive the death of our brain? In G. Doore (Ed.), *What survives?* (pp. 111–121). Los Angeles: Tarcher.

_____. (1998). Experimenter effects in scientific research: How widely are they replicated? *Journal of Scientific Exploration*, *12*, 73–78.

_____. (2001). Experiments on the sense of being stared at: The elimination of possible artifacts. *Journal of the Society for Psychical Research*, *65*, 122–137.

_____. (2005). The sense of being stared at. Part I. Is it real or illusory? *Journal of Consciousness Studies*, *12(6)*, 10–31.

_____, and Smart, P. (2000). A dog that seems to know when his owner is coming home: Videotaped experiments and observations. *Journal of Scientific Exploration*, *14*, 233–255.

_____. and _____. (2003). Experimental tests for telephone telepathy. *Journal of the Society for Psychical Research*, *67*, 184–199.

Sidgwick, H., Johnson, A., Myers, F. W. H., Podmore, F., and Sidgwick, E. M. (1894). Report on the census of hallucinations. *Proceedings of the Society for Psychical Research*, *10*, 25–422.

Siegel, R. K. (1977). Hallucinations. *Scientific American, 23(7)*, 132–140.

_____. (1980). The psychology of life after death. *American Psychologist, 35*, 911–931.

Skinner, B. F. (1953). *Science and human behavior.* Toronto: Collier-Macmillan.

Skrbina, D. (2003). Panpsychism as an underlying theme in Western philosophy: A survey paper. *Journal of Consciousness Studies, 10*(3), 4–46.

_____. (2005). *Panpsychism in the West.* Cambridge, MA: MIT Press.

Smith, M. J. (1968). Paranormal effects on enzyme activity. *Journal of Parapsychology, 32*, 281 (Abstract).

_____. (1972). Paranormal effects on enzyme activity through laying on of hands. *Human Dimensions, 1(2)*, 15–19.

Smith, P., and Irwin, H. J. (1981). Out-of-body experiences, needs and the experimental approach. A laboratory study. *Parapsychology Review, 12(3)*, 1–4.

Snel, F. W. J. J., and Van der Sijde, P. C. (1990–1991). The effect of retroactive distance healing of *Babesia Rodhani* (rodent malaria) in rats. *European Journal of Parapsychology, 8*, 123–130.

Soal, S. G., and Bateman, F. (1954). *Modern experiments in telepathy.* New Haven, CT: Yale University Press.

Solfvin, G. F. (1982). Studies of the effects of mental healing and expectations on the growth of corn seedlings. *European Journal of Parapsychology, 4*, 284–324.

Sondow, N. (1988). The decline of recognized events with the passage of time: Evidence from spontaneous dreams. *Journal of the American Society for Psychical Research, 82*, 33–51.

Spanos, N. P., and Hewitt, E. C. (1980). The hidden observer in hypnotic analgesia: discovery or experimental creation? *Journal of Personality and Social Psychology, 46*, 688–696.

Spence, S. A. (2006). The cycle of action: A commentary on Garry Young (2006). *Journal of Consciousness Studies, 13(3)*, 69–72.

_____, and Frith, C. D. (1999). Towards a functional anatomy of volition. In B. Libet, A. Freeman, and K. Sutherland (Eds.), *The volitional brain: Toward a neuroscience of free will* (pp. 11–29). Thorverton, UK: Imprint Academic.

Spottiswoode, S. J. P., and May, E. C. (2003). Skin conductance prestimulus response: Analyses, artifact and pilot study. *Journal of Scientific Exploration, 17*, 617–641.

Sprigge, T. (2002). Could parapsychology have any bearing on religion? In F. Steinkamp (Ed.), *Parapsychology, philosophy and the mind* (pp. 127–145). Jefferson, NC: McFarland.

Squire, L. (1987). *Memory and brain.* New York: University Press.

Squires, E. (1990). *Conscious mind in the physical world.* New York: Adam Holger.

Stace, W.T. (1960). *Mysticism and philosophy.* Los Angeles: Tarcher.

Stahl, F. W. (1990). If it smells like a unicorn. *Nature, 346*, 791.

Stanford, R. G. (1974). An experimentally testable model for spontaneous psi events. I. Extrasensory events. *Journal of the American Society for Psychical Research, 68*, 34–57.

_____. (1987). The out-of-body experience as an imaginal journey: The developmental perspective. *Journal of Parapsychology, 51*, 135–155.

_____. (1990a). A model for spontaneous psi events. In S. Krippner (Ed.), *Advances in parapsychological research, Volume 6* (pp. 54–167). Jefferson, NC: McFarland.

_____. (1990b). The correlation of lucid dreaming and out-of-body experience: What does it mean? In L. A. Henkel and J. Palmer (Eds.), *Research in parapsychology, 1989* (pp. 9–14). Metuchen, NJ: Scarecrow Press.

_____, and Stein, A. G. (1994). A meta-analysis of ESP studies contrasting hypnosis and a comparison condition. *Journal of Parapsychology, 58*, 235–269.

Stapp, H. P. (1992). A quantum theory of consciousness. In B. Rubik (Ed.), *The interrelationship between mind and matter* (pp. 207–217). Philadelphia, PA: The Center for Frontier Sciences.

_____. (1996). The hard problem: A quantum approach. *Journal of Consciousness Studies, 3*(3), 196–210.

_____. (2004). Quantum leaps in the philosophy of mind. *Journal of Consciousness Studies, 11(12)*, 43–49.

_____. (2005a). Commentary on Hodgson. *Journal of Consciousness Studies, 12(1)*, 70–75.

_____. (2005b). Quantum interactive dualism. *Journal of Consciousness Studies, 12(11)*, 43–58.

Stearn, J. (1967). *Edgar Cayce—The sleeping prophet.* New York: Doubleday.

Steinkamp, F. (2002). Parapsychological phenomena and the sense of self. In F. Steinkamp (Ed.), *Parapsychology, philosophy and the mind: Essays honoring John Beloff* (pp. 59–80). Jefferson, NC: McFarland.

_____, Boller, E., and Bösch, H. (2002). Experiments examining the possibility of human intention interacting with random number generators. Paper presented at the 45th annual convention of the Parapsychological Association, Paris, France.

Stevens, P. (2005). The effect of magnetic field on a random event generator: Reconsidering the role of geomagnetic fluctuation in micro-PK studies. *European Journal of Parapsychology, 20,* 135–149.

Stevenson, I. (1960a). The evidence for survival from claimed memories of former incarnations. Part I. Review of the data. *Journal of the American Society for Psychical Research, 54,* 51–71.

_____. (1960b). The evidence for survival from claimed memories of former incarnations. Part II. Analysis of the data and suggestions for further investigations. *Journal of the American Society for Psychical Research, 54,* 95–117.

_____. (1966). Cultural patterns in cases suggestive of reincarnation among the Tlingit Indians of southeastern Alaska. *Journal of the American Society for Psychical Research, 60,* 229–243.

_____. (1970a). Characteristics of cases of the reincarnation type in Turkey and their comparison with cases in two other cultures. *International Journal of Comparative Sociology, 12,* 1–17.

_____. (1970b). *Telepathic impressions.* Charlottesville: University Press of Virginia.

_____. (1972). Some new cases suggestive of reincarnation. II. The case of Bishen Chand. *Journal of the American Society for Psychical Research, 66,* 375–400.

_____. (1973). Some new cases suggestive of reincarnation. IV. The case of Ampan Petcherat. *Journal of the American Society for Psychical Research, 67,* 361–380.

_____. (1974a). Some new cases suggestive of reincarnation. V. The case of Indika Guneratne. *Journal of the American Society for Psychical Research, 68,* 58–90.

_____. (1974b). Some questions related to cases of the reincarnation type. *Journal of the American Society for Psychical Research, 68,* 395–416.

_____. (1974c). *Twenty cases suggestive of reincarnation.* Charlottesville: University Press of Virginia.

_____. (1974d). Xenoglossy: A review and report of a case. *Proceedings of the American Society for Psychical Research, 31.*

_____. (1975). *Cases of the reincarnation type. Volume 1. Ten cases in India.* Charlottesville: University Press of Virginia.

_____. (1976). A preliminary report on a new case of responsive xenoglossy: The case of Gretchen. *Journal of the American Society for Psychical Research, 70,* 65–77.

_____. (1977a). *Cases of the reincarnation type. Volume 2. Ten cases in Sri Lanka.* Charlottesville: University Press of Virginia.

_____. (1977b). Reincarnation: Field studies and theoretical issues. In B. B. Wolman (Ed.), *Handbook of parapsychology* (pp. 631–663). New York: Van Nostrand Reinhold.

_____. (1977c). The belief in reincarnation and cases of the reincarnation type among the Haida. *Journal of the American Society for Psychical Research, 71,* 177–189.

_____. (1978). Some comments on automatic writing. *Journal of the American Society for Psychical Research, 73,* 315–332.

_____. (1980). *Cases of the reincarnation type. Volume 3. Twelve cases in Lebanon and Turkey.* Charlottesville: University Press of Virginia.

_____. (1981). Can we describe the mind? In W. G. Roll and J. Beloff (Eds.), *Research in parapsychology, 1980* (pp. 130–142). Metuchen, NJ: Scarecrow Press.

_____. (1983). *Cases of the reincarnation type. Volume 4. Twelve cases in Thailand and Burma.* Charlottesville: University Press of Virginia.

_____. (1984). *Unlearned language: New studies in xenoglossy.* Charlottesville: University Press of Virginia.

_____. (1986). Characteristics of cases of reincarnation among the Igbo of Nigeria. *Journal of Asian and African Studies, 20,* 13–30.

_____. (1987). *Children who remember past lives.* Charlottesville: University Press of Virginia.

_____. (1988a). A new look at maternal impressions. Paper presented at the 12th International Conference of the Society for Psychical Research, Winchester, England.

_____. (1988b). Three new cases of the reincarnation type in Sri Lanka with written records made before verifications. *Journal of Scientific Exploration, 2,* 217–240.

_____. (1989). A case of severe birth defects possibly due to cursing. *Journal of Scientific Exploration, 3,* 201–212.

_____. (1990). Phobias in children who claim to remember previous lives. *Journal of Scientific Exploration, 4,* 243–254.

_____. (1992). A new look at maternal impressions: An analysis of 50 published cases and reports of two recent examples. *Journal of Scientific Exploration, 6,* 353–373.

_____. (1993). Birthmarks and birth defects corresponding to wounds on deceased persons. *Journal of Scientific Exploration, 7,* 403–410.

_____. (1995). Six modern apparitional experiences. *Journal of Scientific Exploration, 9,* 351–366.

_____. (1997a). *Reincarnation and biology: A contribution to the etiology of birthmarks and birth defects. Vol. 1: Birthmarks. Vol. 2: Birth defects and other anomalies.* Westport, CT: Praeger.

_____. (1997b) *Reincarnation: Where reincarnation and biology intersect.* Westport, CT: Praeger.

_____. (2003). *European cases of the reincarnation type.* Jefferson, NC: McFarland.

_____, and Beloff, J. (1980). An analysis of some suspect drop-in communicators. *Journal of the Society for Psychical Society, 50,* 427–447.

_____, and Chadha, N. K. (1988). Two correlates of violent death in cases of the reincarnation type. *Journal of the Society for Psychical Research*, *55*, 71–79.

_____, and Keil, J. (2000). The stability of assessments of paranormal connection in reincarnation-type cases. *Journal of Scientific Exploration*, *14*, 365–382.

_____, and Pasricha, S. (1979). A case of secondary personality with xenoglossy. *American Journal of Psychiatry*, *136*, 1591–1592.

_____, and _____. (1980). A preliminary report on an unusual case of the reincarnation type with xenoglossy. *Journal of the American Society for Psychical Research*, *74*, 331–348.

_____, _____, and Samararatne, G. (1988). Deception and self-deception in cases of the reincarnation type: Seven illustrative cases in Asia. *Journal of the American Society for Psychical Research*, *82*, 1–31.

Stokes, D. M. (1982) On the relationship between mind and brain. *Parapsychology Review*, *13(6)*, 22–27.

_____. (1988). Some observations on the "chewing gum" theory of personal identity: A review of some books on mind and multiplicity of consciousness. *Journal of the American Society for Psychical Research*, *82*, 53–69.

_____. (1997). *The Nature of Mind: Parapsychology and the Role of Consciousness in the Physical World.* Jefferson, NC: McFarland.

_____. (2001). The shrinking filedrawer: On the validity of scientific meta-analysis in parapsychology. *Skeptical Inquirer*, *25(8)*, 22–28.

_____. (2002a). [Review of *The afterlife experiments*.] *Journal of the American Society for Psychical Research*, *96*, 81–89.

_____. (2002b). The persistence of consciousness: Guest editorial. *Journal of the American Society for Psychical Research*, *96*, 1–14.

Tandy, V. (2000). Something in the cellar. *Journal of the Society for Psychical Research*, *64*, 129–140.

_____, and Lawrence, T. R. (1998). The ghost in the machine. *Journal of the Society for Psychical Research*, *62*, 360–364.

Targ, R., and Puthoff, H. E. (1977). *Mind-reach: Scientists look at psychic ability.* New York: Delacorte Press.

_____, _____, and May, E. C. (1979). Direct perception of remote geographical locations. In C. T. Tart, H. E. Puthoff, and R. Targ (Eds.), *Mind at large* (pp. 78–106). New York: Praeger.

Tart, C. T. (1967). A second psychophysiological study of out of-body experiences in a gifted subject. *International Journal of Parapsychology*, *9*, 251–258.

_____. (1968). A psychophysiological study of out-of-the body experiences in a selected subject.

Journal of the American Society for Psychical Research, *62*, 3–27.

_____. (1969). A further psychophysiological study of out of-the body experiences in a gifted subject. *Proceedings of the Parapsychological Association*, *6*, 43–44.

_____. (1971). *On being stoned: A psychological study of marijuana intoxication.* Palo Alto, CA: Science and Behavior Books.

_____. (1976). *Learning to use extrasensory perception.* Chicago: University of Chicago Press.

_____, Puthoff, H. E., and Targ, R. (1980). Information transmission in remote viewing experiments. *Nature*, *204*, 191.

Taylor, J. (1975). *Superminds.* New York: Warner Books.

_____. (1980). *Science and the supernatural.* New York: Dutton.

_____. (1995). Precognition and intuitive decisions: An answer to the problem of free will and causality. *Journal of the Society for Psychical Research*, *60*, 353–370.

_____. (1998). A new theory for ESP. *Journal of the Society for Psychical Research*, *62*, 289–310.

_____. (2000). Information transfer in space-time. *Journal of the Society for Psychical Research*, *64*, 193–210.

Taylor, R. (2003). Evolutionary theory and psi: Reviewing and revising some need-serving models in psychic functioning. *Journal of the Society for Psychical Research*, *67*, 1–17.

Tazari, L. (1990). An unusual case of hypnotic regression with some unexplained contents. *Journal of the American Society for Psychical Research*, *84*, 309–344.

Tedder, W. H., and Bloor, J. (1982). PK influence on radioactive decay from short and long distances. In W. G. Roll, R. L. Morris, and R. A. White (Eds.), *Research in parapsychology, 1981* (pp. 148–149). Metuchen, NJ: Scarecrow Press.

_____, and Braud, W. G. (1981). Long-distance nocturnal psychokinesis. In W. G. Roll and J. Beloff (Eds.), *Research in parapsychology, 1980* (pp. 100–101). Metuchen, NJ: Scarecrow Press.

_____, and Monty, M. L. (1981). Exploration of long-distance PK: A conceptual replication of the influence on a biological system. In W. G. Roll and J. Beloff (Eds.), *Research in parapsychology, 1980* (pp. 90–93). Metuchen, NJ: Scarecrow Press.

Terry, J., and Schmidt, H. (1978). Conscious and subconscious PK tests with pre-recorded targets. In W. G. Roll (Ed.), *Research in Parapsychology, 1977* (pp. 36–41). Metuchen, NJ: Scarecrow Press.

Tertullian (1997). The refutation of the Pythagorean doctrine of transmigration. In P.

Edwards (Ed.), *Immortality* (pp. 88–90). New York: Macmillan.

Thalbourne, M. A. (2004). The Thouless-Wiesner shin theory: Can it be saved? *Paranormal Review, 31,* 16–17.

Thaler, D. S. (1994). The evolution of genetic intelligence. *Science, 264,* 224–225.

Thomason, S. G. (1987). Past lives remembered? *Skeptical Inquirer, 11,* 367–375.

Thorton, E. M. (1984). *The Freudian fallacy.* Garden City, NY: Dial.

Thouless, R. H., and Wiesner, B. P. (1948). The psi process in normal and "paranormal" psychology. *Journal of Parapsychology, 12,* 192–212.

Tipler, F. J. (1994). *The physics of immortality.* New York: Doubleday.

Toffoli, T. (1982). Physics and computation. *International Journal of Theoretical Physics, 21,* 469.

Troland, L. T. (1917). *A technique for the study of telepathy and other alleged clairvoyant processes.* Albany: Brandow.

Tryon, E. P. (1973). Is the universe a vacuum fluctuation? *Nature, 246,* 396–397.

Twemlow, S. W., and Gabbard, G. O. (1984). The influence of demographic/psychological factors and preexisting conditions on the near death experience. *Omega, 15,* 223–235.

Tyrrell, G. N. M. (1953). *Apparitions.* New York: Macmillan.

Ullman, M., and Krippner, S. (1969). A laboratory approach to the nocturnal dimension of paranormal experience. Report of a confirmatory study using the REM monitoring technique. *Biological Psychiatry, 1,* 258–270.

_____, _____, and Vaughn, A. (1973). *Dream telepathy.* New York: Macmillan.

Varvoglis, M., and McCarthy, D. (1982). Psychokinesis, intentionality and the attentional object. In W. G. Roll, R. L. Morris, and R. A. White (Eds.), *Research in parapsychology, 1981* (pp. 51–55). Metuchen, NJ: Scarecrow Press.

Vasilescu, E., and Vasilescu, E. (1996). The mechanism of telepathy. *Journal of the Society for Psychical Research, 61,* 289–310.

_____, and _____. (2001). Experimental study on precognition. *Journal of Scientific Exploration, 15,* 369–377.

Vasiliev, L. (1976). *Experiments in distant influence.* New York: Dutton.

Venn, J. (1986). Hypnosis and the reincarnation hypothesis: A critical review and intensive case study. *Journal of the American Society for Psychical Research, 80,* 409–425.

Villars, C. (1983). Nonlocality and ESP. *Journal of the Society for Psychical Research, 52,* 189–193.

Virtanen, L. (1990). *"That must have been ESP!" An examination of psychic experiences.* Bloomington: Indiana University Press.

Walach, H., and Schmidt, S. (2005). Repairing Plata's lifeboat with Ockham's Razor. *Journal of Consciousness Studies, 12(2),* 51–70.

Walker, E. H. (1975). Foundations of paraphysical and parapsychological phenomena. In L. Oteri (Ed.), *Quantum physics and parapsychology* (pp. 1–53). New York: Parapsychology Foundation.

_____. (1984). A review of criticisms of the quantum mechanical theory of psi phenomena. *Journal of Parapsychology, 48,* 277–332.

_____. (2000). *The physics of consciousness.* Cambridge, MA: Perseus Books.

_____. (2003). Dualism, causal loops in time and the quantum observer theory of paranormal phenomena. Paper presented at the 46th annual convention of the Parapsychological Association, Vancouver, Canada.

Wambaugh, H. (1978). *Reliving past lives.* New York: Harper and Row.

Warcollier, R. (1948/1963). *Mind to mind.* New York: Collier.

Watkins, G. K., and Watkins, A. M. (1971). Possible PK influence on the resuscitation of anesthetized mice. *Journal of Parapsychology, 35,* 257–272.

_____, _____, and Wells, R. A. (1973). Further studies on the resuscitation of anesthetized mice. In W. G. Roll, R. L. Morris, and J. D. Morris (Eds.), *Research in parapsychology, 1972* (pp. 153–159). Metuchen, NJ: Scarecrow Press.

Watson, J. (1924/1970). *Behaviorism.* New York: W. W. Norton.

Watt, C. A. (1991). Meta-analysis of DMT-ESP studies and an experimental investigation of perceptual defense/vigilance and extrasensory perception. Paper presented at the 34th annual convention of the Parapsychological Association, Heidelberg, Germany.

_____, and Gissurarson, L. R. (1995). Research note: Exploring defensiveness and psychokinesis performance. *European Journal of Parapsychology, 11,* 92–101.

_____, and Morris, R. L. (1995). The relationships among performance on a prototype indicator of perceptual defensiveness/vigilance, personality, and extrasensory perception. *Personality and Individual Differences, 19,* 635–648.

Wegner, D. M. (2002). *The illusion of conscious will.* Cambridge, MA: Bradford Books.

Weinberg, S. (2001). A designer universe. *Skeptical Inquirer, 25(5),* 64–65.

Weiskrantz, L. (1986) *Blindsight: A case and implications.* Oxford: Oxford University Press.

Weiss, B. L. (1988). *Many lives, many masters.* New York: Simon and Schuster.

Wells, R. A., and Klein, J. (1972). A replication of a "psychic healing" paradigm. *Journal of Parapsychology, 36,* 144–149.

_____, and Watkins, G. K. (1975). Linger effects in several PK experiments. In J. D. Morris, W. G. Roll, and R. L. Morris (Eds.), *Research in parapsychology, 1974* (pp. 143–147). Metuchen, NJ: Scarecrow Press.

West, D. J. (1990). A pilot census of hallucinations. *Proceedings of the Society for Psychical Research, 57,* 163–207.

Westfall, R. (1977). *The construction of modern science.* New York: Cambridge University Press.

Wheeler, J. A. (1983). Law without law. In J. A. Wheeler and W. H. Zurek (Eds.), *Quantum theory and measurement* (pp. 182–213). Princeton, NJ: Princeton University Press.

Whitehead, A. N. (1929/1978). *Process and reality: An essay in cosmology.* New York: Free Press.

Whorf, B. (1956). *Language, thought and reality.* Cambridge, MA: Technology Press.

Wiesner, B. P., and Thouless, R. H. (1942). The present position of experimental research into telepathy and other related phenomena. *Proceedings of the Society for Psychical Research, 47,* 1–19.

Wilber, K. (1990). Death, rebirth and meditation. In G. Doore (Ed.), *What survives? Contemporary explorations of life after death* (pp. 176–191). Los Angeles: Tarcher.

_____. (1996). *A brief history of everything.* Boston: Shambala.

Williams, B. J. (2005). Pueblo parapsychology: Psi and the longbody from the Southwest Indian perspective. Paper presented at the 48th annual convention of the Parapsychological Association, Petaluma, California.

Wilson, D. L. (1999). Mind-brain interaction and the violation of physical laws. In B. Libet, A. Freeman, and K. Sutherland (Eds.), *The volitional brain* (pp. 185–200). Thorverton, UK: Imprint Academic.

Wilson, F. A. W., Scalaidhe, S. P. O., and Goldman-Rakic, P. (1993). Dissociation of object and spatial processing domains in primate prefrontal cortex. *Science, 210,* 1955–1958.

Wilson, I. (1987). *The after death experience.* New York: Quill.

_____. (1988). [Review of *Children who remember previous lives* by Ian Stevenson.] *Journal of the Society for Psychical Research, 55,* 227–229.

Wilson, S. C., and Barber, T. X. (1982). The fantasy-prone personality: Implications for understanding imagery, hypnosis and parapsychological phenomena. In A. A. Sheikh (Ed.), *Imagery:*

Current theory, research and application. (pp. 340–387). New York: Wiley.

Wilson, S. K. (1928). *Modern problems in neurology.* London: Arnold.

Wirth, D. P. (1989). Unorthodox healing: The effect of noncontact therapeutic touch on the healing rate of full thickness dermal wounds. Paper presented at the 32nd annual convention of the Parapsychological Association, San Diego, California.

_____. (1990). Unorthodox healing: The effect of noncontact therapeutic touch on the healing rate of full thickness dermal wounds. In L. A. Henkel and J. Palmer (Eds.), *Research in parapsychology, 1989* (pp. 47–52). Metuchen, NJ: Scarecrow Press.

_____, and Mitchell, B. J. (1994). Complementary healing therapy for patients with type I diabetes mellitus. *Journal of Scientific Exploration, 8,* 367–377.

_____, Johnson, C. A., Horvath, J. S., and MacGregor, J. A. D. (1992). The effect of alternative healing therapy on the regeneration rate of salamander forelimbs. *Journal of Scientific Exploration, 6,* 375–390.

Wiseman, R., and O'Keefe, C. (2001). A critique of Schwartz et al.'s after-death communication studies. *Skeptical Inquirer, 25(6),* 26–30.

_____, Smith, M., and Milton, J. (2000). The 'psychic pet' phenomenon: A reply to Rupert Sheldrake, *Journal of the Society for Psychical Research, 64,* 45–49.

Wolfram, S. (2002). *A new kind of science.* Champaign, IL: Wolfram Media, Inc.

Woodward, M. A. (1971). *Edgar Cayce's story of karma.* New York: Berkley.

Wright, S. H. (1999). Paranormal contact with the dying: 14 contemporary death coincidences. *Journal of the Society for Psychical Research, 63,* 258–267.

Young, G. (2006). Preserving the role of conscious decision making in the initiation of intentional action. *Journal of Consciousness Studies, 13(3),* 51–68.

Zhong, Y., and Wu, C. (1991). Altered synaptic plasticity in *Drosophilia* memory mutants with a defective cyclic AMP cascade. *Science, 251,* 198–201.

Zorab, G. (1962). Cases of the Chaffin will type and the problem of survival. *Journal of the Society for Psychical Research, 41,* 407–416.

Index